Edited by Paula J. Massood

The Spike Lee
Reader

TEMPLE UNIVERSITY PRESS
Philadelphia

Paula J. Massood is Associate Professor of Film Studies, Department of Film, Brooklyn College, CUNY, and author of *Black City Cinema: African American Urban Experiences in Film* (Temple).

TEMPLE UNIVERSITY PRESS
1601 North Broad Street
Philadelphia PA 19122
www.temple.edu/tempress

Photographs: Courtesy 40 Acres & A Mule Filmworks.
Cover photograph: Used by permission of photographer, Denis Charmot.
http//:perso.orange.fr/cjarmot.art/

♾ The paper used in this publication meets the requirements of the American National Standard for Information Sciences—Permanence of Paper for Printed Library Materials, ANSI Z39.48-1992

Library of Congress Cataloging-in-Publication Data

The Spike Lee Reader, edited by Paula J. Massood.
    p. cm.
  Includes bibliographical references and index.
  ISBN-13: 978-1-59213-484-7 (cloth : alk. paper)
  ISBN-10: 1-59213-484-X (cloth : alk. paper)
  ISBN-13: 978-1-59213-485-4 (pbk. : alk. paper)
  ISBN-10: 1-59213-485-8 (pbk. : alk. paper)   1. Lee, Spike—Criticism and interpretation.
I. Massood, Paula J., 1965–
PN1998.3.L44S65 2008
791.43'023308996073–dc22

2007021066

2 4 6 8 9 7 5 3 1

To my parents, Terry and Art Massood

Contents

Illustrations

Acknowledgments

I n 1986 I saw a movie that changed my life. It was called *She's Gotta Have It*, and I can still recall the excitement I felt while watching it. I had never seen anything quite like Spike Lee's first feature film. I was fascinated by its unconventional narrative structure, its black-and-white images, and its sense of style infused with humor. Even more, I was drawn to the film's characters and settings. Here were complex characters, lovingly and beautifully rendered on screen. While I had seen many cinematic images of Brooklyn before, I had never seen the neighborhood as it appeared in Lee's film: the Fulton Mall, the Promenade, the Brooklyn Bridge (from a *Brooklyn* perspective). Furthermore, the film's self-conscious style asked—no, demanded—that I engage with it emotionally and intellectually. For this initial (and continuing) inspiration, I'd like to express my deep appreciation to Spike Lee: His love of film, so evident in *She's Gotta Have It*, was contagious. Thanks also to Spike Lee for his support of film scholarship; for taking an interest in what people have to say about his films, and for generously allowing the reproduction of film stills and Toni Cade Bambara's essay in this collection.

Fast forward two decades, and it can only be a happy twist of fate that finds me working on *The Spike Lee Reader* from a New York vantage point and doing so with a stellar group of scholars. I'm indebted to all of the individuals whose contributions have resulted in a collection of exemplary film scholarship. Thanks in particular to the authors of the new essays: Anna Everett, Mark D. Cunningham, Keith M. Harris, S. Craig Watkins, Christine Acham, Beretta E. Smith-Shomade, and David A. Gerstner. Your enthusiasm for the project and your ability to meet tight deadlines while juggling your own responsibilities has not gone without notice or appreciation. I also express my gratitude to the contributors of already published essays, including bell hooks, Michele Wallace, Wahneema Lubiano, James C. McKelly, Ed Guerrero, Krin Gabbard, Dan Flory, and Tavia Nyong'o. Your insightful analyses of Lee's films have helped to make this a rich and diverse collection. For those who were involved in the early stages of the reader, including Thomas Doherty, Cynthia Fuchs, and Karla Rae Fuller, thanks for your enthusiasm and interest in the project. And finally, thanks to Toni Cade Bambara, whose writing continues to inspire us all.

Without Brooklyn—the borough, the school, the people—there would be no reader. I'd like to thank my colleagues in the Department of Film at Brooklyn College, the City University of New York (CUNY), especially Dan Gurskis, Liz Weis, Virginia Brooks, Bill Hornsby, Matthew Moore, Jay Kim, and Bill Healy. You may not think you contributed much to the project, but your interest in Lee, and your enthusiasm for film more generally, remind me daily of why it is that I do what I do. I'm indebted to former Brooklyn College Provost Roberta Matthews, whose research support was integral to the completion of this project. Many thanks to my research assistant, Hans Staats, for his work in the early stages of the collection, and to Ethan Weinstock, for all the help capturing images. I'm also grateful to the students in the Department of Film at Brooklyn College and in the Film Studies Certificate Program at the Graduate Center, CUNY. Our discussions about Lee, African American filmmaking, and American cinema have helped shape the collection's final form.

I've carried the seeds for this project since the very beginning of my career (and perhaps ever since 1986), but they really didn't take root until 2003, when Beretta E. Smith-Shomade invited me to participate in a workshop on Spike Lee at the Society for Cinema and Media Studies' annual conference. I'm indebted to Beretta for organizing the workshop, and its participants, many of whom appear in the collection, for sharing their research and pedagogical approaches to Lee's work. The workshop's standing-room-only attendance proved what many of us already knew: There's a tremendous interest in Lee's films and the need for a venue to exchange ideas. *The Spike Lee Reader* is my humble attempt to continue the dialogue started that day.

My appreciation is extended to Janet Francendese at Temple University Press for her commitment to the project from the very beginning. Her sharp eye and spot-on editorial sense are a model for all writers and scholars. Thank you as well to Temple's editorial, production, and marketing staff, including Gary Kramer, Matthew Kull, and Elena Coler, for making a large project a pleasure to complete.

Finally, none of this would have been completed without the love and support of my family and friends, here and abroad. In particular, I thank Matthew Boyd Goldie for the love, the laughter, the dinners, and the poetry.

Permission to reprint essays was generously granted by numerous sources, including the authors, South End Press, 40 Acres & A Mule Filmworks, Routledge Publishing, Rutgers University Press, the Johns Hopkins University Press, and McFarland & Company. Essays have been reprinted in their original format.

Introduction

PAULA J. MASSOOD

We've Gotta Have It—
Spike Lee, African American Film,
and Cinema Studies

*Sexist/gynophobes, heterosexist/homophobes, and other witting
and unwitting defenders of patriarchy champion Spike Lee
films. So do nonreactionaries. So do many progressives. Not
because the texts are so malleable that they can be maneuvered
into any given ideological space, but because many
extratextual elements figure into the response. Hunger for
images is one element; pride in Lee's accomplishment is
another. That the range of spectators is wide speaks to the
power of the films and the brilliance of the filmmaker.*
— Toni Cade Bambara, "Programming with *School Daze*"

With the release of his first feature, *She's Gotta Have It*, in 1986,
Spike Lee entered the lexicon of contemporary American filmmaking. Starting as an independent filmmaker at a time when
American independents were gaining global status, Lee helped usher in a
new cinematic look and vocabulary in American filmmaking.[1] More important, he gained visibility at a moment when African American film was at a
nadir. Following the industry's shift into blockbuster filmmaking in the mid-
1970s, the studios abandoned blaxploitation film, their sole investment in
African American cinema during the decade (and only marginally associated
with African American filmmaking, since the majority of the personnel associated with the genre were not black). With the success of films like *Jaws*
(Steven Spielberg, 1975) Hollywood had little need or interest in producing
films with black characters for black audiences. With the exception of
Michael Schultz and Stan Lathan and, to a lesser extent, Warrington and
Reginald Hudlin, African American film production had all but disappeared.[2]
That is, until *She's Gotta Have It*.

From the early stages of his career, Lee has been an outspoken proponent of African American film who continues to be a thorn in the side of an industry that has often paid lip service to diversity without supporting it with funding or screen time. Lee's approach to aesthetics and politics is nowhere more evident than in *Do the Right Thing* (1989), his controversial third feature, which sparked a critical pandemic either praising its complex explorations of the interconnections between race and economics or deriding its purported racism and sexism. Wherever the critics landed on this issue, the film ultimately initiated a seminal and enduring microcosmic (Bed-Stuy, Brooklyn, New York) and macrocosmic (United States) dialogue about race relations. Lee has continued to focus on the complexities of race and representation throughout his career—for example, in *Bamboozled* (2000), his satire of contemporary television and film; in *Inside Man* (2006), a look at the erasures of history enveloped in the narrative and stylistic conventions of an action film; and in *When the Levees Broke: A Requiem in Four Acts* (2006), an examination of the government's (state and federal) and media's responses to Hurricane Katrina's disastrous effects on the people and the city of New Orleans. The body of his work, in myriad ways, identifies the tensions inherent in such a diverse national body.

One of the important components of Lee's filmmaking has been its inward extension of the complexities of race and class toward a self-examination of community not seen in African American filmmaking since the early films of Oscar Micheaux, the intervention of Melvin Van Peebles in the 1970s, or the more recent independent works of filmmakers such as Robert Townsend, Charles Burnett, Julie Dash, Marlon Riggs, or Cheryl Dunye. Lee's cultural critique is geared toward making cinematic and televisual representations of black life more complex by showing its varied looks, sounds, and textures. In this way, the director's films, particularly *School Daze* (1988), *Do the Right Thing*, *Clockers* (1995), *Get on the Bus* (1996), and *Bamboozled* often ask African American audience members to consider the ways in which internalized racism can fragment—or unite—a community. Further, they suggest to audiences unfamiliar with black life—and his films, while geared toward black audiences, attract a diversity of viewers—that African American experiences are heterogeneous and complex.

Yet Lee's films are more broadly American, as well. They require their audiences to question conventional structures of feeling, the normative approaches to life as lived in the United States, and to rethink national mythology. Fiction and nonfiction features such as *Malcolm X* (1992), *4 Little Girls* (1997), and *Summer of Sam* (1999), for example, return us to seminal moments in American history to help us understand the present. *25th Hour* (2002), set in an almost immediate post–9/11 context, provides one of the most heartfelt love letters to a New York and nation still recovering from the horrors of that day. Other films, such as *School Daze, Girl 6* (1996), *He Got Game* (1998), and *Bamboozled*, explore the myths of self-determination and success so integral to American literary and cinematic narratives. In *He Got Game*, for example, Aaron Copland's music situates the story of a African American basketball player from Coney Island within the wider scope of American culture. As this suggests, Lee adapts American aesthetics for an African American context and vice versa, in the process creating a mode of address that acknowledges a black subjectivity as part of a national point of view. That he does so by addressing a variety of audiences, as illustrated by this essay's opening epigraph, is an indication of the ways in which his films have encouraged both intra- and interracial debate.

Lee's career and filmmaking style also must be understood in the context of American cinema from the mid-1970s through the mid-1980s. During this time, American film aesthetics were transforming as young, university-trained directors such as Martin Scorsese, George Lucas, and Steven Spielberg skirted Hollywood's more formal apprenticeship system and (at least) initially made films outside or on the margins of the industry. Often these filmmakers were influenced, if not narratively, then stylistically, by post–World War II national film movements such as Italian Neorealism, the French New Wave, and the films of the Japanese filmmakers Akira Kurosawa and Yasujiro Ozu. By the 1980s, audiences were accustomed to films that revised genre and reworked narrative conventions, and that often did so through quotation, allusion, and homage. Lee, as well, is a university-trained filmmaker who is familiar with a variety of international filmmaking styles. The stylistic imprints of the New Wave, cinema vérité, classical Hollywood, and New Hollywood Cinema (especially early Martin Scorsese) can be found in his films as early as *She's Gotta Have It*, which combines black-and-white film stock, direct address, and jump cuts with a Technicolor homage to Victor Fleming's *The Wizard of Oz* (1939) in a story about a sexually liberated woman in Brooklyn. This formal experimentation, influenced by global cinema movements, remains one of the characteristics of the director's filmmaking and explicitly marks some of his films, such as *Summer of Sam*, which is just as much about Scorsese's New York from the 1970s as it is about the Son of Sam murders from 1977.[3]

She's Gotta Have It was a box-office success (one of the few outright profit earners Lee has produced), earning approximately $10 million in its first year of release. But the film was historic for other, more important reasons: First, it inspired a critical dialogue about its filmmaker, its images, its place in independent film, and its status as an African American film at a time when black films and filmmakers were absent from the national and international scene.

She's Gotta Have It (1986). Tracy Camilla Johns as Nola Darling.

White critics in the popular press mostly lauded the film (perhaps they, like the black press, were also tired of blaxploitation caricatures) while having a less amicable relationship with its outspoken director, who often forced them to reconsider their own attitudes toward race and representation. African American critics and scholars had more mixed responses because the film raised (and in some instances resurrected) often difficult questions regarding African American representation—for example, did Lee's films define a black aesthetic, and if so, how? And how might black women fit into this aesthetic?

At the same time, there's no doubt that the film and the two that quickly followed—*School Daze* and *Do the Right Thing*—were responsible for sparking a renewed interest in African American film production, and it is not an overstatement to credit Lee with influencing a new wave of contemporary black filmmaking, a New Black Cinema movement, over the subsequent years. The combined critical and financial success of Lee's films, along with the attention garnered by Robert Townsend's self-financed *Hollywood Shuffle* (1988) and Reginald Hudlin's *House Party* (1990), ignited Hollywood investment in African American projects in the early 1990s—most notably, John Singleton's *Boyz n the Hood* (1991) and its imitators, such as Allen and Albert Hughes's *Menace II Society* (1993). Lee's stylistic and narrative innovations also have had more far-reaching influence. For example, international filmmakers such as Mathieu Kassovitz (*La Haine*, 1995) of France and Jean-Paul Bekolo (*Quartier Mozart*, 1992) of Cameroon cite Lee as the inspiration for their cinematic explorations of the politics of race, economics, and postcolonial tensions in their specific national contexts. More indirectly, Lee's aesthetic imprint can be found in the urban settings, youth communities, pop-culture references, and reflexive aesthetics of films such as *Amores Perros* (Alejandro Gonzaléz Iñárritu, Mexico, 2000) and *City of God* (Fernando Meirelles and Kátia Lund, Brazil, 2002).

A consideration of the impact of Lee's career, however, should not be limited to aesthetic influence. As the opening epigraph suggests, and the rich critical history of films like *She's Gotta Have It* and *Do the Right Thing* indicate, Lee's career has coincided with, and influenced, a crucial moment in film scholarship. While the articles collected in *The Spike Lee Reader* illustrate the depth and complexity of Lee's oeuvre, they also represent the rich variety of responses his work has inspired over the past two decades. The director's films have raised a variety of questions, from attempts to outline the nature, or "essence," of a black cinematic aesthetics to a re-visioning of American film as a whole. They have sparked critical inquiries into the nature of genres, the role of the auteur, and the interactive mechanics of an active text and an oppositional spectatorship. They have asked us to reconsider spectatorial pleasure; to revel in and deconstruct the complexities of their polyphonic visual and aural fields. They consider not only race, but also the often blurry and fraught interconnections among race, gender, sexuality, and class. In short, they have encouraged and, in some cases, forced us to interact with what's on screen and, perhaps more important, with each other, whether it be in the theater, in the café, in the classroom, or on the street corner. *The Spike Lee Reader* continues this dialogue; the essays are meant to interact with each other and with readers.

Lee has been prolific, directing more than twenty feature films, producing other directors' works, directing videos for musicians such as Branford Marsalis, and making commercials for companies that include Nike, the Gap, and Pepsi. The essays collected here consider a selection of the director's feature films rather than his entire directorial output, since to do so would be unwieldy in a project of this nature. A majority of the films included here are considered by critics and scholars to be major works in Lee's aesthetic and formal development, and many, including *She's Gotta Have It, School Daze, Do the Right Thing, Malcolm X,* and *Bamboozled,* have been the focus of detailed critical assessments elsewhere.[4] Other films, such as *Jungle Fever* (1991), *Crooklyn* (1994), *Clockers, Get on the Bus, 4 Little Girls, He Got Game,* and *Summer of Sam* are important, though critically underexamined, films. They, like the director's better-known work, often ask us to reconsider American history through an African American lens by adapting, according to Keith M. Harris, "African American rhetorical traditions through the medium of cinema."[5] Finally, Lee's *Inside Man* completes the collection because it provides the first example of the director adapting his signature style for a studio-based big-budget action film, in the process becoming secondary to studio machinery. As such, the film raises compelling questions about directorial control and authorship, topics that run throughout the collection—in Anna Everett's consideration of *Malcolm X*, for example—but that coalesce in a film that has been discussed less as a director's project than as either an action film or an actor's showcase.

With a director as productive as Lee, it is inevitable that some films, unfortunately, are not included in *The Spike Lee Reader*. They include some with theatrical releases, including *Mo' Better Blues* (1990), *Girl 6* (1996), *The Original Kings of Comedy* (2000), *25th Hour* (2002), and *She Hate Me* (2004), and the majority of Lee's made-for-television films (*Sucker Free City*, *Jim Brown: All American*, *A Huey P. Newton Story*, *Freak*, and *When the Levees Broke*, among others).[6] Films were selected for the collection because of their place in Lee's oeuvre and the critical coverage they may or may not have received. Most of the examples listed earlier (with the exception, perhaps, of *When the Levees Broke*) are arguably "minor" films according to this criterion. Some, like *Girl 6* and *She Hate Me* feel more like transitional pieces—experimentations with style or narrative structure—rather than fully fledged ideas. In addition, some excluded films are flawed, especially in their treatment of gender, in their development of character, or in their execution of narrative. While it can be reasonably argued that all of Lee's films are flawed in some way—which is what makes them interesting to scholars—the issues raised by the excluded films are covered elsewhere in the collection. For example, essays by Anna Everett, S. Craig Watkins, and Krin Gabbard discuss gender and sexuality in detail.

There has been no end to the critical coverage that Lee has generated. The director and his films have produced active and ongoing scholarly debates, from mass-market biographies to academic articles and books. Reviewing the scholarship devoted to Lee's films is the equivalent to revisiting some of the most important critical and theoretical moments in film studies from the past two decades. Again, because Lee's career has encompassed significant methodological changes in the field (coinciding, for example, with the establishment of cultural studies and the expansion of film and media studies across college and university curricula), a survey of "Spike Lee scholarship" provides an opportunity to review the critical landscape. With this intention, *The Spike Lee Reader* contains previously published pieces dating back to as early as bell hooks's seminal "'whose pussy is this': a feminist comment," an intervention against the early euphoria surrounding *She's Gotta Have It*, and Michele Wallace's discussion of Lee's treatment of gender relations in this and *School Daze*, his next feature film. hooks, Wallace, and other scholars writing during the late 1980s and early 1990s, including Wahneema Lubiano, Ed Guerrero, and Toni Cade Bambara, provide a telescopic rendering of the questions many scholars were asking of black film at the time by surveying Lee's filmmaking precedents, situating his work in the contemporary moment, and opening discussion for future critical assessments of African American life on screen. As such, they form the foundations for later considerations of Lee's work; indeed, one cannot understand contemporary approaches to the director's films without a familiarity with these essays.

The Spike Lee Reader also includes a selection of new essays by prominent film and media scholars. These new pieces reassess Lee's major films, such as *Malcolm X*, while at other times they consider films, including *Get on the Bus* and *Crooklyn*, that have received little or no critical attention. S. Craig Watkins's work on the former and Mark D. Cunningham's on the latter, for example, offer important insight into some of Lee's overlooked films. Other essays, such as Beretta E. Smith-Shomade's discussion of *Bamboozled*, build on earlier Lee scholarship and engage in a metacritical dialogue that extends beyond the texts to the films' reception. Still others, such as Keith M. Harris's essay on *Clockers* and David A. Gerstner's on *Inside Man*, interpret the director's works through wider theoretical frameworks, such as those of Mikhail Bakhtin, Michel Foucault, and Jacques Derrida. A few previously published but relatively unknown pieces continue this trend. For example, Dan Flory situates Lee's *Summer of Sam* among recent philosophical theories of race. As a collective, these critical approaches to the director's work suggest not only the malleability of the texts but also the depth of their cinematic significations.

Because Lee's films raise questions that have been central to African American life and letters for more than a century, many of the articles, both old and new, return to seminal cultural and political figures, including W. E. B. Du Bois, Booker T. Washington, Martin Luther King Jr., and Malcolm X, to remind readers that the desire to author an African American identity has long been bound up in an attempt to define an African American aesthetic; in other words, black identity often has been connected directly to what is on the page or the screen. (In the past, this often became a question of positive or negative representation.) Lee's films play an interesting role in these debates. On the one hand, the films and their director often encourage viewers and critics to identify what is on screen with an essential blackness, or a "Black thing," to quote Lee on *Do the Right Thing*. And yet, as Wahneema Lubiano so eloquently argues, the films also "represent a problematic through which the political difficulties that inhere in African American cultural production . . . can be usefully discussed,"[7] a point James C. McKelly makes as

well in his discussion of the relevance of Du Bois's theory of "double consciousness" to *Do the Right Thing*. While critical reactions to Lee's films often belie the scarcity of black images on screen, and the overdetermined
expectations many viewers bring as a result, their shortcomings, omissions,
and flaws enable—in fact, initiate—a more extended dialogue regarding
representation, stereotype, and caricature. Their skillful and self-conscious
dialogue with representation reminds us, ultimately, that they are commenting on reality and its representations, not representing reality itself.[8]

To this end, Lee often references different filmmaking styles. Like those
of many of his immediate predecessors in American filmmaking, especially
Martin Scorsese (whom he often cites as an influence), his films often reconsider genre, and a number of the essays in *The Spike Lee Reader* discuss this
facet of his filmmaking. Toni Cade Bambara, for example, suggests that Lee
uses the conventions of the musical to "make a wake up call about intracommunity self-ambush."[9] Anna Everett, in her discussion of the genealogy of
Malcolm X's life story and the controversies surrounding the film project,
places Lee's *Malcolm X* within the traditions of the Hollywood biopic, arguing
that the director's attempt to make an African American variant of the genre
was fraught with outside expectations (from within and outside the black
community) on how the leader's life should be portrayed on screen. Mark D.
Cunningham places Lee's semiautobiographical *Crooklyn* in the tradition of
the print and screen fairy tale, linking the film to predecessors such as Lewis
Carroll's *Alice in Wonderland* and Victor Fleming's film adaptation of L. Frank
Baum's *The Wizard of Oz* (and referencing the musical genre via Fleming's
film).[10] Keith M. Harris argues that in *Clockers*, "Lee places the dramatic elements of tragedy and melodrama in dynamic conflict and discontinuous relief" as a means of disrupting the generic conventions of the hood film.[11] And
Dan Flory argues that *Summer of Sam*'s use of *film noir* conventions introduce race into a film that is otherwise considered to be the director's first film
to focus on non-black characters.

Lee's films, however, are more than examples of genre revision, and the
essays collected here seek to understand them as a polyphonic system of cultural and political references engaged in diegetic and extradiegetic dialogues.
His films draw from literature (for example, Zora Neale Hurston, Alex Haley,
Richard Price), music (ranging from Aaron Copland, Bill Lee, and Terence
Blanchard to Public Enemy, the Roots, and Mos Def), visual culture (black
memorabilia, including print materials, sculpture, and other artworks), and
contemporary popular culture, including television (sitcoms and music video)
and advertising (print and television). Many of the essays in *The Spike Lee
Reader* seek to decipher this complex signifying system, including the selection by Krin Gabbard, whose analysis of *He Got Game*'s soundtrack suggests

that Lee's choice of Aaron Copland's music was a strategy of reversing "the familiar Hollywood practice of using the visible . . . sounds of black music to
accompany the actions of white people" through the inclusion of work by a
gay Jewish composer.[12] Tavia Nyong'o interprets *Bamboozled's* references to
the history of blackface minstrelsy and other racist visual culture as a form of
"racial kitsch," a method of "oppositional curating" that seeks to understand
and implement racist content in a critical manner,[13] whereas Beretta E.
Smith-Shomade argues that in the film Lee uses the frameworks of "paradox
and authenticity" to "examine the ways in which Lee both forwards and undermines notions of black progress in twenty-first-century visual culture and
within real-lived actualities."[14]

As this suggests, Lee's films are textual systems employing quotation, allusion, and homage to explore the shared national trauma of racism and its
continuing social, economic, and political affects. While most of his theatrical releases have been fiction films, many refer to actual historical or contemporary events from large-scale global disasters, such as slavery and the
Holocaust, to more localized events (Malcolm X's assassination; church
bombings in Birmingham, Alabama; the Million Man March in Washington,
D.C.; the beating of Rodney King in Los Angeles; the deaths of Eleanor
Bumpers, Michael Stewart, and Yusuf Hawkins in New York City; or the
Bush administration's abandonment of New Orleans following Hurricane
Katrina) with national repercussions. In many cases, such as *Malcolm X* and
Get on the Bus, real-world actualities structure a narrative in which fact is
skillfully blended with fiction. In other cases, such as *Jungle Fever, Summer
of Sam,* and *Inside Man,* historical moments and myths are inspirations for
the narrative; they exist beside the story, always reminding audiences of their
presence. Ed Guerrero suggests, for example, that *Jungle Fever*, following a
cinematic legacy that can be traced back to films such as *The Masher* (1907)
and *The Birth of a Nation* (1915), works against society's ambivalent and often hostile attitude towards interracial romance.[15] And David A. Gerstner
reads Lee's New York in *Inside Man* as the director's (perhaps) indirect comment on the Patriot Act's forced homogenization of national diversity.

This ongoing acknowledgment of the world outside the text reminds us
that one of Lee's consistent goals has been to introduce a distinct, historicized, African American point of view into a medium that is often solely associated with entertainment, at least in its American (and Americanized)
variant. From the floor plan of a slave ship filling the establishing shot of
School Daze to references to the Holocaust in *Inside Man*, Lee's films have returned us to decisive moments in history, often announcing, as in *Bamboozled's* definition of satire, their pedagogical intentions. This strategy extends
to Lee's nonfiction work, as well, which explores important events and figures

in black history. The film *4 Little Girls*, as Christine Acham suggests here, functions like many other African American documentaries in that its purpose is to preserve, remember, and recuperate black stories, especially in a contemporary context where so much of the past has been forgotten. In this film, as in his other nonfiction films, Lee combines contemporary interviews with historical footage to suggest continuities between past events and attitudes and the present context. As in *Bamboozled*, the suggestion is made that we can only move forward as a society by understanding our past.

As early as *She's Gotta Have It*, Lee was aware that to succeed as an African American filmmaker he had to continue making films while also maintaining a level of autonomy from the industry; therefore, he set out on a path that belied the mainstream experience of most black directors who rely on studios to sporadically fund their films. Even before his first feature was released, Lee established 40 Acres & A Mule Filmworks, his production company. This followed, in 1996, with an advertising company, Spike/DDB, through which he directs commercials aimed at urban (i.e., young African American and Latino) markets.[16] While he has often worked with studios such as Columbia Pictures and Warner Brothers, Lee's production and advertising companies (the latter in particular) provide the financial foundations that enable him to make films that otherwise would not be made. They have also guaranteed that Lee retains the right of final cut over his films, a form of directorial control that remains rare in the industry and provides us with, perhaps, one of the strongest cases of a director fully in charge of his work.

Lee is the quintessential inside/outside man, often working with the industry, but just as often looking elsewhere for financing. *She's Gotta Have It*'s patchwork of funding sources was the director's first attempt to make an independent feature film.[17] Since then he has often sought alternative sources of financing, perhaps most famously when the completion-bond company on *Malcolm X* closed down the over-budget production before the film was completed. Lee financed the remaining $3 million by taking a cut in salary and soliciting donations from high-profile African American personalities, including Bill Cosby, Oprah Winfrey, Magic Johnson, and Tracy Chapman.[18] In other instances, especially with his more politically "sensitive" films, Lee has experimented with cheaper technologies as a means of cutting production costs. As Craig Watkins discusses, *Get on the Bus* is an example of just such an innovative approach to low-budget filmmaking. Since Lee received no studio interest in his film about the Million Man March, he and his producers solicited private investors, eventually raising $2.4 million from a variety of African American celebrities, including Will Smith and Wesley Snipes. He shot the film on Super-16 mm film stock, a cheaper and more flexible format, thus enabling his exploration of African American masculinities to make it to the screen. This technological experimentation continued with *4 Little Girls* and *Bamboozled*, both of which were shot using digital video technology, the latter with consumer-grade digital videocameras and some Super-16 mm footage.

Despite his continuing role as the studios' conscience, Lee is also an inside man who wields tremendous power and influence. While many of his films have been low-budget independents, he has also worked on big-budget studio films—most notably, *Malcolm X* and *Inside Man*.[19] Anna Everett, in her consideration of the former film, identifies the multiple effects that the studio had on the making of *Malcolm X* years, even decades, before it went into production. And David A. Gerstner's essay on *Inside Man* asks compelling questions about Lee's status as an auteur, particularly if we take the accepted notion of an auteur as a director working within the studio system and yet having a consistent signature style. The essays in *The Spike Lee Reader* suggest a number of continuities across Lee's oeuvre: a focus on race and representation, technical experimentation, and a self-conscious approach to film form, narrative, and genre. Yet what do we make of Lee's *Inside Man*, a studio-backed action film with a $45 million budget, by far the largest that the director has ever enjoyed? As Gerstner suggests, Lee has been marked as a difficult filmmaker—he's political, didactic, and controversial—so much so that he was "erased" from the film's marketing campaign, which focused on its stars rather than its director. There is no denying, however, that Lee's traces exist throughout the film's narrative, form, and politics. The result is a film that asks important questions about film authorship and the economics of filmmaking.

Throughout his career, Lee has been a "difficult" filmmaker whose films are marked by political, didactic, and controversial subject matter. To some, he's a "polarizing filmmaker . . . someone to whom a large segment of the population won't listen, just because of who he is."[20] To others, however, he's the sole black filmmaker with the power and financial clout to make films focusing on African American people, African American stories, and African American history. This dichotomy is no better exemplified than in the juxtaposition of *Inside Man* and *When the Levees Broke*, Lee's two releases from 2006. The latter film, an HBO-produced, four-part documentary about the destruction of New Orleans caused by Hurricane Katrina, was released in August 2006 and marked the first-year anniversary of the catastrophic event. Like *4 Little Girls*, *When the Levees Broke* is Lee's attempt, through the juxtaposition of contemporary interviews and archival footage, to create a history, an audiovisual record of events to ensure that New Orleans's people and neighborhoods are not forgotten. It was a personal film, driven by Lee's desire to expose the truth about the collapse of the city's levees and the government's massive mismanagement of the situation.

Unlike *Inside Man*, *When the Levees Broke* was a Spike Lee film from very early in the production, and the director was the face of the film in all of its pre- and post-release marketing (including for DVD format). The reasons for this bring us back to many of the concerns laid out in the essays collected in *The Spike Lee Reader*: Lee's concern with history and with telling African American stories; his belief in both the didactic and the entertainment strengths of film; his interest in film form. But why did Lee receive more coverage in the popular press for a $2 million made-for-television nonfiction film than he did for the $45 million *Inside Man*? While some of this might be due to Lee's amicable relationship with HBO, some of the attention paid to the documentary suggests the influence that genre has on the reception of the director's films. Lee's fiction films upset the compact between Hollywood and spectators because they ask uncomfortable questions of their audiences (both black and white) rather than entertain them; in this sense, they are difficult. His nonfiction films, by contrast, are expected to be historical and informative, and therefore visibility is a virtue rather than a limitation.[21] Such differing treatments between the films suggest that Lee's relationship with the film industry remains complex, even as he enters his third decade of making films. It is this characteristic of his work as a filmmaker that allows us (indeed, forces us) to continue reframing the questions we ask of African American filmmakers and American film more generally.

In *Bamboozled*, a frustrated African American television writer creates a satirical minstrel show, *Mantan: The New Millennium Minstrel Show*, in the hope of being fired from his dead-end network job. To his surprise, the show is a success, and blackface minstrelsy becomes almost as fashionable among contemporary audiences of various races and ethnicities as it was in the nineteenth century. The film's use of blackface is at once literal and metaphorical; it is the director's comment on the state of African American representation and cultural production at the turn of the century. As one character observes of the show's content, "It's the same damned thing all over again. The same damned thing." The essays collected in *The Spike Lee Reader* suggest that it's not the same damned thing anymore—not cinematically, not industrially, not intellectually. Spike Lee's filmmaking career, and the exemplary body of scholarship it inspires, attests to the fact that black filmmaking *and* black film scholarship have reached a new level of complexity and self-consciousness in the twenty-first century. If not for Lee, we wouldn't be here. "And that's the truth, Ruth."

NOTES

Epigraph: Toni Cade Bambara, "Programming with *School Daze*," in this volume.

1. American independent filmmaking received a boost in 1985 when Robert Redford's Sundance Institute took over management of the Utah/U.S. Film Festival. The event was renamed the Sundance Film Festival in 1991 and has become one of the defining forums for independent and first-time filmmakers. Following a trend in independent

filmmaking at the time—spearheaded by fellow New York University graduates Susan Seidelman and Jim Jarmusch—Lee entered *She's Gotta Have It* in international film festivals, including the Cannes Film Festival, where it won the Prix de Jeunesse for young directors. In 1982, Seidelman was nominated for the Camera d'Or at Cannes for her feature debut, *Smithereens*. Jarmusch's *Stranger than Paradise* won the Camera d'Or in 1984, and his *Down by Law* was nominated for the Golden Palm in 1986.

2. Michael Schultz was one of the few African American directors who continued working in the late 1970s and early 1980s, most notably on films such as *Car Wash* (1976), *Greased Lightning* (1977) with Richard Pryor, and *Krush Groove* (1985). Ernest Dickerson, Lee's New York University classmate and his long-time cinematographer, worked with Schultz on *Krush Groove* before shooting *She's Gotta Have It*. Stan Lathan had a prolific career directing television series such as *Barney Miller* and *Hill Street Blues* in the 1970s and early 1980s. He also directed *Beat Street* in 1984, a music film that, along with Schultz's *Krush Groove*, was a precursor to later films featuring rap and hip-hop stars. The Hudlin brothers were not a significant presence until 1990 and the release of their comedy, *House Party* (written and directed by Reginald; produced by Warrington). Warrington, however, had been making films since the 1970s, and he helped to co-found the Black Filmmaker Foundation (BFF) in 1978. The brothers knew Lee, and Reginald makes a brief appearance in *She's Gotta Have It*.

3. See, for example, Paula J. Massood, "Review of *Summer of Sam*," *Cineaste* 25, no. 2 (Spring 2000): 62–64.

4. For example, see Ed Guerrero's *Do the Right Thing* (London: BFI Publishing, 2001); Mark Reid's edited anthology, *Spike Lee's Do the Right Thing* (New York: Cambridge University Press, 1997); and Michael Eric Dyson's *Making Malcolm: The Myth and Meaning of Malcolm X* (New York: Oxford University Press, 1995), among others.

5. Keith M. Harris, "*Clockers* (Spike Lee 1995): Adaptation in Black," in this volume.

6. From *4 Little Girls* onward, Lee has enjoyed a positive working relationship with HBO. After *4 Little Girls*, he made *Freak* (1998), *Jim Brown: All American* (2002), and *When the Levees Broke* (2006) for the cable network.

7. Lubiano, "But Compared to What? Reading Realism, Representation, and Essentialism in *School Daze*, *Do the Right Thing*, and the Spike Lee Discourse," in this volume.

8. Here I am echoing W. J. T. Mitchell's "The Violence of Public Art: *Do the Right Thing*," in Reid, *Spike Lee's Do the Right Thing*, 107–28.

9. Bambara, "Programming with *School Daze*," in this volume.

10. As mentioned, Lee referenced *The Wizard of Oz* as early as 1986 in *She's Gotta Have It*.

11. Harris, "*Clockers*," in this volume. The "hood," or "gangsta," film refers to a group of films that gained popularity following the success of John Singleton's *Boyz n the Hood* (1991). Hood films focus on young African American men living in urban centers such as Brooklyn and South Central Los Angeles and facing the seemingly inescapable pressures of poverty and crime. Other notable films in the genre include *Straight out of Brooklyn* (Matty Rich, 1991), *Juice* (Ernest Dickerson, 1992), and *Menace II Society* (Allen and Albert Hughes, 1993). In *Black City Cinema: African American Urban Experiences in Film* (Philadelphia: Temple University Press, 2003), esp. 158–59, I trace the hood film to Lee's early work, including *She's Gotta Have It*. I also argue that stylistic

precursors to the hood film can be found in rap/graffiti films such as *Beat Street* and *Krush Groove* from the mid-1980s. See also Ed Guerrero, *Framing Blackness: The African American Image in Film* (Philadelphia: Temple University Press, 1993); S. Craig Watkins, *Representing: Hip Hop Culture and the Production of Black Cinema* (Chicago: University of Chicago Press, 1998); Todd Boyd, *Am I Black Enough for You? Popular Culture from the 'Hood and Beyond* (Bloomington: Indiana University Press, 1997); and Keith M. Harris, *Boys, Boyz, Bois: An Ethics of Black Masculinity in Film and Popular Media* (New York: Routledge, 2005).

12. Krin Gabbard, "Spike Lee Meets Aaron Copland," in this volume.

13. Tavia Nyong'o, "Racial Kitsch and Black Performance," in this volume.

14. Beretta E. Smith-Shomade, "'I Be Smackin' My Hoes': Paradox and Authenticity in *Bamboozled*," in this volume.

15. Ed Guerrero, "Spike Lee and the Fever in the Racial Jungle," in this volume.

16. Lee established 40 Acres & A Mule Musicworks, a subsidiary of Sony, in 1992. The company's focus was marketing the soundtracks to his films, along with music from a selection of artists. He also founded Spike's Joint, a chain of retail stores (in Fort Greene, Brooklyn, and Los Angeles) in 1989. Both stores closed in 1997, the result of competition from an increasing number of clothing brands, such as Tommy Hilfiger and Fubu, marketed to urban (and suburban) youth.

17. Before he successfully produced *She's Gotta Have It,* Lee spent more than a year attempting to secure financing for a semiautobiographical film called *Messenger.* The project folded for lack of funding.

18. Kaleem Aftab, *Spike Lee: That's My Story and I'm Sticking to It* (New York: W. W. Norton, 2005), 164–65.

19. *Clockers*, for example, was made for $25 million with Universal; *Summer of Sam*, for $22 million with Touchstone; and *25th Hour*, for $15 million with Touchstone. All figures are from http://www.imdb.com.

20. Michael Sicinski, "*When the Levees Broke*: A Requiem in Four Acts." *Cineaste* 32, no. 1 (Winter 2006): 55.

21. Ironically, Lee's filmmaking style tends to be more subtle in his nonfiction films. In fact, except for a few examples of self-conscious camera work, and the framing device that Lee uses to introduce his subjects at the end of the film, *When the Levees Broke* is one of his most conventional films.

"whose pussy is this":
a feminist comment

efore I see Spike Lee's film, *She's Gotta Have It*, I hear about it. Folks tell me "it's black, it's funny, it's something you don't want to miss." With all this talk, especially coming from black folks who don't usually go to the movies, I become reluctant, even suspicious. If everybody is liking it, even white folks, something has got to be wrong somewhere! Initially, these are the thoughts that keep me from seeing the film but I don't stay away long. When I receive letters and phone calls from black women scholars and friends telling me about the film and wanting to talk about whether it portrays a liberated black woman, I make my way to the movies. I don't go alone. I go with black women friends Beverly, Yvette, and Maria so we can talk about it together. Some of what was said that evening in the heat of our discussion informs my comments.

A passionate viewer of films, especially the work of independent filmmakers, I found much to appreciate in the technique, style, and overall production of *She's Gotta Have It*. It was especially refreshing to see images of black people on screen that were not grotesque caricatures, images that were familiar, images that imaginatively captured the essence, dignity, and spirit of that elusive quality know as "soul." It was a very soulful film.

Thinking about the film from a feminist perspective, considering its political implications, I find it much more problematic. In the article, "Art vs.

bell hooks, "'whose pussy is this': a feminist comment," in *Talking Back: Thinking Feminist, Thinking Black* (Boston: South End Press, 1989), 134–41. Reprinted with permission of South End Press.

Ideology: The Debate over Positive Images" (*Black Film Review* 2, no. 3), Salim Muwakkil raises the question of whether a "mature African-American community" can allow "aesthetic judgments to rest on ideological or political criteria," commenting:

> The black cultural nationalists of the 60s and 70s demonstrated anew the deadening effect such ideological requirements have on creative expression. Their various proscriptions and prescriptions aborted a historical moment pregnant with promise. It seems clear that efforts to subordinate the profound and penetrating creative process of black people to an ideological movement suffocates the community's creative vitality.

While I would emphatically assert that aesthetic judgments should not rest solely on ideological or political criteria, this does not mean that such criteria cannot be used in conjunction with other critical strategies to assess the overall value of a given work. It does not imply a devaluation to engage in critical discussion of those criteria. To deny the validity of an aesthetic critique that encompasses the ideological or political is to mask the truth that every aesthetic work embodies the political, the ideological as part of its fundamental structure. No aesthetic work transcends politics or ideology.

Significantly, the film *She's Gotta Have It* was advertised, marketed, and talked about in reviews and conversations in a manner that raised political and ideological questions both about the film and the public responses to it. Was the film "a woman's story"? Did the film depict a radically new image of black female sexuality? Can a man really tell a woman's story? One viewer posed the question to me as: "Is Nola Darling a liberated woman or just a WHORE." (This is the way this sentence was written in a letter to me by a black woman professor who teaches film, who wrote that she was "waiting for the feminist response.") There has been no widespread feminist response to the film precisely because of the overwhelming public celebration of that which is new, different, and exciting in this work. Given the pervasive antifeminism in popular culture, in black subculture, a feminist critique might simply be aggressively dismissed. Yet for feminist thinkers to avoid public critique is to diminish the power of the film. It is a testimony to that power that it compels us to think, to reflect, to engage the work fully.

Recently, the film version of Alice Walker's *The Color Purple* evoked more discussion among black folks of feminist issues (sexism, freedom of sexual expression, male violence against women, etc.) than any theoretical and/or polemical work by feminist scholars. *She's Gotta Have It* generated a similar response. Often these discussions exposed grave ignorance about feminist political movement, revealing the extent to which shallow notions of feminist struggle disseminated by non-feminists in popular culture shape and influence the way many black people perceive feminism. That all feminists are man-hating, sexually depraved, castrating, power-hungry, etc., are prevailing stereotypes. The tendency to see liberated women as sexually loose informed the way many people viewed the portrayal of black female sexuality in *She's Gotta Have It*. To some extent, this perception is based on a narrowly defined notion of liberation that was acceptable in some feminist circles at one time.

During the early stages of the contemporary women's movement, feminist liberation was often equated with sexual liberation by both feminist activists and non-feminists. At that time, the conceptualization of female sexual liberation was informed by a fierce heterosexist bias which saw sexual liberation primarily in terms of women asserting the right to be sexually desiring, to initiate sexual relationships, and to participate in casual sexual encounters with varied male partners. Women dared to assert that female sexuality was not passive, that women were desiring subjects who both longed for and enjoyed sex as much as, if not more than, men. These assertions could have easily provided the ideological framework for the construction of a character like Nola Darling, the main female character in *She's Gotta Have It*. Nola expressed again and again her eagerness and willingness to be sexual with men as well as her right to have numerous partners.

Superficially, Nola Darling is the perfect embodiment of woman as desiring subject—a representation which does challenge sexist notions of female sexual passivity. (It is important to remember that from slavery on, black women have been portrayed in white racist thought as sexually assertive, although this view contrasts sharply with the emphasis on chastity, monogamy, and male right to initiate sexual contact in black culture, a view held especially among the middle classes.) Ironically and unfortunately, Nola Darling's sexual desire is not depicted as an autonomous gesture, as an independent longing for sexual expression, satisfaction, and fulfillment. Instead, her assertive sexuality is most often portrayed as though her body, her sexually aroused being is a reward or gift she bestows on the deserving male. When body builder Greer Childs tells Nola that his photo will appear on the cover of a popular men's magazine, she responds by removing her clothes, by offering her body as a token of her esteem. This and other incidents suggest that Nola, though desiring subject, acts on the assumption that heterosexual female sexual assertion has legitimacy primarily as a gesture of reward or as a means by which men can be manipulated and controlled by women (what is vulgarly called "pussy power"). Men do not have to objectify Nola's sexuality because she objectifies it. In so doing, her character becomes the projection of a stereotypical sexist notion of a sexually assertive woman—she is not in fact liberated.

While Nola is not passive sexually, her primary concern is pleasing each partner. Though we are led to believe she enjoys sex, her sexual fulfillment is never the central concern. She is pleasured only to the extent that she is able to please. While her partners enjoy being sexual with her, they are disturbed by her desire to have frequent sex with several partners. They see her sexual longing as abnormal. One male partner, Mars, says, "all men want freaks [in bed] we just don't want 'em for a wife." This comment illustrates the sexist stereotypes about female sexuality that inform Mars's perceptions of Nola. When Jaime, another partner, suggests that Nola is sick, evoking sexist stereotypes to label her insane, depraved, abnormal, Nola does not respond by asserting that she is sexually liberated. Instead, she internalizes the critique and seeks psychiatric help. Throughout the film, she is extremely dependent on male perceptions of her reality. Lacking self-awareness and the capacity to be self-critical, she explores her sexuality only when compelled to do so by a man. If Nola were sexually liberated, there would be no need for her to justify or defend herself against male accusations. It is only after the men have passed judgment that she begins the process of coming to consciousness. Until that point, we know more about how the men in the film see her than how she sees herself.

To a very grave extent the focus of the film is not Nola but her male partners. Just as they are the center of attention sexually, they are also central personalities in the film. In telling us what they think about Nola, they tell us more about themselves, their values, their desires. She is the object that stimulates the discourse, they are its subjects. The narrators are male and the story is a male-centered, male-biased patriarchal tale. As such, it is not progressive, nor does it break away from the traditional portrayal of female sexuality in film. She's Gotta Have It can take its place alongside a growing body of contemporary films that claim to tell women's stories while privileging male narratives, films that stimulate audiences with versions of female sexuality that are not really new or different (Paris, Texas, for example). Another recently acclaimed film, Mona Lisa, objectifies black womanhood and black female sexuality in a similar way.

Overall, it is the men who speak in She's Gotta Have It. While Nola appears one-dimensional in perspective and focus, seemingly more concerned about her sexual relationships than about any other aspect of her life, the male characters are multidimensional. They have personalities. Nola has no personality. She is shallow, vacuous, empty. Her one claim to fame is that she likes to fuck. In the male pornographic imagination she could be described as "pure pussy," that is to say that her ability to perform sexually is the central, defining aspect of her identity.

These sexually active, sexually hungry men are not "pure penis" because there is no such category. They are each defined by unique characteristics

She's Gotta Have It (1986):Thanksgiving dinner with Jamie (Tommy Redmond Hicks),
Greer (John Canada Terrell), and Mars Blackmon (Spike Lee).

and attributes—Mars by his humor, Greer by his obsession with body building, Jaime by his concern with romance and committed relationships. Unlike
Nola, they are not always thinking about sex, do not suffer from penis on the
brain. They have opinions on a variety of topics: politics, sports, lifestyles,
gender, etc. Filmmaker Spike Lee challenges and critiques notions of black
male sexuality while presenting a very typical perspective on black female
sexuality. His imaginative explorations of black male psyche is far more probing, far more expansive, and finally much more interesting than his exploration of black femaleness.

When Nola testifies that there have been "dogs" in her life—men who
were only concerned with getting into bed—a group of black men appear on
the screen in single file delivering the lines they use to seduce women, to
"get it." In this brief segment, sexist male objectification of females is
exposed along with the falseness and superficiality of the men. This particular scene, more than any other in the film, is an excellent example of how
cinema can be effectively used to raise consciousness about political
concerns—in this case, sexist male objectification of females. Without any
particular character making a heavy-handed statement about how shallowly
these black men think about women and sexuality, this point is powerfully
conveyed. Filmmaker Spike Lee acknowledges that he intended to focus

critically on black male behavior in the film, stating, "I know that black men do a lot of things that are fucked up, and I've tried to show some of the things that we do."

While his innovative portrayal of black men in this scene (which is shot in such a way as to assume a documentary stance—each man appearing in single file before a camera as though they are being individually interviewed) acts to expose and, by implication, critique black male sexism, other scenes reinforce and perpetuate it. The deconstructive power of this scene is undermined most glaringly by the rape scene which occurs later.

Often talking with folks about the movie, I found many people did not notice that there was a rape scene, while others questioned whether it could be accurately described as a rape. Those of us who understand rape to be an act of coercive sexual contact, wherein one person is forced by another to participate without consent, watched a rape scene in She's Gotta Have It. When I first saw the film with the black women friends mentioned earlier, we were surprised and disturbed by the rape scene, yet we did not yell out in protest or leave the theater. As a group, we collectively sunk in our seats as though hiding. It was not the imaginative portrayal of rape that was shocking and disturbing, but the manner and style of this depiction. In this instance, rape as an act of black male violence against a black woman was portrayed as though it was just another enjoyable sexual encounter, just another fuck. Rape, the film implies, is a difficult term to use when describing forced sexual intercourse with a sexually active female (in this case it is called a "near rape"). After all, as many black folks—women and men—stressed in conversation with me, "she called him—she wanted to be sexual—she wanted it." Embedded in such thinking is the sexist assumption that woman as desiring subject, as active initiator, as sexual seducer is responsible for the quality, nature, and content of male response.

Not surprisingly, Nola sees herself as accountable, yet her ability to judge situations clearly has been questioned throughout the film. While she is completely in character when she labels the rape a "near rape," the fact remains that she is raped. Though she is depicted as deriving pleasure from the act, this does not alter the fact that she is forced to act sexually without her consent. It is perfectly compatible with sexist pornographic fantasies about rape to show a woman enjoying violation. Since the sexist mindset places responsibility on the female, claiming that she is really in control, then such a fantasy allows that she (who is in actuality a victim) has the power to change this violent act into a pleasurable experience.

Hence the look on Darling's face during the rape, which begins as a grimace reflecting pain, ends as a gaze of pleasure, satisfaction. This is most assuredly a sexist imaginative fantasy of rape—one that we as passive, silent viewers condone by our complicity. Protests from the audience would have at least altered passive acceptance of this depiction of rape. In keeping with the reality of patriarchy, with sexism in our culture, viewers who were pleased with the rape cheered and expressed their approval of Jaime's action when I saw the film.

As Jaime rapes Nola and aggressively demands that she answer the question, "whose pussy is this," this is the moment of truth—the moment when she can declare herself independent, sexually liberated, the moment when she can proudly assert through resistance her sexual autonomy (for the film has highlighted her determination to be sexually active, to choose many partners, to belong to no one). Ironically, she does not resist the physical violence. She does not assert the primacy of her body rights. She is passive. It is ironic because until this moment we have been seduced by the image of her as a forceful woman, a woman who dares to be sexually assertive, demanding, active. We are seduced and betrayed. When Nola responds to the question "whose pussy is this" by saying "yours," it is difficult for anyone who has fallen for the image of her as sexually liberated not to feel let down, disappointed both in her character and in the film. Suddenly we are not witnessing a radical questioning of female sexual passivity or a celebration of female sexual self-assertion but a reconstruction of the same old sexist content in a new and more interesting form. While some of us were passively disgusted, disturbed, sexist male viewers feeling vilified cheered, expressing their satisfaction that the uppity black woman had been put in her place—that male domination and patriarchal order were restored.

After the rape, Nola ceases to be sexually active, chooses to be in a monogamous relationship with Jaime, the partner who has coerced her. Ideologically, such a scenario impresses on the consciousness of black males, and all males, the sexist assumption that rape is an effective means of patriarchal social control, that it restores and maintains male power over women. It simultaneously suggests to black females, and all females, that being sexually assertive will lead to rejection and punishment. In a culture where a woman is raped every eighteen seconds, where there is still enormous ignorance about rape, where patriarchy and sexist practices promote and condone rape of women by men as a way to maintain male domination, it is disturbing to witness this scene not only because it reinforces dangerous stereotypes (a central one being that women enjoy rape), but because it suggests that rape does not have severe and grave consequences for victims. Without counseling, without support, Nola is restored to her cool, confident self by the end of the movie. Silent about her sexuality throughout much of the film, she suddenly speaks. It is she who will call the rape a "near rape," as though it was really no big deal.

Yet it is the rape that shifts the direction of the film, of Nola Darling's fictional self-exploration. As an expression of her newly acquired self-assertion, she calmly denounces the "near rape," explains that the relationship with Jaime has not worked while stressing her right to be autonomously self-defining. Expressed without the bravado and zest that has characterized her previous actions, these statements do not dispel the pervasive sense that we have witnessed a woman being disempowered and not a woman coming to power. This seems to be reconfirmed when Nola's choice to be truly self-defining means that she will be alone, with no sexual partner.

In perfect contrast to *The Color Purple*, wherein same-sex relationships between women are depicted as a source of mutual, non-exploitative erotic affirmation that serve as catalysts for self-development, the lesbian sexuality in *She's Gotta Have It* is negatively portrayed. It does not represent an alternative to destructive heterosexual practice. The lesbian character is predatory, as much a "dog" as any of the men. Significantly, Nola does not find it difficult to reject unwanted sexual advances from another woman, to assert her body rights, her preferences. Utterly male-identified, she does not value her women friends. Though they are underdeveloped characters in the film, her two female friends are compelling and interesting. The apparent dedication and discipline the bass player shows in relationship to her music stands in sharp contrast to Nola's lackadaisical approach to her art, whereas the bass player appears comfortable with her autonomy in a way that Nola is not.

Autonomy is not depicted as a life-enhancing, empowering choice for Nola. Her decision to be self-defining leaves her as vacuous and as empty as she has previously appeared, without the savvy she had evoked in her role as vamp. Finally we see her at the end of the film alone, wrapped in her sheets, a familiar image that does not suggest transformation. Are we to imagine that she has ceased to long for the "it" she's gotta have? Are we to think that the "it" is multiple in implication after all, that it may not be sex but a sense of self she is longing for? She has had sex throughout the film; what she has not had is a sense of self that would enable her to be fully autonomous and sexually assertive, independent, and liberated. Without a firm sense of self, her attempts at becoming a desiring subject rather than object are doomed to fail. Nola cannot enter the sexual power struggle between women and men as object and become subject. Desire alone is not enough to make her subject, to liberate (the film does make this point, but this is no new revelation). A new image, the one we have yet to see in film, is the desiring black woman who prevails, who triumphs, not desexualized, not alone, who is "together" in every sense of the word. Joan Mellen in her introduction to *Women and Their Sexuality in the New Film* emphasizes that the recent attempt to portray radical and transformative images of female sexuality has proved to be a disappointment, in most instances a failure:

> The language of independent women may be reluctantly allowed, but the substance goes unaltered. If lip service provides a pseudo-anticipation of challenge to old values and images, the real business at hand is to refurbish the established view, now strengthened by nominal reference to "awareness." This sleight of hand is the method of co-option. Cinema is an arena in which the process had been refined. Thus the very image of liberated or self-sufficient women, when it is risked on the screen, is presented unpalatably and deployed to reinforce the old ways.

Even though filmmaker Spike Lee may have intended to portray a radical new image of black female sexuality, *She's Gotta Have It* reinforces and perpetuates old norms overall. Positively, the film does show us the nature of black male/female power struggles, the contradictions, the craziness, and that is an important new direction. Yet it is the absence of compelling liberatory reconciliation which undermines the progressive radical potential of this film. Even though nude scenes, scenes of sexual play, constitute an important imaging of black sexuality on screen since they are not grotesque or pornographic, we still do not see an imaging of mutual, sexually satisfying relationships between black women and men in a context of non-domination. It does not really matter if the woman is dominating and a male submitting—it is the same old oppressive scenario. Ultimately it is a patriarchal tale—one in which woman does not emerge triumphant, fulfilled. While we can applaud Nola's feeble attempt to tell a new story at the end of the film, it is not compelling, not enough—it is not satisfying.

2

Programming with *School Daze*

W̲e heard four things about *School Daze* during the spring of 1987 when 40 Acres & A Mule Filmworks was still on location in Atlanta: that it was a musical, that it was tackling the subject of color caste in the Black community, that it had an anti-apartheid theme, and that it was in trouble. The description was interesting; the bad news, of serious concern. In cases of studio-backed independent projects in trouble, Hollywood executives usually make the panicky decision to cut the elements that originally made the work compelling. Examples of films gutted of social relevance, formal innovations, or both are legion. That *School Daze* is not one of them is fortunate. Alert to the film's potential for countering the positive-images school's assertions that color bias played out decades ago and that "dirty laundry" is best kept in a lidded hamper anyway, community workers who use film in our practice were relieved by the late-summer communiqué that *School Daze* was out of the woods. Programmers of independent film and video began planning how to use the new film to facilitate analyses of intracommunity dynamics.

One of the many valuable things shared in the multiple-voiced casebook *Uplift the Race: The Construction of School Daze* (New York: Fireside/Simon and Schuster, 1988) by Spike Lee and Lisa Jones is how to hang tough when

Toni Cade Bambara, "Programming with *School Daze*," in *Five for Five: The Films of Spike Lee*, ed. Spike Lee (New York: Stewart, Tabori, and Chang, 1991), 47–56. Reprinted with permission of 40 Acres & A Mule Filmworks.

beset by problems—the loss of critical location sites, the persistence of bad-mouthing rumors, severe plunges in morale, and competition with a production paying better rates for student extras. A Columbia Pictures executive dropped in for a mere minute, then went home satisfied. And the production team brought the film in for a February 12, 1988, release. To the screen came a good-looking, ambitiously mounted, imaginatively designed production characterized by a bold mix of both dance and musical idioms and performatory and acting styles.

Set at a Southern Black college during homecoming weekend, *School Daze* takes a serio-comic look at caste, class, and gender contradictions among four rival groups of students: Da Naturals, the Gamma Rays, Da Fellas, and the frat members and pledgees of Gamma Phi Gamma. "*West Side Story* with an apartheid twist," quipped a student DJ on WCLK radio in Atlanta. Whether the remark was facetiously or reverentially intended, *School Daze* is a house-divided pageant. It is a pageant in the sense that the spectacle inherent in traditional ceremonies and rites of homecoming (parades, floats, coronation balls, inductions into secret orders) provides the rationale for the overall style of the film.

It is a pageant, too, in the sense that confrontations between the groups are theatrically staged moments rather than realistic debates about the issues. The disturbances are broken up, either by an intervening character or by a scene shift, leaving the parties unreconciled and the contradictions unresolved. The function of the four groups of students is to enact the divisive behaviors that impede unification of the Black community. The film's agenda is to make a series of wake-up calls that the punnish title suggests is necessary for African folk asleep in the West.

The film begins as the Columbia Pictures logo is still on screen. On the soundtrack is the Middle Passage: the wheeze and creak of the ship plowing through water, the dip of the oars, the sounding of the ship's bell. As the prologue's first visual appears, the familiar black-and-white graphic of the slave ship, the old spiritual "I'm Building Me a Home" begins. Using archival materials, Lee presents a chronicle of a diasporized people's effort to make a home in the "new world." Several things are accomplished during the historical unfolding. A faux history is created for Mission College, the fictitious setting that functions as a microcosm. The viewer is reminded that much of our struggle in this land has been about the rights to literacy and autonomy and further that the educational institutions we have built are repositories for much of that history. The film also claims a position for itself in that history. Mission College becomes one of the "homes" alluded to in the spiritual "I'm Building Me a Home." The emancipatory enterprise, the Black nationalist quest for a collective "home," is presented from the time of Frederick Douglass to the era of the Black Panther Party. The prologue then segues to an anti-apartheid rally, the movie's opening scene, in which a "Free Mandela" banner waves. As *School Daze* unfolds, its depiction of contemporary tribal rites is informed by the Fanonian observation that when we internalize the enemy doctrine of supremacy, we jeopardize the liberation project.

Colorist, elitist, sexist, and heterosexist behaviors are presented—sometimes with a degree of hyperbole to signal satiric intent—through the four groups that constitute a hierarchy. The Gamma Phi Gamma forces command the most prestige and the most space on campus; also, they receive the most attention in the production (wardrobe, props, variety of settings, musical themes, spacious framing). Their agenda is to defend tradition at Mission and to perpetuate the prestige of their fraternity.

Committed to some degree to transforming tradition are members of the anti-apartheid forces, Da Fellas. Their homes on campus are the shanty-town construction, a dorm room, and a second-hand car. Members of this group open and close the film and are the subjects of the longest sequence in the film.

The prestige of the Gamma Rays is derived from two sources: their "preferred" looks (light complexions, weave jobs, tinted contact lenses) and their position as the sister order of G Phi G. Their agenda is the maintenance of the frat: The Rays clean the frat house, assist the pledgees in their initiation tasks, throw parties for the brothers, and make themselves available for sex. Although their labor is indispensable to the maintenance of the frat, they are not; they are replaceable by other female recruits. For the most part, the Rays speak an odd form of ventriloquy and are treated by the film as well as by the frat as groupies.

Called Da Naturals in the casebook, Jigaboos on screen, and "Rachel and them" in spectator parlance is the group we come to know the least. Unorganized and with no discernible agenda, these brown-skinned, working-class sisters frequently utter non sequiturs and a variation of the ventriloquy scripted for the Rays. Their "home" is the dorm. Their members loll on a bed saying, "All men are dogs"; they shout from dorm windows saying, "All men are dogs."

In the intervals between group confrontations are several sketchy stories that function as the narrative outline: the seduction and corruption of a fugitive Jigaboo, Half-Pint (Spike Lee); the punishment of an ambitious Wannabee, Jane (Tisha Campbell); and the blown opportunity of a campus organizer, Dap (Larry Fishburne), to develop political coherence. The stories make useful points about intracommunity contradictions. Unfortunately, the film's agenda to make a wake-up call is undermined by its misogynistic and gay-hating sensibility.

Independent filmmaker Marlon Riggs responds to the homophobic bigotry in *School Daze* in his 1989 film *Tongues Untied*. A scripted performance-art work about tribal rights and the tribal rights of Black gay men, *Untied* uses a clip from *Daze* in a section of the film that catalogues examples of heterosexist aggression by Black film- and video makers. The clip is from the Greek show. Da Fellas launch into a call-and-response: "When I say Gamma, you say fag. Gamma (fag), Gamma (fag), Gamma, Gamma, Gamma, Gamma. . . ." Da Fellas continue their disruption of the step contest by issuing threats to the fraternities they've labeled "fags"—"Get back or we'll kick your ass."

Lee's *School Daze*, Riggs's *Tongues Untied*, and Isaac Julien's *Looking for Langston* (a film frequently programmed with *Untied*)—each makes a claim on history while taking a position on the "dirty laundry" issue. *Daze* positions its statements on colorphobia and divisiveness as a counterpoise to the history of struggle chronicled in the prologue. *Untied*, through an innovative mix of idioms (autobiography, lyrical poetry, dramatic monologue, cinema vérité–like scenarios, archival footage), challenges the attempt by the Black community to exclude its gay sector from Black radical history. Footage of gay-rights marches is superimposed on footage of civil-rights marches during the culmination of Riggs's assertive argument.

Looking is a meditation on Langston Hughes that uses the Harlem Renaissance as a cultural reference point for Black gay artists in Britain. Julien sets up a wished-for call-and-response between Harlem of the 1920s and southeast London of the 1980s. He uses archival materials, clothing, literary utterances, and period music to script the yearned-for dialogue. The quest by contemporary Black gay poets for an ancestor, a forefather, a tradition, a past has to override a double silence: Langston Hughes disclosed little about his sexual identity, and the executors of the Hughes estate demanded, in addition to various cuts, that Hughes's voice be lowered on the soundtrack.

Tradition—Mission College's and the G Phi G fraternity's—is what Julian/Big Brother Almighty (Giancarlo Esposito) continually uses as his source of authority, especially in his war with Da Fellas. The radical tradition that Dap could invoke to strengthen his position is not honored at Mission. The three films together—*Daze*, *Untied*, and *Looking*—make for an excellent program on the issue of negotiating identity, individual and collective, in spite of invisibilized histories.

School Daze is a musical. It does not operate like an old MGM down-on-your-heels/up-on-your-toes sis-boom-bah on a mock set of Claremont College. It is not "good news" on campus that *Daze* is singing and dancing about. More is at stake at Mission than whether Grady (Bill Nunn) makes a touchdown. The college is being held hostage by the "old money" robber barons. A wake-up call occurs in a scene in which the chairperson of the board of trustees (Art Evans) advises the president of the college (Joe Seneca) to squash the student-led divest-now campaign because the venerable personages who finance the college will not tolerate being told where they may or may not invest their money. Actor Evans laments, "Why won't our people support our institutions?" At the time of *Daze*'s filming, Cheney and Fisk were being bailed out of serious financial difficulty.

Lee, to make a wake-up call about intracommunity self-ambush, chooses an enshrined genre of the dominant cinema, musical comedy, whose conventions were not designed to address an embattled community's concerns. Much of the tension on screen derives from his effort to link two opposing discourses: Will the ideological imperatives of Lee's agenda subvert the genre, or will the ideological imperatives of the genre derail his agenda? The linchpin is the cinematic rhetoric (framing, choreographed moves, delivery of choral ensemble, costuming) surrounding the fraternity that links the generic conventions (say, spectacle) to the critique of community divisiveness. The story is grounded in Afrocentric modes and idioms (homecoming events, Da Butt, all-up-in-your-face–isms), as are the devices Lee habitually draws from French bedroom farce, nouvelle vague, and Scorsese, as well as from independents who work outside of the industry. "Face," which has become a Lee signature, for example, is the visual equivalent of the oral tradition that resonates in the opening phrase of Toni Morrison's novel *The Bluest Eye*: "Quiet as it's kept. . . ."

The rival groups at the college are repeatedly in each other's face. In the scene at the women's dorm when Half-Pint attempts to get a date, Lee goes beyond using mainstream film devices—talk, shot-response, shot—so that a series of women appear who say, without having to actually articulate it, "Get out of my face." When Dap figuratively gets in Da Fellas' face because Da Fellas prefer to go to the dance rather than keep a vigil in the shanty town, they in turn get in our face: "Lighten up, Marcus Garvey," "Preach, Jesse," "Chill, Farrakhan," "Teach, Malcolm." The close-ups in this scene reconnect us to the history in the prologue, reminding us of what is at stake. The "face" device is responsible, in part, for the intimacy Lee establishes between filmmaker, film, and spectator.

Lee's decision to link old conventions with new ones allows him to deliver pleasure in some of the forms by which dominant cinema keeps audiences addicted to voyeurism, fetishism, spectacle, mystifying notions of social relations, and freakish notions of intimate relations. The mix also allows Lee to present characters in their milieu and to address socially relevant issues, both of which the dominant cinema rules out. What is lost in the mix is the opportunity to articulate a radical Black discourse. What is gained is the opportunity to position several types of spectators.

Since the test case of television's *All in the Family*, commercial success has depended on the ability of an entertainment industry product to address a polarized audience. White reactionaries seeing themselves on prime time were affirmed in their bigotry, White liberals, reading the show as an exposé, congratulated the inventors of Archie Bunker on their "progress." Many Black people desperately needing to see any sign of U.S. Bunkerism defanged tuned in each week to crack up and to reassure each other.

Sexist/gynophobes, heterosexist/homophobes, and other witting and unwitting defenders of patriarchy champion Spike Lee films. So do nonreactionaries. So do many progressives. Not because the texts are so malleable that they can be maneuvered into any given ideological space, but because many extratextual elements figure into the response. Hunger for images is one element; pride in Lee's accomplishment is another. That the range of spectators is wide speaks to the power of the films and the brilliance of the filmmaker.

Many spectators are willing to provide the interrogation missing in the representations on screen because of progressive features: ensemble (collective) playing, the mutually supportive affection of Dap and Rachel (Kyme), the themes of color and apartheid, the pro-Afro aesthetic of Da Butt, and the cast mix of veterans, newcomers, and performers known in other media. Many spectators do not view the film as separate from the figure, Spike Lee, behind it or the emerging movement that figure is a part of.

The message of *Daze* for large numbers of spectators is entrepreneurial, cultural, political, and emblematic of the resurgence of African American expression by the generation that came of age in the post–1960s era. The mixed-strategy approach in the Lee films has released a voice the dominant industry would prefer silenced—the B boys. Lee's composite push (T-shirts, books, and soundtrack CDs) has helped to create a breakthrough for various forms of cultural expression in the marketplace. His commercial success has helped to create a climate of receptivity for Black filmmakers in Hollywood. His preparation of audiences for more active spectatorship is a boon to hundreds of independent Black filmmakers and videographers working in the independent sector.

The color issue is introduced early in *Daze* in a robust production number called "Good and Bad Hair" ("Straight and Nappy" in the casebook). The two groups of sisters encounter each other in the dormitory hallway; neither will give way. Jane, a blonde with green contact lenses, accuses Rachel, a brown-skinned sister with a short 'fro, of having eyes for her boyfriend, Julian. The others, meanwhile, are cracking on one another's weave jobs, kinks, and attitudes. The close-up is held on the two actresses, Kyme and Campbell, in each other's face. Their cohorts call one another Jigaboos and Wannabees.

School Daze (1988). The Gamma Rays (as Jigaboos).

The face-off triggers a production number in a beauty parlor called Madame Re Res. There the women sing and dance a *femme de guerre* to a 1940s-style big-band swing composition with fall-out lyrics.

The Rays and Da Naturals encounter each other several times. The behavior never varies; they sling color-hair insults, but nothing develops. With the exception of a pained remark Rachel makes to Dap after she has a run-in with Jane, no attempt is made in the film to explore, say, the cost of this pro-racist pathology. Such an exploration could have occurred in three scenes involving Rachel and her roommates (Alva Rogers and Joie Lee), but instead they discuss "men are dogs." And it could have also occurred in one scene involving Jane and the other Rays, but instead they plan a party for the frat brothers.

Colorism is reintroduced as a subject in scenes between Rachel and Dap. Dap does not support Rachel's plan to pledge Delta. "They do good work in the community," she argues. Dap, a campus organizer, is opposed. Sororities are as bad as fraternities, he maintains, although he's helped his cousin Half-Pint pledge. Dap's denunciations include charges of color prejudice. She accuses Dap of being equally color-struck, belligerent as he is about light-skinned folks. She teases him, too, about his claims of being pure African. When he won't relent, it occurs to her that his attraction to her may be PR-motivated. "Having one of the darker sisters on campus as your girlfriend is good for your all-the-way Black nationalist image," she says and exits. Although Dap and Rachel get together again, no further mention is made of her charge.

Not verbally stated but visually presented, color caste combined with gender and class operate in the story of Daryl/Half-Pint. He has working-class origins and middle-class ambitions. The viewer's attention is frequently called to the fact that he is brown-skinned, short, and spare by his placement among light-skinned and husky fellow pledgees and among light-skinned and "healthy" sisters. To "graduate" from a less-privileged caste to a more-privileged caste as a member of the reigning fraternity, Half-Pint perseveres in a grueling regimen. The pledgees wear dog collars and chains; they get down on all fours and bark like dogs; they gobble Alpo on command from pet bowls; they drop their pants to be whacked with a mammoth paddle. Half-Pint is singled out by the president of the campus chapter, Julian/Big Brother Almighty, for taunts about his "manhood." To enter G Phi G, the pledgees will be branded. We see Julian's huge, ugly scar of a "G" during one of his scenes with Jane.

The seduction and corruption of Half-Pint culminate in his participation in sexual treachery engineered by Julian. It is gender coercion—"You're a pussy," "Only a Gamma man is a real man and a real man ain't no virgin"—that drives Half-Pint into the men-as-predators/women-as-prey brotherhood. His supremacist-warped agenda to flee his social origins led him to G Phi G. The extravagant attention that the movie gives the frat forces in terms of production and design makes the seduction and corruption of Half-Pint plausible.

The depiction of the fraternity's abusive order and of Half-Pint's ordeal makes a good argument for men engaging in the feminist enterprise of dismantling patriarchy. But what is made more visible in the film is the vested interest men (and women) have in an order characterized by male power, prestige, and prerogative.

The topic predictably raised in post-screening discussions by spectators who identify with Half-Pint is society's standard of male attractiveness. Art Nomura in his video *Wok Like a Man* tackles the implications of the Euro-American standard of height, weight, and aggression for Asian men. On screen and off, one way to become attractive is to have social power or prestige through male bonding, most usually in terms of a shared sexist socialization to despise and exploit women.

Alien standards of beauty internalized at great psychic cost by African Americans are taken up in Ayoka Chenzira's provocative short *Hairpiece: A Film for Nappy-Headed People*. The politics of color links such works as Julie

Dash's *Illusions*, Denise Oliver and Warrington Hudlin's *Color*, Henry Miller's *Death of a Dunbar Girl*, Maureen Blackwood's *A Perfect Image*, Shu Lea Cheang's *Color Schemes*, and Ana Maria Garcia's *Cocolos y Roqueras*. The politics of female representation is treated in Sharon Alile Larkin's *A Different Drummer*. And the complexity and subjectivity of women's experiences is the forte of Zeinabu irene Davis, Camille Billops, Michelle Parkerson, and Barbara McCullough. These issues are central to discussions about the presentation of Jane (Tisha Campbell). The bases of her characterization are classic features in the construction of the feminine: narcissism, masochism, and hysteria. Her seductive display at the ball singing "I Don't Want to Be Alone Tonight," her ambition, and her voluntary sacrifice ("I did what you told me, Julian") are classic she-was-asking-for-it features of femocidal texts.

Uplift the Race informs us that in the original script the frat members entered the Boning Room and ran a train on Jane. Apparently, the thinking behind this particular wake-up call went like this: Isn't it a drag the way men get over on women and how women allow themselves to be ripped off, so let's sock it to this character Jane to protest the unfair situation. Yeah, right. But the appearance of intended meaning (protest) fails to mask the constructed meaning (punishment).

When the Lee films are programmed together, a disturbing pattern emerges. Posters of naked women nailed to the wall in Joe's place of business in *Joe's Bed-Stuy Barber Shop: We Cut Heads* reappear in *Mo' Better Blues* as pictures the musicians pass around while telling one of the guys he should dump his white lover and get himself "an African queen." They hand him pictures of naked Black women. In *Daze*, a male character says "pussy" in one scene, and in the next the Gamma Rays say, "Meow." A more frightening continuity exists between the gratuitous attack of the woman on the stairs in *Joe's*; the rough-off of Nola in *She's Gotta Have It*, an act assuaged by her term "near rape"; and the scapegoating of Jane in *Daze* after she appears in a porno-referenced sex scene with Julian.

Jane is drawn in the conventional pattern of sexual iconography that hallmarks the industry. Gender issues receive no better treatment in *Daze* than in usual commercial fare. But the possibility, and perhaps the intent, was present. The repetitive and exaggerated attention that Lee gives to statements like "a real man," for example, beginning with the first entrance of the frat and the pledgees, sets us up for an exploration that is merely sketched by the comparison–contrast between Julian and Dap—their styles of leadership and how they maintain intimate relationships. What a "real woman" might be is never raised, and little attention is given to the characterizations of female characters.

It was not necessary, of course, to have the frat brothers run a train on Jane. Their presence outside the door and their readiness to go in and "check out how Half-Pint's doing" are suggestive enough of gang rape, particularly after the earlier command was given to Half-Pint to bring "a freak" back to the dorm. It will take another kind of filmmaker, perhaps, to move to the next step and illuminate the homoeroticism–homophobia nexus at play in gang rape and in the kind of surveillance engaged in by the frat brothers, and in the kind of obsessing Mars, Jamie, and Childs engage in about each other through Nola in *Gotta*. Dap's character doesn't articulate the simple wisdom that gay-hate and dominance aren't really crucial to male development. Dap jams his cousin, but he welcomes Julian into the inner circle of the final wake-up call in the film. Would that there had been as much attention paid to human values as to production values.

The anti-apartheid theme is introduced in *Daze*'s opening scene. It is the first wake-up call. "We're late," Dap informs the student body assembled around the administration building. Other universities have been pressured to divest, but Mission hasn't. Dap urges the students to take action: to march, to disrupt classes, to stage a sit-down, and, if necessary, to close the school down. He is drowned out by off-screen chanting—"It takes a real man to be a Gamma man and only a Gamma man is a real man." The frat marches the pledgees onto the turf; they disrupt the rally, seize the space, and disperse the crowd. Within seconds Dap and Julian are in each other's face; in the background, visible between the close-up of the two actors, is a "Free Mandela" banner. Virgil (Gregg Burge), the student council president, steps in between Dap and Julian and breaks them up. A similar scene occurs during the homecoming parade when Julian takes exception to the introduction of a political banner by Da Fellas at traditional festivities. Virgil steps in again and breaks them up. In pay back, Dap and Da Fellas disrupt the Greek Show and bogart the step contest. We assume that their performance will reintroduce the anti-apartheid theme. It does not. Instead, it reasserts an aggressive machismo ("Daddy Lonnnngstroke . . ." "Get back or we'll kick your Gamma ass . . ." "When I say Alpha, you say punk").

A link, though, is made between South African apartheid and the U.S. sharecropping system. It occurs at the top of the longest, most emotionally varied sequence in the film. This sequence is an audience favorite. Dap insists Da Fellas help him defy the ban issued by the administration. Booker T. (Eric A. Payne) 'lows as how he's not risking being expelled by continuing in the divest-now campaign. He's the first in his family ever to go to college; his family "slaved" to get him there. Dap tries to get him to see that the situations are related, that apartheid is international. Da Fellas walk, fed up with Dap, who speaks of the campaign as a personal mission and of their participation as proof of their loyalty and friendship to him (shades of Julian's "Do you love me, Jane? Well, you're going to have to prove it"). He murdermouths them as they exit. Sulking, he hurls a dart at the board. There's a knock on the door. Dap opens it. Piled in cartoon fashion against the doorjamb are Da Fellas. "Do revolutionaries eat Kentucky Fried Chicken?" Grady wants to know.

At Kentucky Fried Chicken Jordan (Branford Marsalis) leaves the table in search of the salt. A shaker is on a table occupied by local working-class brothers. A local in a cap (Samuel Jackson) is relating some off-the-wall anecdote about how he had to get some "bitch" straight. (A few sisters in the audience suck our teeth. We've been assaulted thus far by "freak," "pussy," "tits and bootays," "meow," "bitch"—and the night is still relatively young.) Jordan asks for the salt. The locals look him up and down and continue to talk. Dap calls Jordan back to the table. The local in the cap calls over in falsetto, "Is it true what they say about Mission [limp wrist] 'men'?" This is the umpteenth anti-gay remark. Dap suggests they leave; Da Fellas grumble but get up. (Members of the audience holler because Da Fellas are leaving behind all that chicken!)

In the parking lot, Dap leads Da Fellas to the car. Edge (Kadeem Hardison) does not want to retreat; he's ready to throw down. In seconds, the two groups are lined up in a face-off. The guy in the cap lets it be known that the locals are sick and tired of college boys coming on their turf every year and treating them like dirt. On-campus distinctions between Jigaboos and Wannabees are of no importance to the locals; all college types are Wannabees and ought to stay on campus where they belong. "On account of you college boys, we can't get jobs, and we were born here," the actor Jackson says, cutting through the artifice of the staging. The actors strain to stay on their marks, adding to the electrical charge of the scene. Stuck, Da Fellas go for the short hairs. Dap cracks on the "'Bama country ass" locals' shower caps and jerri curls and casts aspersions on their manhood. Jordan chimes in with "bitch" here and "bitch" there. The local in red pleather (Al Cooper) endures it all with a stony gaze. His partner (Jackson) resumes his assault—"You're all niggers, just like us." He and Dap are face to face. No student council president is present to intervene. Dap steps in closer and says, "You're not niggers." There's a helpless quality to the delivery; there's a vulnerability to the moment. What is at stake for the entire community that refuses to wake up is sounded here. The scene shifts.

Da Fellas are quiet and reflective in the car. So are spectators in the movie seats. Monroe (James Bond III) breaks the silence: "Do we really act like that?" Dap swears it's a case of mistaken identity. Jordan launches into an "I'm Bennett and I ain't in it" routine. Grady has no sympathy for "losers." He is challenged on the class issue. Things are about to disrupt, but Monroe makes a cornball remark that gives them an out. Da Fellas, relieved, pound on Monroe while Booker T. maintains a grip on the steering wheel. Spotting

Julian and Jane, Dap jumps out and jumps right in Julian's chest, saying Julian better make sure that Half-Pint gets into the frat. We've now seen Dap blow the opportunity to develop political clarity three times: with Rachel, when she challenges him on the color question; with Da Fellas, when they suggest that one of the reasons they won't back him is his personality; with the locals, when they let it be known that the debate between the Greeks and campus revolutionaries has no explanatory power in the lives of most Black folks.

The film's finale begins moments after Half-Pint beats on Dap and Grady's door to announce that he is now a "real man." The next scene takes place in hazy yellow light. Images are stretched. Movement is slowed down. In a wide-angle close-up, Dap shouts, "Waaake Uuuupp." Fishburne here displays his vocal register in the exact way that Esposito has done in previous scenes. Does this signal concord between the two male groups? The college bell is ringing. The entire school rises and goes to the quad. Julian gets out of bed, where he's been sleeping with one of Jane's sorors (Jasmine Guy). He is the last to arrive. The camera adopts Julian's point of view as he moves through the crowd toward Dap. Actor Esposito has a particular expression; it may imply that the character has become aware of his ability to change. As the camera ascends, Dap and Julian turn to us, and Dap says, "Please, wake up."

Within weeks of its release, *Daze* became the subject of extravagant claims by folks who'd seen it and loved it, who'd seen it and not liked it, and who hadn't checked it out yet but had their ear cocked to Communitysay: *School Daze* is going to do more to increase enrollment at Black colleges than an army of recruiters could; *School Daze* is going to outshine "The Mind Is a Terrible Thing to Waste" campaigns for gift giving to Black institutions; *School Daze* is going to revitalize our fraternities, and brothers are going to be stepping all over Harvard Yard. By summer—without recourse to stats or surveys and frequently without recourse to a screening of the film—Peoplesay dropped its prophesizing tone, and the statements rang with conviction.

Conversations in neighborhood movie houses focused briefly on the apartheid theme and the range of contradictions treated in *Daze*. Most of the excitement had to do with Lee's original impulse to make use of his experiences as a Morehouse College undergraduate. Aysha Simmons, a former Swarthmore student, recalls that despite passionate dissatisfaction with the film's sexism and heterosexism, the overwhelming feeling within her circle was envy: "We envied the social life of a Black campus." Elvin Rogers, formerly of the University of Pennsylvania, echoes Simmons: "The hazing practices were horrifying, but after seeing the movie we wanted to enroll in a Black college."

Communitysay's claims weren't far-fetched. Many Black colleges and organizations actually did raise funds in a direct way with screenings of *Daze*. And Black Greeks did commence to step all over the quads at Princeton, Harvard, and Yale. And although the various federal agencies and foundations that commission studies of Black colleges and universities can't support a causality theory, preliminary reports from the U.S. Office of Education, the U.S. National Center for Education Statistics, and the Carnegie Foundation do show an unprecedented spurt in Black college enrollment, in Black student enrollment, and in gift giving in the past two-year period [1988–90]. And according to television newscasts during the Thanksgiving holiday of 1990, the Atlanta University complex has been overwhelmed by applications from transfer students and first-year enrollees. In all probability, the 1990 report from the Research Department of the United Negro College Fund will tell the tale more precisely.

The rest of the story is for the audience to report. The Lee films insist on an active spectatorship by the kinds of questions they pose. *School Daze* asks, so what are we going to do about this color/class thaang? Or as the student council president demanded to know at the homecoming parade confrontation, "What do you want to do—kill each other?"

ACKNOWLEDGMENTS

Special thanks to a number of friends for good talks: Louis Massiah; Cheryl Chisholm; Manthia Diawara; Clyde Taylor; the screeners of the Scribe Video Center in Philly and the African American Culture Institute of the University of Pennsylvania; the Black Student Association at the University of California at Santa Cruz (Oakes College); students at Howard University, Spelman College, Knoxville College, and the University of Ohio, Columbus; Mrs. Beatty's senior English class at East Austin High in Knoxville, Tennessee; the sisters with the cassette player at the laundromat on Chelten Avenue and Pilasky Street in Philly; and the brothers with the VCR at the Metropolitan Pool Hall near the Intervale Avenue El in the Bronx.

3

Spike Lee and Black Women

n *The Crisis of the Negro Intellectual,* Harold Cruse defined and described
the impossibility for Afro-Americans of ever isolating a pure separatist or
integrationist agenda. Yet in his rush to supply prescriptions, Cruse missed
the implications of his own scholarship: "Integration," he warned, "is . . .
leading to cultural negation." As Cruse saw it, integration-minded intellectuals like James Baldwin and Lorraine Hansberry were infected with a lethal
dose of false consciousness—a severe case of neither knowing nor caring
what was really black. Thus Cruse called for profound changes in black self-
perception: Black intellectuals needed to toughen up, think more collectively,
and, above all, black up their political, economic, and cultural projects, which
they promptly did in the context of Black Power.

Almost twenty years after Cruse's initial call, black critic Greg Tate sur-
veyed the results for high and low culture in a list-heavy celebration titled
"The Return of the Black Aesthetic: Cult-Nats Meet Freaky-Deke'" (*Village
Voice Literary Supplement,* December 1986). Tate proposed postmodernism
as a way to heal the apparent schism between assimilation and cultural nationalism. "Black artists," he wrote, "have opened up the entire 'text of blackness' for fun and games," which meant that it was no longer necessary to
insist on African origins or the absence of European influences as the basis of
black identity.

Michele Wallace, "Spike Lee and Black Women," in *Invisibility Blues: From Pop to Theory* (New
York: Verso, 1990). Reprinted with permission of the author.

Tate's most encouraging sign of the new age was *She's Gotta Have It*, a low-budget feature made by a young black filmmaker named Spike Lee, which Tate described as "a populist black poststructuralist dream." Not only had Lee formulated "an uncompromisingly black vision," he had "shot [the film] for jackshit with a collectivist cast and crew," thus demolishing "Hollywood's megabudget mystique." This was consistent with Tate's notion of a cultural resistance that "doesn't aim for transcendence of corporate culture's limits into some mystical liberated zone, but for critical intervention in the process by which capitalism is rationalized through mass culture and modernism." Cultural assimilation and even accommodation were now OK, provided they were in a separatist framework. Yet Tate also applauded Lee's "raceman" views on "Whoopi's blue contacts, Michael's nose" and *The Color Purple*: not black enough.

When it came to apparent transgressions in the field of sexuality, the charge of racial inauthenticity was brought out, brushed off, and presented as though it were brand new. Issues of sexual difference were the special blind spot of Tate's theoretical formulations: Women emerged only as also-rans in his numerous lists of who's getting it right, from Miles Davis to Amiri Baraka to Nona Hendryx. Nor did it appear relevant to mention that *She's Gotta Have It*, the showpiece of the new black aesthetic, was about a black woman who couldn't get enough of the old phallus and who therefore had to be raped. Tate's obsession with the prisonhouse of historical narrative (blacks have only walk-on parts in Western Civilization's version) and the groovy way it could be replaced by filmic spectacle, or "fun and games," rendered superfluous the mundane observation that in such spectacles, women almost always occupy a different status.

Since Tate's 1986 declarations, Spike Lee has provided further proof of some kind of major continental drift. His books, *Spike Lee's Gotta Have It* and *Uplift the Race: The Construction of School Daze* (the latter co-authored by Lisa Jones, both published by Simon and Schuster), as well as his new movie, *School Daze*, all participate in Tate's ambiguous vision of "blackness." This spring, Lee made a black-and-white, vérité campaign commercial for Jesse Jackson, and another movie is in the works. Melvin Van Peebles, whom this movement embraces as spiritual father, is also making a movie this summer. So is Robert Townsend, a West Coast actor who tired of the film industry's racism and decided to make his own vehicle. There are reported spinoffs from both the Lee and the Townsend projects, as well. Perhaps film's indeterminacy and power make it seem the likely place for black American culture to emerge from disadvantage and invisibility. But there's a problem here, too, with which the "blaxploitation" films of the 1960s and 1970s thoroughly acquainted us. Black films are obviously untenable without popular success in somebody's marketplace. I hope Lee, Townsend, and Van Peebles et al. are not intending to demonstrate that black filmmakers can reclaim blaxploitation without revising its use of female humiliation as an inevitable byproduct of plot resolution.

The only way to avoid a renaissance of filmic black sexism—while this is still a movement and not yet a full-blown industry—would be to take on the field of sexual difference deliberately and oppositionally. At first, it seemed that Spike Lee had done exactly that with *She's Gotta Have It*. "It always amazed me," Lee wrote in the journal he kept while making the film, "how men can go out and bone any and everything between fifteen and eighty and it's OK. They are encouraged to have and enjoy sex, while it's not so for women. If they do what men do they're labeled whore, prostitute, freaks, nympho, etc. Why this double standard? Why not explore this?"

Lee thus invents a sex-loving female character named Nola Darling, who has three male lovers: Greer Childs, a narcissistic buppie actor who likes being seen with Nola because she's attractive; Jamie Overstreet, a solid, average guy who wants to marry her; and Mars Blackmon, played by Lee himself, a B-boy on a bicycle who always makes Nola laugh. Nola, her male lovers, and her female friends all address the camera to supply competing versions of who she really is. The structure of the film thus subverts whatever masculine authority Lee, as director, writer, and producer, intermittently imposes.

But this film's fun has its limits. Significantly, *She's Gotta Have It* begins with an epigraph from the beginning of *Their Eyes Were Watching God*, in which Zora Neale Hurston romanticizes the irreconcilability of men and women. Nola's three lovers also remind me of Janie's three husbands in Hurston's novel. Jamie seems most like Logan Killicks, who offers Janie the lackluster security of forty acres and a mule and wants to degrade her when she fails to appreciate it. Greer Childs resembles Joe Starks, who becomes the mayor of an all-black town and wants to put Jamie on a pedestal. Tea Cake, who offers Janie pleasure and companionship "on the muck" among the "folk farthest down" seems a dead ringer for Mars Blackmon, whose love of fun emerges as a critique of conventional masculinity.

Although it is Jamie who finally rapes Nola into submission when she refuses to marry him, Lee's journal clearly suggests that he views Jamie as the best man among her lovers. For instance, Lee often remarks that while Nola has sex with all three men, she has orgasms only with Jamie. He has to caution himself against writing too many scenes in which Nola is crying. He doesn't know how Nola should react to Jamie's rape. Should she enjoy it? He settles for having Jamie reluctantly admit that he enjoyed it. Perhaps most important, Lee never calls it a rape. These matters work out considerably better in the film than in the notebooks—on screen, Lee resists the obvious conclusion, in which the best man marries Nola, the prize. But the film's mistrust of female sexuality is disturbingly obvious in Lee's handling of Nola's relationship with her lesbian friend, Opal Gilstrap, who comes on like the original serpent in the Garden of Eden. In many ways, especially in the scene where Lee's puckered lips traverse her flesh, Nola seems less a character than a dark continent to be explored and conquered. Although she addresses the camera directly, her language seems inane and self-canceling, as if she were selling something in a TV commercial. Still, *She's Gotta Have It* left me eager to see what Lee would do next.

School Daze takes on a scene that is already familiar to readers of the canon of Afro-American literature. It's the black college campus of Booker T. Washington's *Up from Slavery*, W. E. B. Du Bois's *The Souls of Black Folk*, Jean Toomer's *Cane*, Ralph Ellison's *Invisible Man*, Amiri Baraka's *Tales*. But such literary allusions cannot hope to compete with the film's animated pastiche of classic homecoming-football-game movies; slapstick humor and sight gags; Motown and Busby Berkeley production numbers; jazz, R&B, and funk performance; black English, style, and dance. To the perennial question of the classic Afro-American literary text—"What kind of education can a black man expect, even at a black college, except a lesson in how to heel to a white master?" Lee replies, "Not much," in a film pointedly devoid of classrooms, professors, and all the appurtenances of study. My question then becomes, reluctantly, what kind of education can a black woman expect to receive as audience for this film?

School Daze is a postmodern film version of Harold Cruse's *The Crisis of the Negro Intellectual*, with the dichotomies of Pan-Africanism versus accommodationist economics and black pride versus assimilation transposed into the madcap goings-on of pop cult's *Animal House* and the neocultural nationalism of Ishmael Reed's playful *Mumbo Jumbo*. But the accompanying political issues of separatism and integration are all but silenced by the film's all-black universe. Also prominently displayed is postmodernism's vision of women as monster kewpie dolls, whose wayward desires require on-screen punishment in movies such as *Half Moon Street*, *Blue Velvet*, *Mona Lisa*, *The House of Games*, and *Ironweed*. While the film halfheartedly focuses on a conflict between students and administration over whether black Mission College should divest from South Africa, its obsession is with gender and sexuality: The viewer is invited to witness entirely distinct male and female versions of a contest between light-skinned, affluent Wannabees and dark-skinned, nappy-haired, lower-class Jigaboos.

The film's opening scene provides us with an introduction to the major male contingents, who generally devote their attention to global issues of cultural leadership or political responsibility (although a lot of what they do appears to be very silly). Dap, the story's protonationalist hero, and Da Fellas, or male Jiga-boos, are participating in a rally to protest South African apartheid and the fail-ure of Mission College to divest. The president of the college and the president of the board of trustees, either or both of whom participated in the civil-rights demonstrations of the 1960s, are watching from an administration-building window. Trouble promptly arrives in the form of the stylishly dressed Gamma Phi Gammas, the principal contingent of the Wannabees, led by a proto-Nazi Big Brother Almighty and flanked by the glamorous Gamma Rays. They don't give a damn about divestment or the plight of South African blacks. As Ju-lian/Big Brother Almighty so succinctly puts it, "I'm from Detroit! Motown!"

The particular cause of conflict is the display the Gammas are making of breaking in eight baldheaded, sycophantic, slavelike pledgees, who are being led along, chain-gang style, on leashes. "It takes a real man to be a Gamma man!" the Gammites chant at the top of their lungs, "Because only a Gamma man is a real man!" Among these Gammites, occupying a uniquely liminal status in the text (in that he is the only character we see communicating effectively with both groups) is none other than the bigeyed auteur Spike Lee, as Half-Pint, Dap's cousin, who is director, producer, and writer of this film, as well.

The women, both Jigaboos and Wannabees, take no apparent interest in either politics or culture except as passive consumers. The Gamma Rays wear expensive clothes, elaborate Farrah Fawcett hairdos, and lots of makeup. The film's preoccupation is with their falseness, which reflects both their "wanna be whiteness" and their femininity—as though they were black women in white women's drag. Jigaboo women, on the other hand, are natural women with natural hair; the film focuses on them primarily as objects of ridicule, humor, and negation. Rachel, Dap's girlfriend, "the darkest thing on campus," in her own words, seems the leader of the Jigaboo women by default. She doesn't really do anything except march alongside Dap, have sex with him, and argue with him about whether she should finally, in her senior year, pledge a sorority, which seems a puzzling contradiction of the Jigaboo stance.

Women's affairs are epitomized by the film's largest musical number, "Straight and Nappy." Suddenly, Wannabee and Jigaboo women are transported to a mod-colored Madame Re Res Hair Salon to have it out. The Cotton Club music and the Josephine Baker dancing have all the heat and none of the dignity of the confrontation between white and Puerto Rican boys in *West Side Story*. Although a comically fat Jigaboo dancer weighs in against the nappy-headed side, otherwise slender female dancers, black and tan, battle early in the film for this ambiguous turf. At one point, Jigaboos don masks of Vivien Leigh play-ing Scarlett O'Hara to present a mirror image to Wannabee women. The Wannabees respond by donning masks of Hattie McDaniel playing her Mammy. Which would you rather be? For black women, either/or is really neither/nor.

School Daze (1988). Da Naturals (as Wannabees).

On an even lower scale in the film's visual economy are the local yokels, or street bloods. Their confrontation with Da Fellas at Kentucky Fried Chicken begins when one local, feigning femininity, asks, "Is it true what they say about Mission men?" It ends with one of Da Fellas saying that a yokel looks "just like a bitch" because he uses jerri curl on his hair and wears a shower cap in the street. Thus, at the only moment when the film takes on the plight of poor black men, it simultaneously refuses even to consider black homosexual legitimacy.

I saw *School Daze* for the second time in Brooklyn's Fulton Mall, not far from where Jamie's first meeting with Nola in *She's Gotta Have It* was filmed. It was a Friday afternoon, and the audience was packed with black women, teenagers, and children. Every time the Jigaboo women came on the screen, perhaps because of their dark skin and their free-form, unstraightened hair, there was the uncomfortable laughter of disapproval. When the Gamma Rays appeared, there was more often the silence of complete immersion or the cat-calls of men, or the involuntary "oohing" of admiration. After all, the Gamma Rays look more like the women we're all used to seeing on movie screens. They also have their own musical number.

At the coronation of the Homecoming Queen, Gamma queen Jane Toussaint, who has long blond (dyed?) hair and blue eyes (contact lenses?), and the Gamma Rays, svelte and glamorous, sing "Be Alone Tonight" in a slick imitation of a Motown girl group. The four women perform in slinky silver-and-black gowns with bows and ruffles from their knees to their ankles. They wear black patent-leather high heels and sparkles in their long, cascading hair, T&A emphasized by dress cut and pelvis-gyrating choreography. They look like the ultimate Virginia Slims advertisement.

Light-skinned Jane Toussaint—who whispers softly, à la both white and black girl groups in the 1960s, "Boy, you know I love you"—is set up by this resplendent presentation of her wares for the anachronistic rape that will be the film's climax. While the dastardly deed is technically done by Half-Pint, he is commanded to do it by Julian/Big Brother Almighty while fellow Gammas wait in the hall. That Jane is also tricked into agreeing to it by her boyfriend only makes this act seem more like the collective will of the text: figurative gang rape as filmic imperative. Dap, presumably the representative of this film's utopianism—just as Jamie was the ideal image of masculinity in *She's Gotta Have It*—is moved to take the drastic action of waking everybody up at dawn, because he sees Half-Pint's act as going too far. But where does Lee stand in all of this: with Dap or with Half-Pint, whom he plays? And dare we interpret his progress from playing "the man who makes her laugh" to playing the rapist by popular demand?

I sat through *School Daze* twice that day in Brooklyn, wondering about my own increasing willingness to luxuriate in the film's youthful images and its seductive, playful musical score. I stopped in the theater's bathroom before I left. Two women were humming and singing "Do the Butt," one of the film's big musical performances, which has since become a hit on black radio. But there was a third woman who wasn't humming anything. She was standing in front of the mirror trying to comb her hair. Full-figured with dark brown skin, her short hair dyed traffic-light blond and covered with a long blond fall attached to a cloth headband, she was no "wannabee" in any sense that *School Daze* could articulate. She kept trying to comb the fall, which had grown stiff and artificial looking, into a shape that might approximate the one it had been in when she'd purchased it. On her young, pretty face, she had that worried look black women often assume in public places when they look in the mirror.

I couldn't figure out how this woman could fail to see a relationship between her dilemma and the film she'd just seen. Did she resent Jane, identify with her, or perhaps a little bit of both? Moreover, I had the uneasy suspicion that the blond hairpiece and the blond dye had something to do with that curious process by which black female frustration becomes black female fashion. Which leads me to wonder: Can black women survive another dose of "Black Pride"?

But Compared to What? Reading Realism, Representation, and Essentialism in *School Daze, Do the Right Thing*, and the Spike Lee Discourse

Brothers and Sisters, we need to talk.
—Joe Wood, "Looking for Malcolm"

Underneath it all, the posse don't know. Who, in fact,
are "our people"?
—Joe Wood, "Self-Deconstruction"

I

One of the first things to do is to think through the limits of one's power. One must ruthlessly undermine . . . the story of the ethical universal, the hero. But the alternative is not constantly to evoke multiplicity; the alternative is to know . . . that this is a limited sample because of one's own inclinations and capacities to learn enough to take a larger sample. And this kind of work should be a collective enterprise. Other people will do some other work.
—Gayatri Spivak, "In a Word"

I am an African American feminist, with fragments of a recalcitrant cultural nationalism still in my veins, working primarily in the area of African American narrative, and I am interested in cultural studies; those four things account for the nature of my interest in Spike Lee. When I agreed to

Wahneema Lubiano, "But Compared to What? Reading Realism, Representation, and Essentialism in *School Daze, Do the Right Thing*, and the Spike Lee Discourse," *Black American Literature Forum* 25, no. 2 (Summer 1991): 253–82. Reprinted with permission of the author.

write this paper, I felt considerable frustration, because if there is one African American filmic who has gotten press, media, and academic attention to the point of saturation, Spike Lee is that one.[1] My frustration arose also from knowing that the mass media and its discourse around Spike Lee might not be accessible to a critique, for example, of that which makes him a totem. On the other hand, despite my misgivings about leftist and liberal fetishization of Lee,[2] as well as my distaste for the regressive and ultimately useless criticism from reactionary critics and commentators concerned with "negative images,"[3] I think that he and his work represent a problematic through which the political difficulties that inhere in African American cultural production in this moment can be usefully discussed. The Spike Lee discourse and his production offer a site for examining possibilities of oppositional, resistant, or subversive cultural production as well as the problems of productions that are *considered* oppositional, resistant, or subversive without accompanying analysis sustaining such evaluation.

I do not want to be misunderstood. I am not criticizing Spike Lee for his representation of what some have called "damaging" or "negative" images of African Americans, images that drove Stanley Crouch to froth at the mouth in print. I want to consider instead the tendency (and the implications of that tendency) among the majority of critical commentators to uncritically laud Lee's films—especially *Do the Right Thing*—and Lee's presence in African American filmmaking. *She's Gotta Have It* and *School Daze* do raise complicated issues, despite both films' masculinist representations and the rampant homophobia of *School Daze*. I don't address *She's Gotta Have It* in this paper because so many other feminist critics, bell hooks preeminent among them, have said everything (and some more besides!) that I would have said about that film. While I find *School Daze* a more interesting film for my own close reading and, therefore, address it here, I also include *Do the Right Thing* because of the importance of that film to what I'm calling the "Spike Lee discourse."

The first part of my title—But Compared to What?—is taken from a Gene McDonald lyric (sung by Roberta Flack on her album *First Take*): "trying to make it real but compared to what?"[4] The unvoiced of my title, of course, is the "trying to make it real." Trying to make what real? Lee's films' cultural production? Trying to make real African Americans' complicated existence in the minds of others, real in their own minds? Trying to make real the possibility of a counter-hegemonic discourse on race, a critique of race? Trying to make real or concrete a set of abstractions that achieve concrete form in material practices embodied in a film, in language about a film, in the effects of a filmmaker's presence in the cultural domain? And what is race in the United States if not an attempt to make "real" a set of social assumptions about biology?

But compared to what? Compared to what is not real? Compared to other things both real and unreal? Compared to whatever else exists, has existed, or might be able to exist within the present terms of cultural production, or under terms that might be changed by our examination of what is real? Compared to who else exists, has existed, or can exist within the specific histories—past and present—of Black people across the diaspora engaged in filmmaking? "Compared to what?" might just mean compared to whatever you have.

What do issues of realism, representation, and essentialism have to do with the Lee discourse and Lee's films? I am concerned with the difficulty of thinking and saying anything at all about Lee and his work without contextualizing his work's possibilities and problems as well as what Lee himself has come to mean in the current cultural/political climate. Yet much of the Lee discourse has been insufficiently contextualized. And when I say *political,* I mean political in the sense of discourse and cultural production concerned with issues of power. In order to talk about these things, I examine Lee's evaluation of his work (specifically *School Daze* and *Do the Right Thing*),[5] others' evaluations of his work, the problems raised by Lee's place in film production and discourse, and the films *School Daze* and *Do the Right Thing* themselves.

Gayatri Spivak, in the interview to which I refer in the epigraph, addresses the possibilities of politically engaged criticism in the academy. I evoke her language here to consider another kind of politically engaged work: African American film production within the constraints of Euro-American film discourse. She describes an interventionist political cultural project: doing one's "sample" while others, presumably, do theirs. The problem of Spike Lee's "sample," his place in the sun, is that his presence, empowered by Hollywood studio hegemony and media consensus on his importance, can function to overshadow or make difficult other kinds of politically engaged cultural work, not because it is impossible for more than one African American filmmaker to get attention at a time, but because of the implications and manifestations of the attention given to his work.[6] Further, the availability of different strategies of representation is foreclosed by the pressure many African Americans place on any artist to "speak" for the community, a pressure against which countless African American critics have inveighed, but a pressure to which Lee himself contributes when he claims to have "told the truth."

Spivak's discussion can serve to remind us that the *context* of the "samples," their availability or unavailability, and the process of their reception determine how centered, unitary, or authoritative Lee's work becomes. Were a variety of African American filmmakers framed with such a profile, such a salience, critics and commentators (both African Americans and others) might be less likely to insist that Lee's work is the "real thing" and celebrate it so uncritically. That is to say, the recognition of multiple filmic possibilities, created from variant points of view by various filmmakers, could function to preempt the unitary authority of any one of them. This is not to say that the *rhetoric* of the "real thing" would disappear under these conditions, but a reductionist African American representational hegemony would be more difficult to maintain. In other words, the combination of the increasing financial success of Lee's films and the media's fairly general deification of him functions to marginalize other African American filmic possibilities—possibilities, for example, such as those offered by independent African American women filmmakers .[7]

II

School Daze and *Do the Right Thing* are both engaged with problems of race and racism (external and internalized) in the context of a nation where race *as a construction* is not much talked about outside of academic circles and where the idea of racism as intellectual, systemic, or concrete individual practice is cause for far more anger than theory, more recrimination and defensiveness than focus. Against this background, Stuart Hall's reading of the possibilities of Antonio Gramsci's work theorizes race and racisms and enables us to focus on the ways in which race and racisms are historically specific and inconsistent, to understand that manifestations of both change across time and across the complexities of the social formation. Hall argues that, while race is consistently related to class, it is not always the *result* of class difference (nor, I want to add, is race consistently *mediated* by class difference). The political consequences of specific moments of racism differ. At one moment and geopolitical locale racism manifests itself in colonial enclaves; at another, in slavery; at another, in Bantustans; and at still another, in something referred to as an urban "underclass" (Hall 1986: 23–25).

This general line of theory offers a vantage point for connecting more specific arguments about constructions of "Blackness" in the United States context, including Henry Louis Gates Jr.'s arguments about the metaphorical nature of "blackness" in Western metaphysical discourse, Anthony Appiah's work on the construction of race, and Frantz Fanon's arguments about the effects on Blacks of the construction of "negroness."[8] I am not taking any of these arguments to Manichean extremes and suggesting that there is no biology; for, as Spivak (1990: 148) cogently asserts, "biology doesn't just disappear," it simply ought not to be the "ground of all explanations." Hortense Spillers (1987: 65–66), for example, warns against the ideological manipulations of racialized biology. In her close reading of the Moynihan Report she remarks on that text's confirmation of "the human body as a metonymic figure for an entire repertoire of human and social arrangements."

What has not changed in the history of race in the United States is its centrality within our culture, the importance of it to our socialization as produced and reinforced by schools, organizations, family, our sexual lives, churches, institutions—all of which produce a racially structured society (Hall 1986: 25). Race is a cultural factor of overwhelming importance. I raise these issues not only because Lee's work renders visible the African American presence within the terms of Euro-American dominance, but because he sees himself and his work in terms of racial, and hence political, engagement: He is quoted by Salim Muwakkil (1989: 18) as saying, "Someone has to force America to come to grips with the problem of racism." Additionally, Lee and his co-producer Monty Ross told an audience at the University of Texas, Austin, that they wanted to make films with a message and would try to make entertaining what was also thought provoking; they insisted that they would "tell the truth."⁹ Aware of the need to make changes in the film industry by bringing in African Americans, Lee has indicated that he is proud of the part that he plays. As part of his production deal for Do the Right Thing, he has made his films vehicles for African American employment and entrance into film craft unions: Two folks off the streets of Bedford-Stuyvesant are now part of a union because of him (Lee 1989; Tate 1989). Being a voice for the "real," effecting "reality," then, is the way that Lee sees his cultural mission.

His confidence that he has been able to force the United States to come to grips with the problem of racism is repeated in his insistence (in response to questions at the University of Texas) that he can retain his intellectual and political independence and still be financed by the studios as long as he continues to make money. In the first instance, however, he mistakes the media noise around race, racism, and his film for evidence that this country has "come to grips" with race. In fact, he must have realized at some point that his confidence was misplaced; in an article in Mother Jones he says that white people were more upset over the destruction of Sal's property than they were over Raheem's death (Orenstein 1989: 34). In the second instance, his belief that profit might not be somehow tied to how much a mass-distributed film can make itself acceptable to vast numbers of U.S. citizens is simply naive; he needs to consider that, if a production has to return a profit in the millions of dollars, the likelihood of that production's remaining oppositional or subversive with regard to race might well be in inverse proportion to the extent the film relies on the support of a large (of whatever races), politically uncritical audience to turn a profit. I do not want to argue that studio funding always means that a compromise in form and content is inevitable—profits have been made with more politically adventurous material—nor do I want to argue that the relationship between funding and content is a simple one. In fact, in a session at the 1989 Modern Language Association convention, Ann Cvetkovich and I argued that, if one wants to engage politically with the majority of African Americans or any other marginalized group, one has to be prepared to think seriously about working in the mass culture (and, more to the point, mass distribution) arena (Lubiano and Cvetkovich 1989: 13).[10] But I do want to insist that Lee's confidence needs to be mediated by a *complicated* awareness of market pressure.

In that vein, James Snead (1988: 17) has argued that, "without the incessant and confining restraints of box-office considerations, studio agenda, and censoring boards, the range of artistic choice in *independent* films is potentially *widened*, rather than *restricted*." I don't draw on Snead here in order to absolutize independent production as always politically empowered and empowering; I do not want to romanticize the coercive nature of inequitable access to the means of film production, something the Sankofa Film and Video Collective filmmaker Isaac Julien addresses in the Black British context.[11] (He and the other members of Black British video collectives became involved in separatist projects, opting for ethnically and/or racially based organizations, because of their exclusion from "White" institutions (Fusco 1988a: 8). Nonetheless, I think such consideration of the possible costs of studio/institutional support is especially timely when one sees critics such as Nelson George writing in the *Village Voice* about the economics of African American film production: He points out that, while some of Lee's investors have been African American, some of the most crucial have not and, therefore, that it is time for African American filmmakers to learn how to sit down and talk to studio money people because the *"Black Enterprise* crowd" would still rather invest in real estate than in African American cultural production (George 1990).

George's thinking raises a number of other questions. Would the financing from African American capitalists necessarily be more politically adventurous than that from Euro-American capitalists? I am not so sanguine, not so sure that Black nationalism breaches *class* walls. Black nationalist economics raise yet another issue: Both Spike Lee and Keenan Ivory Wayans talk about the necessity for African Americans to be in particular positions of power in relation to African American cultural production; Lee is "appalled by the dearth of Black executives in Hollywood," and Wayans thinks that "the destiny of Black art rests on Black people and Black corporate America" (Greenberg 1990: 23). To that last bit, "Black corporate America," I can only reply that if our cultural production rests on anybody's *corporate* America, then God/Goddess help us.

It is to Lee's dominant position as and his forthright claim to be a "political" filmmaker that I want to return for the next section of my essay. My impetus for thinking about Lee in this way had its genesis in my reading of Manthia Diawara's article "Black Spectatorship: Problems of Identification and Resistance." I found his argument that Eddie Murphy's character in *Trading Places, 48 Hours,* and *Beverly Hills Cop I* and *II* is first allowed to appear threatening, then "deterritorialised from a black milieu and transferred to a predominantly white world" (Diawara 1988: 71), helpful in considering containment and domestication strategies for certain other kinds of characters. It spurred me to consider similar phenomena within what is at least represented as African American milieux—those depicted in *Do the Right Thing* and *School Daze.* How might one account for the domesticating processes of particular kinds of representations unless one rethinks the politics of what constitutes the possible "territory" of a "Black" milieu?

I find the idea of Lee as a politically radical or progressive filmmaker troubling for a number of reasons: (1) The politics of race, gender, class, and sexuality in *Do the Right Thing* and *School Daze* are inadequate to the weight that these films and Lee carry within the discourse of political cultural work; and (2) having Lee and his work deified by the media and critical establishment, especially (as far as my own interests are concerned) by members of the leftist and African American media and critical establishment, is bad news to other African American filmics who remain overshadowed by the attention granted to Spike Lee and bad news also to the larger possibility of more politically progressive and complex film production focused on African American culture and/or issues of race.

To return to the questions that I raise at the beginning of this paper, any evaluation of Lee's work as radical or counter-hegemonic has to be run past the question *Compared to what?* Against the underdeveloped, stymied state of discussion about race, racism, and racialization in the United States at this moment and against the paucity of productions about African Americans which we could invoke to situate Lee's work and stylizations, evaluations of his and his films' politics require considerably more analysis than has been available.

III

School Daze and *Do the Right Thing* were films discussed by most reviewers on the grounds of realism, authenticity, and relation to the "good" of the community represented in them. Many of the arguments that addressed the issue of *reception* fell into the trap of reducing the complexities of hegemony to simple polarities—White vs. Black audiences or Black middle-class vs. Black lower-class audiences—as though these categories are completely understood and separately distinct.[12] That is to say, the blurred lines between unstable categories of people were firmly and falsely redrawn in the Spike Lee discourse. Omitted from discussion were the ways in which aspects of U.S. culture are internalized and contributed to (in some degree) by most of us (after all, how else does hegemony function?), as well as the ways in which culture constitutes contested ground—contested by different groups even within racialized communities under different circumstances. The complex problems of realism, representation, and essentialism were as apparent in the discussions around Lee and the films as they were in Lee's presence and in the films themselves.

Most of the reviews and articles written began, were imbued with, and/or concluded with references to how very realistic or authentic the films were; how much they captured the sounds, rhythms, sights, styles, and important concerns of African Americans.[13] Armond White (1989: 46) tied the film's politics to its depiction of "Afro-American cultural style as triumphant opposition strategy." As Michael Kamber, writing about *Do the Right Thing* in *Z Magazine* points out, "He's so authentic!" seemed to be the refrain among liberal whites. That refrain, however, came from all corners—liberals, progressives/leftists, and even some conservatives and reactionaries (as troubling as such critics found the film's "reality"), and from the political range of African Americans. It came from organs as ideologically dissimilar as the *Guardian*, the *New York Times*, and *Ebony*. More importantly, whether the critic/commentator was heaping encomia on Lee for attempting to portray African American culture without the "distortions" to which we have all grown accustomed (Muwakkil 1989: 24), questioning whether or not the characters were "real" (Staples 1989: 9), or spouting vitriolic accusations of Afro-fascism because of what one critic saw as Lee's "fantastical" (i.e., "not real") distortions (Crouch 1989: 74), "realism" (or its lack) and the effect of the films' representation of the real have been the keynotes of an incredible array of commentary about them.

Realism as the bedrock of narrative is inherently problematic. Realism poses a fundamental, longstanding challenge for counter-hegemonic discourses, since realism, as a narrative form, enforces an authoritative perspective. According to Raymond Williams, while *real* has denoted the actually existing as opposed to the imaginary since the fifteenth century and, at the same time, was contrasted with *apparent*, by the nineteenth century the word additionally established the difference between the "true" or fundamental quality of some thing or situation and the "false" or mistaken quality, while at the same time marking the difference between concrete and abstract (Williams 1976: 216–17).

Reality, as Suzette Elgin (1984: 30–31) puts it, is established via the consensus of a particular group and marks the "real world, the actually existing, true and concrete world" preserved by the absence of existing alternatives. Kobena Mercer argues that the "reality effect produced by realist methods depends on the operation of four characteristic values—transparency, immediacy, authority and authenticity—which are in fact aesthetic values central to the dominant film and media culture." By adopting this practice as a "neutral" or "instrumental" relation for the means of representation, black filmmakers seek to "redefine referential realities of race through the same codes and forms as the prevailing film language whose discourse of racism" they seem to contest (Mercer 1988: 53). Mercer goes on to argue that, "in short, black film practices which incorporate these filmic values are committed to a mimetic conception of representation which assumes that reality has an objective existence 'out there,' that the process of representation simply aims to correspond to or reflect" (Mercer 1988: 53).

Deployed as a narrative form dependent upon recognition of reality, realism suggests disclosure of the truth (and then closure of the representation); realism invites readers/audience to accept what is offered as a slice of life because the narrative contains elements of "fact." Realism, then, temporarily allows chaos in an otherwise conventional or recognizable world, but at the end the narrative moves toward closure, the establishment of truth and order. As Michael Kamber puts it, the morning after the riot (in *Do the Right Thing*) the neighborhood is "back to normal, . . . and the feeling is that, were Sal to rebuild his pizzeria"—and, I would add, slap some pictures of Malcolm X and a few others on the wall—"and were the cops to avoid killing anyone in the immediate future, everyone would go on back and eat there. Ignorant and apolitical, letting the system roll on" (Kamber 1989: 40).

Realism used uncritically as a mode for African American art implies that our lives can be captured by the presentation of enough documentary evidence or by insistence on another truth. The graffiti on Sal's pizzeria asserts, "Tawana told the truth." The implication is that her story was real, was actual and concrete, was *the* story of rape. The problem presented then is further cathected: Must *Tawana* be telling the truth for us to believe the larger truth about sexual abuse of African American women by Euro-American men? Is this "truth" compared to the "truth" of their abuse by African American men? Compared to what other African American women say? Compared to what Alice Walker, for example, says about African American men?[14] Compared to what Jade herself is saying, or trying to say, to Mookie?[15] In the name of preserving the "truth" of Tawana and her reality, is it okay for Mookie to *insist* that he *knows* the truth?[16]

Realism establishes a claim to truth, but it also presents the ground for its own deconstruction—somebody else's truth. Telling it like it is, as John Akomfrah notes, "has to be said with a certain amount of skepticism, because

ultimately one needs to challenge the assumption that you *can* tell it like it is"
(Fusco 1988b: 53). Telling it like it is, for example, can be claimed by narratives that are politically regressive. Shelby Steele, the new African American
conservative media superstar, in his numerous attacks on the victims of
racism (available in a newspaper/magazine near you) claims to be "telling it
like it is" from his reality (Applebome 1990: 18). "Reality" is promiscuous, at
the very least.

Why the historically consistent demand for and approval of realism in
African American cultural production? Fanon argues that the "natives,"[17] in
the face of the colonizer's big lies about the history and culture of the colonized, make a conscious attempt to reclaim their history and aspects of their
culture (Fanon 1968 [1961]: 206–12). Against the constant distortions of
Euro-American ethnocentric dismissal and burial of the African American
presence, we respond with an insistence on "setting the record straight,"
"telling the truth," "saying it like it is." The Harlem Renaissance intellectuals,
artists, and writers went to cultural war with each other over accurate depictions of the African American community; the Black Aesthetic critics in a
subsequent period built a political and intellectual movement around an assertion of a counter-truth against the distortions of cultural racism; and, because the distortions have not ended, African Americans are presently
preoccupied with the need to intervene in the dominant culture's construction of African Americanness. Nonetheless (and it is here that I am most concerned with the salience of Lee and his "truth"), despite the weight of a will
to counter "lies," a marginalized group needs to be wary of the seductive
power of realism, of accepting all that a realistic representation implies because of its inclusion of some "facts."

The reasons for "real" as a positive evaluation are tied, of course, to
scarcity, the paucity of African American presentations of *facts* and *representations* as well as the desire for more of the first category, which in turn allows
the second category to have its "selectiveness" forgotten in the rush to celebrate its mere presence. It is, however, because of the salience of Lee's representations that he and they warrant *critical* attention. In order to give them
that attention, we have to first acknowledge that they are not *generally* "real"
(however "factual" any part of the content might be) but *specifically* "real"—
and that that specific "real" might be criticizable. If Lee's strength is a certain
ability to document some of the sounds and sights of African American
vernacular culture—its style focus—that vernacularity cannot guarantee
counter-hegemonic cultural resistance. One can be caught up in Euro-
American hegemony within the vernacular, and one can repeat the masculinism and heterosexism of vernacular culture. Vernacular language and cultural
productions allow the possibility of discursive power disruptions, of cultural

resistance—they do not guarantee it. The particular politics of the specifics of vernacular culture that Lee represents are problematic. The films' presentation of and the critics' acceptance of these politics without a challenge encourages audiences to consider these representations as African American essences.

Telling the "truth" demands that we consider the truth of something compared to something else. Who is speaking? Who is asking? And to what end? I don't think that the problem of addressing the construction of reality can be answered by more claims to realism without considering how and why both hegemonic realism and resistance to or subversion of the realism are constructed. Reality, after all, is merely something that resounds in minds already trained to recognize it as such. Further, what happens in the shadow behind the "real" of Spike Lee once it becomes hegemonic for African Americans? In other words, what happens when this "representation" is accepted as "real?" What happens to the construction of "Blackness" in the public discourse?

According to Roland Barthes,

> Representation is not directly defined by imitation: even if we were to get rid of the notions of "reality" and "verisimilitude" and "copy," there would still be "representation," so long as a subject (author, reader, spectator, observer) directed his [or her] *gaze* toward a horizon and there projected the base of a triangle of which his [or her] eye (or his [or her] mind) would be the apex. (Barthes 1985: 90)

Representation refers to images that are selected from what we recognize as reality; they are tied to and have meaning within particular settings. They come "from somewhere" (Barthes 1985: 96) and have meaning insofar as "there are differences of meaning" (Culler 1976: 83). Akomfrah argues that representation "is used to simply talk about questions of figuration. How one places the Black in the scene of writing, the imagination and so on. Others saw it in more juridic terms. How one is enfranchised, if you like, how one buys into the social contract" (Fusco 1988b: 43). In other words, we need to consider how one constructs identity through the vehicle of representation. And compared to what? If Lee is working in a small field, if too much rides on the few African American filmmakers working in this cultural domain and this pressure to variously "represent" cannot be met, how might we reconsider the possibilities of African American filmmaking?

In *Invisible Man*, Trueblood tells a white philanthropist a story explaining his incest, his daughter's pregnancy, and his wife's. The unnamed narrator is shocked by Trueblood's frankness in relating his story and wonders, "How can he tell this to white men . . . when he knows they'll say that all Negroes do such things?" (Ellison 1952: 57). The question of representation and what anyone should say about his/her community is a constant pressure under which African American cultural workers produce. But it is a question which constantly disenfranchises even as it reinforces the notion of absolutes—absolutes such as the "African American" community, the non–African American or "Euro-American" community, or notions of the author or film-maker as the one who does "something" which a reader or an audience then simply consumes, resists, or appropriates. Further, if one is enthralled by the idea of absolute representations, then "good" or "real" cultural production is impervious to reader or audience misbehavior (misreading), and "bad" or "non-representative" or "unrealistic" cultural production comforts racist Euro-Americans, or can be appropriated by them, or misleads African Americans. Believing and acting on these assumptions means deifying or demonizing African American cultural production or producers. In other words, it is as foolish to say that Lee has produced "appropriation-proof," *real* African American art as it is to say that he has produced "Afro-fascism" that distorts reality.

Lee is himself to some extent cognizant of how he is placed within the discourse of representation; on the other hand, he also produces representations that suggest particular Euro-American hegemonic politics. His *Do the Right Thing* is imbued with the Protestant work ethic: There is more language about work, responsibility, and ownership in it than in any five Euro-American Hollywood productions. The film insists that, if African Americans just work like the Koreans, like the Italians, like the Euro-American brown-stone owner, these problems could be averted; or, if you own the property, then you can put on the walls whatever icons you want; or, if you consume at (materially support) a locale, then you can have whatever icons you want on the walls. And its masculinist focus could be distilled into the slogan that screams at us throughout the film: "Real men work and support their families." These representations compared to what? Within the representations of *Do the Right Thing*, what are the ideologies being engaged here, or critiqued here, or, more to the point, not critiqued here? Contrary to Salim Muwakkil's assertion that "Lee's refusal to make clear his judgments has limited his popularity among audiences weaned on formulaic narrative" (Muwakkil 1989: 24), I find *Do the Right Thing* relentlessly formulaic in its masculinist representations and its conventional Calvinist realism.

To paraphrase Stuart Hall (1986: 15–16), there is no law which guarantees that a group's ideology is consistent with its economic—or, I would add, its race—position, nor is there any guarantee that the ideology of a group *isn't* consistent with its economic or race position. For the purposes of thinking about representation and Lee's films, we might want to consider the assumption held by his lower-class characters that work is the "right thing," that it means always what we think it means. Drug dealers (absent from this picture) work; global corporate CEOs responsible for planetary and human degradation also work. Work or non-work, but compared to what? We (as audience) could consider this "work" emphasis to be parody, but the film uses "work" or "ownership" to justify intervention.

Or, to return again to identity politics, Hall writes "'Black' is not the exclusive property of any particular social or any single discourse. . . . [I]t has no necessary class belonging" (Hall 1985: 112). He is drawing on his experience in the Caribbean and British context, but it is an argument that has considerable force for race theorizing and the politics of racial representation within the U.S. context. What does "Blackness" mean in *School Daze* or *Do the Right Thing*? *School Daze*, the Lee film that has received by far the least amount of national critical respect, suggests far more complicated *possibilities* around the idea of identity politics than *Do the Right Thing* (despite *School Daze*'s foul gender politics and horrific homophobia, issues to which I will return). It is with regard to identity politics that unselfconscious realism and representation within the distorted discourse of Euro-American hegemony lead inevitably to a profoundly unstrategic essentialism.

Essentialism is, as Diana Fuss (1989: xi) defines it, "commonly understood as a belief in the real, true essence of things, the invariable and fixed properties which define the 'whatness' of a given entity." It assumes that certain characteristics are inherently part of the core being of a group. The idea of authenticity—a notion that implies essence—can derive from the idea that a particular group and individual entities of that group can be recognized by the ways in which they are shown with some measure of the "real" or authentic or essential qualities of that group. Fuss argues additionally, however, that, because essentialism is not in and of itself progressive or reactionary, the appropriate question is: "If this text *is* essentialist, what motivates its deployment?" (Fuss 1989: xi; my emphasis). Because I am mindful of Fuss's careful complications of essentialisms, I want to make clear my consideration of specific problem sites of essentialism—Lee, the discourse about Lee, and two of his films.

Some African American critics have indicated their impatience with criticisms of essentialism. Henry Louis Gates Jr., for example, has stated his suspicions about this charge as part of his defense of African Americanist canon formation or reformation (Gates 1989).[18] He refers to the fact that African Americanists' "attempts to define a black American canon—foregrounded on its own against a white backdrop—are often derided as racist, separatist, nationalist, or 'essentialist'—my favorite term of all."[19] He argues that "you cannot . . . critique the notion of the subject until a tradition's subjectivity (as it were) has been firmly established" (Gates 1989: 15), but he is not clear about *who* cannot critique the subject at issue here, the African American subject, or *for whom* this subjectivity still needs to be established. I am mindful of the fact that Gates is skeptical of a *specific* charge of essentialism—that leveled against the institutionalization of an African American literary canon—and I agree with his arguments about the political usefulness at this moment of such defining. Attacks on African American "canons" are blind to certain political "realities." I am simply picking one small bone here: I think that it is possible to argue for the work of defining African American literary traditions without "saving" essentialism.

I find Gates's argument about the need to "establish" African American subjectivity a little inconsistent, given his tracing (in *Figures in Black* and *The Signifying Monkey*) of the complexity of the historical development of African American subjectivity (African Americans have been already at work developing *subjectivities*) and his deconstruction of the idea of a "transcendent black subject" (Gates 1984: 297). Part of the work of African American cultural criticism has been not only to claim, to insist on, African American subjectivity/subjectivities, but also to elaborate and complicate that subjectivity/those subjectivities by speculating on their varied and fragmented relations to their products—abstract and/or concrete, formalized and/or ephemeral.

Within the domain of African American cultural discourse, African Americans have been about the business of establishing that tradition's subjectivity and have been fighting about the terms of that subjectivity since the seventeenth century. Some African Americans, as various critics (among them Gates, Gloria Hull, Valerie Smith, Deborah McDowell, and Hazel Carby) have documented, historically resisted essences inscribed in African American cultural commentary, even when these essences were meant to counter essences held by the dominant culture. Vernacular culture, in fact, has allowed a space and mechanism for complicating essences. And in literature and literary critical discourse, Zora Neale Hurston, Nella Larsen, Pauline Hopkins, Jessie Fauset, W. E. B. Du Bois, Sterling Brown, Jean Toomer, and Langston Hughes (to some extent) have complicated notions of African American subjectivity even against the African American male cultural and political hegemony of the Harlem Renaissance.

In her interview with Spivak, Ellen Rooney states that

> to contextualize is to expose the history of what might otherwise seem outside history, natural and thus universal, that is the essence. . . . The problem of essentialism can be thought [of], in this way, as a problem of form, which is to say, a problem of reading. Context would thus emerge as a synonym for reading, in that to read is to demarcate a context. Essentialism appears as a certain resistance to reading, an emphasis on the constraints of form, the limits at which a particular form so compels us as to "stipulate" an analysis. (Spivak 1990: 124)

I am moved to consider the particular situation of Lee by Spivak's warning against "anti-essentialism" as yet another form of essence: "To an extent, we have to look at where the group—the person, the persons, or the movement[—]is situated when we make claims for or against essentialism. A strategy suits a situation; a strategy is not a theory" (Spivak 1990: 127).[20] Lee's films and his place in the discourse of African American and American filmmaking are situations which warrant my criticism of their essentialism; and even if what Lee does is a strategy and not an essence, it is still fair to be critical of that strategy and its power to essentialize within the context of Euro-American hegemony and African American cultural discourse. Lee's presentation of images that resonate with factual reality is glossed as the general truth. The deification of Lee as "truth sayer," and his production as "real," means that the indexing of his selections becomes the "essence" of "Black authenticity"—and thus impervious to criticism.

I understand that to be authentically "African American" or "Black" has, at various times in history and in the present, meant and sometimes means to be rhythmic; or to have a predilection for playing craps, drinking, using and/or selling drugs, or raping white women; or being a jungle savage; or being uninterested in marriage; or being on welfare—the list goes on and on. The resonances of authenticity depend on who is doing the evaluating. But I want to foreground the problematic of authenticity and its relationship to essentialism.

Coco Fusco has argued that "the tenet of authenticity is virtually incompatible with the strictures of narrative drama, since 'typical' experiences are presumed to stand for every black person's perception of reality" (Fusco 1988a: 8). To that I would add only that, when further strengthened by facticity, "typicalness" homogenizes differences. Being different within such a narrative economy, then, is read as "White" or "middle-class" or whatever the current sign used to signify "not Black." In any event, dramatic "play" or manipulation (and its political possibilities) is constrained. Authenticity becomes a stranglehold for political analysis and cultural practice beyond the strictures of narrative drama. When Michele Wallace asserts that "intrinsic oppositionality c[an] not be attributed only to the so-called Other" (Fusco 1988a: 9) and Akomfrah asserts that "Blacks are expected to be transgressive" (Fusco 1988b: 55), they, along with Fusco, point to the specific problem of essentialism in the context of Black film production. If, as Akomfrah, argues, we fall into the trap of Kant's categorical imperative—that categories carry with them their own imperatives, and, following that, that the category *Black* carries with it an essential obligation to oppose, to transgress constantly in specific ways—then we are "saddled with the assumption that there are certain transcendental duties that Black filmmaking has to perform, . . . [that] it has to work with the understanding that it's in a state of emergence, . . . [and that] its means always have to be guerrilla means, war means, signposts of urgency . . . the categorical imperative imprisons" (Fusco 1988b: 53). "Black" essence can come to be read from its activity of transgressing another, even less elaborated essence—that of "Whiteness."

The categorical imperative is essentialist, whether imposed by dominance or volunteered for under the terms of Euro-American political or African American cultural hegemony. If we fail to problematize the notion that being African American *always* means *only* being embattled, that African American film is political only insofar as "someone" empowered to make the evaluation recognizes its political "reality" and calls the shots on its transgressiveness, and that "authenticity" is always already known and can therefore be proven, then we have fallen into the trap of essentialism. Both the celebratory and the hostile Spike Lee discourse have been amazingly, although not entirely, uncritically essentialist.

There are "honorable" exceptions: bell hooks and Michael Kamber writing in *Z Magazine*; Herb Boyd writing in the *Guardian*, Mike Dyson writing in *Tikkun*; and some of what J. Hoberman wrote in the *Village Voice*—all regarding *Do the Right Thing*, as well as parts of the multi-voiced exchange on *School Daze* that went on in the *Village Voice*—not only moved past celebration or dismissal based on explicit language about "reality" and "authenticity," but also managed to critique assumptions of progressive or radical cultural politics based primarily on representations of African Americans on the screen in practices that too many of us have been trained to identify as "transgressive."

When I ask, "Compared to what?" I am asking that we consider a larger domain of possibilities than the Spike Lee discourse has made available. The end of such inquiry is not to lead simply to a fuller explication of his films or his "presence" in cultural production—although that's not a bad side effect—but to enable us to think about the terms of African American cultural production and practice generally, and African American film production and practice specifically, without falling back on an uncritical and unstrategic essentialist celebration of any representations—on screen or embodied in a particular filmmaker.

IV

Although *Do the Right Thing* received far more positive press than *School Daze,* perhaps because its working-class subjects seemed more "authentic" to critics[21] than the middle-class subjects of *School Daze*, I contend that *School Daze* is the more complicated movie. While both films are masculinist, and *School Daze* is also explicitly and viciously homophobic, *Do the Right Thing*

stays, for the most part, comfortably within the boundaries of static and essentialist propositions about racial identity, and about the relationship of wages
and ownership to qualities of responsibility, "manhood," and freedom.[22]

Do the Right Thing makes manhood synonymous with having a job (and
being able to take care of one's monetary responsibilities). When one of the
block's hip-hop young men taunts Da Mayor for his drinking and other problems, Da Mayor returns (as explanation) an account of his inability (in the
past) to feed his children because he had no job. The teenager sneers back
that Da Mayor put himself in that position. Unlike Da Mayor, we are given to
understand, the young man would make sure that he had a job and could take
care of his kids; in other words, *he* would be a *man*. In this vein, Mookie's
wages make him responsible enough—or man enough—that he can abjure
others to "get a job," enable him to make some feeble attempts to provide for
his child, and give him the standing to tell Jade what she needs to know about
sexual oppression. Jade tries to make him back down by participating in the
"wages=right-to-speak" discourse: "You can hardly pay the rent and you're
gonna tell me what to do?" Mookie responds, "I get paid." When Jade returns
with, "You're getting paid peanuts," the point, I suppose, is that were Mookie
to have higher wages, *then* it would be all right for him to tell her what to do.
At the same time, Mookie is excoriated by Sal and Pino to do the work for
which they are paying his wages/his peanuts.

Against, I suppose, the long-held racist charge that African Americans
neither work nor want to work, this film spends much of its running time assuring its audience that African Americans in Bed-Stuy certainly do value
work! (By its end, I am so overwhelmed by its omnipresent wage-labor ethos
that I find myself exhausted.) I am not anti-labor; however, this film makes no
critique of the conditions under which labor is drawn from some members of
the community, nor are kinds of labor/work differentiated. Instead, without
any specific contextualization, work is presented as its own absolute good, because work and ownership are what empower *men* to make decisions, to exercise freedom. The Euro-American brownstone owner need only reply to the
block's hip-hoppers that he "owns" his house to have the last word in the encounter; Sal need only respond that he "owns" his pizzeria in order to maintain his freedom over decor; and Sweet Dick Willie is able to have the last
word in a discussion of Korean ownership by insisting that since he has his
own (or "*owned*") money, he has the freedom to ignore any form of critical
analysis on the part of his buddies or Buggin' Out and patronize the grocery
store and the pizzeria, respectively.

"I own," however, complicates neighborhood boundaries and identity politics. The gentrifier both "owns" his house and was born in Brooklyn and,
thus, can be said to "belong" in the neighborhood (if not on this particular

block). And, ironically, the critique of the Korean grocery store owners because they don't "belong" in the neighborhood is begun by M. L., who is himself an immigrant, as his buddies are quick to remark. Yet, while Sal "owns" his
pizzeria, Pino reminds him again and again that "this" is not "their" neighborhood; they don't "belong" here. Still, no one really needs to think about what
might be at stake in these contradictions; it is enough to have the money:
"When you own your own pizzeria, then you can put your own pictures up."

In these contradictions, *Do the Right Thing* raises an interesting issue:
What is the difference, if any, between a person "born" (and thus able to lay
some kind of claim to "belonging") in a neighborhood and a gentrifier who
lays claim by "buying" his belonging? Further, the gentrifier's presence—as
both "born in" (and therefore "native to") Brooklyn and as "buyer" in this
block—raises the larger context of the relations of racial bodies, real estate
and bank practices, and class issues.

Early on, the film promises a class critique of sorts in the discussion of
Sweet Dick Willie and his buddies on the corner. M. L. begins a complaint
that the Koreans, like so many other immigrant groups, move into the neighborhood and seem immediately to "make it," only to lose the focus of his critique. The men make no mention of differential capital bases or accesses to
bank loans—and there is no reason to think that vernacular language could
not handle that analysis. M. L. concludes his discussion (simplistically): "Either them Korean motherfuckers are geniuses or you Black asses are just
plain dumb." The either/or proposition is reductionist: genius or dumb ass.

The discussion around, and the tensions raised by, the behavior of the Korean grocery story owners/employees as well as their economic relationship to
the rest of the block degenerates completely when the film shows the rioting
crowd suddenly stop seeing the Koreans as economically privileged and allow
them instead to claim the common oppression of race: We are all colored
(and therefore essentially equal) together. A moment's class hostility and film
critique of stratification is disrupted and traded in for simplistic race unity
without any of the complications of such change represented.

Nonetheless, it is in the realm of identity politics—of place and race—that
the film both raises possibilities of complicated representation and undermines
them. "Stay Black" is the keystone phrase for the neighborhood, although it
seems to refer to something ineffable. "Blackness" is what? Perhaps it is the roll
call of musicians on the radio, the DJ's rap, the sounds and sights of vernacular
culture, the claims of female genetic "tender-headedness." Yes. But "Blackness"
is also nailed down without specifics in the exchanges between Buggin' Out
and Mookie, Mookie and Raheem, Raheem and Buggin' Out. Jade is "down for
something positive" and Black—and neither she nor Buggin' Out feels the
need to specify exactly what the "Black positive" is. "Blackness" is Malcolm X,

Do the Right Thing (1989): Mookie (Spike Lee), pizza deliveryman and neighborhood peacemaker.

although, as Smiley's picture and Lee's quotes after the conclusion of the film remind us, "Blackness" is also Martin Luther King Jr.; "Blackness," then, is reduced to the sacredness that inheres in the proper icons.

As Joe Wood asserts, "In the ever-evolving vernacular, Malcolm X has come to mean the real (black) thing, the authentic (black) thing, as close to (black) integrity as close can be. . . . Malcolm [is] the Essential Black Man" (Wood 1990a: 43). Wood goes on to argue that, if Malcolm (or, I might add, Martin Luther King Jr., for that matter) is to be treated as a symbol of blackness, then we've backed ourselves into a religion of "essential Blackness" and away from a historical analysis or exploration of its complexities, its construct-edness. Iconography and fetishization are no substitute for history and critical thinking. The film offers no consistent critique of "pictures"—as icons, as fetishes—except for Jade's discussion with and aborted interruption of Buggin' Out's crude analysis. But the movie diminishes her intervention because, after all, within its terms, who is Jade but a sister who ought to but doesn't know when some White man is hitting on her and who has to be warned both by her brother and by the Tawana truth lurking behind and against her back?

Brothers and sisters, we *do* need to talk.

Blackness also seems to demand images that suggest African American males are prone to death by police violence—as bell hooks reminds us (hooks 1989: 31).[23] In fact, Lee dedicates this film to victims of the police, the dramatic high point of the film being Raheem's murder by the police (hooks 1989: 31). Lee has waxed indignant about that murder's dismissal on the part of some Euro-American viewers (Orenstein 1989: 34); on the other hand, Lee has said also that, if Raheem had just turned down the radio, none of this would have happened—so much for any representation of systemic racist oppression. What are we to make of identity politics within the domain represented by this film? For a filmmaker who claims the mantle of transgression, cultural opposition, political righteousness, and truth-telling, the political ambitions of this film are diffuse and, by its end, defuse into nothingness.

It is the film considered less politically ambitious (but equally masculinist and heterosexist), *School Daze*, that offers the possibilities of greater political depth—it at least raises interesting questions about identity politics "within the group." Although the film is undermined by its homophobia and sexism, it is within the terms of a consideration of these areas that identity politics and essentialism are, in fact, deconstructed.

School Daze is sloppy but complicated. It shows us frat hegemony-forging in action: "Q Dogs, that's what we want to be" is the refrain that bonds. "Q-Dogs are real men because it takes a real man to be a Q-dog"— tautological, yes, and therefore full of the comfort implied by unproblematized allegiances. This refrain, however, is followed by insistences that have no basis in absolutes, that could be read as critical of absolutes, having meaning only by stating differences. A "real" man is *not* a virgin, *not* a "fag." Men know themselves by virtue of their comparisons to "others"—gay men and those individuals in states of pre-sexual being, untouched. Women, too, have their absolutes: "He's a man, he's sneakin'!" is clearly exigesis on the nature or essence side of the argument about the ontology of male being. Nonetheless, the women also have their moments of comparison and acknowledgments of constructedness: Some sororities are not "bad," and Rachel wants to "become" a Delta even though she is *not* a wannabee.

The film offers some poststructuralist comforts. Half-Pint begins the film firmly centered: "I'm your cousin, your blood." But he ends it reconstructed and differently centered (however problematically): "I'm a Gamma man *now*" (my emphasis). That new insistence marks a historicized difference. The film offers additional critiques of identity politics. Possibilities include the town–gown split, an explicitly political one that manifests its implicit politics in aesthetics as well: The townies, who are working-class and, therefore, under some rubrics "Blacker" than the middle-class college kids, are also the ones with the "jerri curls" (generally recognized as evidence of aesthetic *disaffection* with "Blackness") protected by shower caps. And a concern with international politics—South Africa and apartheid—gets read by "wannabee" Julian as evidence that the male jigs really aren't "Black," because "Blackness" originates in and is concerned with U.S. geopolitical sites only—like Detroit.

The film's failing, of course, is that it does not explore the ways in which its (male) politics are also tied to its own forms of aesthetization. Males are not only socialized by the *behaviors* of their groups, whether within fraternities or within male-oriented, internationally focused political practices such as protests, marches, or rallies, but they are participants in the aesthetization of these practices. The film, unfortunately and myopically, presents aesthetics as formal matters of physical appearance in which women only participate.[24] Men *do*: They dance the beautifully choreographed Greek stomps, or the fellas' clever parody stomp, or make careful selections of political posters and other room decor items, and arrange that decor for sexual trysts.

Women, on the other hand, *show*. They wear or don't wear makeup; they straighten or don't straighten their hair; they show off the colors of the eyes with which they were born or show different eyes through the wonders of chemical technology. *School Daze* is incapable of making the connection between what the men do and what they are showing as their aesthetics, and the film is incapable of showing that women do anything other than look like components of male aesthetics. The film is allowed its specificity, but it could have chosen to self-consciously represent male constructions of aesthetics; there is work to be done in this area. Still *School Daze*, while not recognizing its own attitude toward the gendering of its discussion of aesthetics, does make the issue available for critique.

The film's homophobia offers a similar site for examining historical identity and gender politics. In its retreat from and fear of homosexuality and the homosexual, it plays out the fear engendered during the course of African American history and concretized by Robert Park's assertion (in the 1920s) that "the Negro is the lady of the races" (Park 1950: 280). The language around African American culture, intellectualism, and politics has been dominated by language analogous to that which has constructed and constrained women. Within a history that has used the same language to delineate the constructions of race *and* gender, that has insisted, against general Euro-American male privilege, that African American males can only share the space reserved for women, this film is a long commercial that reassures African American males that they *can* center themselves by asserting a salient difference: They are straight; all "real" men are straight; "Blackness" is like real manhood—straight. So there, Robert Park.

Again, however, in defense of a critique of the specificities of this film's representations, the feeble excuse of "reality" comes into play. Lee has consistently defended his film against criticism of its homophobia by claiming and privileging its facticity, by defending realism: Those (frat) guys really are that way. In so doing, he lets himself off the hook for the selection criteria at work in any representation. I respond as simply: Yes, some African Americans are like that; some are not; therefore, to what particular end is this specific "real" content being mined? If it is intended as a critique of African American homophobia, "how" (in form and/or content) is the critique available?

V

I would like to end where I began. The historical moment and the attention given to Spike Lee by an entire spectrum of critics, commentators, and media fora; the effects of his presence and deification on possible productions of African American presences in the cultural domain; the reductionist tendency in any U.S. discussions about race and racism—all combine to make it imperative that we continue to think about the issues raised by Lee and his production. It won't hurt and might help to begin by refusing to consider Lee or his production simply within their own terms. Trying to make things "real" has been the problem. What might more contextual criticism of Lee and his production offer us?

The May 1990 issue of *Emerge* points to the recent successes of African American independent filmmakers at Sundance (White 1990: 65–66). The news is cheering. But there were no African American women among their number and, even more troubling, the critic writing the article said nothing about their absence from Sundance or from his discussion of African American filmmaking. Instead, he described and contributed to the uncritical veneration of the work of Melvin Van Peebles, a tradition in African American film criticism that ignores both formal infelicities in Van Peebles's films and issues of sexism and homophobia.

Within the terms of simple celebration of African American male filmmakers, there is no space for the criticism that any artist needs—especially, given present political constraints, artists from marginalized and racialized communities. Yet, as critics we are responsible for the work of analysis and thoroughgoing contextualization lest we run the risk of continuing, in the name of affirming our cultural production, disabling essentialisms. Representations are not "reality"; simple, factual reproductions of selected aspects of vernacular culture are neither necessarily counter-hegemonic art nor anything else. They don't even "set the record *straight*" (pun intended). Therefore, in our critical considerations we do well to heed Fanon's warnings equally

against nationalist nostalgia for a precolonial past and uncritical nativist cele-
brations in the present. While beginning with the question of context—
Compared to what?—does not foreclose productive discussions, it does make
it harder to rest on simple resolutions. And that's the truth, Ruth.

NOTES

1. Amazingly, the *New York Times*, not exactly famous for its in-depth analysis of
African American cultural life or production, invited a group of people, including academics in literature, education, and sociology; a psychiatrist; an administrative judge of
the New York State Supreme Court; and a film director (among others), to "explore issues raised by the film" *Do the Right Thing*. The editors of the Arts and Leisure section
devoted almost two full pages to excerpts from this gathering ("*Do the Right Thing*"
1989).

2. Included in this category are Aufderheide 1988, Canby 1989, Creedon 1989,
Davis 1989, Day 1989, Ewen 1989, Hoberman 1989, Klawans 1989, Muwakkil 1989,
and Tate 1989.

3. Included in this category are Crouch 1989 and Klein 1989.

4. The subtexts of the "Compared to what?" are both dominant cultural production
and the possibilities for politically engaged film explored by the Black British film
collectives—about which I do not write at any length (or in any depth) in this paper, but
against which I look at Lee.

5. Lee sees himself and his work as politically engaged (see, e.g., Orenstein 1989:
43); that is the reason that I take his political claims as well as the critics who deify him
so seriously.

6. I focus only on Lee instead of including a critique of Eddie Murphy, Robert
Townsend, Keenan Wayans, or the Hudlin brothers (all African American male filmmakers getting considerable attention from the general media and African American
cultural commentators) to keep this essay focused and of moderate length.

7. This is an issue Ann Cvetkovich and I raised in a paper presented at the 1989
Modern Language Association convention.

8. I refer to Gates 1987; Appiah 1986; and Fanon 1967 (1952).

9. The truth of his vision was also the theme of his letter-to-the-editor response (to
Joe Klein's hysterical attack) in *New York* magazine.

10. I do not think, however, that all African American cultural production has to
be nationally distributed for it to be a site of resistance to the dominance of Euro-
American cultural hegemony.

11. Cvetkovich and I have argued also against seeing a simple dichotomy between
politically "good" independent and politically "bad" commercial production and against
as equally simple a dichotomy as that between "avant-garde" as an inherently elitist form
and conventional narrative representation as an inherently popular form.

12. There were, for instance, those who thought Euro-Americans or *middle*-class
African Americans needed to learn from *Do the Right Thing*. Consider the example of
Barbara Day, who thought the movie was good because it was "as real as the nation's last
urban Insurrection." Middle-class people (of both races), she opined, "needed to see
what the poor in New York City ghettos see too often: a Black or Latino Raheem being

choked, feet dangling above the pavement." I could expend much ink and theoretical zeal on the tendency (need? pleasure?) on the part of many Euro-American commentators to romanticize African Americans represented at the most coercive sites, sites that bestow "authenticity," but I don't feel strong enough this time around. While there are differences among segments of the African American population, some circumstances of life in the United States for African Americans are fairly general. The existence of racist police practices is one such unifying factor. I will take issue, therefore, with another aspect of Day's myopia: the argument that racist police coercion is always lower- or working-class oriented. Day connects "a Black or Latino Raheem being choked" with ghetto residents only, but one of the Miami "urban insurrections" was kicked off by the police murder of Arthur Little, a middle-class African American who worked in insurance. The violent tendencies of racist police are not unknown to middle-class African Americans: At the National Black Male Conference workshop on police abuse (Kansas City, Mo., July 13, 1990), the largely academic and middle-class African American audience was unsurprised when Don Jackson, an ex-police officer (made famous by the videotape of a Los Angeles Police Department officer pushing his head through a window), said that "almost everyone in this room looks like a criminal to police officers so inclined." Class does not necessarily mediate racism. Even most *middle*-class African Americans understand (and many have suffered from) some form of racist police violence or hostility.

13. Muwakkil 1989, Tate 1989, and White 1989 were the most enthusiastic in this category, followed closely by Davis 1989 and Day 1989.

14. bell hooks examines the differences between critical responses to Alice Walker's representations of African American men and those of Spike Lee.

15. hooks also touches on this point (hooks 1989: 35).

16. How very much Mookie's insistence on the predatoriness of Euro-American males toward African American females echoes (while countering) Euro-American males' insistence on the myth of African American male predatoriness toward Euro-American females! Of course, one might argue, such insistences are meant to be counter-mythologizing, but such countering accepts the original structure—it does not transform or subvert it. Ironically, unlike the deployments of slippery indirections—the keynote of vernacular linguistic play—counter-myths are as *direct,* as centered as the racist myths they mean to displace.

17. Fanon argues that American Blacks might also be considered "natives" in the sense of being part of an internal colony. In *The Wretched of the Earth*, he states that the "negroes who live in the United States and in Central or Latin American in fact experience the need to attach themselves to a cultural matrix. Their problem is not fundamentally different from that of the Africans" (Fanon 1968 [1961]: 215).

18. This defense might or might not be superseded—time will tell—by his more recent calls for a liberal humanist pluralism and attacks on social theory and critiques of race, class, and gender.

19. Gates is right to take issue with some pejorative descriptions of his work as essentialist. To this end, I disagree with Diana Fuss's argument, for example, that Gates's and Houston Baker's analyses inherently romanticize the vernacular (although some of their specific uses of vernacular analysis have done so; see Gates's media pieces on 2 Live Crew, for example) and that they speak *about* the vernacular and not *in* it. Such an argument is itself a romanticization, first, because it is not necessary to write in the vernacular to theorize about it. Most metacommentary systems employ their own jargon;

theoretical discussions about fictional texts, for example, do not necessarily go on in the language of the texts themselves. More importantly, African American vernacular is *not* necessarily synonymous with "Black English" or any form of Black dialect (rural or urban), although the vernacular and vernacular users often employ Black English and/or Black dialects. African American vernacular is an attitude toward language, a language dynamic, and a technique of language use (see Baker 1984; Gates 1988; Mitchell-Kernan 1973). African American fiction writers such as Toni Morrison frequently "signify" in standard English. And both Baker and Gates have also used vernacular signifying practices from time to time in their oral and written presentations. Vernacularity is not simply a marker for African American working-class or "street" verbal practices. To attach it only to such sites is to be caught in a search for false authenticity.

Fuss (1989: 90) further argues that "the quest to recover, reinscribe, and revalorize the black vernacular" is inherently essentialist. The vernacular is not in need of recovery or reinscription: it is alive and well—and multi-class within the African American group. To graph the specificities of African-America cultural production, its textual theoretical possibilities, is not to go on a ghost hunt.

20. I refer to Gayatri Spivak's interview in *Differences*. While I am aware that exigencies of specific political moments and their attendant strategies have historically demanded essentialism on the large scale—nationalism—nonetheless, I want to think about unreflective essentialism as a problematic generally and specifically in regard to the Spike Lee discourse. I try to be very careful about the way that I use Spivak here because her interview is long and complex; I pick and choose parts of it because, while I think that her warnings about essentialism and anti-essentialism are very much to the point, working through the implications of all of her (and Rooney's) discussion would demand more time and space than I have here. I use, therefore, what seems to me to be most to the point. Spivak argues, among other things, that anti-essentialism risks being another form of essence, that antiessentialism's insistence (in some quarters) on the primacy of "over-determinations" leads to paralyzing strategic anarchy. Further, she asserts, "Essences . . . are just a kind of content. All content is not essence. Why be so nervous about it?" (Spivak 1990: 145). I am nervous, however, because within the terms of Euro-American dominance, as far as African American cultural production and reception are concerned, there is no such thing as just a kind of content.

21. Sarah Shulman (1989) is an exception to this generality, although I find problematic her article's insistence that Lee usurped "authentic" working-class voices and substituted his middle-class voice. I am not interested in taking sides on whether or not he does so; however, while I find much useful in Shulman's reading of the film, this issue of African American middle-class lack of authenticity versus African American working-class authenticity simply reinscribes another debate contained in terms of essentialism: Who is the "real" Black person? The insistence that only the working-class African American carries African American culture is one side of a pointless debate that has gone on for more than a century. All African Americans, in their complexity—of which class difference is a part—make up African culture. One need only watch Cornel West and Hortense Spillers (to name just two) make academic presentations in order to see variations of African American academic, middle-class, vernacular culture at work.

22. hooks 1989, Kamber 1989, and Dyson 1989 have all provided excellent extended readings of *Do the Right Thing*. My work here contributes to discussions they have begun.

23. The death of an African American male by police is a television and cinematic cliché, and bell hooks argues that Lee's representation of Raheem's death does not explode or remap that cliché. Further, as Michael Kamber also notes, despite the tragedy of the disproportionately high numbers of African American males killed by police, such murders are still fairly atypical—less than 1 percent of African American homicides (Kamber 1989: 40). The vast majority of African American male and female homicides are committed by African American males, and the relationship of that fact to the representation of African American male homicide in *Do the Right Thing* is a fair enough question, since representation is the "practice" of the filmmaker's selection. Is the simplicity of murder by cops somehow more "real" than the complexities of murder by African American males? I am not ranking factual horrors, but I am interested in the representation "selection" at work in this film. Does the specter of male socialization within African American communities and its participation in hegemonic violence and masculinism seem too "inauthentic" to be represented?

24. Vernon Reid, in Davis et al. 1988, touches on Lee's depiction of African American color line internalization as played out by women only.

REFERENCES

Appiah, Anthony. 1986. "The Uncompleted Argument: Du Bois and the Illusion of Race." Pp. 21–37 in *"Race," Writing, and Difference*, ed. Henry Louis Gates Jr. Chicago: University of Chicago Press.

Applebome, Peter. 1990. "Stirring a Debate on Breaking Racism's Shackles." *New York Times*, May 30, 1990, A18.

Aufderheide, Pat. 1988. "Racial Schisms: The Daze of Our Lives." *In These Times*, March 16–22, 20.

Baker Jr., Houston A. 1984. *Blues, Ideology and African-American Literature: A Vernacular Theory*. Chicago: University of Chicago Press.

Barthes, Roland. 1985. "Diderot, Brecht, Eisenstein." Pp. 89–97 in *The Responsibility of Forms,* trans. Richard Howard. New York: Hill and Wang.

Boyd, Herb. 1989. "Does Lee 'Do the Right Thing'?" *Guardian*, July 5, 8, 24.

Canby, Vincent. 1989. "Spike Lee Tackles Racism and Rage." *New York Times*, June 30, 1989, C16.

Creedon, Jeremiah. 1989. "That Cannes Can of Worms: Sex, Lies and the Right Thing." *In These Times*, October 18–24, 20–21.

Crouch, Stanley. 1989. "Do the Race Thing." *Village Voice*, June 20, 73–74, 76.

Culler, Jonathan. 1976. *Ferdinand de Saussure*. Ithaca, N.Y.: Cornell University Press.

Davis, Thulani. 1989. "We've Gotta Have It." *Village Voice*, June 20, 67–70.

Davis, Thulani, et al. 1989. "Daze of Our Lives." *Village Voice*, March 22, 35–39.

Day, Barbara. 1989. "Spike Lee Wakes Up Movie Audiences, Confronts Questions of Black Power." *Guardian*, July 5, 24–25.

Diawara, Manthia. 1988. "Black Spectatorship: Problems of Identification and Resistance." *Screen* 29, no. 4: 66–81.

"Do the Right Thing: Issues and Images." 1989. *New York Times*, July 9, sec. 2.

Dyson, Michael. 1989. "Film Noir." *Tikkun* 4, no. 5: 75–78.

Elgin, Suzette. 1984. *Native Tongue*. New York: Daw Books.

Ellison, Ralph. 1952. *Invisible Man*. New York: Random House.

Ewen, Stuart. 1989. "'Do the Right Thing' Is an American Movie in the Best Sense." *New York Times*, July 14, A28.

Fanon, Frantz. 1967 (1952). *Black Skin, White Masks*. New York: Grove.

———. *The Wretched of the Earth*. 1968 (1961). New York: Grove.

Fusco, Coco. 1988a. "Fantasies of Oppositionality." *Afterimage*, December, 6–9.

———. 1988b. "An Interview with Black Audio Film Collective: John Akomfrah, Reece Auguiste, Lina Gopaul and Avril Johnson." Pp. 41–60 in *Young, British, and Black: The Work of Sankofa and Black Audio Film Collective*. Buffalo, N.Y.: Hallwalls/Contemporary Arts Center.

Fuss, Diana. 1989. *Essentially Speaking: Feminism, Nature and Difference*. New York: Routledge.

Gates Jr., Henry Louis. 1984. "The Blackness of Blackness: A Critique of the Sign and the Signifying Monkey." Pp. 287–321 in *Black Literature and Literary Theory*, ed. Henry Louis Gates Jr.. New York: Methuen.

———. 1987. *Figures in Black: Words, Signs, and the "Racial" Self*. New York: Oxford University Press.

———. 1988. *The Signifying Monkey: A Theory of Afro-American Literary Criticism*. New York: Oxford University Press.

———. 1989. "On the Rhetoric of Racism in the Profession." *African Literature Association Bulletin* 15, no. 1: 11–21.

George, Nelson. 1990. "Shady Dealin'." *Village Voice*, February 27, 37.

Greenberg, James. 1990. "In Hollywood, Black Is In." *New York Times*, March 4, Arts and Leisure sec., 1.

Hall, Stuart. 1985. "Signification, Representation, Ideology: Althusser and the Post-Structuralist Debates." *Critical Studies in Mass Communication* 2, no. 2: 91–114.

———. 1986. "Gramsci's Relevance for the Study of Race and Ethnicity." *Journal of Communication Inquiry* 10, no. 2: 5–27.

Hoberman, J. 1989. "Pass/Fail." *Village Voice*, July 11, 59, 62, 66.

hooks, bell. 1989. "Counterhegemonic Art: The Right Thing." *Z Magazine*, October, 31–36.

Kamber, Michael. 1989. "Do the Right Thing." *Z Magazine*, October, 37–40.

Klawans, Stuart. 1989. "Review of *Do the Right Thing*." *Nation*, July 17, 98–100.

Klein, Joe. 1989. "Spiked." *New York*, June 26, 14–15.

Lee, Spike. 1989. Presentation and discussion at the University of Texas, Austin, February 26.

Lubiano, Wahneema, and Ann Cvetkovich. 1989. "Black Film Production as Cultural Studies Problematic." Paper presented to Division on Black American Literature and Culture, Modern Language Association convention. Washington, D.C., December 28.

Mercer, Kobena. 1988. "Diaspora Culture and the Dialogic Imagination: The Aesthetics of Black Independent Film in Britain." Pp. 50–61 in *BlackFrames: Critical Perspectives on Black Independent Cinema*, ed. Mbye B. Cham and Claire Andrade-Watkins. Cambridge, Mass.: MIT Press.

Mitchell-Kernan, Claudia. 1973. "Signifying." Pp. 310–28 in *Mother Wit from the Laughing Barrel: Readings in the Interpretation of Afro-American Folklore*, ed. Alan Dundes. Englewood Cliffs, N.J.: Prentice Hall.

Muwakkil, Salim. 1988. "The Black Middle Class and Lee's School of Hard Knocks." *In These Times*, March 16–22, 21.

————. 1989. "Doing the Spike Thing." *In These Times*, July 5–18, 18, 24.

Orenstein, Peggy. 1989. "Spike's Riot." *Mother Jones*, September, 32–35, 43–46.

Park, Robert. 1950. *Race and Culture: Essays in the Sociology of Contemporary Man.* Glencoe, Md.: Free Press..

Shulman, Sarah. 1989. "I Don't Like Spike." *Outweek*, August 7, 48–49.

Snead, James. 1988. "Images of Blacks in Black Independent Films: A Brief Survey." Pp. 16–25 in *BlackFrames: Critical Perspectives on Black Independent Cinema*, ed. Mbye B. Cham and Claire Andrade-Watkins. Cambridge, Mass.: MIT Press.

Spillers, Hortense. 1987. "Mama's Baby, Papa's Maybe: An American Grammar Book." *Diacritics* 17, no. 2: 65–81.

Spivak, Gayatri. 1990. "In a Word: Interview with Ellen Rooney." *Differences* 1, no. 2: 124–55.

Staples, Brent. 1989. "Spike Lee's Blacks: Are They Real People?" *New York Times*, July 2, sec. 2, 9.

Tate, Greg. 1989. "Burn Baby Burn." *Premiere*, August, 80–85.

White, Armond. 1989. "Scene on the Street: Black Cinema from Catfish Row to Stuyvesant Avenue." *Mother Jones*, September, 35, 46.

————. 1990. "New Dawn at Sundance, Black Filmmakers Take Top Prizes." *Emerge*, May, 65–66.

Williams, Raymond. 1976. *Keywords: A Vocabulary of Culture and Society*. New York: Oxford University Press.

Wood, Joe. 1990a. "Looking for Malcolm: The Man and the Meaning behind the Icon." *Village Voice*, May 29, 43–45.

————. 1990b. "Self-Deconstruction." *Village Voice*, April 24, 79.

The Double Truth, Ruth: *Do the Right Thing* and the Culture of Ambiguity

n "Of Our Spiritual Strivings," the famous first chapter of *The Souls of Black Folk*, W. E. B. Du Bois ascribes to the African American consciousness what he perceives to be a fundamental "two-ness." This "double-consciousness . . . two souls, two thoughts, two unreconciled strivings; two warring ideals in one dark body" (Du Bois 1903: 3), is an effect of the contradictory positioning of African American culture within the dominant social order of "white Americanism" (Du Bois 1903: 4). On the one hand, American democratic capitalism promotes to its ethnic constituents its promise of economic opportunity, material satisfaction, and social justice. On the other, it consistently fails to grant black Americans full and equal access to the socioeconomic structures upon which the fruits of this promise depend.

As Du Bois describes it, this political condition, a consequence of pressures exterior to the black community, creates a corresponding interior dilemma for African Americans who achieve authority in American culture despite its institutionalized racism. Which of two competing allegiances does one serve? One's loyalty to the black community, which would benefit profoundly from one's acquired expertise in engaging white America? Or one's duty to one's own future, ironically linked to the esteem of a majority culture violently inimical to the minority community of which one is a part?

James C. McKelly, "The Double Truth, Ruth: *Do the Right Thing* and the Culture of Ambiguity," *African American Review* 32, no. 2 (Summer 1998): 215–27. Reprinted with permission of the author.

In *The Autobiography of an Ex-Coloured Man*, composed some ten years after the publication of *The Souls of Black Folk*, James Weldon Johnson likewise identifies "a sort of dual personality" which "every coloured man" has "in proportion to his intellectuality," a "dualism" which persists both "in the freemasonry of his own race" and "in the presence of white men" (Johnson 1976 [1912]: 21–22). And like Du Bois, Johnson's hero feels a dichotomy at the core of his ambition: "Was it more a desire to help those I considered my people, or more a desire to distinguish myself . . . ?" (Johnson 1976 [1912]: 147).

Du Bois calls this dilemma "the waste of double aims," a "seeking to satisfy two unreconciled ideals" (Du Bois 1903: 5) which can never be reconciled. The powerfully unitary pull of responsibility to community and responsibility to self, when configured as oppositional by a racist symbolic order, must inevitably become self-destructive. Thus, sublated in this polarized crisis of responsibility is an equivalently polarized crisis of identity.

Cornel West has argued that it is precisely this perceived crisis of identity, this "sense of double-consciousness," which led "anxiety-ridden, middle-class Black intellectuals" such as Du Bois and Johnson to construe the African American cultural experience in terms of "simplistic binary oppositions" that forced black attempts at personal and political liberation to "remain inscribed within the very logic that dehumanized them" (West 1994: 72). The implication of West's critique is that the cultural logic of "double-consciousness," as it was promulgated by the intellectuals of the modern black diaspora and as it has been inherited by contemporary African American culture, consigns that culture to an untenable role within the American capitalist symbolic order. It dooms the African American subject to a literally "entrepreneurial" purgatory, eternally situated between the oppositional terms of a complex hierarchy of antinomies which by definition can never be resolved. This weft of irreconcilable binarisms is constituted by the ideologies and oppositional counter-ideologies which govern the subject's relation to the hegemonic socioeconomic order, to the strategies of resistance conceived to combat this order, to the strategies of survival necessary when this resistance is compromised, and to the subject's own evolving sense of identity, inextricable as it is from this intricate fabric of relations.

Do the Right Thing, produced in 1989, is director Spike Lee's attempt to explore the human particularity of this system of binarisms and the culturally entrepreneurial situation of the African American subject within it. Lee's own background reflects this cultural positioning. He was the eldest child in an "uncomfortably middle-class" black family living in the then predominantly white Brooklyn neighborhoods of Cobble Hill and Fort Greene, where most of his friends were Italian (Breskin 1992: 14, 151). He graduated from traditionally black Morehouse College in 1979, after which he entered New York University's film school as one of only two African Americans in his class. (Lee later was to enlist the other, the director Ernest Dickerson, to handle the cinematography of *Do the Right Thing*.) It is not surprising, then, that the young African American novelist Trey Ellis cites Lee as one of "today's cultural mulattoes," during whose public schooling "it wasn't unusual to be called 'oreo' and 'nigger' on the same day." According to Ellis, these young black people are able skillfully to navigate a multiethnic universe due to their education in "a multi-racial mix of cultures" yet despite this unique ability, they "feel misunderstood by both the black world and the white." They are a generation "torn between two worlds," and, depending upon which term of the social binomial they embrace, they either "desperately fantasize themselves the children of William F. Buckley" or "affect instead a 'superblackness' and try to dream themselves back to the ghetto. Either way they are letting other people define their identity" (Ellis 1989: 234–36).

Ellis's commentary confirms the persistent power of the ideology of "double-consciousness" and the ontological and ethical duplicity it promotes. In *Souls*, Du Bois anticipates this very duplicity—he calls it "the peculiar ethical paradox" which results from "the double life every American Negro must live" and he identifies it as a socially generated psychological state which "tempts the mind to pre-tense or revolt, to hypocrisy or to radicalism" (Du Bois 1903: 202), the two extreme poles of a binaristic formula of resistance to oppression:

> Thus we have two great and hardly reconcilable streams of thought and ethical strivings; the danger of one lies in anarchy, that of the other in hypocrisy. The one type of Negro stands almost ready to curse God and die, and the other is too often found a traitor to right and a coward before force; the one is wedded to ideals remote, whimsical, and perhaps impossible of realization; the other for-gets that life is more than meat and the body more than raiment. (Du Bois 1903: 203)

In articulating the features of these "divergent ethical tendencies" (Du Bois 1903: 203), Du Bois prefigures not only the two dominant ideologies of resistance around which African American political discourse of the second half of the twentieth century has been structured, but also the moral categories from which the adversarial terms of this culturally pervasive dyad derive their significance. Martin Luther King and Malcolm X, two authors, two activists who advocated different strategies to achieve a shared end, have since their deaths—and to some degree because of their deaths—transcended the local, pragmatic potency of their respective narratives of African American resistance. Each has achieved a kind of iconic stature; accordingly, each bears a concomitant freight of metonymic cultural implication. In the bilaterally configured semiotics of political discourse, the figure "King" has come to signify the ethics of reform: justice, integrationism, passive resistance, patience, forgiveness, constructive engagement, and an altruistic faith in democracy and in the basic goodness of the individuals who compose the dominant majority. By contrast, the figure "X" has come to signify the ethics of revolution: power, separatism, proactive resistance, decisiveness, responsibility, autonomy, and a realistic awareness of the systemic failures of democratic capitalism and the complicity, whether intentional or de facto, of the individuals who comprise America's capitalist society.

The film's use of the metonymic figures "King" and "X" as well as the ethically divergent metanarratives of which they are the cultural signifiers suffuses its dramatic structure with the ideological tension generated by the trope of "double-consciousness." The vehicle by which *Do the Right Thing* represents the black community reminding itself, so to speak, of the presence of these figures is the ubiquitous Smiley, a young man with cerebral palsy who earns money selling photographs of African American heroes to his Bed-Stuy neighbors. The film calls attention to one image in particular: the famous photograph of King and Malcolm shaking hands and smiling during their first and only meeting. bell hooks gives us a way of fathoming the semiotic power of this image:

> While King had focused on loving our enemies, Malcolm called us back to ourselves, acknowledging that taking care of blackness was our central responsibility. Even though King talked about the importance of black self-love, he talked more about loving our enemies. Ultimately, neither he nor Malcolm lived long enough to fully integrate the love ethic into a vision of political decolonization that would provide a blueprint for the eradication of black self-hatred. (hooks 1994: 245)

Smiley's image of King and Malcolm in apparent collaborative concord speciously presents itself as the objective documentation of just such an integration. As such, the image haunts, both with mockery and hope. It constitutes a simulacrum of a longed-for yet by definition impossible resolution of the culturally inscribed binarisms central to the African American cultural mythos: the ideological antinomies "King" and "X," the complex dialectic of "love" and "hate" (of enemies, of self) with which hooks associates them, and the logic of "double-consciousness" of which these oppositionally situated terms are a culmination.

The immanence of these oppositional terms in the African American cultural climate is suggested by the film in its foregrounding of their symbolic presence in the actual climate of the film's Bed-Stuy locale. On the one hand, there is the weather itself—New York's hottest day of the year. As the racially charged pressures of life in Bed-Stuy mount, we feel the heat bringing them to a furious boil in a series of conflicts among various members of the multi-ethnic, but primarily black, community. The hate thrives in the heat; in a certain way, the hate becomes the heat, supplanting the cement and the sun as its own autotelic source and medium. The block's precarious race relations boil over in the infamous "racial slur montage" (Lee 1988: 43), a multiethnic round of "the dozens," which H. Rap Brown has described as a "mean game because what you try to do is totally destroy somebody else with words" (Gates 1988: 68–72).

The climatological antithesis of this atmosphere of anathema finds its expression on the radio. If hate, in the form of heat, is in the air, love, in the form of cool, is on the air. Mister Señor Love Daddy, the DJ who from his storefront studio at aptly named WE-LOVE Radio, monitors the street scene like a benevolent demiurge and counters the climate of hate in which his neighborhood audience is simmering with the sounds of his "Cool Out Corner":

> Wake up! Wake up! Wake up! Up ya wake! Up ya wake! Up ya
>   wake! . . .
> Here I am. Am I here?
> Y'know it. It ya know.
> This is Mister Señor Love Daddy,
> doing the nasty to ya ears, ya ears to the nasty.
> I'se play only da platters dat matter
> da matters dey platter and That's the truth, Ruth.

Señor Love Daddy's monologues, which are interspersed throughout the film as the temperature—sociological as well as meteorological—continues to rise, are far more sophisticated than the match of malicious dozens he interrupts. Their lexical and syntactical duplicity serves as a rhetorical representation of the culturally inscribed logic of "two-ness" in which Señor Love Daddy himself, even as he attempts through his art to alleviate its tensions, functions ironically as a definitive term.

The character Radio Raheem embodies singly the moral dualism "love/hate" which the heat and Señor Love Daddy mutually delineate. Radio Raheem is a one-man public-address system whose perceived social role is as a broadcaster of the music that Chuck D of the rap group Public Enemy has called "Black America's CNN." Radio Raheem blasts a single song—Public Enemy's "Fight the Power," commissioned by Lee expressly for the film—from his gargantuan boom box as he moves from place to place in the neighborhood. In a cinematic echo of the psychopathic preacher from Charles Laughton's *Night of the Hunter*, Radio Raheem sports two gold "brass-knuckle" rings: The right-hand ring spells "LOVE"; the left-hand ring, "HATE." He explains the significance of the words he wears in this way:

> Let me tell you the story of Right-Hand-Left-Hand—the tale of Good and Evil . . . . The story of Life is this: STATIC! One hand is always fighting the other. Left Hand Hate is kicking much ass and it looks like Right Hand Love is finished. Hold up. Stop the presses! The Right Hand is coming back! Yes, it's Love. Love has won. Left Hand Hate KO'ed by Love.

The moral cosmology Radio Raheem here narrates is very compelling. In it, "good" is not only identifiable and absolute, but ultimately more powerful than "evil," which, correspondingly, is equally pure and clear. The faith and lucidity of this formulation are potent. Yet the film complicates Radio Raheem's vision with its depictions of his role in the confrontation at Sal's Famous Pizzeria and his murder at the hands of the police. It is not clear that Radio Raheem is purely "good"; according to Lee's highly editorial notes for the conflict with Sal, "Radio Raheem, like the large majority of Black youth, is the victim of materialism and a misplaced sense of values" (Lee 1988: 78). This critique, ironized as it is by Lee's highly visible and controversial promotion of various product lines (including his own) which vigorously target the young African American male demographic, nonetheless identifies a salient feature of Raheem's characterization. And it is tragically obvious during the murder scene that "evil," at least in this particular match, is far stronger than Radio Raheem's "story of Life" implies.

Ultimately, the Weltanschauung with which Radio Raheem defines his sense of identity—so decisively, in fact, that he adopts its very signifiers "LOVE" and "HATE" as salient features of his self-expressive style—terminally relegates both society and the individual subject to the "STATIC" resulting from irreconcilable moral antinomies locked in interminable conflict. The "fight" in Radio Raheem's broadcast battle cry appropriately reflects the moral polarity within which he perceives his own life, the life of his community, and the life of culture at large, to be situated.

If Radio Raheem embodies the logic of "two-ness" regarding African American culture's exterior political conflict with white hegemony, it is through Da Mayor and Mother Sister that *Do the Right Thing* characterizes the corresponding relations which take place within black culture itself. In the film's narrative Da Mayor is exactly what his name would imply: a shambling yet dignified exponent of democratic capitalism's urban order. This role is particularly evident during two episodes involving his contact with ten-year-old Eddie Lovell, one of the neighborhood children. In the following conversation, we hear Da Mayor attempting to instruct Eddie in a street version of the subtleties of exchange value and wage negotiation:

> "What makes Sammy run?"
> "My name is Eddie."
> "What makes Sammy run?"
> "I said my name is Eddie Lovell."
> "Relax, Eddie, I want you to go to the corner store. How much will it cost me?"
> "How would I know how much it's gonna cost if I don't know what I'm buying?"
> "Eddie, you're too smart for your own britches. Listen to me. How much do you want to go to the store for Da Mayor?"
> "Fifty cents."
> "You got a deal."

It is not clear by his response that the somewhat mystified boy has understood the rudimentary lesson in the economics of survival which Da Mayor has attempted to teach. Later, this lesson takes symbolic form when Da Mayor leaps in front of a speeding car to push Eddie out of harm's way. In addition, after the police murder Radio Raheem and what Lee describes as "an angry mob of Black folks" turns toward "a defenseless Sal, Vito and Pino" (Lee 1988: 81), Da Mayor attempts to restore civil order—the very order of which the police have acted as brutal enforcers—by deflecting blame from the three white men as individuals: "Good people, let's all go home. . . . If we don't stop this now, we'll all regret it. Sal and his two boys had nothing to do with what the police did." Da Mayor exhibits a sense of integrity, a sense of "right," as the film's title designates it, which seems to transcend the politics of race.

The film identifies the opposite pole of this binarism in its critique of Da Mayor's role in the economic order. The terms of this critique invoke the culturally intramural issues around which the black community's self-critical political discourse revolves. Da Mayor picks up the change he needs to support his alcoholism by sweeping the sidewalk in front of Sal's, gratefully accepting his subordinate place in the economy given to him by virtue of the patronizing generosity of a paternalistic employer. This good-naturedly marginal participation is further ironized when we learn that his alcoholism is a result of the failure of American capitalism to grant him a materially adequate position in the first place: He began drinking as a younger man to kill the "pain" of daily facing the hunger of his five children and his own inability to provide for them. Ahmad, one of the teenagers of the neighborhood, is unsympathetic:

> I wouldn't stand in the doorway listening to my five children go hungry. I'd be out getting a job, doing something, anything, to put food in their mouth. And you're right, I don't want to know your pain. You're the one who put yourself in this situation. . . . This man don't get no respect. I respect those who respect themselves.

Ahmad's response is significant in that it refuses to acknowledge past injustice as a cause for current condition. It is a version of what an angry young Lee himself said in 1986 about the assumption of responsibility: "We're all tired about white-man this, white-man that. Fuck dat! It's on us" (Breskin 1992: 185).

The film places Mother Sister in direct opposition to Da Mayor as a symbol of inflamed resistance to the notions of labor, property, and authority central to the capitalist project. The reason for her persistent scorn for Da Mayor is that he reminds her of her ex-husband, who "lost all my property, all my money in his scheme to build a black business empire." For Mother Sister, African American participation in free enterprise has spelled financial ruin. Whereas Da Mayor counsels Mookie to "always try to do the right thing"—a conception of "good" akin to Radio Raheem's in its obliviousness to the moral coercion effected by a racist capitalism—Mother Sister warns Mookie, "Don't work too hard today, we can't have you dropping off in this heat"—an enunciation of defiant self-interest over involvement in the work ethic which Da Mayor advocates. And during the riot at Sal's, Mother Sister is screaming in the street, encouraging the crowd to "Burn it down! Burn it down!" even as Da Mayor attempts to quell the outrage.

The Da Mayor/Mother Sister dualism embodies the self-critical interrogation which hooks feels is the first step in facing "the self-hatred, low self-esteem, or internalized white supremacist thinking" which a colonizing culture inflicts upon the colonized (hooks 1994: 248). As the film makes the case, neither of the extreme positions regarding "white Americanism" which Da Mayor and Mother Sister represent results in any productive outcome or community empowerment. For all his stalwart belief in free-enterprise democracy, Da Mayor is destitute and powerless. And for all her righteous antagonism against the faith in American capitalism espoused by Da Mayor, Mother Sister ends up anguished in the street, wailing, "No! No! No!" at not only the horror of Radio Raheem's death but the ultimately self-destructive terror of the ensuing riot which she herself helped to inflame.

The dramatic structure of *Do the Right Thing* situates Mookie, the film's protagonist played by Lee himself, in the midst of this architecture of polarities constructed around the cultural logic of "two-ness." Correspondingly, in the social and economic commerce of the neighborhood, Mookie is placed in a similarly entrepreneurial role as the only black employee of the only white-owned business in the area. Even his job itself—pizza delivery—depends upon his ability to mediate the incompatible rhetorical demands of a white-owned workplace and a black clientele. So positioned, Mookie is a Bed-Stuy avatar of Henry Louis Gates's *homo rhetoricus Africanus*, who is able "to move freely between two discursive universes," traversing "the boundary between the white linguistic realm and the black" (Gates 1988: 75). The Brooklyn Dodgers jersey Mookie wears on his way to work in the morning—Jackie Robinson's number 42—suggests, as Nelson George puts it, that "he's a man watched closely by interested parties on both sides of the racial divide. Both sides think he's loyal to them—that's how he survives" (George 1991: 80).

In Mookie's world, Sal, the eponymous owner of the pizzeria, represents the "discursive universe" of American capitalism. He is an embodiment of the white patriarchy to which Mookie must be accountable if he is to be granted a continuing position, trifling as it may seem, in the dominant economic order. As such, Sal functions symbolically as the sole arbiter of the private sector's social responsibility. Yet Sal is never presented as a caricature of dehumanizing capitalist rapacity. In fact, as a result of his dedication to keeping the business in Bed-Stuy despite pressures from several quarters, this Italian American, neighborhood-scale entrepreneur is, like his African American, neighborhood-scale employee, consistently put in a socially entrepreneurial role. He mediates the constant tension between his two sons, the affable Vito, who is Mookie's friend and seems comfortable with the neighborhood, and the overtly racist Pino, who, violently disturbed by his brother's friendship with Mookie, compares Bed-Stuy to a "Planet of the Apes" and thinks the family "should stay in our own neighborhood, in Bensonhurst. And the niggers should stay in theirs."

Sal also attempts to mediate Pino's racist frustration, an unintended legacy of the culture within which Sal himself has raised him—Pino reports that "my friends laugh at me all the time, laugh right in my face, tell me, 'Go feed the Moolies'" and the resolute pride, however proprietary, with which Sal views the role of the family business:

> Why you got so much anger in you? . . . I never had no trouble with these people. I sat in this window, I watched the little kids get old.

And I seen the old people get older. . . . I mean for Christ sakes, Pino, they grew up on my food. On my food. . . . Sal's Famous is here to stay. I'm sorry. I'm your father and I love you—I'm sorry, but that's the way it is.

Sal here gives voice to one of the ideological tropes through which racist, consumption-driven "white Americanism" constructs its own moral self-justification: the specious conflation of the owner's self-serving economic interest in the subject-as-consumer with a paternalistic emotional interest in the subject-as-child.

Do the Right Thing identifies this well-meaning yet ultimately self-deceptive paternalism in Sal's relationships with Mookie's sister Jade, and with Mookie himself. The film's narrative associates Jade more strongly than any character other than Da Mayor with African American acceptance of the values of American free-enterprise. "Is this another of your patented two-hour lunches?" she asks Mookie. "Sal pays you. You should work." She is also very critical of what she perceives to be Mookie's failures as a father and husband. In yet another of the growing number of imperatives Mookie receives from a growing number of the denizens of Bed-Stuy, Jade ridicules Mookie's dependence upon her for housing and warns her brother to "take care of your responsibilities." And when the would-be activist Buggin' Out asks her if she will support the boycott against Sal's which he is attempting to organize, Jade chastises him, suggesting that he "direct [his] energies in a more useful way" by promoting "something positive in the community."

The film makes it clear that Sal feels a sincere emotional connection with Jade. He treats her like a flower which, cultivated in his own garlic-laced garden by his own flour-dusted hands, has blossomed into a rare beauty despite a climate inhospitable to the nourishment his business offers. He seats her and cleans her table personally, insisting that she allow him to make her "something special," and he exaggerates the quality of Mookie's job performance in order that she not be disappointed. Sal's aestheticized objectification of Jade is exactly appropriate; she deserves his worship as the most powerfully evocative figure of the emotional legitimacy of his mercantile presence in the neighborhood—a legitimacy of which Sal must have his human tokens, or else risk the realization that his significance in the community has been more a function of economy than humanity.

Mookie is such a token as well. If Jade represents Sal's objectified projection of the human improvement wrought by his benevolent colonial presence among a race not his own, Mookie represents an analogous projection of the colonialist miracle of unity and progress which Sal perceives that his dedicated labor has fathered. "I'm gonna rename the place," he says. "I'm gonna call it 'Sal and Sons Famous Pizzeria.' . . . And Mookie, there will always be a place for you here, because you've always been like a son to me." This paternal renaming, which masks itself as an unequivocally unifying gesture, actually expresses a simultaneous recognition and diminution, exposing the limit of Sal's paternalism. That limit, to which Sal himself seems blind, is delineated in the difference between being a son and being "like" a son. Mookie is re-signed by the colonial father—yet this re-signation dooms him to continue to labor under the sign of "Sal and Sons" despite the exclusion latent in the father's word.

In his dual role as proprietor and self-conceived father figure, Sal is positioned between the competing ethical valences of a historically racist economic order: a sense of reciprocal commitment, however paternalistic, to the well-being of the individuals and the community as a whole that provide the commerce indispensable to free enterprise, and, conversely, a sense of independence, of "freedom" as configured by the tenets of classical liberalism, from any such commitment beyond the supplying of goods and services at a specified rate of exchange. As W. J. T. Mitchell has put it, Sal is caught between "his openness and hospitality to the public and his 'right' to reign as a despot in his 'own place'" (Mitchell 1993: 894).

This precarious bourgeois balancing act is disrupted only when Sal perceives a threat to two of the ideological constructions most central to American democratic capitalism: "property" and "freedom." The film accomplishes this disruption through the agency of Buggin' Out. After Buggin' Out confronts Sal with the absence of African Americans on Sal's "Wall of Fame," Sal is quick to assert the absolute authority of ownership over whatever claims the community might raise: "You want brothers on the wall? Get your own place, you can do what you want to do. . . . But this is my pizzeria. American Italians on the wall only." When Mookie resists being held responsible for Buggin' Out's demands, telling Sal that "people are free to do whatever the hell they want to do," Sal angrily expresses his conception of "freedom" as it obtains in his corner of the private sector: "'Free'! There's no 'free' here! I'm the boss. No freedom. . . . You want freedom? [He gestures to the counter.] There, that's free. You take an order, and you take it out."

The boycott proposed by Buggin' Out, whose name marks him as frantic and impulsive, is a bust in the neighborhood. The action founders because Buggin' Out's critique is unfocused, and offers little more than simplistic rhetoric in addressing a very complex issue (Breskin 1992: 164, 172). Although it is misdirected, however, as an idea the boycott is strategically sound in that it calls for the suspension of the subject's status as consumer—the bedrock socioeconomic premise upon which the mercantilist tradition is built. This organized suspension is an assertion of the collective power of

community within that tradition, in service of the proposition that "free" enterprise is not so free from responsibility to that community as its doctrine
would imply. And despite the emotional commitment to community which
Sal professes to be his primary motive, when Buggin' Out and Radio Raheem
throw their two-man boycott in Sal's face at the end of a long day, his repressed racism erupts in violence: He smashes Radio Raheem's box to bits,
and calls him "nigger" in front of all of the young black people who have been
his regulars.

In his subversive challenge, however immaturely executed, to the naturalized assumptions crucial to the determination of power relations in American
culture, Buggin' Out exposes as self-congratulatory self-deception in the paternalistic concern for community foregrounded in the rhetoric of colonial
capitalism. As the catalyst of this unmasking of racist "white Americanism,"
Buggin' Out becomes the oppositional "discursive universe" in the dialectical
social situation of Mookie as *homo rhetoricus Africanus*: If *Do the Right Thing*
presents Sal as the authoritarian proponent of the racially hypocritical socioeconomic values of "white Americanism," it correspondingly presents Buggin'
Out as the self-appointed arbiter of "blackness," the essence of which, as he
defines it, is compromised by African American participation in a white racist
economy. "Stay black," he warns his entrepreneurial friend.

As the locality which supports the welter of ideological binarisms that
comprises Mookie's experience, Bedford-Stuyvesant in the course of the film
takes on what Mikhail Bakhtin has described as a "polyphonic" quality. That
is, by the time of the final conflict at Sal's, the neighborhood, seen as we have
seen it, through Mookie's eyes, has become a medium for "the unification of
highly heterogeneous and incompatible material" issuing from a "plurality of
consciousness-centers not reduced to a single ideological common denomi-
nator" (Bakhtin 1984: 17). Throughout the film, Mookie has weathered an
onslaught of imperatives from these various "consciousness-centers"—each
imprinted, as we have seen, by the culturally pervasive logic of "two-ness"—
which signify for Mookie's benefit their particular ideological values. From
Buggin' Out, he hears, "Stay black"; from Mother Sister, "Don't work too hard
today"; from Jade, "Take care of your responsibilities"; from Tina [the mother
of his child], "Be a man"; from Sal, "You're fuckin' up"; and from Da Mayor,
the clincher of this paradoxical parade of morally absolutist signification: "Always try to do the right thing."

In correspondence with the Bakhtinian model (Bakhtin 1984: 17–65), all
of these signifying voices retain their autonomy. They are placed in opposition,
juxtaposed and counter-posed, combined contrapuntally in a "collaborative antagonism . . . a plurality of voices which do not fuse into a single consciousness, but rather exist on different registers and thus generate a dialogical

dynamism" (Stam 1991: 262). Their contradictions are never presented as the various stages of some unified development. The film outlines no ideological evolution toward completion, telos, or dialectical resolution; as Lee has said, "Everybody has a point" (Glicksman 1989: 15). The only unification offered by Bed-Stuy is the unity of place: simultaneity, coexistence, and interaction.

Thus, as the film depicts it, Bed-Stuy becomes what Linda Hutcheon calls a "postmodernist paradox," an "assertion not of centralized sameness but of decentralized community" (Hutcheon 1987: 18) which, in its insistence on a plurality of differences, uncovers the naturalized binary oppositions by means of which the cultural hegemony guarantees homogeneity and perpetuates the status quo of its ascendancy. A decentralized, pluralistic simulacrum of ethnicity, *Do the Right Thing*'s Bed-Stuy "address[es] ethnic consciousness and its changing context directly, foregrounding it as a contradictory, paradoxical, and multivalent experience" (Sobchack 1991: 342–43). The film's insistence upon the polyphony of Bed-Stuy creates the neighborhood as a symbolic space in which a culture of ambivalence, paralyzed in the tension created by the discursive power of its polarized and polarizing metanarratives, becomes a culture of ambiguity, which in its promotion of a heteroglossia of unmerged, unresolved, and hopelessly contradictory ideological voices potentiates finally an evasion of the logic of "two-ness."

The complex form this evasion takes is rooted in the analogous ambiguities of the film's protagonist. A walking synecdoche for his neighborhood's dialogic assimilation of a plurality of cultural signifiers, Mookie himself in the course of the film becomes what Bakhtin calls an "internally dialogic" character (Bakhtin 1984: 32), containing, as it were, an entire "sociology of consciousnesses," a cacophony of autonomous, irreconcilable significations in conflict, each reflecting the persistence of "double-consciousness": Sal/Buggin' Out, Pino/Vito, Da Mayor/Mother Sister, Jade/Tina, "whiteness"/"blackness," "King"/"X," cool/heat, "LOVE"/"HATE," "right thing"/wrong thing.

When considering what is conventionally regarded as *Do the Right Thing*'s ideological denouement—Mookie's decision to hurl a trash can through Sal's plate-glass window, an act which sparks the ensuing riot that destroys the pizzeria—critics have ignored the dialogical ambiguity cultivated in the protagonist throughout the film. Typically, Mookie is seen to have been driven by "Radio Raheem's death . . . his own personal frustrations [and] his underlying lack of self-esteem" to one pole of the system of antinomies which besets his life: "Mookie is a victim of and catalyst for hate-racial, economic, and personal" (George 1991: 80). The logical conclusion of such a view is to limit the film, as Mark Reid does, to a single, thematically univocal

Do The Right Thing (1989) Neighborhood anger in Bed-Stuy (from left: Roger Guenveur Smith, Bill Nunn, Giancarlo Esposito).

implication: In its portrayal of "an important social problem—interethnic rivalry," Reid argues, the film errs in suggesting that "to celebrate black empowerment, African Americans must deny an Italian-American small businessman his property rights" (Reid 1993: 108).

Even critics who take a more complex view of what they understand as Mookie's declarative action—and, by extension, the declarative symbol of Lee's "intent"—see the film as exploring what Mitchell identifies as the issue of "violence and nonviolence as strategies within a struggle that is simply an ineradicable fact of American public life" (Mitchell 1990: 898). For Mitchell, the film succeeds because it "resituates" the two terms of the "King"/"X" binomial in American political discourse. In a response to Mitchell, Jerome Christensen argues that the film fails because this "resituation" actually amounts to an autocratic, irresponsible circumvention of the "obligation" to negotiate these "oppositions" by "democratic dispute" (Christensen 1991: 586–87). In his reply to Christensen, Mitchell refines his conception of Mookie's act as a "dialectical image" which creates public debate (Mitchell 1991: 605)—but the point is moot, since the debate itself, as evidenced by this critical exchange, serves merely to reinscribe the very antinomies that produced this debate's putative "currency" in the first place. Either way, the metanarrative binarism endures, and the diaphonic logic of "two-ness" is confirmed in its structurally "ineradicable" power.

With his concept of signifyin(g), Henry Louis Gates gives us a critical means of avoiding this hermeneutic trap consistent with the dialogic character of the film's protagonist as well as the polyphony of his Bed-Stuy milieu. As Gates describes it, signifyin(g) is a "double-voiced utterance," a "double play" executed by the African American subject in the realm of language and characterized by the "repetition and revision" which Gates proposes to be "fundamental to black artistic forms, from painting and sculpture to music and language use" (Gates 1998: xxiii–xxiv). Signifyin(g) manifests itself as a vernacular stratagem which on the one hand puts to use the modes of discourse which the colonizing hegemonic culture has made available to it, yet on the other hand always already imbues these culturally endorsed forms with a "signal difference" which renders them at once both conventional yet subversive, deferential yet disruptive, comprehensible yet oblique, disciplined yet resistant, assimilated yet other.

For Gates, "whatever is black about black American literature" consists in this black signifyin(g) difference. Signifyin(g) is that trope and interpretive figure by which the African American consciousness subverts the naturalized rhetorical constructions that confine it to a circumscribed set of psychological and socio-political locations. As such, signifyin(g) enables *homo rhetoricus Africanus* to navigate the rhetorically oppositional discursive realms of "white" and "black," precisely by foregrounding the figures "white" and "black" as figures—as particular discursive locations in the system of significances that constitutes hegemonic culture.

Through signifyin(g), then, the African American subject is able to dispel the culturally inscribed "binary political relationship . . . between black and white" as well as critique "the idea of binary opposition" in general (Gates 1988: 70). Like Derrida's deconstructive critique, signifyin(g) "insists on being a double operation," neither denying nor fully embracing the discursive systems of univocal logocentrism, "work[ing] on the edges" (Brunette and Wills 1989: 11) of, in the case of American culture, a racist symbolic order. Signifyin(g) functions also as a kind of blues, which, in Houston Baker's words, comprises "a mediational site" wherein "familiar antinomies may be . . . dissolved" or receive "polyvalent interpretations" (Baker 1984: 6–7). In this way signifyin(g) can be understood as a performance of what Señor Love Daddy calls "the double truth, Ruth": a double-talk that confounds the antinomies resulting from the logic of "double-consciousness"—a duplicity that confounds duplicity itself.

If Mookie's violent act were construed as *Do the Right Thing*'s presiding symbolic image and the univocal consummation of Lee's "intent" as auteur, then bell hooks would be correct in complaining that "the film denies the problematical nature of identity and offers a simplistic view that would have skin color be all-encompassing" (hooks 1990: 177). The image would then represent the protagonist's singular, definitive election of a single one of two conflicting metanarratives of resistance—and therefore constitute a simulacrum of "the right thing." But if Mookie's act is understood as merely the first term, so to speak, of a bilateral, duplicitous act of radical signifyin(g) in the Gatesian sense, a different picture emerges.

Mookie supplies the second term of this Signification when he returns to Sal's early the next morning to collect his back pay. The night before, Mookie had been an influential practitioner in the discursive realm of "blackness" as represented by Buggin' Out. The word he screamed just before he released the trash can—"HATE!"—seemed a declaration of his rhetorical situation, and the act itself seemed to declare his exile from the ethos of free enterprise. His subsequent return to the burned-out pizzeria, however, reinscribes him as *homo rhetoricus Africanus* and constitutes a re-engagement with the "white" discursive realm.

Mookie's revisitation of American capitalism should not surprise us. Throughout the film we witness Mookie's attempts to reconcile the sociopolitical demands of "blackness" with the financial demands of life in a racist, capitalist democracy. James Weldon Johnson's "ex-coloured" hero succinctly defines this tension: "Since I was not going to be a Negro, I would avail myself of every possible opportunity to make a white man's success; and that, if it can be summed up in any one word, means 'money'" (Johnson 1976 [1912]: 193). Always the entrepreneur, Mookie negotiates this binarism which, as Johnson demonstrates, would construe "blackness" and "success" as mutually exclusive properties. Just as Mookie incisively defends his "blackness" when it is assaulted in the workplace by the boss's son, so does he defend his drive to "make that money, get paid" when Buggin' Out tells him about the boycott. "You're wastin' my time. You should leave that shit alone," Mookie tells him.

And Mookie's acceptance of the economic realities of capitalist culture mirrors that espoused by his author:

> Am I a capitalist? [Pause.] We all are over here. And I'm just trying to get the power to do what I have to do. To get that power you have to accumulate some type of bank. And that's what I've done. I've always tried to be in an entrepreneurial mode of thinking. Ownership is what's needed amongst Afro-Americans. Ownership. Own stuff. (Breskin 1992: 188)

Even the name of Lee's production company, 40 Acres & A Mule Filmworks— an allusion to a stillborn legislative proposal after the Civil War to give land and the means to cultivate it to each freed slave—acknowledges, however reluctantly (note the "pause" in Lee's assertion), the free-enterprise economy as that medium of empowerment most pragmatically instrumental to African American culture.

Appropriately, the morning-after completion of Mookie's "double-voiced" act of radical Signification itself takes the form of a signifyin(g) exchange—a transaction between two entrepreneurs, the "currency" of which is both verbal and material. In a boldly oxymoronic request, considering his destructive repudiation of Sal's colonizing presence in the neighborhood the night before, Mookie asks his now former employer for his week's back pay, $250. In a gesture equally oxymoronic for its own reasons, Sal gives Mookie the $250 and $250 more, a kind of ironic severance pay. Rather than hand the bills over, however, he wads them up and fires them one by one into Mookie's face. It is a signifyin(g) action, duplex in both execution and implication, at once both insult and gift, an indictment of perceived hypocrisy and a reward for loyal service. Mookie's response completes the signifyin(g) transaction; he throws two of the C-notes back in Sal's face, and says, "I owe you fifty bucks." Mookie's keeping the $250 he is owed, as well as the extra $50, tells us he feels justified, despite his having given in to "HATE!" the night before, in claiming what he's earned. Yet his unceremonious return of the extra $200 partakes of the same paradox as Sal's unceremonious offering of it, constituting both an expression of outraged integrity and an admission of responsibility and regret. The "stalemate" (Lee 1998: 91) that follows as both Sal and Mookie stare at the $200 lying unclaimed on the sidewalk is evidence of the conflicted ethical situations of both characters; Mookie's eventually snatching it up is, in the best signifyin(g) tradition, both gracious and self-interested.

Through the symbolic "double operation" of Mookie's radical practice, *Do the Right Thing* accomplishes precisely what Gates has identified as the crucial emancipation offered by the signifyin(g) imagination: the deconstruction of the binarisms culturally inscribed by the received, repeated trope of "double-consciousness" (Gates 1998: 238). Ironically, it is through his "entrepreneurial mode of thinking"—his signifyin(g) defiance of the ideological polarities that lay claim to him—that Mookie avoids the "entrepreneurial" dilemma of the African American subject as we have understood Du Bois to have delineated it: "the waste of double aims . . . seeking to satisfy two unreconciled ideals" (Du Bois 1903: 5). As protagonist, Mookie offers a model not for the integral, stable resolution of "the peculiar ethical paradox . . . the double life every American Negro must live," but for the refusal to abide by the schizophrenic cultural logic of which that condition is a profoundly debilitating effect. This refusal, in its alternately playful yet deadly serious eschewal of the notion of a unitary subjective identity, places in suspension the coercive semiotic structures and the otherwise ineluctable devices of a racist symbolic order, and gives the postmodern African American subject room to move within it.

In light of the film's signifyin(g) contestation of the idea of an essential "blackness," hooks's charges that the film "denies the problematical nature of identity" and "offers a simplistic view" of race seem inaccurate. On the contrary, *Do the Right Thing* rises to the challenge of Cornell West's call for postmodern African American cultural productions which "deconstruct earlier modern Black strategies of identity-formation . . . and construct more multivalent and multi-dimensional responses that articulate the complexity and diversity of Black practices in the modern and postmodern world" (West 1994: 74). The film's problematization of the "King"/"X" dualism releases the African American subject into just such "multivalent" and "multidimensional" modes of responsivity regarding these metanarratives of morally intelligent liberation. And the film's interrogation of consensus regarding "right thing"/wrong thing delivers to the politically marginalized an experience of that binarism's arbitrary and constructed quality. Despite its semiotic power, this denaturalization neither promotes moral chaos nor renders the figure "justice" morally indeterminate. Rather, by suggesting what Jean-François Lyotard has called "an idea and practice of justice that is not linked to that of consensus" (Lyotard 1994: 37), the film helps to free "justice" from the violence of its designated confinement within terms forged by a racist symbolic ascendancy and, like Baker's blues, helps to make "justice" available to the "polyvalent interpretations" which proliferate beyond dialectic. Thus, *Do the Right Thing*'s elucidation of the culture of ambiguity, and the internally dialogic subject which negotiates that culture, represents an elegant erasure of the logic of "two-ness" in all of its ideological formations.

REFERENCES

Baker, Houston A. 1984. *Blues, Ideology, and Afro-American Literature*. Chicago: University of Chicago Press.

Bakhtin, Mikhail. 1984. *Problems of Dostoevski's Poetics*, trans. Caryl Emerson. Minneapolis: University of Minnesota Press.

Breskin, David. 1992. *Inner Views*. Boston: Faber and Faber.

Brunette, Peter, and David Wills. 1989. *Screen/Play: Derrida and Film Theory*. Princeton, N.J.: Princeton University Press.

Christensen, Jerome. 1991. "Spike Lee, Corporate Populist." *Critical Inquiry* 17 (Spring): 582–95.

Du Bois, W. E. B. 1903. *The Souls of Black Folk*. Chicago: McClurg.

Ellis, Trey. 1989. "The New Black Aesthetic." *Callaloo* 12: 233–46.

Gates Jr., Henry Louis. 1988. *The Signifying Monkey*. Oxford: Oxford University Press.

George, Nelson. 1991. "*Do the Right Thing*: Film and Fury." Pp. 77–81 in *Five for Five: The Films of Spike Lee*, ed. Spike Lee. New York: Stewart, Tabori, and Chang.

Glicksman, Marlaine. 1989. "Spike Lee's Bed-Stuy BBQ." *Film Comment* 25 (July–August 1989): 12.

hooks, bell. 1990. *Yearning: Race, Gender, and Cultural Politics*. Boston: South End Press.

———. 1994. *Outlaw Culture: Resisting Representations* New York: Routledge.

Hutcheon, Linda. 1987. "Beginning to Theorize the Postmodern." *Textual Practice* 25: 10–31.

Johnson, James Weldon. 1976 (1912). *The Autobiography of an Ex-Coloured Man*. New York: Alfred A. Knopf.

Lee, Spike. 1988. *Do the Right Thing*. Screenplay, 2nd draft. Forty Acres & A Mule Filmworks. Writer's Guild of America no. 45816.

Lyotard, Jean-François. 1994. "The Postmodern Condition." Pp. 27–38 in *The Postmodern Turn: New Perspectives on Social Theory*, ed. Steven Seidman. Cambridge: Cambridge University Press.

Mitchell, W. J. T. 1990. "The Violence of Public Art: *Do the Right Thing*." *Critical Inquiry* 16 (Summer 1990): 880–99.

———. 1991. "Seeing *Do the Right Thing*." *Critical Inquiry* 17 (Spring): 596–608.

Reid, Mark A. 1993. *Redefining Black Film*. Berkeley: University of California Press.

Shohat, Ella. 1991. "Ethnicities-in-Relation." Pp. 215–50 in *Unspeakable Images: Ethnicity and the American Cinema*, ed. Lester D. Friedman. Urbana: University of Illinois Press.

Sobchack, Vivian. 1991. "Modes of Ethnicity." Pp. 329–52 in *Unspeakable Images: Ethnicity and the American Cinema*, ed. Lester D. Friedman. Urbana: University of Illinois Press.

Stam, Robert. 1991. "Bakhtin, Polyphony, and Ethnic/Racial Representation." Pp. 251–76 in *Unspeakable Images: Ethnicity and the American Cinema*, ed. Lester D. Friedman. Urbana: University of Illinois Press.

West, Cornel. 1994. "The New Cultural Politics of Difference." Pp. 65–81 in *The Postmodern Turn: New Perspectives on Social Theory*, ed. Steven Seidman. Cambridge: Cambridge University Press.

Spike Lee and the Fever
in the Racial Jungle

*Let us then say that we can reinterpret ideologies of difference
only because we do so from an awareness of the supervening
actuality of "mixing," of crossing over, of stepping beyond
boundaries, which are more creative human activities than
staying inside rigidly policed borders.*
—Edward Said, "An Ideology of Difference"

Concerning policed borders, one can often find a film's ideological
perimeters early on in the manner and style in which its opening ti-
tles are rendered. In the case of Spike Lee's fifth production *Jungle
Fever* (1991), the titles and credits are lettered on urban traffic signs and
worked into a montage of streetscapes replete with counterpoised maps of
Harlem and Bensonhurst, and an opening dedication to the slain black youth,
Yusef Hawkins, . . . all set to the theme music of Stevie Wonder's soundtrack.
This flow of sounds, images, and inscribed street signs, combined with all of
Jungle Fever's pre-release media hype and press packaging, clearly heighten
audience expectations that Lee is going to deal with the politics of race and
miscegenation, the crossing of boundaries, the stubborn defense of territories. Yet, unlike Said's promise of new definitions and creative possibilities
arising from "stepping beyond boundaries," Spike Lee has something a bit
more closed, confrontational, and melancholy in mind. Symbolizing the fixity
of Lee's perspective, the sign that announces that the production is a "Spike
Lee Joint" has a ONE WAY sign distinctly displayed underneath it. Adding to
this visual cue the film's title itself is templated on the international, red,
WRONG WAY traffic symbol. Moreover, the drift of these opening significations
is re-enforced by the film's title, which taints the issue of intimate interracial

Ed Guerrero, "Spike Lee and the Fever in the Racial Jungle," in *Film Theory Goes to the Movies*, ed.
Jim Collins, Hilary Radner, and Ava Preacher Collins (New York: Routledge, 1993), 155–69.
Reprinted with permission of Routledge Publishing Inc.

relationships—i.e., miscegenation—with the metaphor of disease, a fever that one, presumably, is in danger of catching, but that can be cured.

From the start, though, if one is to question the subtle but problematic argument in this latest of Lee's features, this questioning must occur against the background of brother Lee's serious contributions to the medium, to the persistent and ingenious ways that he has reinvented and expanded the practice of black cinema in America. Riding the broad popular wave of consumer interest in rap music, hip-hop, youth fashions, and black sports stars, in a very pivotal sense Lee has shifted mass thinking about black films and filmmaking in some fundamental ways. First, Lee has clearly demonstrated that, to employ a problematic term, blacks can be *auteurs.* That is to say, that a black director, using varied financing strategies (Lee's term is "guerrilla filmmaking"), can make a rapid series of feature films rendering his or her vision of black life, and that these films can be popularly consumed and supported at the box office. Thus, Lee has opened a gap, however small, in the dominant production system's wall of racism and exclusion, suggesting a strategy that, hopefully, many socially defined and marginalized *others* will be able to replicate according to their needs. As importantly, by exploring in his films a number of socially charged issues that have expanded the nation's perceptions about what it means to be black in America, Lee has been able to place elements of the African American experience at the center of America's popular culture agenda and social imagination. Hot, socially contained or contested issues that Lee has opened up in his films include the sympathetic, sensual depiction of black sexuality; the frank exploration of black-color caste and class hierarchies; the use of narratives rendered from a black point of view and firmly situated in the black world; the cinematic exploration of what Houston Baker Jr. has mapped as "the matrix of the blues," consisting of vernacular blues sounds, images, and forms in black urban language and music (Baker 1984: 3–14).

Yet upon examining the progress of his work, it also becomes clear that for Spike Lee these powerful issues are double-intentioned. Importantly, Lee's complex, multivalent explorations of the socially repressed, unspoken, and unspeakable issue of "race," have also played into his main profit-making, marketing strategies, in that the more his films assert themselves in the pre-release, public imagination through debate or controversy, the more audience interest they generate, and thus, dollars at the box office. This intense media milieu, along with the press-hyped fears of the racial conflagration that the film was expected to provoke, heralded *Do the Right Thing* (1989). At the time of the film's release, the *Oprah Winfrey Show* and *Nightline* dedicated entire programs to *Do the Right Thing*'s alleged explosive social potential. As well, Lee mugged for the covers of *Newsweek* and *American Film,* and even managed to find his way onto the cover of the conservative *National Review*. Additionally, the *New York Times* and the *Village Voice* ran at least a dozen articles and reviews between them covering all aspects of the film. To a less intense degree, this pattern has repeated itself with the release of *Jungle Fever*, as exemplified by the affectionate close-up of the film's co-stars, Annabella Sciorra and Wesley Snipes, on the June 1991 cover of *Newsweek*. And clearly, we seem to be building towards the same media climate with the Lee versus Amiri Baraka pre-production tussle over who owns the interpretation of Malcolm X's life.[1]

Lee's astounding success; his increasing commitment to mainstream cinema's narrative conventions, visual language, and marketing strategies; and the progressively larger budgets he's managed to accrue over the trajectory of his last three films all lead to a series of critical questions that are for the purposes of this essay best answered by looking at *Jungle Fever* and interrogating the film's argument, as well as its position in dominant cinema discourse. Generally, one must wonder where the trajectory of Lee's work is headed, whether the determined incursion of his interpretation of "blackness" into mainstream cinema's vast production system and its attendant markets will do anything to challenge Hollywood's racial hegemony. More specifically, though, is *Jungle Fever* really counter-hegemonic on the issue of miscegenation? In other words, does Lee's film challenge mainstream cinema's historically hostile stance and taboos against interracial relationships and marriage?

In response to these questions, let us, first, place *Jungle Fever*, and its socially charged narrative about a black male/white female interracial relationship, into a historicized frame by citing a moment from the studio film industry's distant past. During the early 1930s, in reaction to a series of star scandals and in order to avoid government censorship, Hollywood decided to self-regulate by initiating a code of production standards that would appease its critics, church organizations, and a growing middle-class audience of movie consumers. Thus by installing their own hand-picked commissioner, ex-postmaster Will Hays, and negotiating with clerical and civic leaders that commonly came to be known as the Hays Office Code, the studio moguls were able to hold off any attempt at censorship and interference from outside the industry. Reflecting the morals of the times, the Code was tolerant of such necessary box-office moneymaking ingredients as expressions of sex and crime as long as they were morally contained or punished in a film's narrative. But most importantly for this discussion, the Code also upheld the strong sense of racial *apartheid* and paranoia of the times by expressly stating that miscegenation, or the mixing of the races, was to be portrayed as in no way desirable (Miller 1980: 3). Over time, through this system of in-house self-censorship, most of the tenets of the Code remained in force until the gradual erosion of its puritanical ethos, starting with the Motion Picture Association of America's introduction of a liberalized production code in the mid-1960s. Notably, though, the taboo against miscegenation, whether explicitly articulated as in the original Hays Office Code or more implicitly just understood and practiced, has remained in force over the long continuum of dominant cinema's reign, from the very inception of commercial film in the U.S. with *The Masher* (1907) or *The Birth of a Nation* (1915) right up to the present— with the exception of a few gaps or counter-currents as exemplified by such infrequent productions as *Broken Blossoms* (1919), *Guess Who's Coming to Dinner?* (1967), or *100 Rifles* (1969).

Thus, one must note that in the Freudian sense repression isn't a total or complete process, in that all forms and instances of miscegenation have not been relentlessly or thoroughly kept from the commercial screen. Rather, in those occasional films when miscegenation is dealt with, the issue is articulated through various narrative strategies of containment that filter it through the perspective, values, and taboos of the dominant, white culture. And while these strategies are multitudinous, the most common one is to depict interracial romance as occurring between a white male and an exotic non-white female (rarely the other way around), as in *Sayonara* (1957), *The World of Suzie Wong* (1960), or the much protested by the Asian American community *Year of the Dragon* (1985). Moreover, consistent with the spirit of the antiquated Production Code, interracial unions usually end in separation or tragedy, with the person of color being eliminated, sometimes sadistically, as in *Mandingo* (1975), or more often just killed off, as in *Rambo 2* (1985). Even the fatal attraction of the monstrously black King Kong for the blonde, symbolically white-clad Fay Wray in *King Kong* (1933) clearly marks the deployment of this trope. Yet more subtly, when occurring between a non-white man and what is presumed by the dominant imagination to be the object of desire of all races of color, the white woman, interracial unions are often flawed by rendering them between subjects who are distinctly unequal in ways that inversely underscore the superiority of the all-powerful white norm. Consequently, the white woman depicted in unions with non-white men is devalued in some subtle way. She is plain; she is blank; she is handicapped, etc., thus suggesting that the sign of her whiteness should be in itself enough of a reward for the person of color. In both of Sidney Poitier's miscegenous forays, *A Patch of Blue* (1965) and *Guess Who's Coming to Dinner*, he is united with white women who are unmistakably devalued or are not his equals. In the former film, Poitier's white girlfriend is blind, and in the latter, while he is an eminent physician and head of the World Health Organization, his fiancée is simply rich, with no accomplishments or qualifications of her own, other than her whiteness. Both films, then, make the point that these uneven matches are the best a black can aspire to when dealing with the sovereign essence of "whiteness." Notably, this strategy is subtly echoed again in *Jungle Fever,* in the extramarital affair between the black architect Flipper and the high-school–educated, white temporary office worker Angie.

The point of this historical excursion through the taboos and repressed fears of Hollywood's filmic psyche is that, in the present instance, no matter what acclaim Lee has earned as an "independent" or "guerrilla" filmmaker, *Jungle Fever* is strictly a dominant cinema commodity that rigorously upholds every expectation and prohibition of the archaic Hays Office Code on the issue of miscegenation. Despite the film's first appearances as a fresh, controversial, or even counter-hegemonic incursion into the discursive tangles of America's racial jungle at the site of one of its most sensitive issues, interracial coupling, dating, loving, etc., ultimately *Jungle Fever* renders miscegenation from the dominant cinema perspective—that is, as in no way desirable. When it comes to portraying intimate interracial relations, Lee's film efficiently does what Hollywood films have always done. For Lee has produced a cautionary melodrama about an interracial romance doomed from its inception, a tale that clearly maintains that blacks and whites are better off sticking to their own races and territories. The cleverness and cinematic illusion of Lee's argument lies in the fact that he accomplishes this rationalization of the eroding, dominant social taboo against miscegenation by upholding it from a binary oppositional "black" perspective that is an amalgam of black political ideas ranging from Afrocentricity and black separatism to a subtle refrain of black neo-conservatism always faintly resonant in Lee's films and interviews.[2]

Lee's argument, as it is depicted in *Jungle Fever,* confronts the discerning spectator with some problematic moments. The film comes off as confused on the issue of exactly how "race" is constructed, as evident in some glaring contradictions in the narrative. The first of these inconsistencies arises when the buppie, Flipper, is questioned by Angie about whether or not they should have children. Flipper answers to the effect that this would be a bad idea and states that their children would be a "bunch of mixed nuts." One is left to ponder this comment, as it elicits a reflex and logical counter-question: Aren't all American black people, including Flipper's "quadroon" daughter, to use his rather confused and insulting rhetoric, "a bunch of mixed nuts"? The issue here is obvious enough. Flipper's statement explicitly and the film implicitly articulate the premise that there is a *biologically pure* essence of "blackness" somewhere out there in America, generally agreed upon and uniformly upheld by black people. Correspondingly, Lee seems to echo this longing for a pure essence of blackness in the very choice of Flipper's last name, which literally is "Purify." Yet given the infinite and irrepressible range of skin tones, hair textures, eye shapes and colors, and so on, among the many diverse physical features that make up the characteristics of the vast collectivity known as African America, Flipper's comment about "mixed nuts," alluding to a supposedly tainted miscegenous type in contrast to a mythical, pure type, has no empirical basis in science or reality.

Notably, Lee's visual sense of the unresolvable black/white tensions and oppositionality of this melancholy discussion is carefully worked out in this moment's mise-en-scène, as Flipper and Angie sit on distant ends of a king-sized bed looking off in opposite directions. A brick wall as background to their medium-framed, shot-reverse-shot dialogue further enhances the distinct feeling that their relationship is contained and going nowhere. In an obvious reversal of the film's advertisement, which plays on the contrasting allure of black and white skin by depicting a close-up of Flipper's and Angie's fingers affectionately interlocked, Flipper now sits at a distance, his skin cast as a blue-black shadow while Angie's is translucent white in the light of the window. Both of these visual constructions fetishize and manipulate the contrast of black and white skin, although for different purposes. Interlocking male/black and female/white fingers as a poster advertising the film are a titillating suggestion of erotic, forbidden entertainments awaiting the spectator inside the theater, while the distance between Flipper and Angie in shadow and light carry the film's moral message about the pain and futility of miscegenation.

Rebuttals to Flipper's "mixed nuts" comment abound in Black Cinema, say, in the way that a range of physical types naturally occurs in the concluding photo in Ayoka Chenzira's film *Hairpiece: A Film for Nappy-Headed People* (1984), or in the way hybridity implicitly shapes the narrative of Julie Dash's *Illusions* (1982), which in part deals with a light-skinned black woman's negotiations in, and passage through, the white world. Correspondingly, in *Jungle Fever*'s story world, Flipper and Cyrus would only have to look at their light-skinned wives to realize how contradictory and out of touch their notion of a mythic physical homogeneity really is. In a related manner regarding the politics of cultural production, it has been argued often enough that there is no pure or transcendent category of "blackness" (or, logically, "whiteness") known exclusively to black (white) people that magically clarifies or overdetermines all texts, identities, or transactions in the racial jungle. African Americans, as the name implies, are a heterogeneous formation, expressing a diverse range of opinions and ideas on any given subject (Gates 1987: 45).

However, this is not to take up the position of those intellectuals and critics who would theorize blacks as a people with a distinct historical subjectivity out of existence, those who articulate the oppositional and problematic "anti-essentialist" argument that there is no such thing as a cohesive, politically conscious, freedom-seeking, plural matrix of "blacknesses" forged by historical struggle taking the name African Americans. The experience of being black in this country, the devaluation, racism, and tension generated by the invisible, governing white norm that a black subject has to face daily, would quickly cure one of any such delusion. What is posited here is obvious enough to the most casual sojourner trying to negotiate the paradoxes and dangers of the racial jungle. Put simply, "race" as we know and live it, is an ever shifting set of *socially constructed* meanings forged out of political struggle (Omi and Winant 1986). And importantly, in the case of African Americans, "race," for example, as revealed by the construction of the white character—Tar Baby in Toni Morrison's novel *Sula* or Steve Martin's comic protagonist in Carl Reiner's 1979 movie *The Jerk*—is loosely inclusive in its boundaries and community membership, as contrasted to the paranoid exclusion of the reigning collectivity known as "whiteness."

It is a sad reality that the exclusivity of whiteness based on the "one drop" rule remains in de facto force in this country to this day and that it applies exclusively to African Americans. As the rule goes, if a person has "one drop" of African blood or an African ancestor, then that person is considered black and thus loses the naturalized privileges of whiteness (Davis 1991: 4–6). How often have black people observed whites in casual conversation volunteer that they have a trace of Native American ancestry or blood in their backgrounds as a way to enter or negotiate a discussion of the repressed and volatile subject of "race"? However, such a gesture would, at best, come off as naive to an African American for the simple reason that, in the dominant psyche, Native Americans do not raise the same social or political challenge to white privilege and hegemony as does the vastly larger, barely contained, and insurgent social collectivity of African America. This obvious truth has not escaped notice and discussion in black literature. In the short story "That Powerful Drop," Langston Hughes's character Simple satirically reflects on the absurd finality of the "one drop" formula when he observes, "If a man has Irish blood in him, people will say, 'He's *part* Irish.' If he has a little Jewish blood, they'll say, 'He's *half* Jewish.' But if he has just a small bit of colored blood in him, BAM!—'He's a Negro!'" (Hughes 1958: 201). For the same reason, as Patricia Williams so eloquently points out in her book *The Alchemy of Race,* it is a trauma close to death for many whites to recognize, let alone reveal, that they have any African blood flowing in their veins (Williams 1991: 61). Interestingly enough, Lee understands the pathological nature of such fears, as rendered in his clever soda fountain scene set in Bensonhurst where Italian American men almost come to blows over the slightest insinuation of African blood in one of their family lines. Conversely, then, would Lee prescribe such an exclusive, paranoid view of race for African Americans? Would he counter the dominant, invisible, yet all-powerful norm of an essential "whiteness" by

proposing that African Americans fall into the equally bogus notion of a binary and essential "blackness"?[3]

Yet in another important way, the absurdity of such a claim, for a *biologically pure* black essence, is further undercut by a powerful, if repressed,
contradiction worked into the film's narrative. Given black middle-class men's
well-documented preference to marry light-skinned African American
women—as revealed in a number of black novels, including Wallace Thur-
man's 1929 classic of the Harlem Renaissance *The Blacker the Berry . . .* , or
the "high-toned" heroines and chorus girls of any of Oscar Micheaux's black
independent, bourgeois melodramas, and as pointedly rendered in *Jungle
Fever* in Cyrus's and Flipper's clearly stated preference for light-skinned
wives—one must ask *the* critical question and, so to speak, play the child
pointing out the emperor's nakedness. Where do all of these light-skinned
African American wives for the black bourgeoisie ultimately come from, if
not from some form the process of miscegenation itself?[4]

Lee inadvertently plays with this contradiction, skirting the fringes of the
issue when Flipper and his wife argue in the department store where she
works and she accuses Flipper of having "finally gone ahead and done it"—that
is, of trading her in for a white woman. In this scene, which has faint intona-
tions of the "tragic mulatto" stereotype, it is clear that Flipper's wife recognizes
the repressed, ultimately miscegenous origins of Flipper's preferences in
women, although, here, Lee backs off from thoroughly interrogating the issue.
So in the final instance, Flipper and Cyrus are themselves lost in the maze of
twisted turns, choices, ideologies, and illusions etched into the terrain of the
racial jungle, as the film's implicit premise unravels under critical scrutiny.

To say all of this, however, is not to overlook the film's subtle complexities, its clever turns and brilliant moments. In an important sense, *Jungle
Fever* contains within it a dialectical, counter-current tension that arises out
of Lee's propensity and talent for visualizing sexuality, an element that is consistently explored in all of his films and that he continually works to refine. In
this case, Lee's inclination for depicting the erotic has produced perhaps the
most frank, seductive rendering of interracial, black-on-white sex on the
Hollywood screen to date. Lee's black male/white female sexual panoramas—
Flipper and Angie locked in spontaneous coitus on a drafting table at the office; their continual, close-up kisses throughout the film; and their working
through a variety of erotic positions in their bare apartment—stand in tempt-
ing contrast to the routine, missionary position, lovemaking scenes between
Flipper and his wife that open and close the film. Moreover, Lee's moments
of black/white eros are light years beyond *Guess Who's Coming to Dinner?*'s
one, tame, 1967 interracial kiss. At that time, Sidney Poitier kissing his white
financée in the back of a taxi was so socially charged that it literally couldn't

Jungle Fever (1991). Flipper Purify (Wesley Snipes), Angie Tucci (Annabella Sciorra), and the forbidden embrace.

be fully represented on the screen. This potent black male/white female kiss had to be contained in a smaller frame within the dominant frame of the screen, distanced to a voyeuristic gaze in the taxi cab's rearview mirror. So considering that any film's most powerful ideological argument is usually em-bedded in the visual—that is, a film always argues for what it *visually repre-sents*, often regardless of a director's intentions, it would seem that Lee's enticing depiction of black/white sex and affection between Flipper and Angie visually undercuts the argument and outcome of the film's separatist narrative. In a subtle, ironic manner, then, Lee is perhaps spreading the "fever" that he wishes to critique if not cure.

Jungle Fever also makes an insistent appeal for social justice in the stark, editorial way that it renders the limited intellectual horizons of Bensonhurst and its denizens, the neighborhood where Yusef Hawkins was so savagely and pointlessly murdered. The film seems to argue here that racism arises out of an explosive mix of personal bigotry with cultural fear and ignorance. But, Hollywood-style, *Jungle Fever* does not go much beyond this in its analysis of the causes of racism; the film limits its exploration of racism to personal expressions of anger without ever taking on its much more powerful and relevant political and institutional dimensions. In this same manner *Do the Right Thing* is brilliant at rendering the drama of racism in the montage of Puerto Ricans, white cops, Koreans, African Americans, etc., all shouting racist invective at whatever oppositional group happens to be the focus of their rage. This is the *how* of racism, and it makes good cinematic spectacle. But what is never explored is the much more political *why* of racism, as in why are all of these people so divided from, and angry at, each other, and, ultimately, who does this benefit?[5] Certainly *Do the Right Thing* foreshadows the barbaric treatment of Rodney King, and to a degree the counterfeit standard of "justice" applies to the case and the massive Los Angeles Uprising that followed it. But black cinema must now go beyond the commodified spectacle of racial violence, which always enriches the media and entertainment industries, in order to challenge the institutional foundations that subtly and relentlessly hold America's *apartheid* system in place.

Also, *Jungle Fever*'s "war council" of black women, held in Flipper's living room, is a powerful articulation of the film's uncontainable excesses, those usually unspoken social truths, energies, and contradictions that in brief illuminating flashes break through the formal surface of the dominant cinema text to pose some unexpected challenge or set of questions to the "official story." Correspondingly, and in part out of Lee's response to gender-oriented critiques of his preceding films, this was the one scene where Lee surrendered directorial control, letting black women improvise on the subject of black men and white women over the course of twenty-five takes. What emerges here is not the director's monologic stance against race mixing, as marked by the ONE WAY traffic sign. Rather, the scene communicates the irrepressible heteroglossia of black discourse as these women articulate a wide range of views—from the satirical adoration of the mythical black "Zulu dick," to the social marginality of black men, to varied perspectives on miscegenation, from anger and repulsion to an open endorsement of interracial dating, sex, love. It must also be said to Lee's credit that he adds another layer of complexity to this film in the subtle way he acknowledges these uncontainable social energies he attempts to define and harness, in that he holds out the vague possibility of a successful interracial union in his depiction of a Bensonhurst couple (figured along the lines of dominant formula), a black woman and white man.

By way of a conclusion, something must also be said about *Jungle Fever*'s framing of the term "interracial," which seems to imply the hookup of blacks and whites *solemente*. By overlooking the numerous, varied interracial combinations of "people of color," who as the oppressed or marginalized often share a certain affinity with each other, the film's narrow interpretation of the issue inadvertently supports the political interests of those who would benefit from keeping non-white collectivities divided. Conversely, Julie Dash's *Daughters of the Dust* (1991), in which one of the daughters elopes with a Native American, and Mira Nair's *Mississippi Masala* (1992), about a young Indian woman who falls in love with an African American man, come as necessary first steps in broadening the range of interracial combinations represented on the commercial screen. Though it is also worth noting that Lee seems to recognize this potential in *Do the Right Thing*, with Mookie's *Puerto Riquenio* girlfriend, Tina, but such possibilities do not emerge in *Jungle Fever*. Ultimately, then, Hollywood continues to repress an obvious social truth by not representing interracial relationships as part of the everyday transactions of a society with multiple, overlapping racial boundaries.

As a corresponding insight, the film's sense of narrowness and racial finality also spills over into the issue of gender politics in the stark way that its resolution returns Angie to the grim, oppressive patriarchy of her father's Bensonhurst clan. Thus, in the final instance, in accordance with dominant-cinema expectations, Angie is punished for crossing racial boundaries, for mixing. At the same time, though, this scene signals Lee's inability to envision Angie with the potential for a liberated future based on her gender. It is highly implausible that a woman of Angie's adventurous character, whose miscegenous affair can, at least in part, be read as an act of rebellion against all that Bensonhurst has come to stand for (including the violent beating she takes at the hands of her father), would not foresee the possibilities of her freedom beyond the dead hearth and home of racist patriarchy.

Yet in a society that is rapidly pluralizing, and where the invisible, dominating social construct of "whiteness" faces the prospect of being just another large minority past the year 2000, we must push our social vision to imagine what soon will become inevitable: an eruptive, almost infinite variety of *miscegenations* spreading across the political horizon, blurring all binaries and oppositions, subverting the norm, transgressing differences not only of color, but of class, gender, and sexual orientations as well. Certainly this is what Mikhail Bakhtin had in mind when he discussed the modern novel (and to extrapolate, narrative cinema) as open-ended and "unfinalized," as working against the strictures and closures of "official culture" (Morson and Emerson 1990). This is certainly what Toni Morrison, whom Lee admires, has in mind when Sula, her visionary character who transcends the norms of gender and race, an "artist without a canvas," declares on her deathbed that the racially closed and polarized little town that has ostracized her will some day come to love her after all the old women have lain with the teen-agers; when all the young girls have slept with their old drunken uncles; after all the black men fuck all the white ones; when the guards have raped all the jail-birds and after all the whores make love to their grannies; after all the faggots get their mothers; trim; when Lindbergh sleeps with Bessie Smith and Norma Shearer makes it with Stepin Fetchit; after all the dogs have fucked all the cats and every weather vane on every barn flies off the roof to mount the hogs . . . then there'll be a little love left over for me. And I know just what it will feel like. (Morrison 1973: 145–46)

So far, these aren't the kinds of social possibilities that Lee imagines in his films. And it must be said that when staring into the threat of an ecologi-cally exhausted, dystopian future, with most of the world's "consumers" lo-cated in industrial, and/or white-dominated nations in a sort of approaching global *apartheid,* the apocalyptic "color line" that W. E. B. Du Bois so bril-liantly forecast, Lee is not wrong to focus his efforts on exploring the limita-tions, injustices, and tensions of being black in this society. For this is what Spike Lee does best, exploring the cultural tensions and specificity of his in-terpretation of "blackness" at a particular locale on the vast heterogeneous map of African America. In this sense Lee is a profound diagnostician of racism in its localized forms and masquerades, as he sees it. Thus any intima-tion of biological essence that Spike Lee may fall into must necessarily be considered against the ever present but naturalized background of a hege-monic "white" essence that relentlessly struggles to proscribe all black dis-course in this country. However, in order, some distant day, to cure the real fever that plagues the land, which is an overdetermining, paranoid racism that sets all against all, thus poisoning all relations in the society; in order to exit the discursive tangles and snares of America's racial jungle, and to heal this land's fractured territories, we are going to have to spawn black filmmakers who, much like Sula, can imagine emergent, irrepressible social combinations and possibilities as well.

NOTES

1. Although seemingly the flames of this debate have been fanned by market forces, one can glean the core issues of Amiri Baraka's and Lee's differences over the legacy of Malcolm X from Ansen et al., 1991 and Lee 1991. See also Anna Everett, "'Spike, Don't Mess Malcolm Up': Courting Controversy and Control in *Malcolm X,*" in this volume.

2. For an excellent critique of Lee's entrepreneurial politics and positioning within dominant cinema discourse, see Wahneema Lubiano, "But Compared to What? Reading

Realism, Representation, and Essentialism in *School Daze, Do the Right Thing*, and the Spike Lee Discourse," in this volume.

3. Film scholar Manthia Diawara succinctly raises the ongoing issue of being trapped by a binary essentialism when he asks, "How might we talk about Blackness without substituting the historical White man as bad object with an historical Black man as good object?" His essay contains an important illumination of the topic (Diawara 1991).

4. Here I credit long discussions about black film with Tommy Lott for helping me to develop this issue. Also relevant to this essay is Lott's fine article, which, in part, explores the social construction of blackness in relation to the formation of black cinema discourse (Lott 1991).

5. Zavarzadeh 1991: 7–8. Here Zavarzadeh urges the critic to go beyond dominant ideology's "own terms" of formalist, aesthetic criticism. He argues that one must explore the suppressed political "tale" under the dominant, narrative surface by not asking "*how* a particular tale means but rather WHY *it means what it is taken to mean.*" He writes that he has found the "political (why) to be a more effective mode of inquiry than the rhetorical (how)."

REFERENCES

Ansen, David, et al. 1991. "The Battle for Malcolm X," *Newsweek*, August 26, 52–54.

Baker Jr., Houston A. 1984. *Blues, Ideology and African-American Literature: A Vernacular Theory*. Chicago: University of Chicago Press.

Davis, F. James. 1991. *Who Is Black?* University Park: Pennsylvania State University Press.

Diawara, Manthia. 1991. "Cinema Studies the Strong Thought and Black Film." *Wide Angle* 13, nos. 3–4 (July–October): 4–11.

Gates Jr., Henry Louis. 1987. *Figures in Black: Words, Signs, and the "Racial" Self*. New York: Oxford University Press.

Hanchard, Michael. 1990. "Identity, Meaning and the African-American." *Social Text* 8, no. 2: 31–42.

Hughes, Langston. 1958. *The Langston Hughes Reader*. New York: George Braziller.

Lee, Spike. 1991. "Who Owns Malcolm X?" *San Francisco Chronicle*, August 21, E1.

Lott, Tommy L. 1991. "A No-Theory Theory of Contemporary Black Cinema." *Black American Literature Forum* 25, no. 2 (Summer): 221–37.

Lubiano, Wahneema. 1991. "But Compared to What? Reading Realism, Representation and Essentialism in *School Daze, Do the Right Thing*, and the Spike Lee Discourse." *Black American Literature Forum* 25, no. 2 (Summer): 253–82, reprinted in this volume.

Miller, Randall, M., ed. 1980. *The Kaleidoscopic Lens: How Hollywood Views Ethnic Groups*. Englewood, N.J. Jerome S. Ozer.

Morrison, Toni. 1973. *Sula*. New York: Plume.

Morson, Gary Saul, and Caryl Emerson. 1990. *Mikhail Bakhtin, Creation of a Prosaics*. Stanford, Calif.: Stanford University Press.

Omi, Michael, and Howard Winant. 1986. *Racial Formation in the United States*. New York: Routledge and Kegan Paul.

Said, Edward W. 1985. "An Ideology of Difference." P. 43 in *"Race," Writing, and Difference*, ed. Henry Louis Gates Jr. Chicago: University of Chicago Press.

Savery, Pancho. 1990. "The Third Plane at the Change of the Century: The Shape of African-American Literature to Come." Pp. 236–53 in *Where We're Bound: Left Politics and the Literary Profession*, ed. Leonard J. Davis and M. Bella Mirabella. New York: Columbia University Press.

Williams, Patricia J. 1991. *The Alchemy of Race and Rights*. Cambridge, Mass.: Harvard University Press.

Zavarzadeh, Mas'ud. 1991. *Seeing Films Politically*. Albany: State University of New York Press.

"Spike, Don't Mess Malcolm Up": Courting Controversy and Control in *Malcolm X*

When Spike Lee made *Malcolm X* in 1991,[1] he was at the height of his popularity, his creative talents, his trademark outspokenness, and his audacious entrepreneurial successes. This timely confluence of Lee's artistic and commercial acumen, which no doubt helped secure his directorship of this long embattled project, also served to position him alongside Hollywood's pantheon of 1990s A-list film directors such as Oliver Stone, Michael Mann, Norman Jewison, and Woody Allen. At the same time, Lee's troubled production became yoked symbolically to the April 1992 Los Angeles Uprising and was instrumental in what Henry Louis Gates has called the "Malcolmania" that gripped American youth and consumer cultures at that moment. Whereas America's disenfranchised black youth and other sympathetic population segments struggled over the larger political implications of the meaning of Malcolm X, the man, opportunistic commercial enterprises rushed to market "X"-brand potato chips, "refrigerator magnets and trading cards, pins and air fresheners."[2]

Among the notable catalysts driving the political and cultural reawakening of Malcolm X's relevance were disaffected and rebellious black youths in urban spaces; white youths elsewhere; popular rap and hip-hop artists, including Public Enemy's Chuck D. and KRS-One; and Spike Lee films.[3] And like the subject of arguably his most important film to date, Lee has earned the reputation of "an enigmatic and controversial figure."[4] Michael Eric Dyson describes the overdetermined figure of unbowed, uncovering, and fierce revolutionary black masculinist nationalism as "explosively controversial."[5]

"Controversy," then, emerges as the adjective of choice for friends and foes, critics and reviewers of Lee's remarkable cinematic output at that historical juncture, and certainly regarding his affiliation with the *Malcolm X* film.

With the 1986 production of his celebrated first feature, *She's Gotta Have It*, and the culmination in 1991 of *Jungle Fever*, his fifth film in six years, Lee achieved a level of critical and commercial success and amassed a range of formidable production credentials that escaped many young directors of the era, black or white. By the time the *Malcolm X* film project was made available, Lee had not only honed his directorial skills, but he had also cultivated a bankable reputation both as mainstream media's favorite artistic combatant and as newsworthy darling of the independent filmmaking set. Unlike many of his black male contemporaries, including Bill Duke, Mario Van Peebles, and even his longtime collaborator Ernest Dickerson, Lee parlayed his love of cinema, shrewd marketing prowess, and media-made personality into a consistent filmmaking force and catalyst for change both within and outside the film industry.

This essay, then, considers *Malcolm X* as a uniquely and particularly salient aspect of "the 'Spike Lee Phenomenon' in popular dominant discourse."[6] Among my key concerns are *Malcolm X*'s discursive function in what I am calling "Lee's auteur vision," the film's position within the larger cultural struggle over the meaning of the political and intellectual legacies of El-Hajj Malik el-Shabazz (Malcolm X), and a number of high-profile controversies circulating around Spike Lee's making and marketing of his magnum opus *Malcolm X*.

Recuperating Malcolm X: Controversy One

Anyone familiar with Lee's successful deployment of "militant rhetorics" will recognize immediately the aptness of contextualizing his work in terms of controversy.[7] Thus, it is not surprising that when it came to the *Malcolm X* film project, controversy attracted Spike Lee like a moth to a flame and, to a degree, with similarly consuming results. Although burned by the pointed criticism from certain vocal members of the black community about his suitability for representing Malcolm—"our own black shining Prince"[8]—and the de rigueur, if heightened, barrage of racialized criticisms in the white mainstream media, Lee nonetheless was undeterred from his conviction that "the story of Malcolm X belonged to Black film, and there was no other way to look at it."[9] In April 1992, during the film's volatile production, even its star, Denzel Washington, commented that it "would not be the most controversial film of the year. [Rather, it's] going to be the most controversial film of the decade."[10] In the intervening years, however, it has been Lee's *Do the Right Thing*, and not *Malcolm X*, that has been included among those film-title matches corresponding to a Web search for "the most controversial films" on Google. Nevertheless, *Malcolm X* remains at the very least *the* most controversial film of 1992.

It is the case that much of the controversy surrounding Lee's replacement of Norman Jewison as the director of *Malcolm X* is legend. However, for our purposes, certain aspects of the story are important for what they can contribute to our understanding of the film's unique status within Lee's oeuvre and the national disposition to embrace, reject, or ignore the film's status as American cultural artifact. Lee became affiliated with the project after Warner Brothers announced its intent finally to green light a dramatic film about the life and times of Malcolm X, with Marvin Worth as producer and Norman Jewison as director. It is important to note here that Warner Brothers had enjoyed earlier success with Worth's Oscar-nominated documentary about the slain black civil-rights leader, also eponymously titled *Malcolm X* (1971). Public disputes about Lee's eventual involvement with the latest iteration of the Worth and Warner Brothers Malcolm X project vary widely. And although Lee, Worth, and Jewison are on record with three separate perspectives, they each recount an essentially civil resolution to the controversy, as excerpts from their narratives reveal.

In *This Terrible Business Has Been Good to Me: An Autobiography*, Jewison comments candidly about the experience: "I had wanted to make this movie. I didn't because Spike Lee also wanted to make it."[11] These remarks are part of Jewison's discussion about working with Denzel Washington on their film *A Soldier's Story* (1984), which convinced him that Washington was a natural to play Malcolm X. Yet the circumstances surrounding Jewison's departure from *Malcolm X* were less than voluntary, despite efforts to cast the outcome as such after the fact. Jewison continues:

> Marvin Worth . . . signed me to direct. We had a screenplay by Charles Fuller, who had written *A Soldier's Story*, and an older script by James Baldwin and Arnold Perl. . . . The media . . . picked it up and chewed it over. A white director making a film about a black hero? And it was now all about me and Spike, and not about the story of Malcolm X that we both wanted to make. Lee was on talk shows complaining that white directors should not make black movies. . . . Prejudice was everywhere. . . . In the end, the two of us met. . . . It was at my invitation, through his agent. He wore his baseball cap and I wore mine. We talked about Malcolm. I wished him well with the movie. "One thing, Spike," I told him, "just don't screw it up."[12]

Recalling the futility of resistance against this gathering storm—some nearly thirty years hence—Jewison's disappointment and acquiescence are clear.

Worth's position on the fracas, as reported contemporaneously in "A Movie Producer Remembers the Human Side of Malcolm X," seems less forthcoming, even contradicting Jewison's retrospective retelling. In the article by Bernard Weinraub, Worth reportedly claims that "Mr. Jewison was ambivalent about directing *Malcolm X*, saying that the film should be made by a black director." Worth, as Weinraub describes it, saw the growing interest in Malcolm X "especially among younger blacks," and Lee's public complaints "that the movie should be made by a black film maker," as rendering Jewison's continuation on the film untenable.[13]

Worth's project, which began more than two decades earlier, was known throughout the industry as one of the most famous unproduced movies in Hollywood. We are told simply, "Mr. Jewison dropped out, Mr. Lee took over and revised the Baldwin–Perl Script. Mr. Worth reluctantly agreed to take Mr. Baldwin's name off the credits, when the writer's family asked him to do so because of the revisions. The film's screenplay [therefore] is credited to Mr. Perl and Mr. Lee."[14] Worth comments, "Nobody can explain Spike. . . . Very difficult to understand. Very complex. . . . He panics the establishment. You're always getting phone calls about Spike from the studio: 'He's talking again to the press,' 'He's making trouble,' 'He's doing this,' 'He's doing that.' But we get along. We're still hugging."[15] For the flamboyant producer, the film's $10 million weekend box-office showing in third place behind *Home Alone* 2 ($30 million) and *Bram Stoker's Dracula* ($15 million) was better than expected, especially since the film opened in half the movie theaters of its competition. Still, the financial success was not the primary motivation behind the producer's twenty-year obsession. For Worth, the *Malcolm X* project was deeply personal. "Even if this movie doesn't make 20 cents, it's still history," he said. "It's something I *had* to do. My memories of this man go so far back." Although quoted as being "enormously proud of the film," Worth would have preferred that it focus on Malcolm X's incredible charisma and charm. He recalls the fated young man as a charmer who was "a lot of fun," a human characteristic that he fears was not adequately conveyed in the film.[16]

For his part, Lee's recuperative impulses regarding *Malcolm X* tracked according to the filmmaker's own life experiences and his specific processes of discovery about the black leader's life and times. In *By Any Means Necessary: The Trials and Tribulations of the Making of Malcolm X*, Lee reminds readers of Malcolm X's thematic prominence in *Do the Right Thing* (where the charismatic leader's image is a powerful diegetic motif). In fact, according to Lee, it was *the earlier film* that persuaded Worth to approach Lee about directing his film even before Jewison became involved. Lee states:

It was because of *Do the Right Thing* that a man named Marvin Worth—who had the rights to the material on Malcolm's life—sent me a letter saying that he wanted me to direct the film, or would at least like to discuss with me the possibility of doing it. I never did receive the letter, but he later showed me a copy of it. . . . Marvin said Norman felt he needed the Black credibility of [Charles Fuller] to get Betty Shabazz on his side. . . . When it got out that Norman was going to direct this film, that's when I started to speak out about it. . . . So Marvin had gone after me before Norman even came on the scene. Marvin wanted me, Warner Brothers would take me, so it was a matter of how we could make the deal, and let it be Norman's decision to leave, to save face.[17]

If both Lee's and Jewison's recollections reveal anything, it is that the manufactured consensus about how they resolved the controversy over who would direct misses some important nuances. The controversy based on a binary construction of Jewison's noble sacrifice and Lee's brash usurpation of the film directorship, due to extant political exigencies and a highly charged and racially explosive social climate of the period, is not so black and white when we consider the foregoing colorful and significant details. As Jewison points out, both men wanted to direct this movie.[18] And as Lee confirms, there was no way he was going to let Warner Brothers' decision to contract a white director "go without saying something about it in public."[19]

For Lee, courting controversy over *Malcolm X* was a necessary act of political and cultural intervention that turned on matters of credibility, authenticity, and even profitability. Entrusting the still volatile and complex life and revolutionary philosophies of Malcolm X to Warner Brothers, Worth, and Jewison was not an option Lee was willing to abide. Fearing that Malcolm X's larger-than-life story would suffer Hollywood's usual diminutions and circumscription to the industry's two preferred genres of the period, the "homeboy shoot-'em up drug movie" or the "hip-hop musical comedy," Lee was advocating a broader vision.[20] After all, he had read *The Autobiography of Malcolm X* as an impressionable youth in public school in 1969–70. Even then he recognized the man's greatness and thought, "This is a great Black man, a strong Black man, a courageous Black man who did not back down from anybody even toward his death. The Man. Malcolm."[21]

Clearly, Lee was not insulated from the burden of blackness in American society and thus could cast himself in the same fearless mold of black masculinist pride, militancy, self-determination, and group uplift that Malcolm X espoused. In fact, Lee followed in his father's footsteps and attended Morehouse College in Atlanta, where his father, Bill Lee, and Dr. Martin Luther

King Jr. were students a generation earlier. Spike Lee, no rigid black nationalist separatist, respected King's views on integration, which informed his own entrepreneurial practices. Nevertheless, Lee knew that it was the voice of Malcolm X that was, as he put it, "much more in line with the way I felt. So it wasn't a question of school loyalty of fellow alumni or knowing I would do a movie about Malcolm X one day. At the time, it was a question of being drawn to his intelligence."[22] Lee had no doubts about his own credibility compared with a white filmmaker's where directing *Malcolm X* was concerned: Not only had he read and apparently internalized much of Malcolm X's autobiography, he also listened to taped speeches by the slain leader as a matter of course to steel himself for battle against racism in the film industry in general, and his particular battles with Warner Brothers executives during the production of *Malcolm X*.[23]

Making *Malcolm X* at the Gilded Plantation: Controversy Two

> Malcolm X causes a reaction, so there is no way the film won't do the same thing.
>
> —Spike Lee, *By Any Means Necessary*[24]

Where one might presume that Warner Brothers' grudging concession to have Lee direct the film would quell some of the controversy, the opposite was true. All the bad press attending Lee's wresting the film from Jewison and his well-publicized troubles making the film served to ramp up the usual level of controversy and criticism about Lee's involvement with the project. Dyson reminds us that there was great concern that Lee was hustling Malcolm X's memory through shrewd and crass commercialization and merchandizing of Malcolm memorabilia, which tainted the filmmaker's integrity.[25] Nonetheless, film and cultural critics and audiences can bracket such compromises in recognition of the fact that "Lee's *Malcolm X* is still an often impressive, occasionally stunning achievement. It is a richly textured and subtly nuanced evocation of the life and times of a supremely American paradox. . . . Lee's Malcolm is inevitably a creation of Lee's own oversized ambition."[26] Nothing manifests Lee's determination to make *Malcolm X* his way more than his ongoing contests of will with Warner Brothers, the production partner that he mockingly dubbed "The Plantation."[27]

At first glance, Lee's derogation of the studio responsible for his first big-budget feature seems typical of his grandstanding publicity seeking, at best, and of his self-serving race baiting, at worst. But on closer scrutiny, Lee's complaints are less self-indulgent and more indicative of the industry's racist double standard for funding film projects predicated on race. No one expected Lee to suffer silently Hollywood studios' willing big gambles on risky white film projects while he was held to an unfeasible budget for an ambitious project that involved, among other things, second-unit shoots on three continents. In lamenting the industry's endemic double standard, Lee writes about his frustrations with studio heads over money. Expressing his gratitude to Oliver Stone for disclosing certain terms of his *JFK* production deal with Warner Brothers, Lee commented:

> And we're going to kick and scream if we don't get the same mother-
> fucking shit they gave Oliver Stone and *JFK*. . . . [W]e're tired of be-
> ing slighted, where we have to take the short end of the stick again
> and again. . . . They always try and say, "Well, Spike, Oliver Stone has
> made more than $100 million with *Platoon*, and *JFK* might make that,
> and Denzel Washington's not the truly great movie star that has the
> box office appeal of Kevin Costner." I've heard this from them, that's
> their feeling, and it's bullshit.[28]

Bernard Weinraub confirms Lee's charge of underfunding: "What got the *Malcolm X* controversy going and has kept it bubbling—always good for business—are issues involving money and personality. . . . Mr. Lee, who has never been shy about his own endeavors, has described it as 'an epic picture.' . . . The problem with epics, though, is they are expensive and run far longer than two hours. . . . Initially budgeted at $28 million, which is not elaborately expensive, the costs have climbed to $33 million."[29]

Not only was Lee justified in rejecting Warner Brothers' financial low-balling, but his insistence on total control was necessary, given Hollywood's earlier ideas for project X. For example, at various stages along the way, Richard Pryor and Eddie Murphy were serious contenders for the film. While Lee's assertion that the "film never got made" in more than two decades of attempts because "it wasn't s'pose to be made until now"[30] reflects his penchant for grandstanding public relations more than the actual facts of project X's troubled production history, few would argue that Lee's *Malcolm X* is not an impressive achievement. In fact, the film garnered two Academy Award nominations—best actor for Washington and best costume design for Ruth Carter. The foregoing cultural and industrial backstory provides an important context for our analysis of the film, and its particular location within Lee's remarkable career trajectory.

Representin' Malcolm in Spike Lee's Auteur Vision: Controversy Three

A number of additional factors must be considered for any fair assessment of *Malcolm X* as an artistic tour de force and economic triumph. And whether or not one accepts Lee's view that historical and other circumstances conspired to thwart production of a major feature film about Malcolm X because he was "s'-posed" to bring it to fruition, one thing is certain: When Lee's *Malcolm X* hit the theaters in November 1992, the necessary historical, political, cultural, and economic preconditions were met, and the film opened amid a cultural maelstrom. It was the nadir of the Bush–Quayle era, as Bill Clinton and Al Gore successfully challenged and ultimately defeated the Republican incumbents; after twenty years and recognizing "Malcolm mania," the film industry finally became less risk-averse about green lighting the film; an all-white Simi Valley jury acquitted white officers in the assault on Rodney King, and a white police officer in Detroit was convicted of killing black motorist Malice Green; federal marshals violently subdued white supremacists at Ruby Ridge; and Dr. Mae Jemison became the first black woman astronaut in space.[31] Subtending these fin-de-siècle occurrences is their revelation about the status of American race relations and, particularly, their affirmation of W. E. B. Du Bois's prescience when he warned in 1903 that *the* problem of the twentieth century was the color line.

It is this truism that Lee unapologetically foregrounds in narratives about both his experiences in making *Malcolm X* and the thematic preoccupations within that text. Houston Baker makes the point convincingly about Lee's work in this regard:

> Now, it is not that Lee's films are devastatingly original, telling us always things we do not know. What is striking about his work is that it is, in fact, so thoroughly grounded in what we *all* know, but refuse to acknowledge, speak, regret, or change. The strong kernel of critique in his films removes him decisively, I think, from the cult of the art-for-art's-sake campness and the Afrocentric posturings and Black filmic extravagance (or ennui) or neo-Black Arts cinematics.[32]

Where Baker provides a cogent read on Lee's cinematic populism and black cultural pragmatism, his view that Lee's work lacks Afrocentric posturings is arguable. In *Black Film White Money*, Jessie A. Rhines discusses Lee's role as "information conduit," willing to take "a public position on the side of the Black dis-advantaged despite the fact that he has never been one of them."[33] In fact, Rhines points out that Lee shares an Afrocentric uplift agenda of sorts in the tradition of "Booker T. Washington, Malcolm X, and Jessie Jackson, among others."[34] Baker's and Rhines's observations are important pointers toward central ideological markers of Lee's auteur's vision that Paula J. Massood has astutely catalogued.

In *Black City Cinema: African American Urban Experiences in Film*, Massood outlines several recurrent themes in Lee's work that are useful for understanding his auteur vision. As Massood observes, Lee often focuses on "core themes that, while adapted over time, still remain seminal to his work." Lee's films, therefore, are notable to the extent that they are addressed to an African American audience (even though many also draw in a substantial mixed audience), they focus on the role of the city and history in shaping black life, they are highly reflexive in form, they often explicitly evaluate and rearticulate African American cinematic representation, they provide sympathetic and detailed glimpses of the [Brooklyn] borough's African American faces, personalities, and communities, they emphasize black community concerns, they emphasize the realities of location, indicated in grainy visuals, and extended to the use of sound as most characters speak in a combination of middle-class and contemporary urban speech idioms, they use music to set time and place, they provide a multifaceted glimpse of a black urbanscape different from other African American spaces most familiar to film audiences, and they craft a rich variety of black male characters.[35]

My construction of this typology is extrapolated from Massood's observations about significant themes in Lee's earliest works (i.e., *Joe's Bed-Stuy Barbershop: We Cut Heads* and *She's Gotta Have It*) that are adapted in and improved on in his later films. This cataloguing, for me, makes perfect sense because to a one, the themes are recurrent and foregrounded in *Malcolm X* to powerful effect. After all, as Andrew Sarris wrote in the early years of auteur criticism:

> The strong director imposes his own personality on a film. . . . The so-called "big" pictures were particularly vulnerable to front-office interference. . . . The auteur theory values the personality of a director precisely because of the barriers to its expression. It is as if a few brave spirits had managed to overcome the gravitational pull of the mass of movies. The fascination of Hollywood movies lies in their performance under pressure.[36]

It is clear that Lee was and remains the sort of strong director that Sarris had in mind in his own adaptation and appropriation of the *Cahiers du Cinema* author-filmmaker's rubric that underpins our appreciation of the film director as the orchestrator of meaning in a film. While I argue that Lee's *Malcolm X* is a biopic constrained by a number of forces and factors, Lee's courting of controversy fits perfectly within Sarris's view of auteurist praxis under pressure. In effect, Lee was able to exert his own personality in the high-stakes contest of wills with the studio over final cut rights on the *Malcolm X* project.

What makes *Malcolm X* an important sociological, cultural, historical, and industrial moment is the film's participation in what Paul Arthur terms

"Jargons of Authenticity" wherein "documentaries and Hollywood narratives do not issue from separate and pristine worlds but over the course of their histories maintained a tangled reciprocity" by defining themselves each against its other all the while sharing technological, thematic, political and cultural codes.[37] As a result of his many professional and personal contacts and the force of his reputation, Lee was able to authenticate his docudrama by enlisting the support of X's widow, Betty Shabazz; his siblings Philbert and Yvonne; his Muslim brethren Benjamin 2X, Charles Kenyatta, and Minister Louis Farrakhan; and "many others who had been in the nation or who had known Malcolm X."[38] Biopics were among the earliest genres of cinema, and in fact the Warner Brothers studio achieved its earliest success with a 1918 biopic, *My Four Years in Germany* (1918).[39] In Lee's case, realizing his artistic vision of a Malcolm X biopic at Warner Brothers was problematic from the outset. Tensions were high not only because of how he became attached to the project, but also because the studio enjoyed a venerable tradition of biopics in general, and in particular it held the rights to its successful 1970s documentary film about Malcolm X. *Malcolm X* becomes even more interesting as a textual object because of its powerful amalgamation of the Alex Haley *Autobiography of Malcolm X*, footage from the Warner Brothers' documentary and Oliver Stone's *JFK*, a resurgent public interest in the life and times of the man, financial rescuing by prominent black celebrities, and Lee's own independent vision of how best to synthesize these disparate and often competing elements. What follows, is a view of Lee's film within the context of these foregoing discussions.

Lee envisioned *Malcolm X* as an epic film right from the start, and with a running time of three hours and twenty-two minutes, it signals one of his most important victories in the battles with Warner Brothers. For the most part, the film hews closely to the as-told-to autobiography of Malcolm X's life as penned by Alex Haley, and the original screenplay written by James Baldwin, and the later screenplay by Arnold Perl. Ultimately, however, the final script is Lee's adaptation of these earlier treatments to accommodate his more updated and dramatic retelling. Lee's version had a fealty to certain pivotal historical facts, though he also took dramatic license to fictionalize, expand, and compress events and temporalities and to construct composite characters. Dyson argues that there are inherent difficulties associated with "cinematically representing a man whose life has been reconstructed by webs of myth and romance . . . and the film's real-life subject impose historical limits, aesthetic constraints, and artistic conventions that work wonders for Lee's treatment of the complexities of race."[40] Indeed, aside from the rich materials that Malcolm X's life engendered for narrative possibilities, Lee's representation of race as an important narrative determinant in *Malcolm X* bridges an important historical chasm between race relations in America as Malcolm X experienced them during the Civil Rights Movement and the so-called post–civil-rights era of our present time.

The film is structured as a narrative triptych, wherein roughly one hour of screen time is devoted to each of the three successive periods of growth and transformation that defined Malcolm X's short but monumental life. For Lee, it was important to eschew a reductive depiction of Malcolm X as either a hero or villain, saint or sinner. Instead, he stressed the fulcrum of the controversial leader's tumultuous life in terms consistent with what Malcolm X himself described as "up from the muck and the mire."[41] Following Haley's rather spectacular narrative, Lee delivers an equally sensational and powerful biographical discourse that engages each of the stages of Malcolm X's life that ended with spiritual and intellectual redemption and sociopolitical martyrdom. Of course, situating the film along a historical continuum of pathological race relations in America was another central concern for Lee, a concern that certainly resonated with audiences in the aftermath of the 1992 Los Angeles Uprising.

Opening Acts: Malcolm X and the Quest for Black Manhood

Malcolm X opens with Denzel Washington's disembodied voice channeling one of Malcolm X's provocative speeches containing the memorable refrain, "I charge the white man," wherein a litany of white crimes against black humanity, including murder, kidnapping, robbery, and enslavement, are inventoried. The voiceover continues, "He can't deny the charges. You can't deny the charges. We're the living proof of those charges." After Washington's star credit fades, a cut to a full-frame shot of the American flag in color fills the screen, with the words "Malcolm X" appearing center frame. Shots of the intact flag bursting into flames are disrupted by grainy clips from George Holliday's footage of the Rodney King beating as the production credits conclude.

The cross-cutting between the King beating and the fiery American flag constructs a visual dialectic wherein this revered American symbol is recoded through its proximity to the shameful video footage of police brutality and state-sanctioned oppression and racism. Juxtaposed in this way the flag and the King beating footage perform what Sergei Eisenstein referred to as a form of intellectual montage, in which the imagistic thesis (the flag) and its antithesis (the Holliday footage) are conjoined to effect a synthesis: America equals racial brutality and oppression. At the same time, the deployment of the flag imagery instantiates Lee's homage to the film *Patton*, Francis Ford Coppola's 1970 epic about another larger-than-life American figure, General George S. Patton Jr. For Lee, such cinematic referents are not merely gratuitous; they serve a central signifying function in his auteur vision.

The opening sequence is also significant in its extradiegetic framing and intertextual references to the urban rebellions that erupted in the wake of the verdicts in the Rodney King trial acquitting white racism. Thus, the visual rendering of the flag burning at the end of this sound–image montage culminates in its transformation into a burned red, white, and blue X icon, suggesting the enduring nature and contemporary relevance of Malcolm's legacy for addressing the historical continuum of white oppression and supremacy. These volatile significations also tap into a "Burn-Baby-Burn" indexicality recalling the violent urban rebellions of the 1960s.

Malcolm X was released amid a cycle of hood, or ghettocentric, films, including *Boyz n the Hood* (1991), *Juice* (1992), and *Menace II Society* (1993), that according to Melvin Donalson "placed more black and Latinos on the screen" enacting a familiar boys-of-color masculinity "based upon nihilism, materialism, and misogyny."[42] *Malcolm X* surely depicted some striking similarities to these films in its presentation of Malcolm Little's early years as Detroit Red. Most important, however, it presented striking alternatives, as well. For example, the film showcases a panoply of black male characters, including Malcolm X's proud and defiant father, Earl Little (an acolyte of a strong model of black masculinity, Marcus Garvey), Cholly and Toomer (the barbershop's old-timers and Greek chorus who witness daily the black male experience of the period), Shorty (young Malcolm's partner in crime), West Indian Archie (the mathematical genius-thug of Harlem's numbers racket), Baines (prison guard and Nation of Islam minister), Elijah Muhammad (spiritual and business leader of the Nation) and other members of the Nation of Islam (NOI), Dr. Payson (conservative Negro academic who debated Malcolm X on TV), cameo appearances by Reverend Al Sharpton and former Black Panther Bobby Seale, and, of course, the various masculinities of Malcolm X himself. I will explore, briefly, Lee's artistic rendering of the masculine discourses through film's look and creative stylizations.

The Look

Spike Lee and his and long-time cinematographer, Ernest Dickerson, state that the look of *Malcolm X* is based on Coppola's 1972 Academy Award–winning film, *The Godfather*, itself an epic film about changing masculinities. In addition, Lee's expressive camera, dialectical montage, and other formal elements demonstrate his virtuoso "mining of Black cultural themes and institutions" to craft nuanced, hyperbolic, and fragile zones of black masculinity.[43] Several scenes in which Lee uses image and sound to reveal the fragile and treacherous bonds of brotherhood for Malcolm as both Detroit Red and Malcolm X are emblematic in this regard. Following the dark chiaroscuro lighting conventions of film noir, Lee renders visually the uncertainty, the untrustworthiness and suspect motives behind Malcolm Little's (a.k.a. Detroit Red's) close male relationships. With striking dramatic clarity, Lee dramatizes much of Malcolm X's psychosocial development in terms of the tragic loss of his father, who is replaced by a series of perilous mentors, beginning with West Indian Archie and his numbers-running minions, a relationship that clearly prefigures his later troubles with Minister Baines and the Honorable Elijah Muhammad.[44]

Where Lee deliberately uses framing and composition to indict Detroit Red with his criminal cronies as they ply their illicit trades and illegal activities in Harlem's salacious underworld, he conveys effectively the spiritually transformed, more intellectually mature stages of Malcolm X's masculine trajectory via extensive individual shots, close-ups, and interior monologues as voiceover. Despite the film's running time of more than three hours, Lee's formal structuring of the biopic necessitates both temporal compressions and realignments and, to some extent, composite characters. Together they affirm Lee's talents at cinematic storytelling and narrative economy such that the film captures most of the crucial historic and biographical moments that follow "faithfully the lineaments of Malcolm's various emergences and conversions as detailed in his autobiography."[45]

Through the visual economy of dialectical montage, Lee juxtaposes key past and present events to explain Malcolm X's complex character. For example, in the first section of *Malcolm X*, Malcolm confesses his love of the movies in a scene that comports with a description from the autobiography:

> It was at this time that I discovered the movies. Sometimes I made as many as five in one day, both downtown and in Harlem. I loved the tough guys, the action. Humphrey Bogart in *Casablanca*, and I loved all of that dancing and carrying on in such films as *Stormy Weather* and *Cabin in the Sky*. After leaving the movies, I'd make my connections for supplies. . . . I'd start my rounds. . . . I didn't sell and run, because my customers were my friends. . . . None of them stayed any more high than I did.[46]

What is particularly telling in this passage is its support of Lee's storytelling choices that might seem arbitrary to someone unfamiliar with the story, especially his exuberant portrayal of the prolonged musical scene at the Roseland dance hall or the treatment of young Malcolm's underworld life. In these scenes from the film we can see the specific aesthetic influences informing Lee's auteur vision, including a penchant for the hyperbolic drama and fast-paced action of the classic Warner Brothers crime dramas of the 1930s. This aesthetic also pays homage to black dance numbers characteristic of independent race films and Hollywood's black cast films of the 1930s and '40s and the more contemporary musicals such as *West Side Story* (Robert Wise and Jerome Robbins, 1961) and *Fame* (Alan Parker, 1980). Black music traditions and popular artists spanning the period of Malcolm X's life are also featured, including Duke Ellington, Ella Fitzgerald, the Ink Spots, Sam Cooke, and Aretha Franklin. The final result is a scene that putatively draws from Malcolm's own words to present the look and sound of black popular culture over a number of decades.

Other scenes continue with this polyphonic referential strategy—for example, a later scene of Detroit Red and Shorty frolicking through a park, playing a Warner Brothers-inspired cops-and-robbers game, is interrupted by a jarring close-up of Red feigning death from Shorty's air bullets. This playful death scene is intercut with an extreme close-up shot of the actual death of Red's father (whose tragic demise occurs as he lies prone facing an unstoppable train). Lee's choice, then, to link through editing Malcolm X's life and death struggles with those of his father is a powerful visual economy and recurrent motif that speaks clearly to repressive apparatuses brought to bear on black masculinity in America—a literal and figurative arresting of black masculine development. For instance, in the final third of the film Lee draws a visual and thematic parallel between the nighttime bombing of his childhood home with Malcolm X's own family fleeing the destruction of a nighttime bombing of their home. Through a creative arrangement of flashback scenes, then, Lee references important historical occurrences in Malcolm's X's past that foreshadow eerily similar tragic outcomes in his later life.

While it is clear that the film follows the autobiography, Lee appropriated the visual and thematic tropes of treacherous masculinity found in Coppola's *Godfather* films. For example, Dickerson used a chiaroscuro lighting design to convey the ruptured relationship between Malcolm X and his spiritual brethren. This is especially evident in the film's dim and ambiguous lighting and claustrophobic framing in several scenes between Malcolm X, Elijah Muhammad, and the fictional character Baines. The scenes' expressionistic lighting distorts Baines's and Elijah Muhammad's faces and shrouds Malcolm X's in a fog of disbelief, rendering visually the duplicitous and increasingly dangerous nature of Malcolm X's one-time allies. Given the tragic fratricidal nature of Malcolm X's death, Lee's complex representation of the excesses of treacherous masculinity is warranted; however, Lee calibrates this masculine problematic that again underscores Massood's point that black masculinity in Lee's discourse countermands dominant views of a one-dimensional black male subject. In *Malcolm X*, Lee also gives us compelling depictions of fierce black male loyalty, compassion, and redemption. Through the dense signifying chain of meaning and visual economies of mise-en-scène, Lee is able to underscore the more affirmative values and qualities that also defined the black masculine experience of that period.

Lee's construction of a masculine zone or sphere of influence throughout the film is called for by the subject matter and genre. From the start, Lee visually unifies black men by placing theme in close physical proximity via tight framing. Lee also frames Malcolm X between his fiercely loyal underministers, the Fruit of Islam (FOI), who flanked him for protection at all public appearances. Furthermore, he uses mise-en-scène and framing to represent black male power. We see low camera angles used to full effect when West Indian Archie is introduced at the height of his powers and made larger than life in the youthful eyes of Detroit Red; a similar camera treatment of Malcolm X during his rise in the Nation of Islam organization appears later; and most dramatically, there is a scene in which Malcolm delivers a speech in front of a gigantic portrait of Elijah Muhammad. More than an evocation of Orson Welles's classic representation of egomaniacal power in *Citizen Kane*, the positioning of Malcolm X between the eyes of Muhammad's painted poster suggests that Malcolm X's spiritual mentor is both a benevolent protector and a jealous, all-seeing rival.

Nothing signifies black masculine unity and black nationalist solidarity more than Lee's framing of the orderly, disciplined phalanx of FOI ministers outside a police station after one of their own falls victim to police brutality. Lee shoots the crowd of FOI ministers standing at rigid attention in military formation and later moving with soldierly precision on the direction of Malcolm X's one black-gloved hand, shots that demonstrate the awesome unity of the FOI. It is in Lee's nuanced visual attention to the representational options for characterizing the various stages of Malcolm X's life that the complexities of black masculinity are played out. This of course leads us to consider briefly how Lee's very troubled discourse on women in general, and on black women in particular, unfolds in *Malcolm X*. Michael Eric Dyson remarks cogently, "As with the films of Dickerson, Lee, Rich, Singleton, and Van Peebles, this focus on black masculinity spells real trouble for black women."[47]

Lee on Women in *Malcolm X*

Lee has been critiqued extensively for his narrow and sexist representations of women by a number of black film critics, and he even acknowledges his own shortcomings. So there is no need to retread through this well-known and important discursive output.[48] I do, nevertheless, want to highlight a particular instance that speaks to Lee's filmic gender bias because it is at odds with his own authenticating narratives regarding his suitability to direct this film. While lobbying to direct the film, Lee linked his credibility to his blackness and community ties to key figures from Malcolm X's life, including his family members, former Nation of Islam members, and especially his widow, Betty Shabazz. It seems hardly surprising, however, that given his gender troubles, Lee's rapport with Shabazz became strained. Discussing the roles of women in his previous films, Lee appeared to be self-conscious of the need for change. Nonetheless, his statements at the time betrayed his sexist prerogative:

> It matters to me what people have said in the past about my depictions of women in my films. The first thing I think they have to understand is, I'm not a woman, so I can't see women as women see women. I can understand women saying there should have been more or better-developed female characters in my films.[49]

As this passage makes clear, Lee is cognizant of his reputation for sexist depictions, but he is not necessarily penitent or interested in modification. Rather, he finds an alibi in the fact that, as he put it, "All I'm really doing is showing that the way it was. You can't really come down on me for this second-class status the Nation of Islam gave women, because the brothers in the Nation always made the sisters ride in the back seat."[50] In this regard, aspects of Lee's gender representations comport with what Dyson has called "the worst traits of Malcolm's lethal sexism."[51] This is particularly the case in the short shrift that Lee gives to Shabazz in the film and the complete narrative erasure of Malcolm's X's sister Ella.

According to Lee, tensions involved with having Shabazz as consultant revolved around their disagreements over the portrayal of marital strife in the couple's relationship, which Lee felt was necessary to the film's dramatic narrative arcs, despite Shabazz's vehement objections.[52] The contrived marital strife was not only Lee's dramatic license for propelling the narrative forward, but it suggests a view of gender politics wherein the heroic male's larger-than-life mission to save the world is invariably thwarted by the nagging self-interest of a female partner–spouse. In a telling scene, Shabazz (Angela Bassett) instigates an argument with her husband about money and the treachery of the ministers in the NOI. The scene, while prefiguring the split between Malcolm X and the increasingly volatile organization, suggests Shabazz's accusatory rather than supportive role in her husband's life. It seems clear why Betty Shabazz might object to this characterization; as an educated and dedicated Muslim woman, she embodied the very antithesis of this flawed construct of self-centered, short-sighted female obstructionism.

In fairness to Lee, the autobiography recounts an instance of a "domestic quarrel" regarding money in which Malcolm X is quoted as saying that he and Betty "nearly broke up over this argument."[53] Lee stresses this discordant note with powerfully subtle visual cues. In the scene of Malcolm X and Betty Shabazz's wedding, for example, the camera pans the room to show a semiotically dense image of the embracing couple's reflection in a glass encasing a close-up photo of Elijah Muhammad. The superimposed imagery invokes a marriage triangle—or, at the least, too much interference in the young couple's lives by the minister. Lee reiterates this potent photo montage later in the film during the scene of the couple's violent disagreement over what Malcolm X described as "the ugly rumor" swiftly spreading about Elijah Muhammad's adulterous affairs.[54] Here Shabazz attempts to enlighten her husband about his need to be more concerned with money matters for their family.[55]

Wahneema Lubiano finds that, in the "Spike Lee discourse," "Men do," or they have narrative agency, whether dancing in "beautifully choreographed Greek stomps" or organizing protests, marches, or rallies. "Women, on the other hand," she argues, merely "show." Discussing *School Daze* specifically, Lubiano argues that Lee is "incapable of showing that women do anything

Malcolm X (1992). Denzel Washington as Malcolm X.

other than look like components of male aesthetics."[56] Furthermore, it appears that women's agency in his films oftentimes bifurcates in terms of that familiar Madonna/whore construct so characteristic of mainstream Hollywood (and, for that matter, New Hollywood, New Wave, and independent) films. Shabazz's Madonna archetype is rendered with soft, flattering key lighting and intimate, close-up framing with Malcolm X and their daughters. By comparison, Laura and Sophia, Detroit Red's earlier partners, are "ghetto ho's" of dubious intent either mystified by low lighting or fully bared and sexualized by harsh lighting and voyeuristic camera movement. The anachronistic 1990s music video from the 'hood or Victoria's Secret costuming during the scene depicting Laura's descent into prostitution as Malcolm X laments the dream deferred of dutiful black wives, black nurses, black teachers, black scientists, and so on makes the point perfectly.

"How to Read Malcolm X": Controversy Four

To hear Spike Lee tell it, the controversy largely led by the poet-activist Amiri Baraka was the last thing he expected, given his close relationship with Baraka and his family before his involvement with the film. Contemporaneous newspaper articles, as well as later publications by black scholars and other critics, were rife with criticism and, in some quarters, downright condemnations of Lee's depiction of "our own black shining Prince."[57] The following press headlines of the period are indicative of the film's "hard sell to some factions," to use Dyson's terms: "The Real Malcolm X? The Search Widens, but Riddles Remain"; "Malcolm X, in the Eyes of Different Beholders"; "Just Whose 'Malcolm' Is It, Anyway"; "'Malcolm X' is Setting an Industry Brushfire Months before Release"; "Malcolm X: The Myth and the Man"; "Loving and Losing Malcolm."[58] Fueled by such headlines, skepticism about Lee's auteur vision and its capacity to do justice to Malcolm X's legacy abounded within the black community. In addition to Betty Shabazz, the press sought commentary from the ranks of the black literati, including Baraka, Cornel West, and Manning Marable. Most of the complaints involved fears that Lee would trivialize, distort, and taint the highly guarded and venerated reputation of the slain freedom fighter. As Dyson indicates, the controversies concerned fears about, "What happens to Malcolm when his life is treated by a cultural nationalist who is also a bourgeois black artist?"[59]

As one of the more vocal critics of Lee's *Malcolm X*, Baraka proffered some valid correctives calling attention to Lee's more suspect representational choices. At the same time, some of Baraka's complaints betrayed an often contradictory critical logic that seemed more about the poet's antipathy toward Lee than with what appears onscreen. Most troubling and unforgivable for Baraka and other critics were certain of Lee's narrative choices and dramatic emphases, ranging from minimizing the role of family in Malcolm X's life to distorting his trip to Mecca and his later political and spiritual maturation. Joining Baraka were such critics of African American literature and culture as Mary Emma Graham and Clark Eldridge White, among others. Graham, for example, questioned the erasure of Malcolm X's sister Ella, an important and constructive influence on the young leader's life. Graham, like others, was concerned that the resurgence of popular interest in Malcolm X's life was not well served by such inaccuracies in the filmic discourse. Graham saw Lee's stereotypical treatment of Malcolm X's early life in Boston, and especially the film's complete disavowal of his sister and other siblings, as a major weakness because this elision of his family's role in Malcolm X's exceptionalism helps reify an errant societal belief in the myth of the naturally pathological black family.[60]

For most black critics of Lee's cinematic discourse, the issue turned on its fealty to the autobiography. Baraka, Graham, and White participated in a 1993 radio program discussing the legacy of the actual Malcolm X versus Lee's film. All three agreed that audiences should consult the book and not the film for accurate historical information. They did not want the legacy to be reduced to just another Hollywood biopic. Despite longstanding complaints about Haley's recounting, they insisted that it was the autobiography, and not the film, that participated in the venerable history and tradition of respected American literary forms, particularly the traditions of the slave narratives and autobiographical literature. Furthermore, for Baraka, "To Spike, Detroit Red is the real Malcolm." According to Baraka, this explains the film's disproportionate screen time devoted to this period of Malcolm X's early life. Baraka also took Lee to task for the prison segment, stating that the scene "of Malcolm in prison is very foul, he did not just read the dictionary."[61] Following the autobiography, Baraka and the others wanted it known that Malcolm X's prison self-education included grappling with the complex philosophical treatises of "Schopenhauer, Kant, Nietzsche . . . Spinoza" and others.[62] And like Graham, Baraka argued that Malcolm X's road to Islam came through his family ties, not through the troubled mentoring of a corrupt Nation of Islam minister or a composite prison-inmate character named Baines.[63]

I will conclude on Clark Eldridge White's observation that "Malcolm is bigger than U.S. history" to address critics' concerns about Lee's treatment of Malcolm X's visit to Mecca during his estrangement from the Nation of Islam in particular, and their more general concerns about his suitability to direct the film in the first place. I had the opportunity to visit Tunisia while completing this essay, where in my capacity as a visiting professor of film studies I screened *Malcolm X* for my Islamic students in the English Department and the Civilization, Linguistics, and Literature programs. I presented students with a questionnaire about the film to try to get an informal sense of its reception more than a decade after its initial global release. My intention was to discern the students' opinion of the film's treatment of Mecca, as well as their assessment of how this relates to the practice of Islamic thought and teaching in a post–9/11 geopolitical context. None of the students had seen the film before (or any Lee films), though most had heard of Malcolm X through their classes in American history, literature, and civilization.

On the question about the film's treatment of Islam and the scene where Lee has Malcolm X in Egypt and Mecca, the students seemed to reach a consensus. By and large, they affirmed Baraka's criticism that Lee reduces Malcolm X's Mecca trip to a mere travelogue, and that the Egypt scenes are flawed because, in Baraka's words, "Spike has him going to Africa to look at the pyramids and the Sphinx"[64] rather than making the trip for spiritual enlightenment and to engage in political dialogues about African unity with black leaders of the Pan-African independence struggle. In response to the question, "What do you think about Lee going to Egypt to film the pilgrimage to Mecca? Does he capture the event effectively and properly?" one student replied: "Actually, I think that the scene of Egypt and showing the pyramids is superfluous and unnecessary, because Egypt, except the fact that it is an Arabic country, has nothing to do with the pilgrimage." Another wrote, "I think Lee selected Egypt among the other Arabic countries because it is the emblem of the Arab world's cultural heritage." Finally, one student's comments sum up the majority view: "Unfortunately, the film does not provide a true/real understanding of Islam, especially in the first part where E. Muhammad is presented as the 'GOD.' Nevertheless, the part which was filmed in 'Mecca' is quite good and authentic."

That the Tunisian students could respect this aspect of the film speaks volumes for Lee's tenacity and uncompromising stance with Warner Brothers in keeping to this element of filmic authenticity. Lee was able to lend authenticity to the look of the film through his choice of cutting between black-and-white and color film stock during the shooting in Egypt and at Mecca. Lee heightened the drama of the trip through this visual economy so that he could portray the FBI's grainy surveillance film, Malcolm X's saturated home-movie footage, and the putative invisible camera work of the main film's A-roll, 35mm film stock. For Lee, who understood his primary audiences' sophistication and knowledge of film culture and history, it is not surprising that he crafted the visuals of Malcolm X's pilgrimage to Mecca according to well-known imagery from Ingmar Bergman's famous film *The Seventh Seal*, and that the Hajj trek across the desert landscape with Malcolm X and the devout throngs of Muslims walking in single file against the horizon also references a similar visual stylistic in the beach scene in Julie Dash's *Daughters of the Dust*. Such intertextual referents remind us of Lee's professional education and training as a world-class filmmaker, one steeped in classic and contemporary film history and praxis.

To return to Baraka's and other black critics' concerns, one might be tempted to wonder about Lee's dealings with these controversies and challenges to his suitability to the task of directing this film in light of his own challenges to Jewison on similarly weighty, if not identical, grounds. As Baraka and other critics point out, the film should answer to some of the necessary and fair criticism because, among other considerations, it is a biopic, based on the life of a venerated, controversial, and beloved historical figure. Therefore, people expect verisimilitude, as difficult as this concept is to define when put to the test. Still, it is important to understand that Lee's *Malcolm X* is not the one-to-one narrative retelling of Malcolm X and Alex Haley's autobiography; nor is it the Warner Brothers documentary *Malcolm X* produced years ago. Consequently, the director was confronted with myriad creative, political, economic, and ideological choices during his struggles, from preproduction to theatrical exhibition. And although the familiar refrain that the book was better than the film comforts some, it seems important in retrospect to consider just how much better the film is, given Lee's ability to make a three-plus–hour epic and to raise the funds from other African American celebrities to avoid delaying the cinematic realization of an acceptable Malcolm X's film indefinitely. Without his insistence on controlling the central aspects of the film's production, Warner Brothers is unlikely to have green lighted shoots across the three continents that resulted in visually sumptuous scenes in Egypt, the historic access and permission to film the Hajj to Mecca, and the touching scenes with Nelson Mandela in South Africa (which contributed much to film's effective articulation of Malcolm X's global impact toward the end of his life).

To close, I will draw from Angela Davis's latter-day reflections on the influence of Malcolm X on her life:

> Hearing him speak as an undergraduate at Brandeis University before an audience composed of the almost entirely white student population had a profound effect on my own political development. No one could have convinced me then that Malcolm had not come to Brandeis to give expression to my own inarticulate rage and awaken me to possibilities of militant practice. I therefore feel repelled by the strong resonances of unquestioned and dehistoricized notions of male dominance in this contemporary iconization of Malcolm X. This is not to imply that Malcolm was not as much a perpetrator of masculinist

ideas as were others—men and women alike—of this era. What disturbs me today is the propensity to cloak Malcolm's politics with insinuations of intransigent and ahistorical male supremacy that bolster the contemporary equation of nationalism and male dominance as representative of progressive politics in Black popular culture.[65]

Davis's thoughts may help us to decide for ourselves whether or not Lee "messed Malcolm up."

NOTES

1. Once the word got out that Spike Lee would be directing the film, he was warned often to get it right and not "mess up" Malcolm X's life. Most notable were the admonitions by Amiri Baraka and Norman Jewison, among others. See, e.g., Amiri Baraka, in "The Real Legacy of Malcolm X versus Spike Lee's Film X," a panel discussion recorded for *Radio Free Maine*, dir. Roger Leisner, Brookline High School, Boston, February 10, 1993; Norman Jewison, *This Terrible Business Has Been Good To Me: An Autobiography* (Toronto: Key Porter Books, 2004).

2. Phil Patton. "Who Owns 'X'?" *New York Times*, November 8, 1992, sec. 9, 1.

3. "Just Whose 'Malcolm' Is It, Anyway?" *New York Times*, May 31, 1992, H13.

4. James Tyner, *The Geography of Malcolm X: Black Radicalism and the Remaking of American Space* (New York: Routledge, 2006), 2.

5. Michael Eric Dyson, *Making Malcolm: The Myth and Meaning of Malcolm X* (New York: Oxford University Press, 1995), viii.

6. Sharon Willis, "*Do the Right Thing*: A Theater of Interruptions," in *Film Analysis: A Norton Reader*, ed. Jeffrey Geiger and R. L. Rutsky (New York: W. W. Norton, 2005), 778.

7. Mark A. Reid, *Redefining Black Film* (Berkeley: University of California Press, 1993), 108.

8. Ossie Davis, quoted in Malcolm X and Alex Haley, *The Autobiography of Malcolm X* (New York: Ballantine Books, 1964–65), 494.

9. Spike Lee and Ralph Wiley, *By Any Means Necessary: The Trials and Tribulations of the Making of Malcolm X* (New York: Hyperion, 1992), 11.

10. Bernard Weinraub, "*Malcolm X* Is Setting an Industry Brushfire Months before Release," *New York Times*, April 20, 1992, C11.

11. Jewison, *This Terrible Business*, 217.

12. Ibid., 217–18.

13. Bernard Weinraub, "A Movie Producer Remembers the Human Side of Malcolm X," *New York Times*, November 23, 1992, C11.

14. Ibid.

15. Ibid., C16.

16. Quoted in Weinraub, "*Malcolm X* Is Setting an Industry Brushfire," C11.

17. Lee and Wiley, *By Any Means Necessary*, 9–10.

18. Jewison, *This Terrible Business*, 217.

19. Lee and Wiley, *By Any Means Necessary*, 10.

20. Ibid., 11.

21. Ibid., 3.

22. Ibid.

23. Ibid., 28–31.

24. Ibid., 11.

25. Dyson, *Making Malcolm*, 131.

26. Ibid., 132.

27. Lee and Wiley, *By Any Means Necessary*, 30.

28. Ibid., 31.

29. Weinraub, "*Malcolm X* Is Setting an Industry Brushfire," C11.

30. Lee and Wiley, *By Any Means Necessary*, 9.

31. Weinraub, "A Movie Producer Remembers," C11; Lee and Wiley, *By Any Means Necessary*, 27–28.; Wikipedia: The Free Encyclopedia, s.v., "1992," available online at http://en.wikipedia.org/wiki/1992.

32. Houston Baker, "Spike Lee and the Commerce of Culture," in *Black American Cinema*, ed. Manthia Diawara (New York: Routledge, 1993), 166–67.

33. Jesse Algeron Rhines, *Black Film/White Money* (New Brunswick, N.J.: Rutgers University Press, 1996), 106, 112.

34. Ibid., 115.

35. Paula J. Massood, *Black City Cinema: African American Urban Experiences in Film* (Philadelphia: Temple University Press, 2003), 124–26.

36. Andrew Sarris, "Towards a Theory of Film History," in *Movies and Methods*, vol. 1, ed. Bill Nichols (Berkeley: University of California Press, 1976), 246–47.

37. Paul Arthur, "Jargons of Authencity: Three American Moments," in *Theorizing Documentary*, ed. Michael Renov (New York: Routledge, 1993), 108.

38. Lee and Wiley, *By Any Means Necessary*, 33.

39. George F. Custen, *Bio/Pics: How Hollywood Constructed Pubic History* (New Brunswick, N.J.: Rutgers University Press, 1992), 6.

40. Dyson, *Making Malcolm*, 133.

41. X and Haley, *Autobiography of Malcolm X*, 313.

42. Melvin Donalson, *Masculinity in the Interracial Buddy Film* (Jefferson, N.C.: McFarland, 2005), 101.

43. Baker, "Spike Lee," 167.

44. Dyson, *Making Malcolm*, 137.

45. Ibid., 134.

46. X and Haley, *Autobiography of Malcolm X*, 110.

47. Dyson, *Making Malcolm*, 126.

48. See, for example, Ed Guerrero, *Framing Blackness: The African American Image in Film* (Philadelphia: Temple University Press, 1993); Reid, *Redefining Black Film*; bell hooks, *Black Looks: Race and Representation* (Boston: South End Press, 1992), among many others.

49. Lee and Wiley, *By Any Means Necessary*, 92.

50. Ibid.

51. Dyson, *Making Malcolm*, 127.

52. Gary Leva, dir., *By Any Means Necessary: The Making of "Malcolm X"* (Warner Home Video, 2005), 30 min., DVD.

53. X and Haley, *Autobiography of Malcolm X*, 318.

54. Ibid., 323.

55. While Shabazz's on-screen treatment is spared the worst of Lee's and Malcolm X's sexist constructions, such is not the case for Laura and her white rival for Malcolm Little's (a.k.a. Detroit Red's) affections, Sophia. These young, attractive women from Malcolm X's youthful days are emblematic of a particular mode of gender essentialism that Wahneema Lubiano, in a different context, observes is part of the "the Spike Lee discourse." See also Malcolm X's troubling views on women in ibid., 103, 246.

56. Wahneema Lubiano, "But Compared to What? Reading Realism, Representation, and Essentialism in *School Daze, Do the Right Thing,* and the Spike Lee Discourse," in this volume.

57. Davis, quoted in Malcolm X and Haley, *Autobiography of Malcolm X*, 494.

58. Caryn James, "The Real Malcolm X? The Search Widens, but Riddles Remain, *New York Times*, December 3, 1992; Felicia R. Lee, "Malcolm X, in the Eyes of Different Beholders," *New York Times*, November 1, 1992; "Just Whose 'Malcolm' Is It, Anyway," *New York Times*, May 31, 1992; Weinraub, "'Malcolm X' Is Setting an Industry Brushfire"; Nick Charles, "Malcolm X: The Myth and the Man," *Cleveland Plain Dealer Magazine*, February 2, 1992; Betty Shabazz, "Loving and Losing Malcolm" (as told to Susan Taylor and Audrey Edwards), *Essence*, February 10, 1992.

59. Dyson, *Making Malcolm*, 128.

60. Graham discusses the film and Malcolm X's autobiography in Leisner, "The Real Legacy."

61. Baraka, in ibid.

62. X and Haley, *Autobiography of Malcolm X*, 196.

63. Baraka, in Leisner, "The Real Legacy."

64. Ibid.

65. Angela Y. Davis, "Meditations on the Legacy of Malcolm X," in *Malcolm X: In Our Own Image*, ed. Joe Wood (New York: St. Martin's Press, 1992), 42.

Through the Looking Glass and Over the Rainbow: Exploring the Fairy Tale in Spike Lee's *Crooklyn*

*C*rooklyn (1994) may very well be the least regarded film in Spike Lee's oeuvre. Yet it presents a rarely explored territory in American film-making: a story about a young black girl in the city. In its focus on the coming-of-age experiences of Troy Carmichael, a young girl living in Brook-lyn, the film broke away from the more common African American subject matter being produced by Hollywood at the time; violence-laden hood or "gangsta" films, such as *Boyz n the Hood* (John Singleton, 1991) and *Menace II Society* (Allen and Albert Hughes, 1993), featuring stories of inner-city African American males. Despite the obvious industry lack of interest in films about young black girls, Lee and his co-screenwriters and siblings, Cinque and Joie Lee, managed to bring the semiautobiographical story to the screen with Universal Pictures for a reported $14 million. The result was a film that critics and viewers alike praised as enlightening, uplifting, and poignantly funny. Roger Ebert, for example, heralded the film for its many "wonderfully observed" scenes, while Peter Travers found it "rich in funny and touching entertainment."[1]

So what accounts for *Crooklyn*'s appeal? First, unlike Lee's previous films, many of which were either controversial before release (*Malcolm X*) or imme-diately on release (*Do the Right Thing*), *Crooklyn* took on subject matter that was neither politically nor socially problematic.[2] Indeed, perhaps because of its semiautobiographical nature (which Lee doesn't admit to), the film takes a much more gentle look at African American life than the director's earlier films. Moreover, *Crooklyn*'s presentation of Brooklyn's residents and streets in the 1970s takes on an almost mythical aura. This is perhaps because we are asked to view the world through the eyes of ten-year-old Troy, the film's young narrator, but it is also because the narrative is drawn from the conventions of the classic fairy tale, particularly *Alice's Adventures in Wonderland* and *The Wizard of Oz*.

In *Spike Lee: That's My Story and I'm Sticking to It*, Lee makes a direct connection between his film and *Alice's Adventures in Wonderland*. At one point in *Crooklyn*, Troy leaves Brooklyn to visit family in Virginia. Lee and cinematographer Arthur Jafa used an anamorphic lens to shoot the Southern scenes, resulting in an elongated vertical image that Lee found to be "almost like *Alice in Wonderland*."[3] The film also draws on another childhood classic, Victor Fleming's 1939 film adaptation of L. Frank Baum's *The Wizard of Oz* to embellish Lee's narrative.[4] While it might be difficult to make direct comparisons between *Crooklyn* and Carroll's and Fleming's texts, I'd like to suggest that the film is influenced by certain themes relating to girlhood and coming of age that have been examined in these fairy tales. Furthermore, I'd like to flip Lee's analogy and suggest that Troy's Wonderland may actually be her Brooklyn neighborhood, while the Southern sections are much more reminiscent, at least in look, of Fleming's Oz. But first, how might Brooklyn, of all places, be considered a Wonderland?

As it pertains to this essay, Brooklyn as Wonderland has little to do with literary allusion; instead, it is suggestive of the film's nostalgic rendering of the past (in this we must remember that it is semiautobiographical). When juxtaposed against the contemporary imagery of today's urban setting, especially in films such as Matty Rich's *Straight Out of Brooklyn* (1991), which describe a more dystopian space, the Brooklyn in Lee's film appears to be from another realm. The opening credit sequence is excellent testimony to this statement. Children play in front of rambling brownstones and bodegas while the adults look on, observing from their windows, playing dominoes, and lounging outside with cold cans of Budweiser. There are street signs reminding the residents that "a healthy block is a clean block" and that "a cleaner block is up to [them]." This collection of shots suggests a time when streetlights were the sign to head home for young folk playing after dinner, when every adult was responsible for the well-being of every child, when imagination was the cure-all for boredom, or, quite simply, when Brooklyn was a better, safer place (at least in Lee's memories).

Troy in Wonderland

Crooklyn tells the story of the Carmichaels. Carolyn (Alfre Woodard), a schoolteacher, and her jazz musician husband, Woody (Delroy Lindo), struggle to raise their five children—sons Clinton (Carlton Williams), Wendell (Sharif Rashed), Nate (Christopher Knowings), and Joseph (Tse-Mach Washington), and daughter Troy (Zelda Harris)—in this enchanted Brooklyn, but that ideality is disproved by the continual intrusion of the strains of financial problems and marital contention within their home. These occurrences are often invisible to the children who inhabit the multistoried Carmichael brownstone. Instead, they are involved in the activities associated with childhood, such as arguing over which television show to watch or how to divide a bag of candy. The film's early scenes depict Troy's life as a Wonderland filled with play and a comical collection of characters.

Initially, Troy lives in a world where gender doesn't seem to be a determinant. Consider a moment during the film's opening when Nate taunts Troy during a game of stickball. When he releases the ball into the air, he also sets forth a string of statements decrying his sister's athletic abilities. "You ain't hittin' nothin'! Look at that! You hittin' air!" He lets loose one last shot that she pummels into a nearby window. Through the sounds of shattering glass and her brother's minor remorse about the destruction of property, Troy exclaims, with a throw of the hip, "I told you so!" As this suggests, Troy is capable of handling herself when faced with the acrimony of her young male counterparts; in fact, she actually enjoys showing them up. In another scene, one of the neighborhood boys, Greg, and some of his cronies throw a cat onto Troy and a group of girls while they are jumping rope. A melee erupts, and Troy stands face to face with Greg, who sends an insult her way. She volleys back with, "Shut up, Greg, with you and your welfare self! How many times have you been left back? You stupid ass dummy!" After having that declaration meet the approval of her friends, she retorts to Greg's dismissal of her words with, "So, you mother's a ho!"

Still, despite this ability to rebut the macho posturing of the young boys, Troy is on the receiving end of many torments and insults. Tan Lin reminds us that most of the characters in Wonderland "are male, older than Alice, and contentious, imperious, or condescending in their adherence to strict rules."[5] The same holds true for Troy. The males in her world make her the object of their contempt and dissatisfaction. Her brothers and the neighborhood boys repeatedly refer to her as "Troy the Boy" when they want to ridicule her abilities (Nate uses it during the stickball game) or as retaliation for her getting the best of them or denying their affections. (After Troy demands that Greg stop following her around the neighborhood, he denies the accusation and punctuates it with the moniker.) Troy's two eldest brothers, Clinton and Wendell, are often the main instigators of trouble. In one scene, for example, Wendell pushes Troy onto a bed and threatens to strike her after she verbally and physically protests his act of grabbing a cereal box from her hands.

Perhaps the best example of this brotherly torment, however, is a debacle concerning Clinton's basketball-championship game tickets. In a series of scenes, Clinton is shown annoying Troy. Clinton, a devout New York Knicks fan, discovers his tickets are missing and accuses his sister. Correct in his assumption, he puts Troy into a headlock, releasing her only after she screams, "You're hurting me!" After she returns the tickets, he concludes his torment with a threat, "You better stay out [of my room or] next time I'm gone punch you in your face! Heifer!" And he reinforces the last insult with a push onto the bed, again verbally and physically abusing her.

Her brothers are not the only source of Troy's discomfort. Much like *Alice*'s Duchess and (especially) the Queen of Hearts, Peanut (Kewanna Bonaparte), the neighborhood bully, is a source of intimidation for Troy. Despite her presence in only one scene in the movie, Peanut uses violence and myriad scare tactics to ensure respect, fear, and occasionally financial gain. Troy crosses paths with Peanut by chance. Embarrassed to be sent to the grocery store with food stamps ("Ain't nobody gone laugh at you that ain't on food stamps themselves!" her mother tells her), Troy decides to resort to thievery by smuggling a package of liver and a bag of onions under her shirt. As she starts to leave with the hidden food, the scene of the store manager arguing with Peanut and pulling stolen goods from her shirtsleeves distracts Troy. Peanut singles Troy out by asking her what she's looking at, threatening her and the store manager all in the same breath. Meanwhile, Troy manages to leave the store with her stolen goods undetected.

Troy's victory, however, is immediately cut short by Peanut's battle cry ("I'll get you, you ugly bitch!") and forceful hand. After a short tussle, the storeowner rescues Troy, comforts her, and (unknowingly) sends her home with the food she has taken from his store. Carolyn has little sympathy for her daughter's distress. After Troy exaggeratedly sizes Peanut up to be about six foot two and two hundred pounds, her mother, on hearing that Peanut is a girl, dismisses her daughter's protests. The evidence she uses: "You 'round here wrestling and punching your brothers all the time and you let some girl named Peanut take my groceries and my food stamps? I oughta whip your butt my damn self." Troy's inability to defend herself against Peanut stands in direct contrast to how she relates to her brothers and the other neighborhood boys. As the only girl in a household filled with boys, it can be expected that Troy has a grasp on how to deal with their personalities, attitudes, and behavior. Because of her unfamiliarity with similar behavior in girls, there is a level of fear involved in terms of how to respond to Peanut's violence.

Troy's Wonderland is populated with a bevy of interesting personalities, such as Tony Eyes (David Patrick Kelly), a lonely geek of a man with exaggeratedly thick eyeglasses and unusual taste in clothes who fights constantly with the Carmichael children about his property, and Vic (Isaiah Washington), a shell-shocked Vietnam War veteran who is afforded the hero's welcome in the neighborhood the United States largely failed to show returning black soldiers. Yet as eccentric as they and those like them are portrayed in the film, their purpose extends beyond simply being the source of laughter or whimsy. The racial, ethnic, and personality construction of the neighborhood suggests a place that is accepting of people who may not be valued or otherwise noticed. Further, this construction also exemplifies a neighborhood that is truly indicative of the population of New York City—an amalgam of people of different backgrounds, languages, classes, and ethnic groups. More specific to the film, all of these people shape Troy's understanding of the world and provide her with a catalogue of rich, and often magical, experiences. And yet, all is not as magical as it first appears.

Phantasmagoria: Dreaming "Crooklyn" Style

In *Crooklyn*, dreams are a means by which Troy tries to make sense of the events that influence her life. Dreams manifest in two ways in this film. First, there are the more conventional types, often nightmares, which occur while Troy is asleep. The second type could be classified more as daydreams, as we see Troy completely consumed by a particular sight, event, or action in an almost trancelike state. Early in the film, Troy is so engrossed in a dream that it causes her to sleepwalk. She goes into the room where two of her brothers sleep and, thinking she is in the bathroom, urinates on the floor. Only Nate's drowsy exclamation of disgust and a demand that she "better clean that mess up" wakes Troy, and she, just as lethargically, apologizes. Lee never makes us privy to what leads Troy to sleepwalk, and it is the only time she does it in the entire film. This initial appearance of the subject simply suggests an occasion for humor. It is funny (and might I say, even charming) to see Troy in such a deep, deep sleep that she is unaware of her actions. But that Lee uses humor to introduce us to Troy's experience with dreams serves as a suggestion of impending unrest and an introduction to the more serious way this condition will later manifest itself.

Later, we see Troy thrashing about the bed in a fitful sleep after she has suffered Peanut's wrath, Greg's worrisome pestering (not to mention the forced apology by her mother for calling his mother a "ho," among other insults), and various other tense moments at home and throughout the neighborhood. Also, Troy's parents are in the middle of a separation sparked by the lack of domestic and financial support felt by her mother and the lack of respect her father feels he receives for his work as an artist. These occurrences are pressurized in Troy's psyche, and they explode in her nightmares. As

Freud explicates, "A child's dream is a reaction to an experience . . . which has left behind it a regret, a longing, a wish that has not been dealt with."[6] This prophesized bout of fitful sleep reflects the turmoil permeating Troy's world, and her age, lack of understanding about certain life experiences, and feelings of subjection have rendered her unable to find an immediate solution to these problems.

Troy's daydreams also suggest her state of mind. One occurs while she witnesses a bizarre episode in the bodega between a statuesque woman and her miniature Puerto Rican associate. As Troy walks into the store to buy candy, she is distracted by the sight of Connie (RuPaul), clad in an enormous white Afro wig and bright pink shorts and dancing with Tito (Hector M. Ricci), her much shorter companion. Tito moves feverishly around the wanton Connie, who is making jerking motions with her body and singing along with Joe Cuba's "El Pito (I'll Never Go Back to Georgia)." Suddenly, in response to an insult we do not hear, Connie grabs Tito's face and tells him, "What you talking 'bout? I ain't no *puta*! I ain't no *puta*! I keeps my panty clean!" Troy is so engrossed in the duo's suggestive dance and conversation that she has to be "awakened" by the cashier to complete her transaction. Troy walks out of the store still in a trance, listening as Connie and Tito continue to engage in their love–hate war.

Troy's fascination with this brazen display suggests her increasing awareness of her own sexuality. In her demonstration, Connie represents a female performativity that differs from what Troy sees in her own mother.[7] Troy is never witness to her mother as a sexual being, as Carolyn is only ever seen by her daughter (and us) as a dutiful, frustrated, often tired disciplinarian. In contrast, Connie is sexually uninhibited. She is also in control of the entire exchange with Tito, unlike Troy's mother, who struggles to maintain control over the household. This behavior is attractive to Troy, who later emulates it. After returning from the store, for example, she locks herself in the bathroom and stuffs her shirt with toilet paper, suggesting the alluring connection she sees between Connie's womanhood and her power over Tito. Later, she imitates the scene between Connie and Tito again during her visit south. This time her performance is in a context so different from Connie's portrayal that the audience clearly knows that Troy has little understanding of what she has witnessed.

"We're Not in Brooklyn Anymore": Troy in Oz

Midway through the film Troy is sent, at her mother's insistence, to visit relatives in Virginia. Lee's comparison of the Southern scenes in *Crooklyn* to *Alice in Wonderland* is amply supported by the text. Certainly, the moments of youthful dissidence and acclimation to new surroundings in this portion of the film bear more than a passing resemblance to Carroll's fantasy. But, as stated earlier, I want to expound on Lee's observation by suggesting that Troy's escapades in Brooklyn—at least, in the first part of the film—are akin to the frolicsome adventures Alice has in Wonderland, while her vacation with relatives in Virginia is analogous to the journey Dorothy takes down the Yellow Brick Road in *The Wizard of Oz*.

We meet the hosts of Troy's Virginia excursion, Aunt Song (Frances Foster), Uncle Clem (Norman Matlock), and Cousin Viola (Patriece Nelson), in genial circumstances: Pleasantries are exchanged, compliments are given, and food is served. This Southern household is a mild and unassuming enough setting to suggest that Troy will be safe in its embrace. In fact, Carolyn tells Troy how lucky she is to be getting out of Brooklyn. "I barely know these people," Troy pleads, but Carolyn's lovingly rendered response dismisses Troy's uneasiness: "They're your relatives, come on. I'm the one you oughta feel sorry for. I have to go up there with all those boys." This disregard reminds the audience that this visit is double-edged. On one hand, it's a reprieve for Troy from her brothers' rambunctiousness; on the other hand, Carolyn's words convey her exhaustion and foreshadow something worse to come. Still, this environment is unfamiliar to Troy. So, no matter how beneficial this vacation has the potential to be for the both of them, Carolyn understands the trepidation Troy feels about staying with her Southern relatives.

The differences between Virginia and Brooklyn are communicated through cinematography and mise-en-scène. In Fleming's *The Wizard of Oz*, Dorothy leaves the sepia-toned comforts of Kansas for the Technicolor brilliance of Oz. Moreover, in addition to color, the film uses other visual elements such as shape and size to convey the differences between Kansas and Oz through Dorothy's eyes.[8] In a similar manner, Lee's *Crooklyn* uses cinematography, in the vertical stretch of an anamorphic lens, to denote Troy's view of her new surroundings.

Yet it does not take the visual styling of an anamorphic lens to let us know that Troy is in unfamiliar territory. (She's already said so in the first scene that takes place in Virginia.) For twenty-seven minutes the vibrant colors, attitudes, and people of Brooklyn are replaced by the solitude of Virginia. In this version of Oz, the inhabitants hardly need signs to remind them "a healthy block is a clean block" because the homogeneous, colored-coordinated architecture of the homes and the manicured lawns suggest that the neighborhood's residents already subscribe to this belief. Ironically, there are signs that warn drivers to watch for children and basketball hoops, but there are no children playing in the neighborhood. When Troy and Viola play, it is very orderly and "appropriate": They ride bicycles, play badminton, torture little dogs with water hoses (perhaps the most disorderly activity of their playtime), and jump rope to Little Sally Walker–type songs ("All, all, all in together now, how you like the weather now? January, February, March . . .). But, children aside, with the exception of a man washing his car in his driveway and Uncle Clem mowing the lawn, the streets are empty of community life, another difference from Troy's Brooklyn home. This Southern Oz features a triumvirate of appealing characters. Uncle Clem, for example, combines the stalwartness of the Tin Man and the cuddly appearance of the Cowardly Lion. A balding cherub of a man, he is the peacemaker between his wife and daughter, giving the deciding word in the prickliest of situations. Aunt Song is the Wicked Witch of the West, although she is less Margaret Hamilton than a cross between Gregory Maguire's misunderstood Elphaba and Lawrence Otis Graham's "kind of people."[9] Aunt Song speaks without thinking, holds strong opinions, and is the perfect embodiment of the black bourgeoisie. With her beloved canine companion Queenie in one hand and her high principles in the other, she emerges as a source of laughter while simultaneously managing to be a tremendous thorn in Troy's side. The young Viola is, perhaps, the Scarecrow. She and Troy immediately connect through their mutual dislike of Aunt Song (so much so that Viola tells Troy at the very start of her visit that it is all right if she does not like Aunt Song because she was adopted). Viola admires Troy for reasons that extend from her pierced ears to the sheen of urban adventure that coats her very aura. She longs for a different existence, one that is the direct antithesis of her mother's identity with a middle-class status. In this way, the anamorphic lens symbolizes not only Troy's displacement within this milieu, but Viola's as well.

Crooklyn (1994): Bedtime in Oz (from left: Zelda Harris, Frances Foster, Patriece Nelson).]

And who or what represents the man behind the curtain, the all-powerful Wizard of Oz? I would argue that the family's unconscious need to identify as middle class determines the shape and texture of the Virginia landscape, and the ways in which this differs from the Carmichaels' way of life can be seen in the film's many references to popular culture.[10] For example, the television programming showcased in Uncle Clem and Aunt Song's house is a Christian children's show featuring a televangelist and his wife singing with a group of (all white) children, "One, two, three the devil's after me / Four, five, six, he's always throwing sticks / Seven, eight, nine, he misses every time / Hallelujah, hallelujah, hallelujah, Amen!" This piety stands in direct contrast to the violent war movies and episodes of *Soul Train* enjoyed by Troy and her brothers in Brooklyn, a more secular space. In addition, Viola's room is filled with white dolls and one lone Black Barbie doll, and while the girls get ready for bed, there is a record playing with an ostensibly white male voice encouraging the girls to have good manners, to put their clothes away, and to be on time for school. The differences between the two spaces are further demarcated when Carolyn sends both girls jade earrings for Troy's birthday. Aunt Song immediately balks, saying, "Viola, you don't have pierced ears. You know how I feel about that." When Viola points out that Troy has pierced ears, Aunt Song condescendingly observes, "Well, Troy was also wearing them funny braids and beads and shells and thangs," suggesting her class pretensions in her assessment of the young girl's appearance.

This tension between the different spaces, which can be read as tensions between assimilation and cultural nationalism, is also alluded to on the film's soundtrack. When the film is set in Brooklyn, Lee uses the grittier soul styling of such artists as the Chi-Lites, the Stylistics, the Delfonics, Curtis Mayfield, and the Staple Singers. The scenes in Virginia, by contrast, are accompanied by two Jackson Five songs, "ABC" and "Never Can Say Goodbye." This use of Motown suggests a certain notion of crossover blackness. As S. Craig Watkins explains, Berry Gordy, the founder of Motown, "package[d] Black culture and style for mainstream America" and "developed artists that white America found pleasing and assimilable." Thus, the music here further marks the distinction between the assimilationist views of Troy's Southern relatives and the more nationalist expressions of her family in Brooklyn.[11]

Aunt Song's value system—her strictures on hair, clothing, skin tone, and behavior—also comments on the strivings of a certain, more integrationist component of the black bourgeoisie. Michael Eric Dyson suggests that the black middle class is diverse, running the gamut from "barely a paycheck or two from poverty [to] one in the upper stratum, with high-level professional employment," with identifying factors that include style and behavior as well.[12] Aunt Song's preoccupation with decorum and propriety signifies her status in—or, at least, her striving to become—the upper echelon of the black middle class. Conversely, we cannot ignore the class status of the Carmichaels, as exemplified by Carolyn's career as a teacher and Woody's work as a musician. Despite their financial problems, the Carmichaels have managed to buy a Brooklyn brownstone and a Citroën. If Aunt Song's "seditty" and snobbish ways give her automatic admission to the assimilated middle class, then the Carmichaels' more "nationalist" middle-class lifestyle is just as affirmed, particularly in the film's 1970s timeframe, when identification with one's blackness was a marker for a politically engaged cultural elite.

As in *The Wizard of Oz*, the Wicked Witch of the West in *Crooklyn* is defeated, but in a way that suggests rebellion as opposed to the defeat of evil. During Troy's birthday slumber party, Aunt Song discovers that her much adored Queenie is the victim of suffocation after being stuffed in a fold-out couch. Lee never reveals the actual culprit, but the blank stares on the faces of Viola and Troy as Aunt Song dissolves into a blubbering mess suggests their guilt. Queenie's death is the "water in the face" that results in the "I'm melting, I'm melting" deterioration into hysterics or "death." This defeat of the Wicked Witch of the West can be read as the girls' act of retaliation against what she represents: assimilation and conformity. Viola, at the very least, accomplishes a small victory against the rigidity of her mother's value system, while Troy is able to return home to brave the streets and attitudes of Brooklyn stripped of the sensibilities forced on her by Aunt Song.

There's No Place Like Home

Aunt Song's grieving, Troy's insistence on returning to her family, and Uncle Clem's consent are the three clicks of the ruby-red slipper that send Troy back to Brooklyn. But Brooklyn is no longer the free-spirited space it once was. Upon her return, Troy's Uncle Brown (Vondie Curtis-Hall) and Aunt Maxine (Joie Susannah Lee) take her to the hospital, where she confronts the sight of her ill mother. Troy tells her mother that she works too hard and that she will start helping her around the house. This offer implies that Troy obviously missed her mother during their time apart, but that she has also matured during her visit to Virginia. In reply, Carolyn explains to Troy that she is to look after her youngest brother, Joseph. This inheritance of duty along the female line is not uncommon in the black community: "Grandmothers, sisters, aunts, or cousins act as othermothers by taking on child-care responsibilities for one another's children," and young girls "are often carefully groomed at an early age to become othermothers."[13] Still, Troy's acceptance of this charge initiates the beginning of the loss of her childhood in ways more significant than her fantasies of womanhood inspired by Connie earlier in the film.

Troy's transition from youth to adulthood is facilitated by Woody's announcement to the children that Carolyn has been diagnosed with cancer. The boys break into fast tears, insisting that their mother's illness is not their fault. This need to extract blame from themselves—particularly the oldest boys, Clinton and Wendell—implies feelings of guilt for their sometimes volatile relationship with their mother. Troy, by contrast, is stoic, her face registering a look that suggests she knew such news was coming all along, and quite frankly, this could be exactly the case. Troy has nothing to feel guilty about, as throughout the film she and Carolyn have had the more affectionate and understanding relationship. Further, the hospital conversation has prepared her for her mother's death. When Carolyn succumbs to cancer, Troy's stoicism begins to crack under the strain of her grief. On the day of her mother's funeral, Troy feigns illness and refuses to attend. After her father explains that her attendance would make her mother happy, Troy's grief and anger grows to the point that she forlornly states that assuring her mother's contentment is a fruitless endeavor. Her father states the contrary, and in moment of solidarity expresses his own hatred for funerals and extends comfort to his grieving daughter. As the scene ends, the Five Stairsteps begin their promise of "Ooh child, things are gonna get easier / Ooh child, things will get brighter."

Earlier I discussed the appearance of dreams and how Troy's are a manifestation of the fears and inconsistencies in her life. In a scene late in the film, Troy tosses to and fro in a state of erratic slumber. She hears the voices of her mother and father in argument. In a series of quick edits that suggests she is still in the dream state, Troy moves quickly down the staircase, pleading with her parents to stop fighting with one another and punctuating her cries with, "Mommy! Mommy!" When she finds, instead, Woody noisily attempting to kill a rat, he has to break the news all over again to her that Carolyn is gone. The sickness that Troy gave earlier as reason for not attending her mother's funeral reappears, sending her to the bathroom. Troy's stoicism finally gives way to the grief that can no longer be denied. Lee follows the scene with Troy sitting on Woody's lap in a cramped half bathroom, framed in such a manner as to suggest a more intense closeness. The exchange that occurs as Woody comforts his daughter reflects the completion of her transition into adulthood:

TROY: Mommy was in a lot of pain, wasn't she?
WOODY: Yes, she was.
TROY: Then it's good she died. So she wouldn't have to suffer.
WOODY: That's a nice way of putting it, baby. Yeah, that's real nice.

It is in this moment that Troy begins to think in a fashion that belies her age and speaks to a forced maturity.

In *Crooklyn's* final scenes, we once again see children in various states of play. Brooklyn is a Wonderland once again, and things seem to have come full circle—that is, for everyone except Troy. For example, we see her sitting in her mother's barber chair, literally taking her mother's place, combing Joseph's hair and chastising him for not tending to it better. When he tells her, "Well, it never hurt when Mommy combed it," Troy corrects him, stating, "Well, I'm sorry, Joseph, but I'm not Mommy." But Troy *has* become the mother. This role is further solidified when we hear the kids from the street asking her permission to let Joseph come outside to play. Her response is a very maternal: "All right, don't go too far. Dinner's almost ready." At this point, Troy has assumed the role of "othermother," and her childhood is over.

Crooklyn is most poignant in these last scenes, especially because we begin to understand the nostalgic tone of the earlier parts of the film. There is a sadness in seeing Troy stand behind the gate like the rest of the adults, watching the children play. She is no longer a participant but an observer of the amusements she once enjoyed. We are left with a final look of pensiveness marked by a smile that suggests that Troy has accepted her new role as caretaker of her family. Just as Alice understood that one day she would, indeed, have to grow up, and Dorothy realized "there's no place like home," Troy has seemingly made peace with the disappearance of her Brooklyn Wonderland. Unfortunately, for all three girls, the loss of childhood fantasy seems to be the price of adulthood.

NOTES

1. Roger Ebert, *Roger Ebert's Video Companion: 1995 Edition* (Kansas City: Andrews and McMeel, 1994), 155–56.; Peter Travers, "Crooklyn," *Rolling Stone*, no. 683, December 8, 2000, available online at http://www.rollingstone.com/reviews/movie/5947313/review/5947314/crooklyn (accessed February 4, 2007).

2. For more on the controversies attending *Malcolm X*, see Anna Everett, "'Spike, Don't Mess Malcolm Up': Courting Controversy and Control in *Malcolm X*," in this volume.

3. Spike Lee, *Spike Lee's Gotta Have It: Inside Guerrilla Filmmaking* (New York: Fireside/Simon and Schuster, 1987), 146.

4. Indeed, Lee has shown in previous films his predilection for the fanciful images found in Fleming's opus. In his book recounting the writing and production of *She's Gotta Have It* (1986), Lee divulges that the colorful dance sequence that comes in the mid-section of the black-and-white film is meant to be a "homage to *The Wizard of Oz*." Lee continues this homage in his second film, *School Daze* (1988), which again quotes Fleming's film with its splashy musical numbers and fantasy sequences.

5. Lee, *Spike Lee's Gotta Have It*, xvi.

6. Sigmund Freud, *Introductory Lectures on Psycho-Analysis* (New York: W. W. Norton, 1966), 157.

7. This is noteworthy because the actor portraying Connie is RuPaul, a well-known drag queen. For more on drag and the blurring of gender, sexuality, and masculinity in the visual arts, I recommend Andrew Ross, "The Gangsta and the Diva," in *Black Male: Representations of Masculinity in Contemporary American Art*, ed. Thelma Golden (New York: Harry N. Abrams, 1994).

8. Suzanne Rahn, *The Wizard of Oz: Shaping an Imaginary World* (New York: Twayne Publishers, 1998), 81.

9. This comparison refers to the novel *Wicked: The Life and Times of the Wicked Witch of the West* by Gregory Maguire (New York: Regan Books, 1996) and the book *Our Kind of People: Inside America's Black Upper Class* by Lawrence Otis Graham (New York: Harper Perennial, 2000). Maguire's novel is the satirical retelling of *The Wizard of Oz* in which the Wicked Witch, whose given name is Elphaba, is revealed as having had a troubled childhood and is working to free the land from a politically corrupt Wizard of Oz. Graham's *Our Kind of People* is a meditation on the social construct of the black bourgeoisie. Graham discusses the history of and requirements for joining elite black social organizations (such as the Links, Jack and Jill, and Boulé) and black fraternities and sororities (such as Alpha Phi Alpha, Omega Psi Phi, Alpha Kappa Alpha, and Delta Sigma Theta) while also analyzing what it means to belong to the right family, go to the proper schools, and possess the approved (i.e., light) skin color.

10. The discussion of assimilationism versus nationalism has been the source of tremendous attention within the black community. The speeches, writings, and teachings from sources as diverse as Marcus Garvey, Malcolm X, the Nation of Islam, the Black Panthers, and others have extolled the virtues of black nationalism and the need for black people to take control of the economic and social development of their communities, relying less on the influence and benevolence of white culture. For competing philosophies, on the side of assimilation, one can look at Booker T. Washington, *Up from Slavery* (New York: Penguin Books, 1986), which asked that black people accept their second-class citizenship and seek to educate and train themselves in the ways of industrial service, while on the nationalist front is W. E. B. Du Bois, *The Souls of Black Folk* (New York: Signet Classic, 1969), which speaks of the need for black "conscious self-realization" and for black people to be formally educated and take control of their lives and communities socially and economically. Other scholars who have addressed this issue include Frantz Fanon, *Black Skin, White Masks* (New York: Grove Press, 1967); E. Franklin Frazier, *Black Bourgeoisie: The Book That Brought the Shock of Self-Revelation to Middle Class Blacks in America* (New York: Free Press Paperbacks, 1997); and Wilson Jeremiah Moses, *The Golden Age of Black Nationalism 1850–1925* (New York: Oxford University Press, 1988). Finally, in keeping with the present consideration of Spike Lee, I must also add that this discussion provides the framework for his second film, *School Daze* (1988), and its companion book written with Lisa Jones, *Uplift the Race: The Construction of School Daze* (New York: Simon and Schuster, 1988).

11. S. Craig Watkins, *Hip Hop Matters: Politics, Pop Culture and the Struggle for the Soul of a Movement* (Boston: Beacon Press, 2005), 47.

12. Michael Eric Dyson, *Is Bill Cosby Right? Or Has the Black Middle Class Lost Its Mind?* (New York: Basic Civitas Books, 2005), xv.

13. Patricia Hill Collins, *Black Feminist Thought: Knowledge, Consciousness, and the Politics of Empowerment* (London: HarperCollins Academic, 1990), 119–21.

KEITH M. HARRIS

Clockers (Spike Lee, 1995):
Adaptation in Black

The initial press releases announcing that Spike Lee was heading the project *Clockers* were a surprise to fans. The film had been developed and finally passed on by Martin Scorsese and Robert De Niro and inherited, as it were, by Lee. Herein lies the surprise: Lee's films are noted for his autuerist building of the film from the early stages of development (including writing and casting) to production, post-production, and press. In addition, the press surrounding the "change of hands" suggested that Lee's eighth film was going to be his take on the gangster film, the "hood" film that was so prevalent in the 1990s. However, when viewing Lee's adaptation of Richard Price's ready-made *Clockers*, the film is an adaptation that not only transforms the novel, switching the medium to the screen, but also adapts the screen, transforming the historical image, narrative, and genre to Lee's cinematic aesthetic. Furthermore, when one considers the African American social critique and cultural traditions on which Lee draws for his cinematic aesthetic, *Clockers* serves as an adaptation in black, a displacement of the novelistic dialogue, and description onto the cinematic and into a visual tradition of innovation, revision, and direct address.

I

I refer to Price's novel as "ready-made" because of the author's prior success as a writer whose novels are adapted to films and as a screenplay writer who has developed scripts for successful films. His adapted novels include *Blood*

Brothers (1978) and *Clockers*; his screenplays include *The Color of Money* (1986), *Sea of Love* (1989), and *Night and the City* (1992), to name a few. Price's *Clockers* is a New Jersey tale, a crime/cop novel chronicling the impact of "crack" cocaine not only on the neighborhood, dealers, children, and families involved, but also on the police officers enforcing the law. The novel is grand and ambitious, told primarily from the point of view of a jaded homicide detective, Rocco Klein. The dialogue, the density of street language, and the careful attention to the details of the drug trade are the most striking features of the novel. In its gritty yet clinical attention to language, action, and character motivation, the novel is a throwback, of sorts, to literary naturalism. The emphasis on naturalism can be seen in the ways in which the lives of the characters are determined by their environment and in the special attention that Price pays to the racial representations and stratifications of the crack epidemic.

In addition, in keeping with the ready-made quality of the novel, the narrative is structured along the lines of a screenplay, divided into five distinct parts, and it is "cinematic" owing to its attention to aspects of lighting, description, and physical perspective (as opposed to first-person or second-person narrative point of view). For example, in the opening paragraphs of the novel, the reader observes Strike on the housing-project "block":

> Strike was seated on the top slat of his bench, his customary perch, looming over a cluster of screaming kids, pregnant women and too many girls, drinking vanilla Yoo-Hoo to calm his gut, watching The Word try to think on his feet. The white guy, a scrawny redhead wearing plaster-caked dungarees and a black Anthrax T-shirt, looked too twitchy and scared to be a knocko, but you never knew.[1]

The scene reads like an omniscient camera establishing shot of the block, complete with a pan around the block in medium close-up of characters, describing the surroundings and costumes. Yet this detailed "cinematic" or "filmic" narration still remains particular, or peculiar, to novelistic narration in that it is pictorial, imagistic.

It is scenes like this one that are transformed in Lee's adaptation. If we turn to the same scene in Lee's film, indeed we see this as an establishing shot. Furthermore, the shot not only establishes location, tone, and mood, but it also initiates a dialogic between novelistic realism and cinematic anti-realism. In other words, the film appropriates the realism found in language, description, and action of the novel to anti-realism and the service of reflexivity, calling attention to the subject matter and to film itself. I emphasize this dynamic between realism and anti-realism because the dynamic itself comments

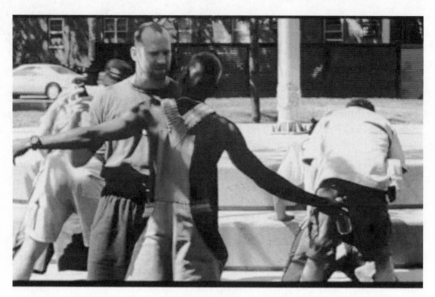

Clockers (1995). A routine shake-down and strip search by New York's finest.

on the limitations of realism and because anti-realism as a technique is important to the broader project of revision inherent in the film.[2]

From this establishing shot, the film leads into the first sequence of a routine cop shakedown in which Strike is strip searched. In the novel, this scene reveals hierarchical relations between the police and the clockers, the dynamics of control through intimidation and humiliation. The scene is rich in dialogue, description, and characterization:

> "Open your mouth there, Strike." Big Chief checked his teeth as if he was a horse, or a slave. . . . "OK." Big Chief looked right, left, then moved close. "Drop your drawers there, Strike. Dicky check." Strike hesitated as always, holding it in, weighing his options, finally unzipping and pulling down, some of tenants in the crowd looking away and talking under their breath, some cursing out the Fury, some cursing out Strike. "Drop your drawers, bend over, say ah-h-h," Thumper said, getting into it now. Strike held his underwear band out so Big Chief could look in. "Short and sweet there, Strike." Big Chief frowned. "Let's see under your balls, there. See what you got taped under your balls." "Strike's ball," Thumper drawled. "Strikes and balls, three and two, full count." Strike pulled up his scrotum, caught Peanut grinning on the sidewalk and then looking away quick when he saw Strike watching him.[3]

Lee's rendition of this scene is telling of the cinematic, dialogic trajectory that emerges in the total film. This opening sequence, with the establishing shot that gives us the view of the housing projects as a series of towers, facing in on a centrally located block, makes frankly literal the implied metaphor of the scene in the novel, for the use of the 360 degree shot of the crowd watching the search and encircling the action restages the spectatorial practices of a slave auction. However, there is deliberate irony in the fact that the onlookers are the housing community's members, some bearing disdain for Strike and his kind, some with contempt for police officers. The housing-project block becomes the slave block, but ambiguously so. This scene, though realistic in its adaptation from the novel, emphasizes the cinematic and references the visual legacy of black men on display and, as a consequence, opens the text of the novel to a performative medium.

One strategy, then, at the core of Lee's adaptation is the manipulation of story and the double-timing structure of narrative. Here I refer to the distinction between story time (*histoire*) and discourse time.[4] This distinction is both narratological, through the use of flashbacks and the treatment of time in the unfolding of the story, and rhetorical in that it is an argumentative and persuasive strategy.[5] Lee remains true to the spirit of the story, with its realistic emphasis on the ordinary, daily life of the characters, cops, and clockers; it is in his manipulation of discourse time, the narrative ordering and the cinematic rendering/ordering of the events, that Lee relocates the focus of *Clockers* from that of Rocco Klein, the police officer, to that of Ronald/Strike, the clocker. In doing so, Lee not only changes the point of view of the original text but also discursively revises and revitalizes the hood/gangster film and aesthetically envisions a black cinema that deploys all of the properties of the medium to the service of visualizing Strike's "black experience."

II

The hood film, variously identified as ghetto film or black gangster film, was an established New Black Cinema form by the time of the arrival of *Clockers* in 1995.[6] Films like *Boyz n the Hood* (John Singleton, 1991), *New Jack City* (Mario Van Peebles, 1991), and *Menace II Society* (Allen and Albert Hughes, 1993) not only perfected the genre but also circumscribed the prospects of New Black Cinema as masculine narratives about fatherless sons trapped in the social legacies of race and postindustrial America. One can trace the origins of this cycle of films to the antiheroes of the blaxploitation-era narratives, antiheroes such as Shaft, Superfly, and Sweetback. The relationship between these two cycles of films would be the formation of a character caught between two worlds—one of crime, the other of community. The hood film

updates the blaxploitation-era films with social-realist strategies of story similar to the social-problem film, the content of which has an immediate social
relevance emphasizing the antiheroic choices as those that plague black masculinity in contemporary America. In doing so, arguably, the African American gangster film, with its location of action in the inner cities and the focus
of subject matter on African American male, is already revisionary of the
more traditional American gangster-film genre.[7] The hood film is usually urban, set in Los Angeles or New York most often. Furthermore, with the 90s
cycle of hood films, there are the common masculinist narratives of redemption. These films often employ the narrative strategies of the masculine melodrama, as Jackie Byars has outlined them. The strategies provide a mode of
constructing moral identity. Byars discusses the melodramatic form as family
situated, as conflict over social values, and as a genre that serves to define and
redefine gender roles.[8] In addition, the male-oriented melodramas are those
in which men are coming of age and establishing identity and relationships
with their fathers.[9]

   In contrast to its predecessors, *Clockers* does not include an overt, didactic discourse of the absent father. This is illusion, however, in that the absent
makes itself present. There is no messianic figure like *Boyz n the Hood*'s Furious Styles or demonic figure like *Menace II Society*'s Tat Lawson. The fathers
are absent, and while there are apparent father figures (both paternal father
figures such as the police officer Andre and paternal, criminal father figures
such as Rodney), there is no rhetorical or polemical film language or story
about the absent fathers or about role modeling. No value is placed on the
presence or absence of the black male as father, natural or surrogate. The lack
of a discourse on the father may appear pessimistic, and it would be redun-
dant were it there. Neither pessimism nor redundancy is the trajectory of this
lack, however. Instead, the film allows for an observation of the various outcomes of the lack of a father figure. It does not assume Patrick Moynihan-
esque, cyclic black family dysfunction as other films in the genre do. The film
maintains itself as a masculine narrative, but there is great effort to bring this
narrative into question.

   Much of the early and later film press was about the shift in character focus from Rocco to Strike and the shift from New Jersey to Brooklyn. The shift
in locale, as Paula J. Massood suggests, indicates not only the place of Brooklyn in Lee's body of work, but also the significance of Brooklyn as an end
point in African American migration patterns and terminal destinations
within New York City.[10] More significant for my interests, the focus on Strike
allows for an emphasis on the young black male, rendering *Clockers* as a black
cinematic *rites de passage,* which is quite common in black gangster films.[11]
Upon closer examination, however, these two simple maneuvers of adaptation

render the film "black" (with the emphasis on Strike) and broaden the genre of the black gangster film as a mode of storytelling in black cinema history. With these slight changes in form and references to form, Lee's *Clockers* disrupts the hood-film genre. Indeed, Lee argues that with the film he wanted to "[demystify] this whole romantic vision of gangsters, drugs, hip-hop, you know, shoot-em-up."[12] Massood notes, "*Clockers* deconstructs and problematizes [the hood films]. It may be, in fact, just this process of revision that transforms the hood film into something else entirely."[13] Massood continues to locate the revision of the genre and black cinema in the envisioning of the city, mobility, and migration. I want to expand on the revision of genre and cinema and elaborate on the significance of *Clockers*, because in this space of revision the hood-film genre is problematized and black cinema is given greater, more fluid significatory possibilities.

III

As mentioned earlier, there is dynamic exchange in the film between the novel's naturalism and realist reflection and the film's self-conscious anti-realism. The significance of anti-realism has been noted about other Spike Lee films.[14] Of interest here is the critique of realism, an aesthetic toward which black cinema tends. Furthermore, Robert Stam notes that this exchange between reflection and reflexivity, as realism and anti-realism, oftentimes is to the service of metatextual critique.[15] I would argue that in the case of *Clockers*, this critique is historical and aesthetic: historical in the reference to black cinema, its history, its conventions, and the legacies of African Americans in film; aesthetic because of the African American rhetorical traditions that the film adapts to the visual medium of cinema. Lee's opening credit sequences often perform a visual historiography, a critical writing of history on the subject of the film through imagery. This is seen in *Malcolm X*, *Get on the Bus*, *Girl 6*, and *School Daze*, especially. In the opening sequence of *Clockers*, we begin with the music, Stevie Wonder's "Searching." The lyrics to the song are otherworldly, utopian, indeed spiritual, with emphasis on a movement, a migration, to somewhere beyond. Next there are restaged autopsy and crime-scene photographs of dead clockers.[16] The photographs are intercut with shots of graffiti and murals, which in the images and in the community portrayed serve as a form of memorial, tribute, or altar in marking the spot of a murder. These images are followed by faces of the community, women, men and children, directly facing the camera as it pans across police tape: the spectators and the filmic community are onlookers, observing the scenes of the crime and the scenes of the community. Through the use of music, photography, cinematography, and the images of the onlookers, Lee visualizes the community of "Nelson Mandela Houses" (the Gowanus Houses, along Atlantic Avenue in Brooklyn) as an African American community, searching for someplace beyond the crack-plagued, constantly surveilled here and now of the film.

If we examine the rhetoric of this sequence, it becomes evident that there are argumentative and persuasive aesthetics at play. There is great effort on the part of the sequence to convey a tone of respectfulness and seriousness to the audience at the same time that there is an effort to convey an investigative and critical attitude toward the subject matter (not only gangsters and drug dealing, but also the generic representation of gangsters and drug dealing). The reproduction of the crime-scene and autopsy photographs references a "real," a social reality outside the film. At the same time, the use of these photographs references the hood film. The double-valenced referentiality of the photographic discourse of crime and social death and the cinematic discourses of realism and genre call attention to the "doubling" theme and technique throughout the film.

In the narrative following the opening credits, there is the prominence and distinction between the tragic and the melodramatic as they are deployed by dialogue, characterization, settings, and recurring motifs. As for the subject matter of the tragic, tragedy is about the human divided, a conflict within, divided between different forces or values. Characters are guilty and innocent in one, and these characters are defeated by this division. Tragedy raises ethical questions—questions that are resolved in the doing and suffering, in the plot and action of the events, and in the cathartic resolution of events. Melodrama, by contrast, assumes a whole, a lack of inner conflict, and furthermore, it externalizes conflict as one between humans or between humans and things.[17] Melodrama emphasizes the character and the moral side, good or bad, on which that character falls. Melodramatic characters are iconic and archetypal. Whereas tragedy is plot driven, melodrama is expressed in characterization and spectacle. Accordingly, Robert Heilman notes, the two forms establish different structures of feeling: Melodrama is monopathic in its singular emotional drive, in its tendency toward wholeness, evoking unified feelings of hope or hopelessness, joy or sadness. Tragedy is polypathic in its emotional structure, generating complex, conflicting emotional reactions—for example, contempt and pity.[18]

Lee deliberately does not sustain these modes and structures of feeling as genre or convention throughout the film. In other words, Clockers is not categorically a tragedy or a melodrama. Instead, the director places the dramatic elements of tragedy and melodrama in dynamic conflict and discontinuous relief to the service of presenting character depth and generic disruption. The tragic elements are seen in the actions of the character Strike, who is literally eating himself from the inside because of guilt, self-doubt, and moral conflict. His consumption of a Yoo-Hoo-like beverage and its function of quelling his ulcerated stomach metaphorically signifies on his embodied, divided allegiance to two different value systems: one of the individual, entrepreneurial aggressivity of the drug trade, and the other of his community and familial ties, which are lost or in jeopardy because of his clocking. Formally and structurally, the most significant scenes, where Strike's tragic characterization is seen to adhere to dramatic unities of time and space, are while he is on the block monitoring drug trafficking or in confined spaces where his internal division is brought into question, the spaces of the police interrogation room or the spaces of loyalty interrogation (those spaces, the shop and car, when Rodney, Strike's drug boss, challenges his loyalty to him). Furthermore, the scenes on the block are punctuated with a chorus of clockers, arguing or signifyin(g) on their jobs, or masculinity, or on everyday things such as music and clothing. What is significant is that this chorus remains apart from, often physically surrounding or framing, Strike and the dilemma of his internal division.[19]

The melodramatic elements of the film are seen in the characterization of Strike as one who is maintaining himself, first and foremost. Strike's dilemma is social, one of conflict between loyalties: in the contrasting and conflicting characters of Strike and his brother, Victor; between Strike and Rodney, the drug-dealing kingpin; between Rocco and Strike; between the housing-authority police officer, Andre, and Strike; between Strike and the mother of the young boy that Strike takes under his wing (Tyrone Jetter). These are dichotomies of victim–victor, good–bad, legal–criminal, right–wrong, and innocent–guilty, respectively. In addition, melodrama is often seen in the film's cinematic spectacle. For example, swirling camera movements encircle character action and movement in the scenes between Strike and Tyrone's mother, and the stylized acting and drama of those scenes, as well, deliberately intensify their passion. The final scene between Strike and his mother in the interrogation room, where he is enclosed on one side by his family and on the other by Rocco, operates in a similar fashion. I want to emphasize that not only is it the acting and settings, but also the camera movement and cinematography, which render these scenes as melodramatic spectacle.[20]

The internal movements between tragedy and melodrama are rhetorical strategies and manipulations of discourse time that direct the viewer to the breakdown of the hood film/gangster genre. The tragic emphasis on plot locates the action in the unreconciled interiority of the characters, as opposed to the external action of shootouts and car-chase spectacles so common in the genre. The melodramatic emphasis on character and spectacle is tempered by the tragic, as the characters are rendered through explosive and/or

intimate scenes of *dialogue* (instead of explosions, violence, or big action sequences) that are cinematically composed. The special attention to lighting,
film stock, camera angle, and set design allow the viewer to observe the conflicts, the fears, angers, and passions of the characters through the characters'
slight actions and language. The dialogue and conversations are shot with two
cameras, in medium close up, often in the enclosed or tight spaces of rooms,
doorways, elevators, cars, or across interrogation tables. In this fashion, the
film may be said to be theatrical, deploying reflexivity through the non-
cinematic use of set and performance. By theatrical, in this instance, one may
say the sets and performances are artificial in comparison with the naturalis-
tic, realist cinematic styles found in contemporary black cinema. The use of
framing and two shots is typical of film and inherited from the theater. However, the deployment of the frame here is as a proscenium arch, as opposed to
an illusionist frame/window onto a world and, therefore, separates the action
on the screen as that on a stage, as that at a distance.

Furthermore, the film's theatricality displaces the action of violent movement and grand spectacle often associated with the gangster genre and shifts
it onto the performance of dialogue. In addition, the theatricality of these
scenes breaks the illusion of cinema and is attuned to the other anti-realist
techniques of the film. Performance through dialogue is coupled with distinct
visual styles of color, mixed media (including film, video, and animation),
shot distance, and camera movement. The result is that the interior thoughts
of the characters are made transparent. For example, the scene of the interrogation of Victor, Strike's brother, by Rocco Klein is subtle and quiet in that
Rocco feels that Victor is lying about the murder, and the interrogation becomes one in which Rocco determines to prove Victor's innocence, even
though Victor has confessed to the crime. Through Rocco's constant questioning of Victor, pointing out the inconsistencies of his confession, the scene
asks the viewer to look deeply into Victor's motivations. At the same time,
"looking deeper into the character" is repeated in the complex spectacle that
is rendered when the medium close-up, two-shot dialogue scene cuts to an
enormous, extreme close-up of Victor's eye in which we see the reflection of
Rocco's face, probing to the point of abstraction, to point at which spectacle
becomes narrative reflection as the viewers see what Victor sees and see the
limit of Rocco's vision into Victor's interior.

The movements from realism to anti-realism, from interior to exterior,
and from tragedy to melodrama establish a set of dichotomies roughly
equivalent to the universal and the particular. The oscillations between the
tragic and the melodramatic are analogous to the universal timelessness of realism and to a particular historical past and cinema and generic formation
found in anti-realism, respectively. The discontinuous discourse of genre (be

it tragedy, melodrama, or the hood film) challenges the universal versus the particular dichotomy by foregrounding the failure of both discourses; however, it does so aesthetically. The hood film, like *Boyz n the Hood* or *Straight Out of Brooklyn*, is referenced for its redundancy, its use of social realism, its didacticism, and its form as a timely, relevant story and genre. The hood film is not dismissed but given over to a critique of black cinema and the reliance on genre and realism. *Clockers*'s critique is one of the hood film and, by extension, black cinema.

IV

When I speak of black cinema, I follow a periodization and refer to aesthetic expressions of film identified as black. The periodization I draw from Tommy L. Lott.[21] His definition of black cinema has the advantage of being informed by a "theory of contemporary black cinema that accords with the fact that biological criteria are neither necessary, nor sufficient, for the application of the concept of black cinema."[22] This opens up the possibility of raising questions of aesthetics beyond the "race" of the director and of focusing on cinematic form and its relation to other African American expressions in literature, the visual arts, and visual culture. In reference to black cinema as an aesthetic expression, I step away from conversations about black cinema as genre, which implies not only convention in form, but also in story content. The idea of genre restricts black cinema to films *about* black people, without allowing for films that *address* the audience in an African American cultural tradition of critique.[23] This latter idea of black cinema is one in which it is configured as a signifying practice.

Gladstone Yearwood defines signifying practice as follows: "Signifying practice describes the process we use to make our films, the sum of cinematic languages, aural and visual languages, languages of color, and languages of imagery. It is through various language systems that existing social relations are represented and reproduced."[24] Yearwood's black film as signifying practice inserts black cinema into rhetorical and literary traditions of African Americans, allowing us to move beyond the limiting, often essentializing black film as genre formulations of black cinema. As a signifying practice, black cinema is immediately aligned with Henry Louis Gates's notion of signifyin(g) as a master rhetorical trope in African American vernacular and literary tradition. Gates describes signifyin(g) as a double-voiced practice, wherein the sign is doubled. Signifyin(g) is a rhetorical strategy above the semantic; it is repetition with a difference; it combines or utilizes elements of parody and pastiche; it is a method of revision.[25]

If we return to Lee's rhetoric of film, we find this use of doubling and repetition with a difference on a number of levels. Foremost is the use of anti-realism to exaggerate the realism of the novel and of the hood film. This doubling of reflexivity through cinematic reflexivity and the reflexivity of generic revision and reflection reveals the limits of realism, or the exhaustion of it as an aesthetic mode of representing the young, urban black male. All points of signifyin(g) in the film lead to this critique: the double, discontinuous use of the genre conventions of tragedy and melodrama; the resulting discursive doubling of the universal versus the particular; the present absence of the black male father and the discourse of that absence; the use of repetition of locations and choral figures (such as the signifyin[g] boys on the block). Furthermore, there is a broad sense of orality in Lee's cinema that lends itself to appreciating the strategies of dialogue, the use of rap music, and visual idioms of color as engaging rhetoric and an African American aesthetic. What emerges is a complex reading of the gangster as he is inhabited by young, urban black men and as black cinema visualizes him.

However, Lee's use of signifyin(g) is not just postmodern play, pastiche, or bricolage. In Gates's terms, it is motivated signifying, parody, a signification on other texts, a "close reading" of sorts.[26] Indeed, it is through signifyin(g) that cinematic and generic conventions are rendered as visible trope and rhetoric. With visual rhetoric of editing and cinematography, through the discontinuous doubling and revision of generic figures, such as the father, the gangsta, the single mother, etc., the film aligns itself to African American literary traditions. The end point of signifyin(g) in the film is something akin to a jeremiad. According to Sacvan Bercovitch, the American jeremiad is a political sermon with "unwavering faith" in the errand, the message to the messenger, a Puritanical expression of self as the chosen people.[27] The African American jeremiad, abolitionist in origins, is an adaptation of the form to protest the inhumanity of slavery in the antebellum South; it is a warning and lament.[28] David Howard-Pitney describes the basic tenets of the jeremiad as having three elements: a citation of "the *promise*; criticism of present *declension*, or retrogression from the promise; and a resolving *prophecy* that society will shortly complete its mission and redeem the promise."[29] Furthermore, in an American tradition, African Americans, as presented in the rhetoric of the jeremiad, are the chosen people of the chosen people, arguing the promise of America and the New World would not come to fruition without the fair treatment of African Americans.[30] In contrast to the European jeremiad, a moral lament leading to the horrors of the apocalypse, the American and African American jeremiad is inciting and moralizing, but its prophecy is optimistic.

Clockers, though it does not adhere to all of the formal qualities of the jeremiad, uses cinematic and generic conventions to call attention to how they can be used in maintaining themselves, the forms of knowledge that they embody, and the social and cultural discourses that they perpetuate. The film reasserts the "chosen people of the chosen people" rhetoric of the African American jeremiad by placing emphasis on Strike's tragic dilemma as one that concerns everyone (think of Rocco's refusal of *The Final Call* in the end sequence of the film: It is not a final call, end time apocalypse for Rocco, but instead a wake-up call for his complicity in and his duty to fighting the crack epidemic).

Furthermore, Lee's critique of the black hood film harkens back to the promise of black cinema as a tool of change, as an oppositional aesthetic, as a challenging, critical aesthetic that has lost its way in mire of convention, repetition, and redundancy. At a glance, the film fails in the area of prophecy in that it is not overtly Christian or sermonic in its rendering (and in this sense, Lee's *Do the Right Thing* would be more appropriate). Yet there is prophetic commentary in the story and visuals of the film. Through the film's ambiguous ending—Strike is given a way out, bathed in suffuse light, taking a train for the first time, intercut with shots of Tyrone playing with trains (inherited from Strike), with Scientific (the inheritor of Strike's "block" and "clock"), and with Victor gaining his freedom from jail for murder—*Clockers* prophesizes the possibility of these young black men: Strike as mobile and potentially self-inventing in his mobility; Tyrone as the future, a future scarred by the present and nostalgic for the past; Scientific and drug dealing as already dead; and Victor as the father figure, scarred by the failure of his own self-realization. Granted, this is bleak prophecy, but it is a charge to the medium of film and the aesthetics of black cinema. The ambiguous ending opens the possibility of multiple outcomes, multiple subjective formations from a given situation and from given social conditions. Furthermore, the film opens the possibility of black cinema beyond genre, beyond the conventions of genre, to the possibility of black cinema as a metacritcal form, to the possibility of black cinema as transgeneric expression of an artistic commitment to the chronicling, envisioning, visualizing, and aestheticizing of the black experience, dispersed across genres.

The difficulty of Lee's *Clockers* is perhaps its ambiguity and ambition, a difficulty that the director has formulated across his body of work. However, when ambiguity, especially, is interrogated, Lee's adaptation of *Clockers* provides an opportunity to examine the social and cultural transformation of a text. Richard Price's *Clockers*, arguably not a novel in the African American literary tradition, is rendered black through innovation, through an application of a black ethos of conflict and self-invention and revision and critique. In doing so, the film charges black cinema with the mission of moving beyond itself, beyond a kind of phenomenal locality of blackness in generic conventions to that of an aesthetic, a mode of being and expression.

NOTES

1. Richard Price, *Clockers* (New York: HarperCollins, 1992), 4.

2. Anti-realism refers to the highly aesthetic use of reflexivity in *Clockers* and the resulting critique of novelistic realism and naturalism and cinematic social realism overwhelmingly present in the "hood film." As a strategy in film, reflexivity calls attention to the cinematic apparatus itself, to the constructedness of film and the film-viewing experience. In doing so, reflexivity, often times artistically, ideologically, and politically, serves as critique or corrective to illusionism, as illusionism posits film narration as the seamless, unmediated reproduction and re-presentation of reality. As I elaborate later, the use of anti-realism in *Clockers* is not a denunciation of realism, illusionism, or social realism; instead, anti-realism shifts the cinematic emphasis from objectivity, mimesis, and verisimilitude, and the illusions of these in realist film texts, to a subjective expression of reality through an emphasis on the plasticity of film, an emphasis on cinematography, character point of view, and performance. The result, I argue, is a revision of the hood film's realism that only serves to mimetically represent the "experience" of the young, black, urban male, without interrogating the attending discourses of race, gender, racial pathology, and social and economic disenfranchisement, to name a few.

3. Price, *Clockers*, 12.

4. The narratological distinction is made between story time (*histoire*) and discourse time in the "double-time structuring" of narrative: "What is fundamental to narrative, . . . is that these two times are independent. . . . [T]he time of the story is fixed, following the ordinary course of a life: a person is born, grows from childhood to maturity and old age, and then dies. But the discourse-time order may be completely different: it may start with the person's deathbed, the 'flashback' to childhood; or it may start with childhood, 'flashforward' to death, then end with adult life": see Seymour Chatman, "Novels and Films," in *On Narrative*, ed. W. J. T. Mitchell (Chicago: University of Chicago Press, 1980), 118.

5. Here I refer to traditional Aristotelian rhetoric, which, as I understand it, is a way of communicating and a form of persuasion. In addition, I imply Adam Banks's use of African American rhetoric "as the set of traditions of discursive practices—verbal, visual and electronic—used by individuals and groups of African Americans toward the ends of full participation in American society on their own terms." I emphasize rhetoric here because, as I will discuss later, Lee's "rhetoric of film" becomes part of the adaptation of the film informing not only how the film makes meaning but the goal of the meaning made: see Adam Banks, *Race, Rhetoric, and Technology: Searching for Higher Ground* (Mahwah, N.J.: Lawrence Erlbaum Associates, 2006), 2.

6. New Black Cinema refers to the films that emerged between *She's Gotta Have It* (Spike Lee, 1986) and, arguably, *Clockers* or *Devil in a Blue Dress* (Carl Franklin, 1995). New Black Cinema is a periodization and demarcation of a kind of black film. See Keith M. Harris, *Boys, Boyz, Bois: An Ethics of Black Masculinity in Popular Film and Television* (London: Routledge, 2006), 79–97.

7. Mark Winokur, "Marginal Marginalia: The African-American Voice in the Nouvelle Gangster Film, *Velvet Light Trap* 35 (Spring 1995): 19–32.

8. Jackie Byars, *All that Hollywood Allows* (Chapel Hill: University of North Carolina Press, 1991), 8.

9. Ibid., 217–26.

10. Paula Massood, *Black City Cinema: African American Experiences in Film.* (Philadelphia: Temple University Press, 2003), 192–193.

11. Here I refer to Manthia Diawara's discussion of "new realism," the 1990s cycle of hood films, and the masculine rites of passage that these films signify: see Manthia Diawara, "Black American Cinema: The New Realism," in *Black American Cinema*, ed. Manthia Diawara (London: Routledge, 1993), 3–25.

12. Spike Lee, quoted in Delroy Lindo, "Delroy and Spike Lee," in *Spike Lee Interviews*, ed. Cynthia Fuchs (Jackson: University of Mississippi Press, 2002), 161–77.

13. Massood, *Black City Cinema*, 189.

14. Sharon Willis, "*Do the Right Thing* (1989), Spike Lee," in *Film Analysis*, ed. Jeffrey Geiger and R. L. Rutsky (New York: W. W. Norton, 2005), 776–93.

15. Robert Stam, *Reflexivity in Film and Literature* (New York: Columbia University Press, 1992), 1, 159–62.

16. For Lee's discussion of the choice to restage these images, see Stephen Pizzello, "Between a 'Rock' and a Hard Place," *American Cinematographer* 76, no. 9 (September 1995): 36–46.

17. For these distinctions, I am drawing on Robert Heilman's revision of tragedy and melodrama: See Robert Bechtold Heilman, *Tragedy and Melodrama: Versions of Experience* (London: University of Washington Press, 1968).

18. Ibid., 88–91.

19. Willis notes Lee's use of "classical" drama early in his career with *Do the Right Thing*: see Willis, "*Do the Right Thing* (1989)," 776–93.

20. For a discussion of the cinematography and the choices made by Lee and his director of photography, Malik Sayeed, see Pizzello, "Between a 'Rock' and a Hard Place."

21. Lott's demarcations are as follows: "Early Silent Films (1890–1920), Early Soundies and Race Films (1920–45), Post War Problem Films (1945–60), and Contemporary Film." I would add a slightly more nuanced reading to the period Lott identifies as "Contemporary Film": the Los Angeles Rebellion filmmakers (1968–71), New Black Cinema (1986–95), and Post New Black Cinema (1995–present): Tommy Lott, "A No-Theory Theory of Contemporary Black Cinema," *Black American Literature* 25, no. 2 (Summer 1991): 223.

22. Ibid.

23. For a more elaborate discussion of the shift from genre to signifying practice, see Harris, *Boys, Boyz, Bois*.

24. Gladstone Yearwood, *Black Film as a Signifying Practice* (Trenton, N.J.: Africa World Press, 2000), 115.

25. Henry Louis Gates Jr., *The Signifying Monkey* (Oxford: Oxford University Press, 1988), 47–48.

26. Ibid., 107–11.

27. Sacvan Bercovitch, *The American Jeremiad* (Madison: University of Wisconsin Press, 1978).

28. David Howard-Pitney, *The African American Jeremiad*. rev. 2nd ed. (Philadelphia: Temple University Press, 2005), 95.

29. Ibid., 7.

30. Ibid., 95.

Reel Men: *Get on the Bus* and the Shifting Terrain of Black Masculinities

I n 1996, Spike Lee celebrated his tenth anniversary as a feature filmmaker by releasing his tenth theatrical release, *Get on the Bus* (Columbia Pictures). During that ten-year period, Lee had emerged as a genuine icon in American film and earned the reputation as the most prolific African American feature-film maker in Hollywood. His output, though spotty at times, was an astonishing achievement and a testament to Lee's dogged determination to make films. Not coincidentally, the opening date of his tenth feature film, October 15, 1996, was also the anniversary of another iconic moment in American history. One year earlier, approximately 1 million African American men (and women) convened on the National Mall in Washington, D.C., for what organizers called "a day of atonement." The Million Man March was the biggest political demonstration ever held in the nation's capital and generated substantial controversy, national publicity, and debate about the state of Black America. Many of the issues tapped by the march—intra-racial relations in the black community, the historical and contemporary role of racism in the African American experience, and the plight of black men, women, and families—were reoccurring themes in Lee's ten-year body of work.

Indeed, Lee had built a career out of making racially charged topics and the intimate aspects of black American life the centerpiece of his cinematic and political projects. Still, even though the thematic issues of *Get on the Bus* were familiar terrain for Lee, the production of the film and the ideological work that it performed broke new ground for the filmmaker.

The making of *Get on the Bus* was inspired by the remarkable success of the Million Man March. An estimated 1 million African American men (and women) came from all over the United States to participate in the event. They came for many different reasons. Some, for instance, viewed the march as an expression of political protest against the rising tide of social conservatism in American politics, marked in 1995 by the ascendancy of Newt Gingrich and the Republican-led "Contract with America." Other African Americans approached the march as a chance to establish greater racial solidarity. For some, the march represented the opportunity to enlist greater involvement from black residents in their communities. The march was a means for others to counter the media portrayals of black men as dangerous, criminal, and irresponsible. The event was a much more personal experience for a number of participants creating an opportunity to establish a stronger spiritual connection to black Americans.

The Million Man march was one of the biggest news stories of 1995. Starting on October 10, a mere five days before the march, the three major network news programs—ABC, CBS, and NBC—began to produce a number of stories in anticipation of the upcoming event. Several of the stories led the news broadcast, suggesting that the march emerged as a major news story in a constantly churning twenty-four–hour news cycle that was redefining both the production and consumption of news.[1]

Several factors explain the degree and intensity of the coverage. The Million Man March occurred during a period in which the attention cycle of the news media was focused on race relations in America, especially between blacks and whites. Twelve days before the march, O. J. Simpson was acquitted on the charges that he had killed his wife and her male friend. The verdict, rendered by a predominantly black jury, unleashed a flurry of post-trial dialogue about racial polarization in America. An additional factor that drove coverage of the march was the proposed size of event. Indeed, the specter of 1 million black men, in the words of one news reporter, "descending on the nation's capital" established the dramatic qualities and newsworthiness of the event for the major news outlets.[2] However, the most significant factor driving the coverage was the presence, leadership, and racial politics of the man who called the march, Louis Farrakhan. Despite the various reasons that attracted men to the march, the national news media developed a one-dimensional storyline in their coverage of the event. That storyline pivoted on the Nation of Islam leader. Several news stories featured sound bites of some of Farrakhan's most incendiary remarks, along with a selected range of commentators and sources that characterized Farrakhan as racist, sexist, or anti-Semitic. In the end, the news media's personality-driven reporting shifted public focus onto Farrakhan and away from a more productive dialogue about race or the conditions of black men. In effect, a demonstration designed to bring attention to questions about racial inequality was filtered through a frame that restricted news discourse to a single, polarizing figure.

Though *Get on the Bus* was billed as a film about the Million Man March, it was, in reality, an attempt to engage the state of African American men. Unlike the personality-driven frames of the news coverage, *Get on the Bus* used the occasion to excavate the lives of those who made the march a genuinely newsworthy event—ordinary black men. If the march posed the question: "What is the role of black men in the African American community?" the film pursued a slightly different query, "What constitutes legitimate black manhood?" The latter question is infinitely more complex insofar as it challenges many of the ideas about black men presumed in the former question.

Though Lee was the figure most people identified with *Get on the Bus*, the actual catalysts for the film were the longtime Hollywood producers Bill Borden and Guy Rosenbush. One evening while at home, Borden saw a local television news report about a group of men who took a bus trip from Los Angeles to Washington, D.C. The men departed for Washington as strangers and returned to Los Angeles as close friends. The story captured his imagination and planted a seed in his head. Borden and Rosenbush then called Reuben Cannon to see if would be interested in helping to produce the film. Once Cannon was on board, he reached out to the one director he believed could translate the story to film, Spike Lee. Intrigued by the pitch and the premise of the film, Lee came on board as director and executive producer. The producers calculated that having Lee, a well-known filmmaker and celebrity in his own right, as part of the executive team could convince a major studio to put up the money for the film. Lee's involvement with the project caught the eye of studio executives, though not necessarily for the right reasons.

Over the course of his ten-year career as a feature-film maker, Lee had written and directed some of the most talked-about films in America. His endeavors outside filmmaking, such as his partnership with Nike and Michael Jordan, made him a cultural icon and household name. No filmmaker, with the exception of maybe Steven Spielberg, had generated more press than Lee during his career. Though Lee was a recognizable figure in American pop culture, his star in Hollywood was showing signs of fading in 1996. His three prior films—*Crooklyn*, *Clockers*, and *Girl 6*—had performed poorly at the box office, suggesting that Lee's ability to turn real-life headlines and racial drama into box-office magic was waning. Making matters worse was the fact that his seven-year relationship with Universal Pictures ended in 1996, and the project closest to his heart, a biopic about Jackie Robinson, appeared unlikely after Turner Pictures walked away from the project after it became clear that budget disputes could not be resolved. Lee's personal struggles to secure financing for his films symbolized the larger struggles of black filmmakers in Hollywood. Significantly, it underlined the fact that there were still no African American powerbrokers in the film industry: no one, more specifically, who had the authority to green light a film.

From the beginning of his feature-film—making career, Lee's relationship with the commercial film industry had been contentious. Early in his career, Lee spoke openly about the institutional racism in Hollywood, and he had to battle constantly with studio executives for creative control. *She's Gotta Have It* was initially rated X because of the strong sexual content. The lightning-rod climax in *Do the Right Thing* provoked at least two studios to demand that he soften the ending or look elsewhere for distribution. But the real turn in his relationship with Hollywood was the debacle that ensued over *Malcolm X*. Fearful that Warner Brothers was going to pull the plug on the long-awaited and highly publicized feature on Malcolm X, Lee took his battle with the studio, the industry, and charges of racism public. Many insiders believe that Lee's handling of the situation burned some crucial bridges in the industry.[3]

When Lee and the producers of the film first approached the studios about financing *Get on the Bus*, they received very little interest. Convinced that the concept for the film was viable, the producers were undeterred by Hollywood's lack of enthusiasm. Borden's key contact at Columbia managed to secure a negative pick-up deal. If the producers could finance and make the film, the studio agreed to pay $3.6 million for the distribution rights. In the spirit of the march, especially the idea that black men should take responsibility for their own fate and that of the community, Cannon and Lee decided to solicit private investors. Specifically, they mined their contacts with successful African American men. Eventually, fifteen men joined the effort to finance the film. Cannon and Lee incorporated the group that agreed to be named—what else?—15 Black Men.

With the support of investors that included Will Smith, Wesley Snipes, Johnny Cochran, and Bob Johnson, the producers raised $2.4 million. Cannon was able to convince the potential investors that the $100,000–$200,000 figure that he and Lee were asking them to contribute was a no-risk investment. Lem Daniels, a vice president at Merrill Lynch and one of the investors, explained his decision to invest this way: "I just looked at the numbers. It was difficult to lose money on this movie based on its budget.

Statistics on minority films with budgets in the $2 million range say they seem to consistently bring in returns of $6 million."[4] Cannon's business proposal assured the private investors that the combination of box-office receipts, international distribution rights, and auxiliary sales in the home video and DVD market all but guaranteed some degree of return on their investment. A few days before the film was released in theaters, the producers held a luncheon for the investors and presented them with a check that included their initial investment plus 8 percent interest.

The pursuit of investors for *Get on the Bus* was aided by the shifting economics of Hollywood. On the one hand, the emergent economic system in Hollywood, especially the pursuit of expensive blockbusters, renders small black film projects obsolete. On the other hand, the new sources of profit in the industry make it possible for small, low-risk films to generate healthy revenue. By 1995, Hollywood was entering a new era in which the most reliable profits were coming from the international and home-viewing (video rentals, DVD sales, and pay-per-view) markets rather than the domestic box office. This development meant that the chances of a relatively inexpensive feature like *Get on the Bus* losing money were unlikely.

The creation of 15 Black Men raises a provocative question: Why doesn't the black business and entertainment elite pursue this model more frequently? In other words, given the oft-stated complaint that Hollywood refuses to invest in imaginative films about black life, why can't African Americans put together a pool of investors who could finance small independent features at a relatively low cost and little, if any, financial risk? While African American filmmakers may not have any executive authority to green light films, some of them do have access to the financial capital necessary to produce small features.

The problem with institutionalizing this financial strategy is highlighted by the changing landscape of feature-film making. In today's digital media environment, producing film and video content has become widespread and common. Young students armed with only a small handheld camera are posting all kinds of material—experimental, recreational, sexual, and violent—on popular video-streaming websites. But for filmmakers like Lee who are interested primarily in producing theatrical releases, the barriers to entry persist because of several factors. The investment strategy pursued by Cannon and Lee, in reality, resolved one-third of the feature-filmmaking business—production. But millions of dollars are also required to address the other two-thirds of the business—distribution and promotion. The production of even a small independent theatrical release is still an expensive enterprise. In the case of *Get on the Bus*, the producers cut a deal with Columbia Tri-Star for a negative pick-up. As a result, they did not have to worry about the costs related to distribution and promotion. This suggests that truly independent theatrical film production still requires collaboration with the studios to distribute and market product, thus making the continuation of the private-investment strategy in any permanent manner unlikely or, at best, contingent on the ability to establish and maintain partnerships in Hollywood.

As he has on many of his films, Lee faced a series of challenges as he prepared to shoot *Get on the Bus*. Many of the tensions surrounding the making of his tenth feature pivoted around the two themes that define Lee's relationship with the film industry: the politics of money and race. As has always been the case between Hollywood and Spike Lee, a major factor in the production of the *Get on the Bus* was money—or, to be more exact, the lack of money. This fact along with the volatile racial and gender politics of the film placed Lee on familiar ground. While money and political issues have never been exclusive to Lee, the bold and public manner in which he has addressed them has made these matters especially visible.

Still, as he poised himself to begin production on *Get on the Bus*, it would be an experience like no other one in his ten-year career.

After securing the money, Lee's next challenge was the shoot itself. The specifications of the shoot were unlike any other Spike Lee Joint. *Get on the Bus* was his first road movie. Filming was scheduled to take place in Los Angeles, Nashville, and the Baltimore–Washington, D.C., area. The bulk of the story, 75 percent, takes place on a bus. For this project, the director had to figure out ways to make the cross-country bus trip engaging and entertaining to viewers. The idea of a narrative film unfolding in a confined space was not unprecedented. In his 1944 feature *Lifeboat*, Alfred Hitchcock shot an entire film based on seven survivors stranded in a deserted lifeboat. In situations like these, the director has to come up with inventive ways of translating the story; thus, the use of camera movement and angles, sound, editing, and other technical details become even more crucial. However, the challenges of both shooting and selling *Get on the Bus* were enormous in the context of an industry that relies heavily on special effects, action, and spectacle to remain relevant in a hyper-competitive entertainment economy.

The lack of space was not the only challenge. There was also very little time for production and post-production. In order to have the film in theaters by the one-year anniversary of the Million Man March, the production, which did not begin until April 1996, had to move swiftly. Because many of the actors, crew, and Lee himself were working for scale, the window of time on the shoot was unusually short: eighteen days. Along with putting together a cast and crew, the project needed a script. To handle the screenplay-writing duties, Lee and his fellow producers turned to Reggie "Rock" Bythewood. The young writer had cut his teeth in television first writing for the NBC sitcom *A Different World* and later the short-lived but popular Fox serial drama *New York Undercover*. The Fox drama was one of the first prime-time network programs to incorporate hip-hop music, aesthetics, and sensibilities into its televisual style.

In spite of the fact that Lee conducted himself as a classic auteur, the production of a feature film is an intensely collaborative process. Though famous for the number of films that he wrote, directed, and starred in Lee, shared the writing credits in some of his earlier work (*Crooklyn* and *Malcolm X*), and the playwright Suzan-Lori Parks wrote the screenplay for *Girl 6*. But while he did not write the screenplay for *Get on the Bus*, Lee helped to sketch out the story by supplying Bythewood with anecdotes and other thematic ideas that he wanted to incorporate into the film.

As Lee prepared to immerse himself in the shoot, he found himself, strangely enough, back where he had begun ten years earlier when he wrote and directed his breakout hit, *She's Gotta Have It*: on the outside of the commercial film industry looking in. It was an odd position for a filmmaker who had broad name recognition and critically acclaimed work. After ten years in the business, he was still making films under relatively adverse conditions. But his marginalized position also gave him something that he prized: greater creative control and autonomy. Lee used his freedom to make films that were not only thematically provocative but also aesthetically rousing.

Starting with the highly unconventional look and texture of *She's Gotta Have It*, Lee's approach to filmmaking has been highly stylized. That is, his distinctive approach to directing cinema occasionally intrudes on the filmmaking process by interrupting and subverting some of the norms and conventions that dominate the aesthetic organization of classical Hollywood cinema. The director's filmmaking techniques, particularly early on in his career, were expressive, self-conscious, and attention seeking. While some view Lee's filmmaking as gratuitous or self-serving, his films nevertheless represent a form of authorial action, a sense of agency that deliberately contests the intensely regulated manners of classical Hollywood film. Lee has never approached cinema or any other form of popular media culture as an innocent, objective, and non-biased view of the world. In fact, his position has been the exact opposite: that popular media culture and the representation of the world are inherently political.[5]

It would, however, be a mistake to view Lee's stylistic and aesthetic choices as purely political. In reality, there has always been an economic dimension to Lee's guerrilla filmmaking inclinations. Faced with limited resources, Lee has been forced to be wildly creative, even downright subversive at times regarding how he combines classical Hollywood with art, European, and experimental cinema. His unconventional style of filmmaking has not only earned him a signature voice among Hollywood directors, it has also worked to promote him and his films as a unique entertainment experience.

The strict timetable and budget meant that the production schedule and costs had to be streamlined. Lee shot *Get on the Bus* on Super-16 mm film stock. The smaller handheld camera was affordable and flexible enough to handle a film shot primarily on a moving bus. The decision to go with Super-16 also gave the film a cinema vérité style that enhanced its power of realism. Although it is a fictional narrative, *Get on the Bus* has the look and texture of a documentary. The last time he had shot a film in Super-16 was *She's Gotta Have It*.

Lee approached *Get on the Bus* as an opportunity rather than an obstacle to be hurdled. In addition to the crew, he was able to assemble a multitalented cast that included Andrew Braugher, Bernie Mac, Isaiah Washington, Charles S. Dutton, and the legendary Ossie Davis. "The biggest problem," Lee noted, "was trying to get the same caliber of performance in such a short shooting schedule, because even though the film had a low budget we didn't

Get on the Bus (1996): D.C. bound (front row, from left: Andre Braugher, Hill Harper, Hosea Brown III, DeAundre Bonds, Charles Dutton, Steve White; back row, from left: Gabriel Casseus, Thomas Jefferson Byrd, Ossie Davis, Isaiah Washington, Roger Guenveur Smith, Harry Lennix, Bernie Mac).

want the acting to look that way. Everyone's aspirations were high in spite of the budget."[6]

Lee employed a variety of unconventional shots, methods, colors, film stock, and angles to make *Get on the Bus* visually arresting. Some reviews of the film noted that the look, style, and pace of the film possessed the vigor and imagination that harked back to Lee's earlier and more critically acclaimed work. *Variety* wrote that *Get on the Bus* is "a vital regeneration of a film maker's talent as well as a bracing and often very funny dramatization of urgent sociopolitical themes," and called it "his most satisfying work since *Do the Right Thing*."[7]

In addition to figuring out ways to make the movie interesting from a filmmaking and aesthetic point of view, Lee had to devise a way to make the story compelling. On that front, *Get on the Bus* also broke new narrative and political ground for the filmmaker.

Lee understood that a film about the Million Man March would have been difficult to sell. "I knew that we could not re-create the march," Lee said. "We felt that the journey was in a lot of ways more important than the destination, because everyone had seen the march on TV. The drama would come from what happens to this unique mix of individuals, this diversity of men who we feel represent African-Americans at this time."[8] The narrative focuses on the intimate life stories that encouraged black men of diverse backgrounds to participate in the Million Man March. Despite the charismatic appeal and controversial legacy of Farrakhan, what ultimately made the march such a compelling and historic event was the increasingly complex plight and experiences of black men in America. Whereas most news accounts of the Million Man March focused on the inflammatory rhetoric and racial politics of Louis Farrakhan, *Get on the Bus* aimed to explore the social and psychological makeup of the black men who came to the march. At its core, *Get on the Bus* offers a microcosm of the diverse identities, experiences, and histories that mark the shifting contours of black masculinity.

Strategically, Bythewood and Lee wanted to expand the representational discourse about black masculinity. Several factors—age, politics, region, class, skin color, religion, education, occupation—render the principal characters in *Get on the Bus* distinct and diverse. Among the passengers is a former gang member who converts to Islam and a life of faith. The juxtaposition of the University of Southern California (private) and University of California, Los Angeles (public), students is a reference to the class and status divisions among black men. Age is also a distinguishing variable ranging from a seventy-plus victim of corporate downsizing to a teenage hip-hop head whose problems with the criminal-justice system force him to ride the bus shackled, literally, to a father who had abandoned him as a young boy. The biracial character struggles with his identity and connection to black men. There is even a black Republican, albeit a largely caricatured representation, who is eventually kicked off the bus for his harsh comments about blacks. The idea that this particular collection represents, in Lee's words, the "diversity of men who we feel represent African-Americans at this time" is inherently political and bound to encounter some serious shortcomings, given the complexities of black men's lives.[9]

The presence of so many different black men on the bus, however, invites a conceptual shift away from the notion of black *masculinity* and toward a due consideration of black *masculinities*. The former assumes an ideal or essential black male identity that reigns superior and above any other formation. The latter, alternatively, suggests that there is no singular black male identity or experience. Thus, *Get on the Bus* suggests that the idea of an authentic black man is illegitimate and irreconcilable with the everyday realities of life. As a result, each of the men on the bus, irrespective of their differences, stakes a particular claim in black masculinity.

In his earlier work—the "frat boyz" in *School Daze* or the classic masculine hero type in *Malcolm X*—Lee invests an enormous amount of his capital as a filmmaker in dominant notions of black masculinity. One of the most enduring criticisms of Lee throughout his career has been of his gender politics. While this particular critique has focused mainly on the filmmaker's portrayal and treatment of women, Lee's representation of black men has escaped sustained and critical engagement. Furthermore, Lee's attempt to trouble the notion of black masculinity places him on new thematic and political ground: black homosexuality.

Get on the Bus aims to critique previous representations of black men, including, ironically, the work of Lee. Throughout his career, Lee has maintained that his films provide a more responsible if not accurate portrait of black American life. But in the celluloid world that Lee has imagined, black men have generally been the catalyst for narrative transmission. *School Daze*, his second theatrical release, is a prominent example. In that film the male protagonists define their blackness and their masculinity in close tandem with their domination of the black public sphere and women. In this microcosmic portrait of black life, African American men are dominant in every sense of the word. They dominate the screen, the dialogue, and the story and are clearly the agents who drive the narrative. Typical of Lee's work, gay men are either invisible or the source of derision and mockery in *School Daze*. The repeated references to "punks," "sissies," and "fairies" was rightfully criticized for the homophobic tendencies that belittle and marginalize black gay men.[10]

The negation of black gay men is certainly not unique to Spike Lee. The topic of homosexuality remains a volatile one in the African American community. Black religious institutions, a viable center of cultural and political power in the African American community, consistently condemn homosexuality. Moreover, the black church and mainstream black political leaders have adamantly rejected any effort to align the push for gay rights with the struggle for black racial equality and civil rights. The harsh anti-gay tone in some African American quarters has prompted a few commentators to assert that blacks are the most homophobic or anti-gay segment in America. While anti-gay currents certainly run strong in the African American community, the idea that they are somehow deeper or more hostile than other anti-gay sentiments lacks credibility.

Still, the dominant tropes of blackness often evoke masculine imagery and sensibilities. In most instances, authentic blackness is equated with manliness. Current configurations of black masculinity in black popular culture can be traced back to the tumultuous decade of the 1960s, a period when the black male image underwent a dramatic overhaul. With the rising demand for black power came bolder expressions of black identity. Blackness, increasingly, was associated with openly defiant figures such as Malcolm X, H. Rap Brown, and members of the Black Panther Party. This more potent articulation of black masculinity embodied in the "Shining Black Prince" figure articulated in Ossie Davis's memorable eulogy to Malcolm X but was later subjected to caricature in popular formations ranging from blaxploitation films to hip-hop culture. In this particular claim on masculinity, black homosexuality is an oxymoron, an identity that is inconsistent with the preferred representations of black masculinity.

Like most representational forms, *Get on the Bus* relies on individual characters to symbolize social identities and cultural experiences that, in truth, are varied and complex. In Bythewood's script, the characters Randall (Harry J. Lennix) and Kyle (Isaiah Washington) represent black gay men. When we meet the two men, their quiet quarrel about the collapse of their relationship erupts and turns noisy when Randall announces out loud to Kyle, "You are afraid to admit that you love me." The reaction on the bus (and among film audiences) is predictable, as passengers express emotions ranging from dismay to disgust. Though some of the harshest critics of *Get on the Bus* lambasted Bythewood for creating types rather than real people, there is nothing in particular about Kyle and Randall that marks them as gay. In their opening scene, Randall is dressed in very standard business attire, and we learn that Kyle spent ten years in the Marine Corps and recently fulfilled a tour of duty in the Persian Gulf War, where he was wounded by not so friendly "friendly fire" from two American soldiers who suspected he was gay.

Speculation about the same-sex couple abounds on the bus. In one of the improvisational scenes in the film, Xavier, a young college film student, interviews Kyle. Determined to learn why gay men would want to attend a march called by Farrakhan, an outspoken critic of homosexuality, the young student asks Kyle, "What role do gay men have in the black community?" Kyle calmly answers the question with a question aimed at all heterosexual black men, "What's yours"? The initial question is problematic on several fronts. Most significantly, it assumes that gay men have to justify and defend their role in the black community. Once again, the humanity of black gay men—indeed, their status as legitimate black men—is called into question.

If Lee's attitude toward gay men can be read as indifferent or even hostile in his earlier work, *Get on the Bus* represents an effort to strike a more inclusive tone. The film, albeit in problematic form, asserts that gay men are a part of the black community. This position, while certainly more laudable, is problematic for many African Americans. In fact, Lee noted that one of the most notable trends in the audience feedback to *Get on the Bus* was the negative reaction to the two black gay characters. According to Lee, many members of the audience did not like their insertion into the story and objected to any claim that gay men have a legitimate role in the African American community.

In *Get on the Bus*, Kyle earns his racial stripes by defeating his chief antagonist in the film, Flip (Andre Braugher), in a fight. From the moment Flip discovers that Kyle and Randall are gay, he bombards them with epithets that challenge both their manliness and their blackness. After ignoring many of Kyle's warnings about the constant name calling, the situation between Flip and the ex-marine turns violent, literally, as they decide to handle their differences in a duel.

In the fight scene, arguably the most disturbing and emotionally charged scene in the film, Kyle prevails, thus establishing the masculine and racial credentials of gay men. Though problematic, the scene admittedly is supposed to be read symbolically and not literally. Lee also uses music and humor to enhance the power of the moment and the message. As the other men on the bus form a circle around the two combatants, Stevie Wonder's magnificent version of Bob Marley's classic cry for mental and political emancipation, "Redemption Song," is playing in the background. In this instance, the song implies that African Americans, despite years of progress and struggle, continue to be victims of slavery, especially mental imprisonment, by succumbing to many of the racial myths and ideologies that have oppressed African Americans. Black men, the scene reminds us, can be their own worst enemy at times.

But the scene is also marked by a touch of humor. As Kyle begins to gain the advantage in his duel with Flip, he proudly mentions black gay men such as Langston Hughes and James Baldwin as signs of strengths and viable man-hood. After delivering the final blow, he tells Flip, "That one was for Dennis Rodman." Flip, bent over in pain, utters in disbelief, "Dennis Rodman is gay?" The reference to Rodman is recognition of how the former basketball star bent the strict gender codes in professional sports by wearing makeup, wigs, and wedding gowns and even publicly discussing his homosexual fantasies.

The film also provides clues that Kyle may be bisexual, practicing what has become known in black gay subculture as the "down low." This is a refer-ence to a generation of black men who build heterosexual lives publicly while pursuing homosexual lives privately. This particular development has gener-ated considerable attention in the popular press. In "down low" culture, it's not the simple fact that black men are in the closet but, rather, that they ac-tively refuse to identify as gay or bisexual. Several factors explain the "down low" phenomenon—most notably, the fact that black gay men have to con-tend with the fear of rejection in the black community, heterosexism, and the restrictive images of black masculinity circulating in the cultural landscape.

In "down low" culture, we see how far hegemonic notions of black masculinity reach. In this particular world, homosexuality is associated with effeminate white men, an identity, in short, that is irreconcilable with common-sense notions and expressions of black masculinity. It is interesting to note that many black gay men choose the "down low" lifestyle because of the racial rather than sexual costs of homosexuality in the black community. African American men engaging in same-sex sexual relations actively culti-vate a hyper-masculine exterior—popularly referred to as "homo thugs"—that subscribes visually and behaviorally to the dominant scripts of black mas-culinity. In this case, dominant notions of black masculinity—tough, hard, urban, aggressive personalities—shape and influence a homosexuality iden-tity that runs counter to it.

But even as *Get on the Bus* strives to make the case that black men make up a complex mix of identities, values, and experience, it also maintains that they are bound together by the powerful history of race and gender in Amer-ica. The point is effectively conveyed in the scene titled "Pulled Over." As the bus is making its way through the middle of the night in Tennessee, it is sud-denly forced to pull over by state troopers. The scene is a reference to the racial-profiling practices that have become common along many interstate highways across America.

The men on the bus, despite their differences, are vulnerable to a familiar figure in the American cultural imagination: the criminal black male. All of the men are innocent of the alleged reasons the bus has been stopped and searched. According to the trooper, drug smuggling across state lines has been on the rise. What the scene powerfully depicts is what most African American men, despite their income, class, status, or sexual differences, have had to endure at least once in their lives—the presumption of guilt by virtue of the fact that they are black and male. While this type of racial profiling does not always lead to a Rodney King–type episode, the underlying result is the same: Black men are constantly under surveillance, policed, disciplined, and marked as a threat to the social order.

In the face of state-sanctioned authority, the men are essentially powerless to confront the injustice of armed law enforcement. The presence of the police dog further dehumanizes the bus passengers and evokes images of the dogs that were used in the 1960s to attack nonviolent civil-rights activists in the South. The music choice, once again, adds an important layer of meaning to the scene, "People Get Ready," by the proto-gospel soul group the Impressions. The resilient falsetto of the lead vocalist, Curtis Mayfield, like that of a number of black artists in the 1960s, injects the racial pride and social consciousness of the period into black rhythm-and-blues music. Once the bus is allowed to resume its course Lee's blue-tinted close-ups of the passengers aptly captures the humiliation, anger, and despair that underscores the blue mood that fills the bus after the encounter with state troopers.

In its own peculiar way, the state-trooper episode soothes over some of the divisions and hostilities on the bus and draws the passengers closer together. Later, when the bus reaches Washington, D.C., Xavier discovers that Jeremiah (Ossie Davis), the oldest member on the trip, has passed out. Jeremiah's health, and not the march, becomes the primary interests of the passengers. Eventually, each man on the bus opts to stay in the hospital in a show of support for the ailing Jeremiah, who eventually dies from heart complications. Though they have all missed the march, the cross-country journey achieves one of the goals of the march: It creates a special bond between the men and a renewed sense of fellowship, strength, and commitment to community and personal responsibility.

Despite all of the financial and production obstacles, *Get on the Bus* opened in American theaters on the one-year anniversary of the Million Man March. It was an amazing accomplishment. Unfortunately, the film's $2,837,711 opening weekend across 1,207 screens produced a paltry $1,905 per-screen average.[11] By the third week, the box office total was $5,402,971, and theaters began pulling the picture. On virtually every financial and box-office measure, *Get on the Bus* was a failure. What went wrong? And, more important, what lessons did it reveal about Spike Lee and the changing landscape of black cinema, a landscape that, ironically, he helped to shape?

According to Lee, many black moviegoers stayed away from theaters because they believed the film was a documentary. Translation: not a film intended to entertain the audience. Over the course of his career, Lee has been
an advocate of films that resonate with the African American experience and
break from the representational ethos that typically treats blacks as a mono-
lithic community. But Lee has also been in the business long enough to know
that the black filmgoing audience, like most audiences, goes to the movies to
be entertained and not educated. Trying to make sense of the poor box-office
performance, Lee explained, "Maybe the black audience didn't want to see a
movie like this. Not now, I mean. They want to see shoot 'em up stuff,"
adding with a tinge of sadness, "The African-American audience for the most
part was unresponsive."[12]

A lot had changed in the world of entertainment and black American life
in the ten-year period in which Lee rose to become one of America's most
recognizable filmmakers. The most significant changes, arguably, were the ascendancy and spreading influence of hip-hop culture and the fact that young
African Americans drove commercial representations of blackness and wider
popular culture trends. Even though Lee had been a catalyst in the commercial revival of black cinema, by 1996 he was no longer its most bankable director. A new generation of filmmakers whose cinematic eye and attitude
connected more effectively with hip-hop vied for that distinction. The rise of
F. Gary Gray illustrates the point.

Three and a half weeks after the theatrical release of *Get on the Bus*, New
Line Cinema released Gray's female-driven action crime drama *Set It Off*.
Starring Jada Pinkett Smith and Queen Latifah, the picture opened on
Wednesday, November 10. By the end of business at the box office that weekend, *Set It Off* had earned $11,807,451, for an impressive $8,342 per-screen
average on 1,019 screens.[13] By week three, the small-budget feature had generated more than $25 million at the box office.

The strong showing of *Set It Off* and the emergence of Gray was an indication of the cultural and commercial impact of hip-hop in the film industry. Gray
cut his directorial teeth making music videos for artists such as TLC, Coolio, and
Ice Cube. His decision to shoot music clips in 35 mm displayed a cinematic
touch and the ability to tell a story visually. His body of work in music opened
the door for his first feature, the hip-hop comedy *Friday* (New Line Cinema)
starring Ice Cube. Shot for about $3 million, *Friday* became a surprise hit, earn-
ing nearly $28 million at the box office. *Set It Off*'s focus on four women's strug-
gle for their families, economic survival, and individual worth brought a new
narrative twist and sensibility to he growing body of hip-hop–influenced cinema.
Lee studied the box-office performance of *Get on the Bus* and *Set It Off* and
openly pondered what it meant for the state of black cinema.

Realizing that *Set It Off* was on course to make more that seven times what *Get on the Bus* would generate at the box-office gate, Lee speculated out loud: "It's disturbing because studio heads are looking at these numbers, and the next time a black filmmaker tries to make a film with any substance, they'll say, 'Well, the last time somebody tried a film like that was *Get on the Bus,* and nobody came.'" He added, "But you know, they sure did come to see *Set It Off,* so we've got to have more shoot 'em ups, more violent pieces."[14]

Lee believed the message gave Hollywood producers the license to bypass complex scripts about black life in favor of films that emphasized urban violence and villainy. While some critics would certainly debate whether *Get on the Bus* was a film of substance, Lee's larger point, that the industry preferred violent, action, and youth-oriented vehicles, was more difficult to dispute. The new realities confronting black cinema, however, also point to audiences and what kinds of film and entertainment they prefer.

Research on the black moviegoing audience is sketchy, at best. For at least two decades, popular accounts contend that African Americans make up a disproportionate share of the box office. Even if the claim is true, it usually makes very little distinction within the audience, especially the fact that, in all likelihood, the majority of black moviegoers are young and often motivated, from a consumer-behaviorist perspective, by their identification with hip-hop. This explains in part why a film many young blacks may have believed was a documentary did so poorly compared with an entertainment- and action-oriented vehicle such as *Set It Off*.

After ten years in the feature-film–making business, then, Spike Lee, like many of his peers, was approaching a crossroads as black cinema, Hollywood, and popular culture were changing directions. On a more personal and professional note, the shifts driven by hip-hop raised an intriguing dilemma for Lee's cultural and commercial relevance, as well as for his vision of black cinema. More specifically, was the most productive black feature-film maker in history still relevant as black American cinema and black American life crossed over into the new millennium?

NOTES

1. For more on the news media's coverage of the Million Man March, see S. Craig Watkins, "Framing Protest: News Media Frames of the Million Man March," *Critical Studies in Media Communication* 18, no. 1 (2001): 83–101.

2. "World News Tonight," ABC, October 13, 1995, transcript no. 5205-1.

3. For a more elaborate discussion of Lee's relationship with the film industry early in his career, see S. Craig Watkins, *Representing: Hip Hop Culture and the Production of Black Cinema* (Chicago: University of Chicago Press, 1998). See also Anna Everett,

"'Spike, Don't Mess Malcolm Up': Courting Controversy and Control in *Malcolm X*," in this volume.

4. Matthew S. Scott, "Are You Ready to Invest in the Film Industry?" *Black Enterprise*, December 1996.

5. See Watkins, *Representing*, 159–66.

6. Erich Leon Harris, "Spike Lee Speaks, Demystifying the Man," *MovieMaker* 24 (March 1997), available online at http://www.moviemaker.com/magazne/editorial.php?id=297.

7. Todd McCarthy, "Lee Back on Track in 'Bus,'" *Variety*, October 7–13, 1996.

8. Harris, "Spike Lee Speaks."

9. Ibid.

10. See Toni Cade Bambara, "Programming with *School Daze*," in this volume.

11. Andrew Hindes, "'Sleepers' in a Walk; 'Bus' Stalls," *Daily Variety*, October 21, 1996.

12. Harris, "Spike Lee Speaks."

13. *Hollywood Reporter*, November 11, 1996.

14. Harris, "Spike Lee Speaks."

We Shall Overcome: Preserving History and Memory in *4 Little Girls*

> *Perhaps more than any other people, Americans have been locked in a deadly struggle with time, with history. We've fled the past and trained ourselves to suppress, if not forget, troublesome details of the national memory, and a great part of our optimism, like our progress, has been bought at a cost of ignoring the process through which we've arrived at any given moment in our national existence.*
>
> —Ralph Ellison, Shadow and Act

September 15, 1963, was Youth Day at the Sixteenth Street Baptist church in Birmingham, Alabama. Denise McNair, Cynthia Wesley, Addie Mae Collins, and Carole Robertson were in the ladies' lounge in the basement of the building freshening up, knowing that, along with their friends, it was their responsibility to help with the services of the day. At a little past ten in the morning, dynamite exploded in the church, instantly killing the four young girls and injuring over twenty.[1] To those African Americans living in "Bombingham," Alabama, and all across the country, it was another tragic reminder of how little their lives meant to the racist white residents of their city and to apathetic Americans as a whole. Indeed, a week before the bombing, as the federal government ordered that schools desegregate, George Wallace, then governor of Alabama, said in an interview with the *New York Times* that a "few first-class funerals" would end integration in Alabama.[2]

Robert Chambliss, a.k.a. "Dynamite Bob," was arrested in 1963 for the bombing of the Sixteenth Street Baptist church and for having dynamite without a permit. However, on October 8, 1963, he was only fined $100 and a given a six-month sentence for possession of the dynamite. While a 1965 FBI memo to J. Edgar Hoover indicated that four Ku Klux Klan members— Robert Chambliss, Bobby Frank Cherry, Herman Frank Cash, and Thomas E. Blanton—were responsible for the bombing, no charges were filed. Indeed, in 1980, a Justice Department report indicated that Hoover had prevented the prosecution of the men responsible for the bombing. It was not until 1977 that Bill Baxley, attorney general for the State of Alabama, reopened the case against Chambliss. Based on information from FBI files, Chambliss was found guilty and sentenced to life in prison, dying there in October 1985.[3]

The four girls were martyrs to the cause of desegregation and would never grow to see the changes that resulted from their sacrifice. It was a case that shocked many across the United States and is now considered a moment that changed the course of the Civil Rights Movement in the nation. Along with the televised images of Police Chief Bull Connor's attacks on civil-rights pro-testors in Birmingham, these incidents brought the reality of black people's plight home to white Americans unwilling to acknowledge their complicity in the U.S. racial dictatorship.[4]

The revelatory and shocking nature of these images led to repeated viewings throughout the country at large and within the African American community specifically, first to comprehend, then to instigate change and eventually to remember and pay tribute to those who lost their lives for black survival and to open doors for future generations in this country. Over time, these images have become an important part of the national memory. How-ever, in a disturbing trend in the 1990s and in this new century, many people have become desensitized to the horrors of the civil-rights struggle, and these scenes and stories do not seem to evoke what one would think to be an ap-propriate response. Indeed, many people do not even know of some of these specific stories, such as that of the four little girls.

One day while teaching the class Black Popular Culture, I casually re-ferred to Jesse Owens and noticed the blank looks on the faces of many in front of me. When I asked who knew who Jesse Owens was, only one or two students raised their hands. I mentioned a few other black historical figures—Stokley Carmichael, Medgar Evers, Emmett Till—and received the same re-action. I quickly realized that when I teach my African American studies classes, I shouldn't assume that African American stories, no matter how sig-nificant, are passed down. Unfortunately, while from the days of slavery oral histories were a given part of the African American life, in this highly medi-ated world, these important traditions have fallen by the wayside.

It has also become clear that some African American students in my classes, while enjoying the fruits of the civil-rights struggle, consider this an-cient history and a topic that does not need to be addressed. Although a sig-nificant black underclass still exists, the successes gained in certain areas of American industry and politics, the high visibility in sports and music, the embrace of hip-hop by mainstream America seemingly negates the presence of underprivileged black people, the high rate of black incarceration, and the reversal of affirmative action. Many African Americans assert that to address these issues and to keep this history alive is to stir up an ugly past. Forgetting is colluding with the forces that wish to overlook the nation's legacy of racism.

Preserving, remembering, and recuperating black stories has been the work of African American documentary-film makers from the earliest days of the medium. Whether it was reporting on life at the Tuskegee institute in *A Day at Tuskegee* (1910), black military recruits in *The Negro Soldier* (1944), or the black freedom movement in *Eyes on the Prize* (parts I and II; 1987, 1990), black filmmakers and screenwriters have considered documentary film a political and social tool.[5] In their book *Struggles for Representation: African American Documentary Film and Video*, Phyllis R. Klotman and Janet K. Cutler argue that black documentary-film making follows a tradition within African American society by creating historical narratives that address white American representations of black culture:

> Many socially and politically committed film/videomakers view documentary as a tool with which to interrogate and reinvent history; their work fills gaps, corrects errors, and exposes distortions in order to provide counter-narratives of African American experience.[6]

While the authors acknowledge that documentary theory challenges that idealistic nature of documentary production as a whole, they alternately argue that within black society, documentary has been and continues to be a mode of political and social agency. Following within this tradition is the genesis of Spike Lee's *4 Little Girls* (1997).

Moved by an article he read while in film school at New York University, Lee wrote to Chris McNair, father of the bombing victim Denise McNair, in hope of getting permission to make a film about the incident. Although McNair knew and respected Lee's father and aunts, he did not trust Lee with the story. McNair reveals:

> Spike was still in school when he sent me a letter asking me if I'd be willing to participate in a documentary. It wasn't as though I didn't want to talk about it. . . . [I]t's cathartic for me. But I don't guess I was ready to talk about it on film, and at that time Spike wasn't ready to make the film.[7]

McNair, who became a politician in Birmingham in 1973, also did not want anyone to think that he would use the case to advance his own career and protected the girls' legacy fiercely.[8] Years later, Lee approached him again and met with both Chris and his wife, Maxine, who agreed to have their story told. In 1995, McNair met two Birmingham women who were almost thirty years old and had never heard of the bombing.[9] As he stated, "I realized it was stupid to forget. I want people to know who the four little girls were, and to understand that this could have happened anywhere in the United States. Those girls . . . my daughter should not have died."[10]

Spike Lee's *4 Little Girls* succeeds in shaking both black and white viewers out of their contemporary apathy to U.S. racial history. Lee moves the viewer between the personal history of the families of the victims and the more recognized, public, political history of Birmingham. Focusing on the individual puts a face on the atrocities of the civil-rights struggle. In doing so, Lee nuances the viewers' memory of civil rights, which is typically enmeshed with larger-than-life symbols of the movement, such as Martin Luther King Jr. and Rosa Parks. A unique part of the film is that it attempts not to portray the girls as symbols but as flesh and blood, which in turn forces the viewer to become reconnected to the past and to have a renewed appreciation for civil-rights struggles. Released in 1997, in the midst of the bombings of black churches across the United States, the film also reminds viewers that without vigilance we are forced to repeat our past.

Personal and Public History and the Structure of *4 Little Girls*

> African Americans are far too quick to want to forget. We don't want to remember. It's always: "Let's forget about slavery, Emmett Till, Rosa Parks, Medgar Evers. Why you wanna go back and bring that up—dredge up that stuff?" Consequently, we have a generation of black kids who think this is the way it always was—that we could always live where we wanted, eat where we wanted, have church where we wanted. We need to remember.
>
> —Spike Lee[11]

If you ask the average American what he or she knows about the Civil Rights Movement, more often than not the first thing the person will say is that he or she knows about Martin Luther King. King, like Rosa Parks, has become a standard part of school curriculum in primary through secondary (and post-secondary) education. He is a "Think Different" Macintosh computer advertisement. He is a public holiday. Unfortunately, this familiarity with a figure who represents a movement can also lead to apathy. Why choose to discuss a topic we all know so well? The structure of *4 Little Girls* works against this indifference as it associates the personal stories with the larger political movement, encouraging empathy and understanding, if not outrage.

Lee's opening-credit sequences have often stood out as metanarratives that comment on the films. For example, the encapsulated African American history lesson at the beginning of *School Daze* places dilemmas inherent in black educational institutions within the context of African American history. Lee also addresses larger contemporary societal issues, such as police brutality with the inclusion of the Rodney King footage during the opening credits of *Malcolm X.* The opening sequence of *4 Little Girls* reveals the film's overall structure, which shifts between the personal history of the four families whose girls died in the bombing and the more recognizable public history of civil rights in Alabama. In doing so, Lee creates a bridge between the personal and the political in black history.

The film begins with a black-and-white tracking shot of what is revealed to be a cemetery. Joan Baez's "Birmingham Sunday" (1964), written to pay tribute to the four girls, provides the soundtrack. Images that have come to be almost instantly, perhaps naturally, tied to the Civil Rights Movement follow: Black people are attacked by police dogs and assaulted by policemen, and young children march in protest. The film reverts back to color footage of the cemetery to indicate the shift from the historical to the contemporary time period, and the camera zooms in on individual gravestones of the four girls, making the audience more than aware of how young the victims were when that bomb took their lives.

The lyrics of Baez's song introduce the viewer to the four girls. "And Addie Mae Collins, her number was one." Collins's black-and-white photograph is superimposed on the left side of her headstone, which reads, "Civil Rights Martyr Addie Mae Collins Apr. 18, 1949–Sept. 15, 1963." The film then cuts to images of anonymous youth associated with the movement. Rather than showing images of major civil-rights figures to mark the era, Lee makes this a story of everyday people caught up in the struggle. The black-and-white image of Denise McNair follows, juxtaposed, again, with her headstone. The subsequent footage focuses on children marching and school desegregation. The gravestone of the Wesley family represents Cynthia and is followed by images of black children blasted by fire hoses. Finally, Carole Rosamond Robertson's gravestone bears the dates of her short existence while the historical footage that follows becomes more specific to the topic at hand: images of the Sixteenth Street Baptist church, the funeral of three of the girls, and the mourners. These are interspersed with contemporary images of a memorial sculpture and a plaque that displays school pictures of the four girls. By juxtaposing the gravestones and photos of the young victims with the public history, *4 Little Girls* encourages the audience to meditate upon this specific tragedy within the wider context of the Civil Rights Movement and, by doing so, personalizes an era whose relevance is becoming diminished. As Lee suggests, "I want the audience, especially the parents, to think about

4 Little Girls (1997). In Memoriam.

what they might have done had their child been taken away from them like that. I want the audience to come to know and love those four little girls."[12]

This concern for its subjects and subject matter provides the emotional impact of *4 Little Girls*. It is clear that Lee was able to build trust with his subjects in the documentary that allowed him access not only to information, but also to their interior personal worlds. By introducing the viewer to the girls and their families, Lee hopes that his film will not only make them a permanent part of the audience's memory but also create a link between the past and the present. One of Lee's stated concerns is the loss of connection between African Americans and the struggles of their ancestors. Lee's secondary task is therefore to re-engage the viewer with the civil-rights past.

An example of this structure can be seen in the first segment of *4 Little Girls*. The film begins by introducing the audience to the McNair family. A jazz score by Terence Blanchard plays on the soundtrack as a yearbook opens and focuses on a college photograph of Christopher McNair. As he explains, he went to school at Tuskegee and met his wife. The shots switch between McNair and his wife, Maxine, as they discuss their courtship, marriage, and the birth of their child. Like many traditional American wives of the 1940s and '50s, what Maxine wanted in life was the American dream—a husband, a house, and children—and chose to have Denise in Birmingham to be near her mother. As Denise's parents, aunts, friends, and neighbors discuss their memories of the girl in voiceover, photos of Denise as a baby and a young girl appear on-screen. The effect of this audiovisual combination encourages audience identification with the girl.

The film fluidly moves between the personal and public history of Jim Crow by calling on the families to recall their memories of living in Alabama during the era of segregation. Chris McNair discusses how difficult it was for a black man with an education to find a job in the blue-collar town. His reminiscences are set in opposition to the comments of Circuit Court Judge Arthur Hanes Jr., who was also the defense attorney for Bob Chambliss. Hanes calls Birmingham the Magic City and describes the early 1960s as "a time of quiet, a wonderful place to live and raise a family." In the film Hanes represents the idealized, white version of the Birmingham of the past. While Hanes describes the city in voiceover, Lee ironically inserts photographs of various lynchings and KKK marches, including footage of a young child in a KKK uniform. The effect is to support McNair's observations while also questioning the validity of Hanes's comments. A larger and perhaps more compelling result of the juxtaposition is to remind viewers that historical memory is not only subjective but subject to revisions over time.

The McNair family and neighbors present a black perspective on segregated life in Alabama—for example, a neighbor of the McNairs' remembers, "It was an awful time, an awful time for young people to grow up in this city." Chris McNair describes shopping at a local store with Denise, who, after using the bathroom, smelled the onions cooking at the lunch counter and asked to have a sandwich. It can be assumed that the audience has heard the stories or seen pictures of civil-rights sit-ins at restaurants. However, this very personal story of a man having to explain segregation to his child brings home the reality of the situation to an audience who may have either become desensitized over time or may not have a true understanding of how dehumanizing or emasculating it was for a man not to have the power to give his child what she wanted. Reinforcing the depth of the hurt that this caused him, McNair explains, "That night I knew I had to tell her she couldn't have that sandwich because she was black. That couldn't have been any less painful than seeing her with a rock smashed into her head."

A similar connection with each of the girls in the film personalizes many of these well-known indignities of segregation in the South. For example, during a subsequent segment, Carole Robertson's older sister Dianne Braddock remembers going to the movies with Carole and having to sit in the segregated balcony. Braddock recalls venting her frustration by throwing ice and popcorn on the white patrons below. Dr. Freeman Hrabowski III, one of Cynthia Wesley's friends, discusses the time that Bull Conner spit on him, as well as his fear during his incarceration with the other children arrested for marching in Birmingham.

These everyday individuals are given the power as witnesses on the level of the "icons." Whereas the majority of public histories of the movement rely on the stories, testimony, or recollections of the better-known participants of the Civil Rights Movement, such as Rosa Parks or Andrew Young, the film allows these "ordinary" citizens a voice in their history. The Civil Rights Movement was always a grassroots movement; over time, the concentration on figures such as Martin Luther King Jr. has diminished the power of the movement that came in the sheer numbers of black people who sustained it. The film *4 Little Girls* balances the picture for a young, contemporary audience who, if taught about the movement in a public-education setting, is told the stories of icons and not necessarily of the power of the individual within the movement.

Ethics and Memory in *4 Little Girls*

It's not easy because we had put so much of this behind us, and we don't remember, we don't remember anymore. You know what I am saying? But you know how you felt. You may not remember details, or what step-by-step of what I had to go through. But I do know that it affected me so bad.

—Junie Collins on being asked to remember her sister Addie Mae

By choosing to make *4 Little Girls* a documentary, Lee entered a different world of filmmaking from his previous fiction projects.[13] While he made *Malcolm X* as a dramatic adaptation, based in part on others' scripts, Lee felt differently about this topic and thought, "The best treatment of the story would be to let people who were there tell it. There is no way I can write dialogue that can describe the pain of a parent losing a daughter at a young age."[14] To this end, he choose to let the subjects speak for themselves, often setting up the camera and holding the shot for long moments to capture a situation's nuances.

With the kidnapping of Africans and their loss of home, the one way to pass on stories of the past was through an oral tradition. This cultural, social, and political act is at the core of African American society and African American aesthetics. As times changed and access to education increased, some of these stories were written down to preserve them for future generations. The first-person retelling of these stories through documentary film closely replicates this form of history keeping, allowing for the continuation of this black tradition. However, the use of this filmic form brings a distinct level of responsibility to the filmmaker. The issue of film ethics takes on a new meaning when one is dealing no longer with characters, but with people. As the documentary theorist Bill Nichols suggests, "Ethical considerations attempt to minimize harmful effects. Ethics becomes a measure of the ways in which negotiations about the nature of the relationship between filmmaker and subject have consequences for subjects and viewers alike."[15] In creating the level of emotional realism for his audience, Lee had to consider the impact on the lives of those he has chosen to represent.[16] Through his decisions about what types of questions to ask (or to avoid) during the interview process, as well as his choice to shoot many interviews with long takes, Lee pushes the degree to which the film expresses the psychological reality of the families. The result is the film's emotional impact.

The interviews focusing on the aftermath of the bombing and the funerals are perhaps the most difficult to witness because family members and friends who at one point in the film joyfully remember the girls now begin to confront their painful memories. Far from his better-known and dynamic cinematography, in these scenes the camera remains static, and the image is often held for several seconds more than is comfortable to the viewer. Cynthia's sister, Shirley Wesley King, reads her mother's description of the last conversation she had with Cynthia. On the day of the bombing, Cynthia's slip was showing, and her mother made her come back inside and fix herself, telling her, "You never know how you're coming back." As she reads from her mother's memoirs, Shirley begins to cry on camera and must pause on several occasions, but the camera steadily holds its position. Lee says, "What was difficult on my part was to ask probing questions knowing that on several occasions it was going to make people break down and cry on camera."[17] He admits that he "had no qualms about keeping the camera running at intense moments. However, in respect to his subjects, he suggests that 'it was just a question of when you cut. I didn't want anyone onscreen crying for a great length of time.'"[18] The length of these scenes creates a strong sense of empathy with the families, revealing the contemporary reality of those living with this historical tragedy.

In another example, the film focuses on the aftermath of the bombing by returning to the McNairs' memories of the events. Chris McNair remembers seeing his daughter's body, and Maxine recalls going to her mother's and just crying, "hollering and screaming." Lee's use of extreme close-ups and long takes intensifies the viewer's connection with the families: The audience sees Maxine McNair relive the event on camera up close and personal. At first she cannot look at the camera; then the audience sees the pain in her tear-filled eyes and her rigid and trembling body and hears the anguish in her cracking, shaky voice. The camera zooms in slowly to a close-up as her story concludes and her emotional intensity is at a high point. Janie, Addie's sister, says that although she assumes that her parents identified the body, her older sister Junie also did, and it had a major impact on her. Lee again zooms into a close-up that reveals a numb, almost static, Junie Collins, who discusses her panic attacks since the event and reveals that she was afraid to be inside or outside, as she had assumed that the church should have been safe.

Brief still images taken of the bodies at the morgue are intercut sporadically during these interviews with the families. Lee found the photos unexpectedly at a public library in Birmingham. As he describes:

> You can't imagine what 20 sticks of dynamite can do. But when you see the results, it literally brings tears to the eyes. I have to be honest with you, I was not 100 percent sure whether I should include those shots. The postmortem photographs. But I decided I would not linger on them, it would be tasteful. They reinforce the horror and the crime that was committed.[19]

His choice to include images of the girls' mangled bodies was important because the brutality of the moment might have been lost without some sort of verification of its horrors. As Lee noted previously, the contemporary viewing audience has become desensitized to violence, as we are surrounded by it everyday through all aspects of the media.[20] Seeing these images, even for the briefest of moments, is something not easily forgotten. While he felt that it was important for the audience to see this, the decision was difficult for Lee to make, as he was primarily concerned with the impact on the victims' families.[21] Chris McNair discusses the morgue photos "as the hardest part to look at." Although he says that he understands the importance of including the images, his eyes tear up when he admits, "It wasn't a pleasant thing."[22] Clearly, the relationships that Lee created with families resulted in a level of openness and trust. This was also reciprocal, as Lee's ultimate concern for the families determined many of his choices. "I didn't care about the critics," he said, "but I wanted the participants' approval. It really mattered to me that Chris McNair and Maxine and the other parents would love the film. No one else lost their daughter when the bomb went off."[23]

As Klotman and Cutler discuss, "African American documentarians tend to express an identification with their subjects and a sense of shared concerns. [The films] illuminate communal values and subjectivities . . . the reciprocal relationship between creative agents and their subjects."[24] Three particular interactions with the parents reinforce this relationship. While learning that Carole was a part of the Girl Scouts, played clarinet, and was scheduled to perform with the school band at her first sporting event on the day after the bombing, we also experience a touching and disturbing moment when Mrs. Alpha Robertson not only shows Lee Carole's last Girl Scout sash, but also the Bible that she had with her on the day of the bombing. Mrs. Robertson states that she kept it with her for a long time. This is clearly a very personal artifact for Mrs. Robinson, something that she has kept close, not placed in some museum for the viewing public. That she shared such a personal piece of history suggests the closeness of her relationship with Lee and the sense of trust he managed to develop between his subjects and himself over the course of the shoot.

Maxine McNair shows Lee her collection of Denise's old dolls, toys, pictures, piggy banks, and school projects. She leans over and opens a red cloth that she describes as the "strange brick that penetrated her [Denise's] skull, that a friend of mine at the cemetery saved and gave to my mother, and my mother some years later gave it to me." Like the scene with Mrs. Robinson, this is something that viewers might not have witnessed had Lee not formed such a close relationship with the family. In a final interaction, Alpha Robertson says, "I worked hard not to feel anger and hatred. The hating of people wasn't going to do me any good. It would hurt me worse than it would hurt them." She does admit the reality to Lee, though, that her anger still comes out at times. These moments allow for empathy with parents who have opened the most personal and painful parts of their lives in the hope of sustaining the memories of their children.

Both Lee and Chris McNair further emphasize the importance of the reciprocal relationship between black documentarian and his subject. Lee understood that he needed to gain the trust of McNair for the project to work and for others in the Birmingham community to open up and trust him. McNair stated:

> During the process I had the chance to evaluate him, to find out what his philosophy was. I trusted his ability because I knew he took that very, very, very seriously. But I wanted to know about his [dedication to] accuracy. . . . Thank God for Spike Lee, whom I could trust to do this.[25]

The film *4 Little Girls* was a result of this collaboration. McNair's trust provided Lee with the keys to the doors of the families and friends on whom this incident had an impact. In turn, the contemporary viewing audience is given access to this painful but historically critical moment in black history.

In comparison with his treatment of the families of the victims are Spike Lee's ethical decisions about the interview with George Wallace, former governor of Alabama. Lee was at first surprised that Wallace agreed to the interview, but the director believed that Wallace and his advisers were "trying to do some revisionist shenanigans, trying to undo some stuff that he did in the past which was responsible for people dying."[26] Wallace is introduced to the audience with the historical footage of his infamous gubernatorial inaugural speech of 1963 in which he declared, "Segregation now, segregation tomorrow, and segregation forever." Wallace used his opposition to integration as the cornerstone of his political platform, and the image of Wallace symbolically standing in the door of the University of Alabama to prevent integration is an iconic image of the civil-rights era.

The film cuts between historical footage of Wallace and interviews with local black citizens who comment on his role in Alabama. One man claims that "George Wallace was the cause of many peoples' deaths and certainly much suffering." Another states, "George Wallace was a dynamic expression of the mental derangement of white people." The film immediately cuts to an extreme close-up of a present day Wallace, whose image is somewhat blurred. This is followed by a black-and-white image of Wallace, from the 1960s, in a similar close-up. The voiceover continues, "In that people who are afraid of change. . . . George Wallace expressed that mental illness, he was the best in the business." The editing of this sequence calls on the audience to interrogate these images and voiceover, which go far to suggest Wallace's "mental derangement."

News footage of Wallace's speech at the University of Alabama follow, then the film returns to the contemporary image of Wallace at his desk, reading a typed question from Lee. In his now stilted speech (the film is subtitled because Wallace was suffering from Parkinson's disease at the time of the shoot), he explains that segregation was all that he knew and that he had understood that it was the best for both races. Wallace clearly wants the audience to believe that he is not racist, and he resorts to clichés when he says that his best friend is black: "Over there is my black friend." Wallace says that this friend, Eddie Holcey, went all over the world with him, and he gestures to the individual to come onto camera. Holcey is actually the nurse who had taken care of Wallace over the years. Ed, as Wallace refers to his aide, looks incredibly uncomfortable in front of the camera.

> When he calls him over . . . we were all amazed. I was biting my lip to keep from laughing. When you watch the film, you should watch [Holcey's] face. He was really being put on the spot. That's what makes the scene poignant—that he is being led out like he is in a circus.[27]

This scene is followed by historical footage that clearly overrides the contemporary Wallace's claims. For example, it shows Wallace as he makes his stand at the University of Alabama. This juxtaposition reminds the viewer of the many black domestics who toiled to provide care for white families. Many of those same white people, who often referred to their black employees as one of the family, albeit a subjugated member of the family, worked to uphold Jim Crow and keep black people repressed in the South.

As the families continue to comment on Wallace, he appears in a medium shot so we can see him behind his desk with a nameplate identifying him as "George C. Wallace, Governor," in the foreground and the state seal of Alabama hanging on a wall in the background. At this point, the film cuts between black-and-white and color footage in these images of the contemporary Wallace, a distinct difference in style from the film's more common use of black-and-white and color to demarcate a change between past and present. The blending of footage in this scene acts as a metacommentary by suggesting a lack of change in Wallace's character, despite the effects of Parkinson's disease and his paralysis from a 1972 assassination attempt.

The segment concludes as Wallace again calls on Holcey as visual proof of his nonracist ways. But the structure of the scene suggests that Holcey is actually proof of everything Wallace represents: He calls this man his best friend, but Holcey is clearly in a position of servitude. He stands in the far-left corner, off-screen at first; is dressed casually; and cares for Wallace's physical needs (almost like a modern-day mammy). Holcey's clear discomfort is evidence of his awareness of being used by Wallace as visible evidence of the man's supposedly changed relationship with black people. That Wallace perceives or claims that his relationship with Holcey is one of friendship instead of a working relationship reinforces the old white myth that the black caretaker's relationship with the white employer is more important to him or her than the needs of his or her own family.

As Lee remembers, "He called Eddie twice in front of the camera to show his love for black people. You saw his face. I felt sorry pulling him into this."[28] Clearly, Lee's subjectivity is visible in this moment. While particularly careful about his treatment of his African American interviewees, he leaves an obviously uncomfortable Holcey in the film. However, his decision to shoot the interview in this manner goes far to reinforce Wallace's continued legacy of bigotry.

Conclusion

The FBI reopened its investigation of the bombing in 1993 after meeting with local Birmingham black leaders and ironically made the official announcement in July 1997, a month following the release of 4 Little Girls. Herman Frank Cash, one of the accused, died in 1994 before charges could be brought against him, but in May 2000 both Bobby Frank Cherry and Thomas E. Blanton surrendered after murder indictments were handed down by a grand jury in Alabama. Blanton was convicted in May 2001 and sentenced to life in prison.[29] Cherry went to trial and was convicted and sentenced to life a year later.[30]

In 1996, civil-rights leaders and ministers met with Attorney General Janet Reno to discuss the spate of church fires that had occurred in Southern, primarily black, churches over the previous year and half. Believing that these were racially based, the group requested federal protection for the churches and more deliberate investigation into the fires. As a result, the National Arson Taskforce was created in June 1996.[31] The inclusion of footage of these contemporary fires at the conclusion of *4 Little Girls* reminds the viewer that racial hostility is far from over within this country and that forgetting is not an option.

Lee's *4 Little Girls* illustrates that it is the responsibility of all to keep these memories alive—not to engender bitterness, but to honor those who paved the way for black progress. Black political, social, and economic success, while certainly viable, is still a struggle, and the conservative politics of the country constantly attempt to reverse the advances made by our predecessors. We must not allow ourselves to be lulled into the belief that racism is a thing of the past. While acts of racism may not appear as frequent or as visceral as those in Birmingham during the 1960s, racism continues to exist. It has just taken on a different but still insidious visage, the fact of which *4 Little Girls* seeks to remind us and a point that is reinforced by *When the Levees Broke: A Requiem in Four Acts* (2006), Lee's Home Box Office (HBO) documentary project. Through an impressive collection of interviews with the everyday citizens of New Orleans, victims of Hurricane Katrina and the Federal Emergency Management Agency (FEMA), politicians, artists, news reporters, and cultural critics, Lee again interweaves tales of the personal and the political, reminding the viewer that issues of race and class still matter in this country.

NOTES

Epigraph: Ralph Ellison, *Shadow and Act* (New York: Vintage International, 1995).

1. For information on the bombing of the Sixteenth Street Baptist church, see Taylor Branch, *Parting the Waters: America in the King Years 1954–1963* (New York: Simon and Schuster, 1989); Diane McWhorter, *Carry Me Home: Birmingham, Alabama, the Climactic Battle of the Civil Rights Revolution.* (New York: Simon and Schuster, 2001).

2. Dan T. Carter, *The Politics of Rage: George Wallace, the Origins of the New Conservatism and the Transformation of American Politics* (New York: Simon and Schuster, 1995), 115.

3. For information on the Chambliss case, see McWhorter, *Carry Me Home.*

4. Michael Omi and Howard Winant, *Racial Formation in the United States* (New York: Routledge, 1994), 53–76.

5. *A Day at Tuskegee* was commissioned by Booker T. Washington and shot by George W. Broome. *The Negro Soldier* is not normally considered an African American film, yet its script was written by Carlton Moss, perhaps better known for his role in Oscar Micheaux's *Harlem after Midnight* (1934). Parts I and II of *Eyes on the Prize* were produced by Henry Hampton's Blackside Inc., one of the oldest minority-owned production companies in the country (est. 1968).

6. Phyllis R. Klotman and Janet K. Cutler, *Struggles for Representation: African American Documentary Film and Video* (Bloomington: Indiana University Press, 1999), xvii.

7. Henry Cabot Beck, "Edgy Spike Lee Shifts Gears to the Factual," *St. Louis Post Dispatch, Everyday Magazine*, July 13, 1997, 3C.

8. Bruce Kirkland, "Dad Watches over *4 Little Girls*," *Toronto Sun*, March 12, 1998, 56.

9. Peter Howell, "Spike Lee's Learning How to Listen," *Toronto Star*, September 12, 1997, D3.

10. Denene Millner, "A New Documentary Finally Puts a Face on the Racial Terrorism That Claimed the Lives of Four Little Girls," *New York Daily News, Sunday Extra*, July 13, 1997, 2.

11. Lee, quoted in ibid., 2.

12. Ibid.

13. The director subsequently made other documentaries, most of them, like *4 Little Girls*, in collaboration with HBO Films. Other titles include *A Huey P. Newton Story* (2001), *Jim Brown: All American* (2002), and, most recently, *When the Levees Broke: A Requiem in Four Acts* (2006), about Hurricane Katrina and its aftermath in New Orleans. Lee also directed *Freak* (1998), a performance film starring John Leguizamo, for the network.

14. Lee, quoted in Ruthe Stein, "Lee Explores Lingering Grief from Killing of '4 Girls,'" *San Francisco Chronicle*, October 7, 1997, B1. This was also the first time that Lee worked with the HBO cable network.

15. Bill Nichols, *Introduction to Documentary* (Bloomington: Indiana University Press, 2001).

16. In *Introduction to Documentary*, Nichols suggests that documentary films are built around different elements of realism, two of which are emotional and psychological realism. Emotional realism deals with the impact on the viewer, while psychological realism deals with how the film represents the emotional world of the subject of the film.

17. Spike Lee, "Special Features: Making the Documentary," *4 Little Girls*, dir. and prod. Spike Lee (40 Acres & A Mule, 1997), 102 min., DVD.

18. Lee, quoted in Stein, "Lee Explores Lingering Grief."

19. Brandon Jundell, "An Interview with Spike Lee, Director of '4 Little Girls,'" IndieWire: People Archives, 1997, available online at http://www.indiewire.com/people/int_Lee_Spike_971212.html.

20. Two years earlier, Lee had explored the issue of audience desensitization to violence in the opening sequence of *Clockers*, which includes reenacted images of actual crime scenes. The images self-consciously reminded viewers of the voyeuristic pleasure attached to violent spectacle, a pleasure often used by films focusing on inner-city youth and black-on-black violence. For more on *Clockers*, see Keith M. Harris "*Clockers*

(Spike Lee 1995): Adaptation in Black," in this volume, and Paula J. Massood, *Black City Cinema: African American Urban Experiences in Film* (Philadelphia: Temple University Press, 2003), 175–205.

21. Lee, "Special Features."

22. Ibid.

23. Steve Murray, "Movies: Time Is Finally Right to Revisit the Bombing," *Atlanta Journal and Constitution*, October 24, 1997, 10P.

24. Klotman and Cutler, *Struggles for Representation*, xix.

25. Kirkland, "Dad Watches over *4 Little Girls*," 56.

26. Stein, "Lee Explores Lingering Grief," B1

27. Ibid.

28. Lee, quoted in Marty Rosen, "Film's techniques Evoke Emotions, Controversy," *St. Petersburg Times*, February 23, 1998, 2B.

29. Angie Cannon, "Church Bomber's Conviction May Aid Other Cases." *U.S. News and World Report*, May 14, 2001, 24.

30. Ellie Cose, "A Reckoning in Birmingham," *Newsweek*, June 3, 2002, 31.

31. Tom Morganthou, "Fires in the Night," *Newsweek*, June 24, 1996, 28.

12

KRIN GABBARD

Spike Lee Meets Aaron Copland

At the beginning of *He Got Game* (1998), written and directed by Spike Lee, the credit sequence contains an unusual juxtaposition. In consecutive title cards the American composer Aaron Copland (1900–90) is credited with "Music," and the rap group Public Enemy is listed for "Songs." These credits link a composer widely associated, perhaps inaccurately, with the American heartland to an urban, highly political rap group. A correspondingly diverse set of images appears behind the credit sequence. Usually in balletic slow motion, young Americans play basketball in a variety of locations, including pastoral landscapes in the Midwest and concrete playgrounds in the inner city. Behind the title card with Copland's name a young black man dribbles a ball along the Brooklyn Bridge, perhaps an acknowledgment that both Copland and Spike Lee grew up in Brooklyn and that they may have more in common than audiences expect. Throughout the credit sequence the audience hears the steel-driving clangor of Copland's *John Henry*. Although this composition is among Copland's more dissonant works, it has an appropriately portentous quality, not unlike the beginnings of many big-budget American films. Copland in fact specialized in the auspicious, often opening his compositions with grand gestures, even fanfares. He was also familiar with the conventions of film music. He wrote the soundtrack score for

Krin Gabbard, "Spike Lee Meets Aaron Copland," in *Black Magic: White Hollywood and African American Culture* (New Brunswick, N.J.: Rutgers University Press, 2004). Reprinted with permission of Rutgers University Press.

Of Mice and Men (1939), *Our Town* (1940), and *The Red Pony* (1949), as well as for a few short films, and his score for *The Heiress* (1949) won an Academy Award. Portions of the soundtrack music for *Our Town* can even be heard in *He Got Game*.[1]

He Got Game takes place during the few days when Jesus Shuttlesworth (Ray Allen) must decide where he will attend college. The most sought-after high school basketball player in the nation, Jesus is recruited by a large group of college coaches, many of whom appear as themselves in the film. Even his girlfriend, Lala (Rosario Dawson), is involved with an agent who wants to profit from Jesus's decision. Jesus's father, Jake Shuttlesworth (Denzel Washington), is in a state penitentiary serving a long prison sentence for killing his wife in an incident of domestic violence when Jesus and his sister, Mary (Zelda Harris), were children. The warden (Ned Beatty) tells Jake that the governor, who is a graduate of "Big State," wants Jesus to play basketball at his alma mater and that Jake may have his sentence reduced if he can convince Jesus to attend Big State. Carefully watched over by prison guards in civilian clothes, Jake is taken to a sleazy motel on Coney Island where he must overcome the enduring bitterness of a son who still blames him for the death of a beloved mother. At the motel Jake becomes involved with Dakota (Milla Jovovich), a prostitute who returns to her home in the Midwest after she makes love to Jake. At the climax of the film, Jake challenges Jesus to a game of one-on-one basketball, telling Jesus that he will permanently stay out of Jesus's life if he loses. If Jake wins, the son must sign the letter of intent for Big State that Jake carries with him. Jake loses the game and is taken back to prison, but the next day Jesus announces at a press conference that he will attend Big State. The warden, however, tells Jake that since he did not actually get Jesus's signature on the letter of intent, the governor may not honor his promise to reduce Jake's sentence.

With its multicultural cast of basketball players, including young white women as well as African American men, the opening sequence of *He Got Game* does not actually racialize the music of Copland, in spite of the fact that the legendary John Henry was black. But about ten minutes into the film, after the principal characters have been introduced, Spike Lee is more didactic in mixing Copland's music with images on the screen. When a group of black youths arrive on a court at night and begin a vigorous game of full-court basketball, the soundtrack music is "Hoe-Down," the final movement of Copland's 1942 ballet *Rodeo*. Spike Lee has made a powerful statement by combining images of young black men playing basketball with music written by the one composer in the classical tradition considered by many to be "the most American." Writing in the *New York Times* in anticipation of the centennial of Copland's birth, Anthony Tommasini referred to the composer as

"Mr. Musical Americana" (Tommasini 1999: 2:1). Copland's music, especially a composition as robust as "Hoe-Down," can signify the American spirit
at its most positive. Wit, energy, spontaneity, romance, bravado, optimism,
and grace all seem to emanate from the music, as if Copland's dancing cowboys transparently express the soul of the American people. These kinds of
associations have more to do with the reception of Copland's music than with
anything intrinsic to it, but Spike Lee has made the most of commonly accepted associations by linking "Hoe-Down" with exuberant young black men
on a basketball court. In a move that would have pleased Ralph Ellison, Lee
may be asserting that these African American youths are as uniquely and
thoroughly American as anything that Copland's ballet music might signify.
For Ellison, African Americans are most themselves when they improvise and
play changes on the bricolage of American culture. And Lee has said, "When
I listen to Aaron Copland's music, I hear America, and basketball is America"
(Sterritt 1998: 15). But just as Lee has made the obvious statement—all
African Americans are American—he is also stating the inverse—all Americans are African American. Like Ellison before him, who said that being truly
American means being somehow black, Lee has made his assertion knowing
that many white Americans cannot accept it. So long as this remains the case,
even flawed films such as *He Got Game* deserve our attention.

The Invisible Signifier

In his choice of Aaron Copland, Spike Lee may also have sought to reverse
the familiar Hollywood practice of using the invisible and "inaudible" sounds
of black music to accompany the actions of white people (Gorbman 1987:
73). As composers of film music frequently point out, if audiences listen too
closely to the background score, something has gone wrong. The most successful composers find subtle ways to supplement the action on the screen,
often playing to cultural assumptions of which audiences are scarcely aware,
certainly not while the film narrative is in full gear. This convention is at its
most benign when an unseen African American singer provides a romantic atmosphere for white lovers. Clint Eastwood has made broad use of this practice in *Play Misty for Me* (1971) and *The Bridges of Madison County* (1995).
So have the people who made *Next Stop Wonderland* (1998), *The Talented
Mr. Ripley* (1999), and *The Green Mile* (1999). To cite one more example
among many, in *Groundhog Day* (1997), Bill Murray romances Andie Mac-
Dowell in a small-town location that includes virtually no black people even
though at the most romantic moments the soundtrack includes Ray Charles
singing "You Don't Know Me" and Nat King Cole crooning "Almost Like Being in Love."

In a more sinister use of the voices of blacks to signify something other than black subjects, a film will make a menacing group of youths seem even more menacing by playing rap music on the soundtrack even if all the youths are white. Andrew Ross has pointed out that in *Batman* (1989) the Joker is played in whiteface by the white, middle-aged Jack Nicholson, but that the character arouses white anxieties about black youths by speaking in rappish rhymes and spray-painting graffiti on famous paintings in a museum while prancing to the funk of Prince (Ross 1990: 31). In all of these films, music says what the filmmakers are unwilling or afraid to say with images. While Eastwood and the makers of films such as *Groundhog Day* engage in "permissible racism" by benignly associating African American artists with intensified romance and sexuality, the singers are acknowledged only in the end credits, their black bodies kept off screen in order to maintain the centrality of white characters. In *Batman,* director Tim Burton and his collaborators have avoided charges of overt racism by *not* showing black hooligans on the screen, but they have made the Joker more threatening by linking him to African American musical performances that scare the hell out of many white Americans.

In *He Got Game,* Spike Lee has turned these conventions upside down. Instead of using black music as a supplement for white characters on the screen, Lee allows the music of a white composer to enhance the playfulness, grace, and masculinity of black youths on the basketball court. Lee may even have supposed that the early scene with "Hoe-Down" would be widely excerpted outside of its original context. Even for those who do not know the plot of the film or the identity of the ballplayers, the meaning of the scene is clear. When I presented a shorter, spoken version of this essay, I made the case for Lee's reversal of standard Hollywood practice most forcefully by showing that scene. There are surely any number of academic presentations on Lee, Copland, and/or film music that have made or will make use of the same scene. By simply bleeping out the one use of the word "shit" on the soundtrack, the clip could even be a useful teaching tool in a grade-school music appreciation class. This would bring the music of Copland home to a generation of American students more in touch with black urban culture than ever before. But even this scene must be understood in the larger context of *He Got Game,* of Spike Lee's other films, and of Aaron Copland's career. By combining the music of Copland with images that do not immediately appear apposite, Lee has made viewers think about new sets of associations. By tracing out an even larger group of associations, this chapter is in effect continuing the work of the film. Ultimately, I have little interest in what Spike Lee actually knows about Aaron Copland. I care more about how racial, sexual, political, and musical discourses play off one another in and around *He Got Game.*

Constructing America

As the theorists of postmodernism have argued, sounds and images do not adhere to grand narratives but circulate freely among systems of meaning that
escape the conventional boundaries of academic disciplines. And as the new
musicology has taught us, musical meaning has as much to do with listening
communities as it does with well-established attempts to "anchor" it in reas-
suring discourses.[2] Spike Lee has made several attempts to anchor the compositions of Copland to specific meanings at crucial moments in *He Got
Game*, often lifting music out of a more familiar context so that it can signify
in new ways. In the "Hoe-Down" sequence, however, Lee follows traditional
practice and casts Copland as an "American" composer in the most positive
and unproblematic sense. But Copland's identity as Mr. Musical Americana
becomes highly problematic if we examine his own story.

Copland did in fact seek new ways of creating a music that was recogniz-
ably American, even in his earliest works. Rejecting many of the Eurocentric
elements in American classical music, Copland paid special attention to
American folk melodies and quoted them in his compositions without irony
or patronizing gestures.[3] He also found tonalities that gave his music a spacious, uplifting quality that is today considered "American" even if the same
chords that seem to symbolize the wide-open plains of the American country-
side can have different meanings in other contexts.[4] Copland's Jewish roots
have also been connected to passages in his music, as when Howard Pollack
suggests that a central motive in *Piano Concerto* of 1926 hint at "the calls of
the shofar" (Pollack 1999: 522).

But if Copland intended his music to represent the essence of America,
he did so in a spirit that was by no means blandly jingoistic. Especially in the
1930s his politics were well left of center, leading him at one point to write
what he called "my communist song," a setting for a Marxist lyric by Alfred
Hayes (Pollack 1999: 276). Although he never joined the Communist Party,
his 1934 song "Into the Streets May 1st" won the prize in a competition spon-
sored by *New Masses,* a prominent magazine for "the proletarian avant-garde"
(Denning 1997:140). In writing this music, Copland succeeded by combining a musical style that might be called "revolutionary" with an appeal to mass
taste (Pollack 1999: 276). Copland later disavowed the song, but its composition foreshadowed certain stylistic aspects of *Fanfare for the Common Man*
(1942). Although *Fanfare* was written to bolster the morale of Americans in
the early stages of World War II, and although by the end of the millennium
the piece was being used in television commercials for the U.S. Marine
Corps, the music must also be regarded as a powerful statement of the composer's leftist sentiments. Pollack suggests that even Copland's invocations of

Abraham Lincoln, Billy the Kid, and John Henry can be understood alongside the Communist Party leader Earl Browder's efforts to bring ultranationalist sentiments into the party's rhetoric (Pollack 1999: 279).[5]

Nor should Copland's homosexuality be overlooked in the consideration of a music that has been characterized as "manly" as well as American. Keep in mind that the sounds of *Rodeo* and *Billy the Kid* that wash over the robustly masculine bodies in *He Got Game* were written for the ballet. Compared to the black athletes in Lee's film, the actual dancers who have performed these ballets look like gay men in cowboy drag, which in many cases they are. Indeed, as Susan McClary instructed Robert K. Schwartz when he wrote his article about the sexuality of male composers, "The straight boys claimed the moral high ground of modernism and fled to the universities, and the queers literally took center stage in concert halls and opera houses and ballet, all of which are musics that people are more likely to respond to." As a gay man, Copland was surely fascinated by men who performed their masculinity in the dance, the cinema, and the opera, and he wrote memorable music for all of these genres. Pollack even suspects that there are homosexual subtexts to much of Copland's work:

> This would include the macabre eroticism of *Grohg*, the portrait of a rebel in *Billy the Kid*, the acceptance of difference in *The Second Hurricane*, and the male bonding in *Of Mice and Men* and *The Tender Land*. Moreover, *Rodeo*, *The Heiress*, *The Tender Land*, and *Something Wild*, all of which concern a young woman's sexual and emotional self-discovery, could be seen as "coming out" tales of one kind or another. (Pollack 1999: 526)

Of course, it is also possible to hear much of this same music as a "beard" to help Copland survive in a culture where Jews and homosexuals often have to pass for heterosexual gentiles. Regardless, in finding musical codes to express masculinity and heterosexual romance, Copland was demonstrating that he, like innumerable other gay composers, filmmakers, and performers, was highly sensitive to the performative nature of sexuality and gender.

Not every critic was comfortable associating a gay Jewish leftist from Brooklyn with the most basic sounds of America. A variety of writers have denounced Copland's attempts to create a uniquely American classical music. Many of these attacks were un-selfconsciously anti-Semitic, such as the statement by E. B. Hill that in his *Music for the Theatre* (1925) Copland was guilty of "the usual clever Hebraic assimilation of the worst features of polytonalité" (Oja 1990: 335). Perhaps the most vicious assault on Copland came from the Jewish writer/composer Lazare Saminsky, who wrote in 1949 that

Copland possessed "a small, cool creative gift, but an ego of much frenetic drive, a devious personality with a feline *savoir faire,* with his fine commercial acumen and acute sense of the direction of today's wind" (Pollack 1999: 520).

Half a century after these attacks, the music of Copland has won the admiration of a sufficient number of critics to overcome the old slurs on his politics, ethnicity, and sexuality. More significantly, he influenced a large contingent of younger composers who understood his ability to capture what could pass for the authentic American vernacular. If Copland is considered today to be the most American of American composers, it is primarily because so many other writers of music felt his influence in this way. In fact, even the less positive aspects of Copland's compositions have been conceptualized as *echt* Americana. Wilfrid Mellers has said that Copland's "fragmentary, cubistlike forms and the static, nonmodulatory harmonies" represent "uprootedness and disintegration, reflective of American alienation" (Pollack 1999: 529). It may have been these aspects of Copland's music that inspired Spike Lee to use the opening, conflicted section of *Billy the Kid,* the ominous *Orchestral Variations,* and the less celebratory portions of *Lincoln Portrait* for a story about the tensions between a father serving a long prison sentence and a son in constant danger of being used up and tossed aside by a culture that values him only as a commodity.

Corporate Populism or Revolutionary Art?

Spike Lee's choice of Copland's music for a film about black basketball players might seem surprising in the light of perceptions about the director's politics. Lee is known as the director of *Malcolm X* (1992), a biopic of the black Muslim leader, and *Get on the Bus* (1996), a film about black men journeying to hear Louis Farrakhan at the Million Man March of 1995. Lee ends all his films with Malcolm X's phrase, "By any means necessary." *Do the Right Thing* (1989), which inspired some white commentators to charge Lee with inciting racial violence, is surely the most controversial film that Lee has made to date. That film paid close attention to the only surviving photograph of Malcolm X with Martin Luther King Jr. In most discussions of identity politics, King is associated with the hope that black Americans can survive comfortably within the American mainstream, while Malcolm X represents the nationalist view that African Americans must survive on their own apart from white America. At the end of *Do the Right Thing,* Lee ran two quotations, one from King and one from Malcolm X. King's eloquent endorsement of nonviolence is *followed* by Malcolm's powerful defense of violence in self-defense, suggesting to some that Lee was endorsing Malcolm's statement. The fact that Lee ends his films with a quotation from Malcolm and that he made a film about Malcolm and not about King also suggests that Lee is more comfortable with the nationalist sentiments of Malcolm.

But many critics found Lee's *Malcolm X* to be a conventionally bland Hollywood biography. Amiri Baraka denounced Lee as the "quintessential buppie" who brought his own "petit bourgeois values" into the film (Baraka 1993:146). And it is surely significant that Smiley, the character in *Do the Right Thing* who constantly holds up the photograph of the two black leaders, can barely speak because of a severe stutter. The film's regular association of Smiley with the photograph may represent the inability of Lee or anyone else to articulate a satisfying synthesis of what the two extraordinary black men had to say.

The release of *Do the Right Thing* also inspired Jerome Christensen to charge that Spike Lee was a "corporate populist," more interested in selling the Nike Corporation's Air Jordan sneakers than in making politically responsible films (Christensen 1991). The same charge could be aimed at *He Got Game,* especially when Jake Shuttlesworth expresses great delight as he purchases a pair of "the new Jordans" shortly after his temporary release from prison. Throughout the 1990s, Spike Lee and Michael Jordan were the two public figures most associated with Nike sports shoes. Lee directed television commercials for Nike that featured Jordan, and Jordan himself appears in *He Got Game*. In fact, Jordan can be seen in the film twice, once in a brief clip when he utters the three-word title of the film and again as the subject of a heroic statue in front of the United Center in Chicago that appears in the opening credit sequence. In the statue, Jordan strikes the same pose that appears as an icon on Nike products.

Even the use of Copland's music in *He Got Game* can be interpreted as a corporate maneuver, since Copland is a great deal more accessible than any number of composers who could have been arrogated by Lee to signify American values. Although George Gershwin might have been even more accessible, Lee probably did not choose him because Gershwin was too implicated in the old game of "love and theft" with which whites have approached black culture. Furthermore, Woody Allen had already made extravagant use of Gershwin's music in *Manhattan* (1979). Lee certainly could have made a more daring choice than Copland if he had used the music of, say, Charles Ives. Once Copland's music was chosen, however, many of his recordings heard in the film were issued on the CBS/Sony label and made available for purchase on the CD *He Got Game: Spike Lee Presents the Music of Aaron Copland* (Sony Classical SK 60593). *Elvira Madigan* (1967) sold a Mozart piano concerto, *Ordinary People* (1980) sold Pachelbel's *Canon,* and *Platoon* (1986) sold Samuel Barber's *Adagio for Strings*. Why should *He Got Game* not sell *Rodeo* and *John Henry*? Lee surely knew that CDs with music from a film

could be as financially remunerative as the film itself, even if Lee's Copland
CD would probably enrich the music publisher Boosey and Hawkes and the
Copland estate more than it would the filmmaker.

But the charge that Lee is merely a shill for corporations such as Nike and
Sony must be considered alongside the film industry's commitment to corporate advertising that virtually began with the birth of the American cinema
(Hansen 1990: 51–71). For an artist to survive today in *any* marketplace without some connection to corporate interests is scarcely possible. Todd Boyd
compares Lee to Charles Barkley, who appeared in *He Got Game* prior to his
retirement from professional basketball in 1999. Aggressive and voluble both
on the court and off, Barkley was fond of making statements such as, "I'm a
'90s nigga. . . . I told you white boys you've never heard of a '90s nigga. We do
what we want to" (Boyd 1997: 132). Writing about Spike Lee, Boyd says,
"Lee's presence is quite like that of Barkley, a compromised image of Blackness for mass consumption in return for the financial power to challenge the
racial status quo elsewhere" (Boyd 1997: 138). W. J. T. Mitchell has even
suggested that *Do the Right Thing* can be read as a *critique* of corporate populism, in which "no utopian public image or monument is available to symbolize collective aspirations" and in which purchasing a pair of sneakers is,
sadly, among the few ways for dispossessed individuals to find a sense of personal identity (Mitchell 1997: 124).

In *He Got Game,* Jesus has no mother, does not trust his father, and is beset by predatory individuals who have little concern for him as a person. He
can rely on no stable institution or, in Mitchell's words, "a monument" to
make sense of his predicament. Instead he must contend with a cast of self-
interested characters that includes his girlfriend, his uncle, his high school
coach, a sleazy agent, college coaches, the media, and promiscuous white coeds, not to mention the governor of New York. Even his little sister tells Jesus
that she hopes his money will buy them a home on Long Island so that she
can leave the projects of Coney Island. Other than his cousin, the only character who does not seek a profit from Jesus and seems genuinely concerned
about his welfare is "Big Time Willie," a local godfather who drives a red Mer-
cedes and claims to have put the word out on the street that Jesus must be left
alone. Willie warns Jesus about drugs, alcohol, and the HIV-infected women
who lie in wait for him and cautions the young man about the ballplayers who
thought they could "make it out of Coney Island" but "didn't amount to shit."
Jesus smiles when he corrects Willie by naming Stephon Marbury, even
though he is the only athlete he can identify who provides a valid role model.

The mention of Marbury, the high-scoring National Basketball Association (NBA) point guard who, like the fictional Jesus Shuttlesworth, played for
the Lincoln High School Rail-Splitters on Coney Island, is one entry in a virtual

encyclopedia of basketball lore that runs through the film. The familiar faces of Dean Smith, Lute Olson, John Chaney, John Thompson, Nolan Richardson, Rick Pitino, Reggie Miller, Charles Barkley, Bill Walton, Shaquille O'Neal, and of course Michael Jordan all appear in *He Got Game*. Lee even stops the progress of his plot to let high school players speak directly to the camera about what the game means to them. There is a sense of pride and possibility in this early sequence when the five young men on the championship high school team talk about the game. Jesus, for example, says that for him "basketball is like poetry in motion." We later learn that Jesus Shuttlesworth was not named for the biblical character but for Earl Monroe, whose nickname was "Jesus" when he played in Philadelphia prior to becoming a star with the New York Knicks. When Jake tells Jesus about the origins of his name, he points out that the press referred to Monroe as "Black Jesus," but that the people in Philadelphia simply called him "Jesus." The discourses of big-time athletics can be meaningful to marginalized groups and, as Boyd powerfully argues, they can provide sites of resistance to dominant culture. Stanley Crouch has even suggested that "the game of basketball is Negro history itself, a thing of inspiration and horror, magic and disillusionment, compassion and sadism. . . . Discipline, wariness, compassion, and good judgment are of absolute importance" (Crouch 1999: 257).

It is significant that Big Time Willie, who speaks so compellingly of the dangers that Jesus faces, is played by Roger Guenveur Smith, the same actor who played the stuttering Smiley in *Do the Right Thing* and who has appeared in most of Lee's films. A character who is basically incoherent in one film can be uniquely articulate in another. Hollywood films rarely dramatize the conflicts faced by a young black man, especially one like Jesus Shuttlesworth who is portrayed as largely instinctual and unreflective. In many ways, he recalls Ellison's Invisible Man, who learns little as he tries to find his way in a culture of predators until wisdom comes as "I began to accept my past" (Ellison 1972 [1952]: 496). Jesus cannot speak with the eloquence of the Invisible Man, but he, too, finally learns to accept his past and reconciles with his father.

If we look for a political statement in a film such as *He Got Game,* we must find it within the complex web of achievement and co-optation that surrounds Lee's characters. Victoria A. Johnson has written:

> Lee's "politicized" voice is most conflicted . . . as his films grant expression to the voices that are typically marginalized in relation to the mainstream, only for those oppositions to be subsumed by larger commodification practices that recoup them for popular sale as black history and politics. Perhaps in spite of themselves, however, Lee's

films may represent a provocative, positive fusion of a prolific, chameleon-like visual-aural aesthetic—a fusion that incorporates diverse youth concerns (in terms of response rather than generational affiliation) and plays with spectator activity and popular knowledge in an unprecedented fashion. (Johnson 1997: 70)

He Got Game exposes the predicament of Jesus Shuttlesworth, who would seem to be among the most successful members of black youth culture. The film regularly contrasts Jesus's anxieties with the popular media's upbeat view of college athletics, embodied most memorably in the manic figure of Dick Vitale, the sportscaster and former college coach who is even more over the top than usual in his brief appearance in *He Got Game*. A fictional character standing in apposition to Vitale is John Turturro's Billy Sunday, the coach at "Tech U" who tries to recruit Jesus with rhetoric more reminiscent of his namesake than of a basketball coach. Chick (Rick Fox), the college player who is escorting Jesus on his campus tour, smirks at Jesus during Sunday's speech. Like Smiley, Radio Raheem, and many other characters in Lee's films, the black athletes must find alternative means to speak their minds.

Nevertheless, for all its celebration of the game and its flamboyant personalities, *He Got Game* does not hold out much hope for Jesus Shuttlesworth. As Big Time Willie persuasively argues, and as the film continually demonstrates, Jesus is entering a cutthroat world of agents, coaches, and hangers-on. Any number of mishaps can quickly end his career, even before he arrives in the NBA. As many have pointed out, an African American male has a better chance of becoming a successful doctor or lawyer than of playing in the NBA. The film is much more about the oedipal reconciliation between father and son than about a young man's rise to success in professional athletics.

Intertexts, Oedipal and Otherwise

Even if Spike Lee is not entirely devoted to reaping the corporate benefits of his interventions, he cannot be expected to survive in the American film industry without making some accommodations with global capital. Nevertheless, he has consistently taken chances in his films, and he is not afraid to experiment at the edges of the Hollywood style. The visual feel of *He Got Game* is in many ways as experimental as its soundtrack. Lee takes chances with different types of film stock and with flashes of light throughout the film, and he presents the opening moments of his film in staggered sequence, jumping back and forth between Jake's first conversation with the warden and the events leading to his arrival at the motel on Coney Island. But there are other aspects to *He Got Game* that cannot be ignored once we acknowledge that the presence of Copland's music opens up a number of intertexts. I have already mentioned the montage of white and black ballplayers that the credit sequence links to Copland's *John Henry*. Although the lyrics for the tune reproduced in Copland's music tell the story of a black man, Lee associates the legendary steel-driver with both black and white athletes.

Later, in the scene in which Jesus hears the appeal of Coach Billy Sunday at Tech U, the young athlete is exposed to an elaborate video played over the gymnasium's huge monitors and public address system. Although it features Copland's much honored *Fanfare for the Common Man,* the video primarily reflects the histrionic religiosity of Coach Sunday. Playing with the connotations of the name Jesus, the video includes bits of footage from George Stevens's kitsch epic *The Greatest Story Ever Told* (1965). In the fast montage of images, we even see a mock cover of *Sports Illustrated* in which Jesus poses on a cross wearing his basketball uniform and a crown of thorns. Lee has made Copland's music part of a postmodern pastiche, deflating the auspicious sounds associated nowadays with individuals and institutions more well heeled than the average "common man." *Fanfare for the Common Man* has been recruited, after all, for bombastic purposes by the Rolling Stones; Woody Herman's New Thundering Herd; Emerson, Lake, and Palmer; Elvis Presley; and Grand Funk Railroad, not to mention the producers of numerous television news programs. The popular media's transformations of *Fanfare* constitute a set of intertexts that Lee happily acknowledges at the same time that he treats the rest of Copland's music without irony.

But Lee may not have intended to unleash all the intertextual possibilities in a film with so much of Copland's music. For example, by using "Hoe-Down" to ennoble a spirited game of playground basketball, Lee and his collaborators inevitably suggest comparison with Agnes de Mille's scenario for *Rodeo.* The "Hoe-Down" section of the ballet was basically a dance of sexual aggression in which the cross-dressing, adventuresome Cowgirl reveals her femininity, only to be subdued in a vigorous dance by the overbearing Buck. In *He Got Game* Copland's music for *Rodeo* has been joined to an action that has nothing to do with women but everything to do with phallic aggressivity and male display. That Copland was writing as a gay man intrigued by staged masculinity undermines the black athletes' seemingly natural display of gender. At the same time the music looks forward to the subordination of women that is an all-too-significant element in *He Got Game.*

The film's final music before the end credits is from *Billy the Kid,* the ballet that Copland wrote in 1938 to a scenario by Eugene Loring. Like Jesus Shuttlesworth, the Billy of Loring's scenario witnesses the accidental death of his mother when he is still a child. In a rage, the twelve-year-old Billy publicly kills the man who shot his mother as she passed by during a gunfight. Billy is protected from the crowd by Pat Garrett, who functions in the early stages of the ballet as a surrogate father for the boy. Garrett rides with Billy for a period, but then becomes disillusioned, takes a job as a lawman, and ultimately fires the shot that kills Billy. This narrative begins and ends with a solemn procession of people headed westward, some of whom fall by the wayside or succumb to madness. The music of this processional plays prominently throughout the final scene of *He Got Game* after Jesus seems to have definitively rejected his father. We first hear it on the soundtrack as the camera shows Jake, back in prison for we know not how long, writing a letter to his son. When we see Jesus reading the letter, he is clearly moved by his father's words. The music continues as Jake risks being shot by a guard when he walks into the off-limits area of the prison basketball court and hurls a ball over the wall. The basketball magically arrives at the gymnasium at Big State where Jesus practices alone. He picks up the ball, examines it, and smiles. He may even be crying, but it is difficult to identify tears among the streams of perspiration on his face. The events of the film end here along with Copland's music.

In its original incarnation as music for a ballet, the processional from *Billy the Kid* depicted the epic movement of settlers across the American continent. Copland surely wrote it in the spirit of the radical populism of the 1930s,

He Got Game (1997). Ray Allen as Jesus Shuttlesworth.

dramatizing the struggles of ordinary men and women who built America before capital turned their descendants into exploited members of the working
class. Some who made the westward journey were slaves and freedmen who
helped settle the West and who formed a large contingent of the men called
cowboys (Durham and Jones 1965). Some of the black men who journeyed
west surely ended up like Jake in *He Got Game* and fell by the wayside. The
Billy the Kid ballet is usually staged so that dancers, following the westward direction of the early settlers, move right to left, from the audience's point of
view, during the processional. On the one hand, it is significant that Jake
throws the ball toward the left of the frame and that it lands to the right in the
gymnasium where Jesus is practicing; the processional from *Billy the Kid* com-
plements the frustrated westward aspirations of a black man in prison. On the
other hand, it is ironic that music associated with oedipal aggressivity is recruited to add emotional depth to the reconciliation between father and son at
the end of *He Got Game*. I have no idea if Spike Lee or Alex Steyermark, who
is listed as the film's music supervisor, were aware of the oedipal struggle between Billy the Kid and Pat Garrett that is central to the ballet's narrative. For
that matter, I do not know if Copland's politics, sexuality, or ethnicity were under consideration as Lee and Steyermark picked out the music for *He Got
Game*. Nevertheless, by combining Copland's music with the incidents in the
film, Lee and his collaborators have activated subtexts involving racial politics
and gender construction, as well as oedipal conflict.

The Filmmaker and His Father

With its powerful oedipal elements, *He Got Game* might be regarded as the
third in a series of partially autobiographical films by Spike Lee. The director
has long regarded his own father with a great deal of ambivalence. Bill Lee,
who has been an important bass player in the New York jazz community for
several decades, refused to play electric bass or accommodate himself to
more popular musics in the 1960s (Lee and Jones 1990: 163). As a result, the
Lee family could not live on his income, and Spike Lee's mother, Jacquelyn,
went to work as a schoolteacher to support Spike and his siblings. Spike Lee
has said that his mother was "the heavy" in the household in contrast to his father's passivity (Lee and Jones 1990: 43). She died of cancer when Spike Lee
was nineteen, and a few years later Bill Lee began living with a Jewish
woman, much to the chagrin of his son, who resented what he perceived as an
insult to his mother's memory as much as he resented the color of his father's
new companion. (I cannot help wondering if the white prostitute with whom
the father has sex in *He Got Game* may—in the thoughts of Spike Lee—bear
some relationship to Bill Lee's white companion.) Even a largely hagiographic

biography observes that Spike Lee and his father could barely speak without arguing, even during the years when Bill Lee was writing memorable music for his son's early films (Haskins 1997: 35).

I have argued that *Mo' Better Blues* (1990) is a wish-fulfillment fantasy in which Spike Lee rewrites his own story (Gabbard 1996: 155–56). Bleek Gilliam (Denzel Washington), the jazz musician protagonist of the film, grows up in a house in which the father and the son are dominated by the mother, played with great authority by the vocalist/composer/actress Abbey Lincoln. Unlike Spike Lee's father, however, Bleek Gilliam abandons jazz and grows up to become a strong father who gently gives orders to his wife in a final scene that precisely reproduces all but the matriarchal dominance depicted in the film's opening. In *Crooklyn,* an even more overtly autobiographical film from 1994 written by Spike Lee's sister Joie Lee, the father is a jazz pianist who greatly disappoints his oldest son by insisting that the family sit through the father's sparsely attended recital on a night when the son would much rather be watching the New York Knicks play in the NBA finals. Spike Lee was in fact the oldest son of Bill and Jacquelyn Lee, and his lifelong devotion to the Knicks is well known.

Alfre Woodard plays the mother in *Crooklyn* as a loving but overwhelmed and often angry woman who struggles mightily to keep a large family afloat. Although Woodard's character is not entirely sympathetic at first, her death is played for great pathos toward the end. Significantly, the father in *Crooklyn* is played by Delroy Lindo, the talented but sinister-looking actor who would later play a murderous drug dealer in Lee's *Clockers* (1995). If *Crooklyn* can be read as incidents from Spike Lee's childhood, *He Got Game* might be regarded as a narrative of Spike Lee in young adulthood. The later film dramatizes the crises of a talented young black man from Brooklyn who must cope with all those who would profit from his fame. The protagonist's mother in *He Got Game* is even more idealized than the mothers in Lee's previous films. Seen briefly in flashbacks, Martha Shuttlesworth sends her son loving letters while he is away at camp. In the film she is played by Lonette McKee, who appeared in Lee's *Jungle Fever* (1991) as a successful career woman with a white father and a black mother who explodes when her husband (Wesley Snipes) takes up with a white woman (Annabella Sciorra). In *He Got Game,* McKee looks much younger than the Abbey Lincoln of *Mo' Better Blues* and is perhaps more strikingly beautiful than the Alfre Woodard of *Crooklyn.*

Although the father in *He Got Game* has actually killed the mother, the film is told primarily from his point of view. And as played by Denzel Washington, the character is among the most complex figures in any of Lee's films. Crouch was abundant in his praise for Washington's performance as Jake Shuttlesworth: "Pathetic, arrogant, insecure, stoic, brutish, tender, suspicious, disciplined, sadistic, fatherly, and choking with desire for his son to forgive him, this character has classic American dimensions, wide like the country but intensified by the laser precision of an ethnic authority so fundamentally human that it bores through all walls of class and social division" (Crouch 1999: 258). In the flashback that precedes the mother's death, Copland's grim *Orchestral Variations* plays on the soundtrack as Jake drives Jesus mercilessly on the basketball court, calling him "a little bitch" and at one point hurling a ball directly into his face. But we also see that the end result is mostly positive; Jesus is the nation's most sought-after high school player. The audience's sympathy is drawn immediately to Jake if only because he is played by Washington, who certainly possesses more charisma than Ray Allen, the real-life NBA basketball player who plays Jesus. The intense dislike that Jesus expresses for his father alongside the extremely sympathetic treatment given to Jake by the film suggest that Spike Lee is as ambivalent as ever about his own father.

Perhaps as a result of the powerful oedipal content in *He Got Game,* the women of the film do not fare well. Like Freud's male child, Jesus must renounce the oceanic feeling associated with the mother—and her surrogates—and embrace the values of his father in order to achieve manhood. Jesus is given many reasons to move beyond the stage of dependence upon a woman. During the scene in which Big Time Willie lectures Jesus about the dangers of women, he asks, "How you spell pussy? H.I.V." Jesus's girlfriend, Lala, openly cavorts in a swimming pool with D'Andre (Leonard Roberts), whom she identifies as her brother, while Jesus looks on. Presumably looking after the best interests of his son, Jake later breaks D'Andre's nose and then reminds Jesus of the story of Samson and Delilah. Jesus subsequently understands the extent to which Lala cares only for herself and sends her away with the phrase "Good riddance." In addition to sexual experiences with the duplicitous Lala, Jesus has sex with two large-breasted coeds at Tech U who are obviously interested primarily in recruiting him to their college. Jake has sex with the prostitute Dakota, who professes her love for a vicious pimp with a pockmarked face. These sexually degraded women stand in stark contrast to the idealized Martha, whose photograph Jesus kisses shortly after he has seen Lala in the pool with D'Andre.[6] When Jake visits Martha's grave and embraces the headstone, we hear "Grover's Corners" from Copland's score for *Our Town,* perhaps the most lyrical music in the film. But Martha is dead, the victim of the film's brutal oedipal struggles. She is the only positive female character in the film perhaps because she is safely out of the picture during the film's crucial scenes. *He Got Game* suffers most from its unapologetic embrace of misogyny and unreconstructed masculinity.

Annotating White Music

A well-trained deconstructionist could follow many other chains of signifiers at each of the links between Spike Lee and Aaron Copland. I conclude this exercise by identifying another set of associations that follows from the work of this essay but that may be more consistent with the intentions of the film-makers. Although they do not take up as much time on the soundtrack as do the compositions of Copland, the songs of Public Enemy drive home many of the film's ideas. As with much of rap music, the songs are highly didactic. Consider Chuck D's lyric:

> People use, even murder's excused
> White men in suits don't have to jump
> Still a thousand and one ways to lose with the shoes

Indeed, the world painted by Public Enemy holds almost as little promise for Jesus Shuttlesworth as it does for his imprisoned father. But within the film, the songs provide a microcosm of the interracial connections that grow out of the juxtaposition of Copland and black basketball. Public Enemy comments on white music, especially a tradition of popular music in the white main-stream that tends to hide its debt to African American traditions. This com-mentary provides a relevant and perhaps even oppositional comment on the use of Copland.

Public Enemy is surely Spike Lee's favorite rap group. Their version of "Fight the Power" was the anthem for *Do the Right Thing* even if that film was dominated musically by the symphonic jazz of Bill Lee, which strongly sug-gested the influence of Aaron Copland.[7] The musicians who make up Public Enemy have taken their role seriously as spokesmen for marginalized and ex-ploited people, often denouncing record companies that prevent artists from interacting more directly with their audiences. At the end of the 1990s, the group was fighting with Def Jam Records, which refused to release some of the group's music. Group member Chuck D received some public attention when he took the music to the Internet and made it available in high-quality audio format to anyone with a computer, a sound card, and a modem. Def Jam subsequently released the withheld music.

For *He Got Game*, Public Enemy composed a number of songs in which they articulate values of revolutionary youth and present themselves as candid commentators on urban life. Their song "He Got Game" is especially signifi-cant for its title as well as for its prominence in the end credits. In fact, the song kicks in immediately after the last strains of Copland's *Billy the Kid* and the image of Jesus holding the basketball magically delivered to him by his father fade away. Public Enemy's "He Got Game" is the last music audiences hear as they leave the theater. The opening sounds of the song are a sampling of the 1967 recording of "For What It's Worth" by the folk-rock group Buffalo Springfield. Actually, Public Enemy does more than just sample the recording. The entirely of "He Got Game" is layered over the earlier record. The chime-like whole notes alternating between E and B in portions of "For What It's Worth" can be heard throughout all of Public Enemy's record. Chuck D actually convinced Stephen Stills to join the group in the studio so that he could re-record his thirty-one-year-old lyrics to "For What It's Worth" (Brunner 1998). Even so, Public Enemy's Flava Flav plays the trickster, engaging in call and response with Stills. When the aging rocker sings, "There's a man with a gun over there," Flava responds with a knowing, "Yeah, that's right. Hah hah."

The rapper's intrusions into the mild protest rock of the 1960s become especially plangent when the female voices of the Shabach Community Choir of Long Island are heard late in the recording. Although they sing the same lyrics as Stephen Stills, the choir was added to the mix by Public Enemy. The female singers embody the African American gospel traditions that have found their way into white popular music, usually as a means of validating the "authenticity" of the white singer. Innumerable white vocalists have performed in front of a group that consists primarily or exclusively of black singers and dancers, including the Rolling Stones, Laura Nyro, Carole King, Talking Heads, Madonna, and more recently Vonda Shepherd, who was a regular presence on the weekly television program *Ally McBeal*.

By essentially holding up Buffalo Springfield's music to the scrutiny of black artists, the appropriation of African American voices by white artists becomes especially obvious, not at all like the invisibility of black singers in Hollywood's *The Bridges of Madison County*, *Groundhog Day*, and so many other films. Similarly, Public Enemy's annotations of "For What It's Worth" allude to the role of the Civil Rights Movement in the rhetoric of the student protest movements of the 1960s. When Stephen Stills sang about the ominous presence of men with guns, he was referring to the Sunset Strip Riots of 1966, in which police harassed young people, many of them in hippie mufti, who were attracted to the region's nightlife. Later, the song became associated with the attacks by police and National Guardsmen on Vietnam-era protestors. Regardless, Stills was poaching on the much greater fears that African Americans felt as they faced down police in the civil-rights struggles of the 1950s and 1960s. The knowing responses of Flava Flav to the lyrics of "For What It's Worth" register the gap between the anxieties of white hippies like Stills and the daily exposure to racism experienced by black Americans.

But then Public Enemy has also done its share of poaching by appropriating the white musicians of Buffalo Springfield for their performance. By employing

Public Enemy, Spike Lee has again called attention to the common but invisible practice of mixing black music into performances by white artists. Lee and Public Enemy reveal the inseparability of "white" popular music and African American traditions, a synthesis so profound that to separate the two would be, in the words of Ellison, an attempt at "a delicate brain surgery with a switchblade" (Ellison 1995: 283). I am quoting Ellison's review of *Blues People,* the book by Amiri Baraka (then LeRoi Jones) that first made a powerful case for the centrality of the black experience in jazz and blues. Ellison was charging Baraka with overlooking the extent to which African American culture has become an inseparable part of the American mainstream. Aaron Copland did after all look to jazz in his early years to find an American vernacular. He later looked to folk traditions that had effectively absorbed Negro influences long before Copland got to them. By the time he was writing his great ballets and film music, it had become impossible to identify which elements in Copland's music were indisputably "white" and which were the undiluted products of black culture. Because Ralph Ellison was writing as a high modernist in his critique of Baraka, he was less interested in the identity politics and institutional boundaries that Baraka was then developing, ultimately with great success. But I am convinced that Ellison, as a modernist and an integrationist, would have been very pleased with Spike Lee's appropriation of Aaron Copland.

NOTES

1. It would be difficult to overstate the influence of Copland's music on the history of music for American films. To choose just one example, in the same year as the release of *He Got Game,* John Williams's score for Steven Spielberg's *Saving Private Ryan* (1998) was extremely Coplandesque.

2. In "Rhetoric of the Image," Roland Barthes argues that the polysemy of a photograph in a magazine can be stripped of a wide range of possible meanings and anchored to a specific few by means of the caption below the picture. Claudia Gorbman has employed this concept of ancrage by arguing that soundtrack music can anchor the profusion of images in a film to selected sets of meanings: see Gorbman 1987: 32.

3. Compare Copland's quotations with those of jazz musicians who relish the opportunity to insert fragments of inapposite melodies into their compositions. Perhaps the best example is Charlie Parker's frequent references to Percy Grainger's "Country Gardens," as if to conjure up a bourgeois drawing room while playing in a smoky nightclub full of bohemians: see Gabbard 1991.

4. Tommasini has argued that chordal structures that suggest the American heartland in Copland's work can also be found in music that Palestrina wrote in sixteenth-century Italy (Tommasini 1999: 36).

5. But in *The Cultural Front,* Denning argues that invocations of Lincoln were more typical of "the official Americanisms of the Depression" (Denning 1997: 131). Members of the Popular Front and other radical groups were more likely to associate themselves with the abolitionist John Brown.

6. The sexual politics of the film are further complicated by the racial dynamics at Tech U, where Jesus is surrounded by white coeds who are, in the words of Chick, "freaks." When Chick and Jesus walk across the campus with two white girls, they encounter a group of black coeds, one of whom says, "That's not right, Chick." While Jesus speaks with one of the white girls, Chick attempts to mollify the black girls by saying that he will see them at church on Sunday. Later, Chick explains in detail why he prefers white girls, who will wash his "dirty drawers," as opposed to black girls, who "make you work too hard."

7. Writing at least a year before the release of *He Got Game,* Victoria Johnson referred to Bill Lee's score for *Do the Right Thing* as "Coplandesque" (Johnson 1997: 55).

REFERENCES

Baraka, Amiri. 1993. "Spike Lee at the Movies." Pp. 145–53 in *Black American Cinema,* ed. Manthia Diawara. New York: Routledge.

Boyd, Todd. 1997. "The Day the Niggaz Took Over: Basketball, Commodity Culture, and Black Masculinity." Pp. 123–42 in *Out of Bounds: Sports, Media, and the Politics of Identity,* ed. Aaron Baker and Todd Boyd. Bloomington: Indiana University Press.

Brunner, Rob. 1998. "Game Boys." *Entertainment Weekly,* May 1, 61.

Christensen, Jerome. 1991. "Spike Lee, Corporate Populist." *Critical Inquiry* 17, no. 3: 582–95.

Crouch, Stanley. 1999. *Always in Pursuit: Fresh American Perspectives.* New York: Vintage.

Denning, Michael. 1997. *The Cultural Front: The Laboring of American Culture in the Twentieth Century.* London: Verso.

Durham, Philip, and Everett L. Jones. 1965. *The Negro Cowboy.* Chicago: University of Chicago Press.

Ellison, Ralph. 1972 (1952). *Invisible Man.* New York: Random House.

Gabbard, Krin. 1991. "The Quoter and His Culture." Pp. 92–111 in *Jazz in Mind: Essays on the History and Meanings of Jazz,* ed. Reginald T. Buckner and Steven Welland. Detroit: Wayne State University Press.

———. 1996. *Jammin' at the Margins: Jazz and the American Cinema.* Chicago: University of Chicago Press.

Gorbman, Claudia. 1987. *Unheard Melodies: Narrative Film Music.* Bloomington: Indiana University Press.

Hansen, Miriam. 1990. "Adventures of Goldilocks: Spectatorship, Consumerism, and Public Life." *Camera Obscura* 22: 51–71.

Haskins, Jim. 1997. *Spike Lee: By Any Means Necessary.* New York: Walker.

Johnson, Victoria A. 1997. "Polyphony and Cultural Expression: Interpreting Musical Traditions in *Do the Right Thing.*" Pp. 50–72 in *Spike Lee's "Do the Right Thing,"* ed. Mark A. Reid. Cambridge: Cambridge University Press.

Lee, Spike, and Lisa Jones. 1990. *Mo' Better Blues: The Companion Volume to the Universal Pictures Film.* New York: Fireside/Simon and Schuster.

Mitchell, W. J. T. 1997. "The Violence of Public Art." Pp. 107–28 in *Spike Lee's "Do the Right Thing,"* ed. Mark A. Reid. Cambridge: Cambridge University Press.

Oja, Carol J. 1990. "Virgil Thomson's Harvard Years." Pp. 331–46 in *A Celebration of American Music: Words and Music in Honor of H. Wiley Hitchcock,* ed. Richard

Crawford, R. Allen Lott, and Carol J. Oja. Ann Arbor: University of Michigan Press.

Pollack, Howard. 1999. *Aaron Copland: The Life and Work of an Uncommon Man*. New York: Henry Holt.

Ross, Andrew. 1990. "Bullets, Ballots, or Batmen: Can Cultural Studies Do the Right Thing?" *Screen* 31, no. 1: 31.

Sterritt, David. 1998. "Spike Lee Chooses Copland Classics for Soundtrack." *Christian Science Monitor*, May 8, 15.

Tommasini, Anthony. 1999. "Aaron Copland, Champion of the American Sound." *New York Times* , November 21, 1999, sec. 2, 1, 36.

13

Race and Black American *Film Noir*: *Summer of Sam* as Lynching Parable

A lthough the "new black film wave" inaugurated in the mid-1980s by directors such as Spike Lee has received a good deal of critical attention, one overlooked aspect is its ongoing cycle of Black American *films noirs*.[1] These works have transformed *film noir* itself by redirecting its conventions and themes to explore what might be called an epistemology of race. While some academic work has focused on this cycle's development among African American scholars (most notably, the work of Manthia Diawara) and mainstream *noir* studies, much of its significance has been misunderstood.[2] In particular, few critics seem interested in examining why filmmakers as diverse as Spike Lee, Carl Franklin, Bill Duke, Charles Burnett, and Kasi Lemmons have found *noir* conventions useful in portraying the struggles African Americans often face as they confront the injustices of everyday racialized life. How is it possible for Black *film noir* to bring an explicit social criticism of race into the Hollywood mainstream? What are the conditions of knowledge that provide a foundation for an ongoing Black *noir* investigation of race?

Two points should be made clear from the outset. First, I argue that these films offer audiences new ways of seeing and understanding the role of race

Dan Flory, "Race and Black American Film Noir: *Summer of Sam* as Lynching Parable." Originally published as "The Epistemology of Race and Black American Film Noir: Spike Lee's *Summer of Sam* as Lynching Parable," in *Film and Knowledge: Essays on the Integration of Images and Ideas*, ed. Kevin L. Stoehr (Jefferson, N.C.: McFarland & Company, Publishers, 2002). Reprinted from *Film and Knowledge: Essays on the Integration of Images and Ideas* © 2002, Edited by Kevin L. Stoehr, by permission of McFarland & Company, Inc.

in contemporary American society. Second, I suggest that while Black *noirs* utilize elements found in such classic American *noir* films as *Double Indemnity*, *Out of the Past*, and *The Naked City*, they do so in ways that transform *noir* tropes through the category of race. Both traditions often address issues of power, confinement, determinism, and marginalization. Both also typically feature powerful or inadequately understood forces that threaten their protagonists, who are inexorably drawn toward fates that seem inescapable. In recent Black American films, however, *noir* elements attribute confinement, marginalization, and determinism to social injustice, thereby ascribing a racialized dimension to the trappings of power. This is a striking difference from standard American *film noir*. While some classical *noirs* aimed at criticizing problems of class,[3] a socially critical strain of this tradition that could have been directed toward problems of race was neglected during its heyday as well as its revival beginning in the "New Hollywood" of the late 1960s and early 1970s.[4]

In contrast, the current cycle of Black *noir* has not only reinvigorated and reconfigured the workings of *film noir* into critical investigative mechanisms focused on race but also provides illuminating analogues to arguments advanced by recent theorists of race working in philosophy, including Charles Mills, David Theo Goldberg, and Lewis Gordon. Similar to Black filmmakers' *noir* intervention into the Hollywood mainstream, critical examinations of race in philosophy have moved to center stage and created a new subfield that is beginning to reshape the discipline. Moreover, studies in the cognitive aspects of race aim directly at laying bare what Mills has identified as philosophy's "epistemology of ignorance" regarding race by providing insights into an alternative system of knowing that profoundly challenges dominant forms of cognition.[5] Epistemologists of race have offered philosophy access to that overlapping yet distinct parallel universe of human experience where racist oppression radically alters everyday life, even as this oppression is overlooked by those professing to describe, theorize, and explain "universal" human experience. Ultimately, these critics argue, the revelation of this parallel universe of experience—a crucial example of which is ordinary Black life—demands a reconceptualization and redirection of what we think of as moral and political philosophy, an assessment that concurs with the perspectives offered by Black *film noir*.

By juxtaposing one such film with elements deriving from critical examinations of race in philosophy, I hope to bring into focus some of the details involved in addressing the questions posed above and illuminate aspects of white presumptions of privilege, particularly their distorting effects on moral thinking. Here I offer three main points, which I will illustrate by means of Spike Lee's *Summer of Sam* (1999). First, I sketch some relevant epistemological

conclusions advanced by recent philosophical theorists of race. Second, I describe some of the ways in which Black filmmakers have reinvigorated *noir*
conventions by using them to challenge typical American conceptions of race
and their underlying moral epistemologies. Third, through this redeployment
of *noir* conventions, I argue that African American filmmakers have provided
critical evidence for claims advanced by work in the epistemology of race. Because I have written elsewhere about several earlier works in this film cycle,[6]
and because *Summer of Sam* represents an advance in the overall critique put
forward by Black *noir*, I concentrate here on the more recent example Lee's
film provides. Based on its analysis, I then offer some concluding remarks
about epistemology, race, and Black American *film noir*.

Recent Philosophical Theories of Race

Let me begin by offering an analogy that I think illustrates the longstanding
relation between race and philosophy. Black detective-fiction writer Chester
Himes wrote in 1976 in the second volume of his autobiography, *My Life of
Absurdity*, that problems of race had created such an existential absurdity in
his life that he often could not tell the difference between what was real and
what was absurd.[7] Himes's observation about his own life fittingly describes
the status of race in modern Western philosophy.[8] On the one hand, until
well into the 1990s race had at best a marginal place in most philosophical
discussions, particularly those discussions taking place in the United States.
Problems linked to the concept of race were considered to be of peripheral
interest—empirical, non-philosophical matters to be discussed after the
"real" theoretical disputes had been settled.[9] On the other hand, since the
seventeenth century Western philosophy has profoundly influenced the treatment of non-whites and their status as human beings, even while it outlined
and established the bases for "universal" human rights and theories of liberalism. While providing the foundations for these cornerstones of modern Western society, philosophers such as Locke, Rousseau, Hegel, and Kant also
established the theoretical underpinnings for modern racism.[10] This contradiction continues to induce dimensions of absurdity and realism into discussions of race in Western philosophy, the examination of which theorists have
only recently begun to force onto the discipline.

In contrast to this way of treating racial matters, many contemporary philosophers examining race argue that while Western philosophy's influence on
people of color has been profound, that influence has been consistently evaded
or obscured. They suggest that modern liberalism has historically and concep-
tually presupposed the systematic and racialized oppression of entire groups of
human beings from whose domination whites, as the main beneficiaries of

modern liberalism, have long benefited and from whose circumstances they continue to benefit. For these thinkers, the everyday realm, as reconfigured through the category of race, emerges as a primary battleground. They argue that, like liberalism, the typical American day-to-day life of whites presupposes systematic and racialized oppression. The everyday life of persons counted as white takes for granted a system of dominance and privilege that has as one of its dimensions the award of full human rights to whites and a lesser schedule of rights to non-whites, a social structure that continues today in multiplicitous forms. Being white, then, has social, political, and moral privileges, a conclusion that should surprise no one. Yet the astonishing consequence raised here is that whiteness also imposes *cognitive* requirements with moral consequences for both whites and non-whites. When looked at institutionally, whiteness amounts to an epistemological stance that affects the ethical.

These theorists contend that one overlooked aspect of race is the way in which it permeates everyday cognitions as well as dominant sensibilities: that is, ordinary ways of thinking, believing, and acting. Mills argues that whites normally operate by means of a structural blindness to their own power and privilege as well as to the consequences of that lack of vision. "An idealized consensus of cognitive norms" informs their beliefs and actions, constituting a system of knowledge that imposes misperceptions, insensitivities, and presumed incapacities regarding persons counted as non-white.[11] This epistemological blindness is a *condition* of whiteness in its idealized form, in the sense that to think and perceive from that subject position presupposes that one possesses such a cognitive incapacity. Whiteness, considered as a set of institutionalized power relations rather than as an aspect of biology or heredity, has profoundly disturbing epistemological as well as moral consequences.[12]

Thomas E. Hill Jr. and Bernard Boxill concur with Mills's assessment of this cognitive blindness on the part of whites, even while working from a strict Kantian perspective.[13] They argue that knowing the right thing to do is often difficult for whites because knowing the relevant moral facts is deeply problematic for those comfortably ensconced in power. Hill and Boxill elaborate that "confident, complacent, well-positioned white people will not only find it difficult to do what they know to be right; they will find it still more difficult to know what is right, even when they sincerely claim that they are trying to do so."[14] This difficulty arises because whites may be easily deceived by their own advantage into believing that it accrues to all, and unable to see with adequate vividness cases of racial injustice because these seem so far removed from white experience.[15] Such obstacles place whites at a cognitive disadvantage as a price of their privilege. They are prone to self-deception regarding racial injustice because they lack an ability to grasp the morally relevant facts, and their advantages blind them to the absence of such privileges for others. As a result, their capacity to act morally becomes seriously impaired.

From a phenomenological perspective Lewis Gordon argues similarly that ordinary white perceptions of everyday matters involving African Americans mask those perceptions' proper status as systematic forms of misanthropy, abnormality, social pathology, and injustice.[16] Rather than seeing what in the situation of fellow whites would be deemed unfair, iniquitous, or even perverse, one sees merely the ordinary life of blacks, normalized by its presumed pervasiveness as well as by waves of alleged explanation aimed at justification. In other words, it is those people's living conditions, their nature, social relations, economic circumstances, family structures, or overall potential for intelligence that are to blame. Gordon notes that such "ordinary" perceptions also truncate whites' social world to the point of moral retardation, for under such epistemological regimes human beings live lives cut off from complete actualization of their humanity, which renders them incapable of appreciating its full possibility. Whites, as he puts it, possess a "misanthropic consciousness" that lacks significant aspects of the social world.[17] Whole dimensions of human interaction, lifestyles, sensitivity, and even language become off limits as a condition of acceptance for whiteness. Thus, one aspect of being white is that it requires a cognitive, moral, and social amputation of one's full potential for humanity, the results of which have fundamental effects for one's self and for others.

David Theo Goldberg explores related points in the field by examining how some racist exclusions may be justified by rational means. While many, perhaps most, forms of racism are indeed not rational, others turn out to be consistent with accepted criteria of rationality such as providing sufficient evidence, accepting reasonable doubt, being open to criticism and revision, and the like. Those forms of racist belief that pass standards of rationality become cognitively "normalized" by means of endorsement from the highest standard of human behavior. It becomes "perfectly reasonable," in other words, for whites to assume in everyday life that new, expensive clothing and valuable possessions operate as markers of criminal accomplishment if possessed by African Americans; that skin color operates as a sign of criminal guilt or at minimum suspicion; and that neighborhood locations operate as indicators of good or bad morals.[18]

More recently, Jody David Armour has augmented Goldberg's argument by considering how some versions of Bayesianism may support "rational discrimination" by whites. If one uses certain forms of probabilistic reasoning to weigh statistics of violent felony convictions, overall criminality, and the like, then believing that Blacks possess a far higher potential to be violent assailants of one's person or property passes the test of rationality.[19] While Armour goes on to argue that such reasoning fails to meet a higher standard of reason,[20] the point I wish to underscore here is that some forms of racism have at least a prima facie claim to being rational, which Armour points out has been accepted by U.S. courts as well as some philosophers (e.g., Michael Levin).[21] This revelation would seem an unfortunate discovery to almost anyone working in moral and political philosophy.

The shared conclusion of these theorists working with the epistemology of race is that instances of unfairness and injustice in Black life often escape detection by whites due to a kind of cognitive blinkering. The task of the theorist, then, is to bring attention to the epistemological misperception of everyday details, so that critics may reformulate and redirect white moral vision in ways that acknowledge the unjust and unfair circumstances constituting many people's everyday lives, rather than letting what I will here call the "white gaze" determine dominant moral perception and sweep over such details obliviously.[22] Philosophical theorists of race have worked to reveal to their readers what Mills has called a "racial fantasyland" that undergirds white dominance and privilege. This fantasyland constitutes the epistemology of ignorance that prevents whites from perceiving the reality and effects of their own beliefs concerning racial difference.[23] Such cognitive blindness requires fundamental revision, for it rests on what Mills calls a "consensual hallucination," an invented delusional world where white moral consciousness is filtered by norms of social cognition that derive from an unconscious sense of dominance in the world.[24] The necessity of redirecting and reformulating this flawed white moral vision is forcefully brought home by many Black American *noir*-influenced films.

Film Noir's Subversive Possibilities

From its inception in the 1940s, classical American *film noir*'s convergence of diverse techniques and themes has offered ways of persuading audiences to see protagonists cross lines of bourgeois acceptability, transgress established laws, and infringe on underlying moral codes. Outlaw and marginalized groups have regularly counted *noir* characters among their members and have just as often drawn others into their orbit. Moreover, the doomed or damaged fates of many *noir* protagonists reflected a pessimism and dissatisfaction felt by audience members against prevailing established orders. While *noir* films typically cause audiences to sympathize with moral transgression as well as underworld economies, here I want to suggest a slightly different but related point—namely, that these standard themes and conventions of classical *film noir* may be directed toward critical examinations of knowledge.[25] For instance, a convention such as confinement to circumstances from which there seems no escape may function in *film noir* to compel characters and/or audience members to seek knowledge that might profoundly alter their systems of belief, perception, or action. Such conventions open up possibilities for *noir* narratives to serve as cognitive searches aimed at epistemological transformation.

These possibilities arise frequently in classical *noir* as well as its post–1960s descendants, generally known as neo-*noir*. *Out of the Past* (Jacques Tourneur, 1947) depicts its main character trying to uncover details that will allow him to escape his sordid past. *Try and Get Me* (Cy Enfield, 1950) explicitly condemns (non-racialized) lynching.[26] *In a Lonely Place* (Nicholas Ray, 1950) examines the latent violence that typically informs American masculinity. *Chinatown* (Roman Polanski, 1974) reveals a dispiriting corruption that thrives in the way most municipalities are run. *Noir* narratives often become cognitive investigations that aim at some sort of epistemological transformation, particularly of their audiences. Some are explicitly so (e.g., *Try and Get Me*), while others may be more subtle (e.g., *In a Lonely Place, Chinatown*), but many offer up to their viewers knowledge and perspectives meant to change how they think, perceive, and act.

In spite of this well-established subversive capacity, *noir* functions in both radical and conservative manners. Usually, it is noticeably duller as right-wing critique: Who, after all, admires *film noir* for such works as *I Was a Communist for the FBI* (Gordon Douglas, 1951)? Like many critics, I find *noir's* radical affinities more attractive, and African American filmmakers have likewise been drawn to these elements. In one of the best articles written describing this appropriation, Manthia Diawara explains how the new black film wave often redeploys *film noir* tropes to depict social injustice against African Americans and the need for its rectification.[27] Rather than highlighting moral or legal transgression, black and darkness tropes are used to foreground the oppression forced on African Americans by white society. For example, *noir* conventions may serve to show how institutions of white authority impose criminality and law-breaking on African Americans by granting them virtually no other viable choices. By depicting Black life through *noir* conventions, Diawara argues that many films by African Americans deconstruct white racism and its intricacies by exposing the ways in which forces of white privilege fracture and distort African American existence, thereby making possible improved reflections by audience members regarding the immorality and injustice of these dominant institutions.[28] Unlike typical Marxist or feminist forms of *noir* criticism, Diawara focuses mainly on thematic elements in *film noir* narrative to support his analyses, rather than offering a form of criticism based more squarely on *noir's* style.[29] This is a strategy I follow in my own analysis, to which I now turn.[30]

Summer of Sam as Lynching Parable

Spike Lee's recent film offers a subtle and oblique form of racial analysis, for on the surface the narrative is not about race at all. Instead, it focuses on how suspicion and fear of difference itself cause violent tensions in an Italian American neighborhood in New York City during the hot summer of 1977. Using *noir* techniques that at times tacitly quote from Jules Dassin's classic *The Naked City* (1948), particularly in the framing story narrated by Jimmy Breslin which parallels producer Mark Hellinger's voiceover narration of the older film, Lee depicts how several young men who grew up together begin to suspect an old friend of the serial murders taking place in their neighborhood after he returns from living in Manhattan with ideas and an outward appearance that are entirely foreign to them. Afraid of the unfamiliar and unable to assimilate their friend into the simple-minded stereotypes with which they were raised, these young men reflexively treat him with suspicion, distance themselves from him, and presume his guilt based on their own fear of those not like them.

However, Lee introduces the element of race into the film by thematizing this suspicion of difference through *noir* narrative, thereby transforming this Bronx tale into a parable for racial lynching. With scenes of white neighborhood gangs roving the streets with baseball bats looking to beat up anyone who might not "belong" there and individuals who look different being refused service at diners while police officials collude with vigilantism and mob hysteria, the allusions to the history of Black lynchings are striking. For example, most of the characters repeatedly criticize the anomalous appearance adopted by their old friend Ritchie [sic] (Adrien Brody). With his hair spiked and his body adorned with the regalia of punk rock, Ritchie embodies a look they cannot assimilate. At first, they try to fit him into ready-made outsider categories by calling him a "freak," a "vampire," and a "fag." Later they tell him that he is no longer welcome in the neighborhood because the way he looks upsets them. Eventually they suspect him of being a Satanic cult member because his otherness is so foreign that they can find no other place for it. They put him at the top of the list of suspects who they believe might be the killer roaming the streets of New York City that hot summer, the Son of Sam, even though the narrative makes clear that this suspicion has no basis in fact. Tellingly, Spike Lee portrays Ritchie as the most sensitive, caring, and thoughtful of these young men. Ritchie openly objects to their violent actions against those weaker or different from them, sees people for who they are instead of by means of stereotypical categories, and thoughtfully listens to his friends' problems rather than using them as the basis for ridicule and advantage.

Ignoring all that, however, the other young men browbeat Ritchie's best friend Vinnie (John Leguizamo) into betrayal with taunts such as "killer, fag,

Summer of Sam (1999). Richie (Adrien Brody) as the target of the neighborhood's suspicions.

pimp, punk rocker . . . queer, pervert, degenerate, whatever the fuck it is. I mean—c'mon: who wants something like that around here anyway?" *Summer of Sam* is thus transformed thematically into a *film noir* about racial lynching. Lee uses themes of confinement and determinism as in other *noirs*: Fate slowly closes in on Ritchie as his progressive marginalization culminates in being beaten mercilessly, and his best friend Vinnie inexorably succumbs to the dictates of the dominant "white gaze" by giving in to the idea of seeing Ritchie as someone punishable for being different.

Characters in the narrative also specifically reference the theme of lynching. The first time Vinnie betrays Ritchie and leads a group of vigilantes to one of his hangouts, Ritchie responds, "So you [brought] a fucking lynch mob down here to string me up." In this instance Ritchie manages to escape, due to the ineptitude of his would-be assailants, but out of frustration they severely beat another punk who crosses their path and provocatively claims to be a Boston Red Sox fan. Near the end of the film, the news reporter John Jefferies (Spike Lee) describes the crowd awaiting the arrival of the person who was later proved to be the real Son of Sam, David Berkowitz. Jefferies refers to this roiling mass outside the police station as a "potential lynch mob" full of "rage and vengeance." While he goes on to describe them as "going crazy" at Berkowitz's arrival and giving in to "pandemonium . . . hysteria . . . [and] chaos," we hear the crowd screaming "Kill him" and "Lynch him" while on the soundtrack The Who's ironic "Won't Get Fooled Again" comments on the in-tercut screen images of not just one but two hysterical groups. One is the crowd outside the police station, nearly out of control and demanding the im-mediate death and burning of someone who has yet to be tried for the actions of which he stands accused. The other is the neighborhood gang that, igno-rant of the events being televised, has actually spun out of control as it finally catches up with Ritchie and beats him senseless.

The film also subtly emphasizes how this mentality embraces virtually all whites: men and women, adults and children, gays and heterosexuals—even junkies—so long as they are able to gain acceptance by means of some sem-blance of normalcy, a normalcy that is subtly raced as white. Moreover, the film returns again and again to the matter of Ritchie's punked-out hair as the marker of anomaly and how upsetting it is to those who desire the sort of hair "normal people" (i.e., those raced as whites) possess. Characters repeatedly comment on how they cannot get used to Ritchie's spiked (and later Mo-hawked) hair, as if his choice of haircut were a clear offense against them. This rejection of non-standard hair uncomfortably alludes to dominant white rejections of Black hair on alleged aesthetic grounds and perhaps to its erst-while souvenir value as evidence of lynchings.[31] Acceptable-looking hair must be the sort that fits within the parameters of whiteness, which Ritchie's punked-out hair, like typical Black hair, does not do.

When the television reporter played by Spike Lee, John Jefferies, goes to the Bedford-Stuyvesant neighborhood to obtain what he describes as "a darker perspective" on these serial murders, one of his respondents tells him: "I am going to give you your darker perspective. The darker perspective is: . . . I thank God that it is a *white* man who kills all of those *white* people, because if it were a *black* man who kills all of those *white* people, there would be the biggest race riot right here in New York City." This observation reveals one way in which the city's community is riven with racial tensions that could eas-ily result in mob hysteria and lynching. Such commentary by Black New York City residents enlists them as a Greek chorus whose remarks illuminate the panic and paranoia felt by whites in the city, who perhaps for the first time begin to acquire a sense of the fear and stress that is inextricably linked to the normal lives of persons of color in America. The threat of violence is latent, but palpable, and any individual could be the potential carrier of it. There is simply no way to tell. In this fashion *Summer of Sam* further alludes to his-torical Black sentiments regarding lynching and everyday life.

In a brief discussion of racial lynching in his book *Bad Faith and Anti-Black Racism*, Lewis Gordon observes that "the victim is anonymous except insofar as he can be identified as a member of a hated *group*."[32] Consistent with this idea, characters in *Summer of Sam* repeatedly tell Ritchie, "I don't know you," even though they have known him all their lives as close friends. Instead they place him in the category of some misunderstood, marginalized outsider group (cult member, punk rocker, degenerate), in an effort to distance themselves from him. In this manner they remove Ritchie's individuality, making him the anonymous member of a hated group. As Gordon points out, the *racial* dimension of this human diminution reveals itself through the ways in which the power relations of such symbolic persecutions mimic those of white privilege. The anonymous outsider moves into the subject position of being Black, while the enraged mob as an instrument of retribution becomes empowered as white.[33] The punishment becomes a punitive action by those with power, who act as if they were white by imposing it on an individual for being different, who is thereby treated as if he or she were Black.

Bernard Boxill extends these observations by noting that "the symbolic meaning of a lynching is that its victims, and those like them to whom it is meant as a warning, have no rights." Conversely, its perpetrators "admit no wrong." Rather, they hold "themselves up for approval and [declare] their righteousness." As such, "the effectiveness of lynching as an insult lies in the special vehemence and perverse eloquence with which it makes its point."[34] Persecution of this sort is not meant merely to harm the individual involved, but is meant as a warning to *all* those in the group of which the individual is a member who would even hint at challenging the status quo: This will happen to you, too, if you so much as dare to question your station in how things are. Like some members of the Black community, punks like Ritchie openly challenge how power relations stand, doing so in ways that range from emulating contrary hairstyles, clothes, bodily adornments, and music to violating notions of respectability and propriety (in other words, that range from aesthetics to politics). Ritchie's persecution, then, parallels that of blacks who respond similarly to the power relations confining them in the sense that he is punished symbolically for the same reason—that is, for daring to think, act, and look differently. When looked at symbolically, then, the persecution of one individual stands for the persecution of all in his or her marginalized group, for it is meant as a warning—a threat—by those in power against challenges of any sort against them.

Another element the film raises is the issue of how vigilantism and lynching have symbiotically co-existed with white officialdom. Early in the narrative, two police detectives appeal to the neighborhood capo, Don Luigi (Ben Gazzara), to help them catch the serial killer. With officialdom's blessing he forms roving gangs armed with baseball bats to "protect" the neighborhood from anyone who does not belong there. Charles Mills has interpreted the collusion between white officialdom and vigilantism as part of the physically violent aspect of coercion that enforces artificial racial differentiation.[35] Lynching operates as "massively disproportionate retaliatory violence" that is intended to force non-whites to remain obediently in their subaltern positions by stressing the violence's difference in scale and ferocity.[36] As a technically illegal activity, lynching is something that may occur—particularly with its intended force—only through the collusion and at times encouragement of those in power. Lynching also helps to enforce the cognitive dimensions of racial differentiation, which include for non-whites learning to see one's self as undeserving of the privileges enjoyed by whites through providing a strong physical incentive to believe that the dominant position's formulations are accurate.[37] Mills likens this second form of coercion, which is ideological as well as cognitive, to the intellectual equivalent of "seasoning," or slave breaking. He quotes Frederick Douglass as describing this process of darkening one's moral and mental vision and annihilating one's power of reason, a necessary process if non-whites are to see themselves as appropriately subordinated by this sort of racial differentiation.[38] Such cognitive enforcement of differential rights is greatly facilitated by white officialdom's open and willful blindness to violent acts such as lynchings.

A related aspect of the film's racially inflected exploration of themes surrounding lynching is its calling to viewer attention a disproportionate horror at the death of whites, as opposed to those of non-whites. Sadly, as Mills would note, this disproportionality is a consequence of the differential valuation of human beings that is built into our social epistemology.

Conclusion

If we view *Summer of Sam* in conjunction with studies in the epistemology of race, its analysis brings out the ways in which its viewers—particularly its white viewers—need to attend to aspects of race in ordinary life. As such, this film joins forces with other Black American *noirs*, among them *One False Move* (Carl Franklin, 1992), *Deep Cover* (Bill Duke, 1992), and *Devil in a Blue Dress* (Carl Franklin, 1995), in exposing how a distorted social epistemology undergirds institutional forms of white supremacy.[39] Such attempts to broaden critiques of race as one finds in *Summer of Sam* show a conscious effort on Lee's part to come to terms with the problem of difference in general, very much in line with the efforts of philosophers who theorize race.[40] *Summer of Sam* bespeaks an effort to achieve a broader understanding of the human condition rather than one that rests content in a parochial perspective. What Lee recognizes here is that similarities exist between the problems of many different marginalized groups. Those goals and efforts of such groups aimed at greater fairness and liberation may then be shared. This broadened perspective is essential if problems of race (and for that matter difference in general) are to be fully understood and eradicated. Although *Summer of Sam* focuses predominantly on whites, it highlights their racial attitudes by analyzing an underlying fear of difference in order to criticize and change it.

Juxtaposing Black American *film noir* with recent discussions of race in philosophy, then, can highlight elements depicting undetected aspects of daily life that betray a raced sense of knowledge and cognition. Particularly when observed through the lens of certain philosophical texts, Black *noirs* can help viewers, especially white viewers, see what the relevant moral facts are regarding racial injustice, to use Hill and Boxill's phrasing.[41] These films can also fulfill at least some of the conditions that Adrian M. S. Piper describes as the cognitively transformative possibilities possessed by contemporary works of art. For sympathetic viewers and under the proper conditions (e.g., having read recent discussions of philosophy and race), Black *noirs* have the capacity to encourage viewers to confront their own racist beliefs.[42] These films might assist in convincing whites to learn to listen or observe sympathetically those who may be somehow subordinate to them, so that whites might acquire a better sense of moral relevance. Laurence Thomas has explained this sympathetic listening more elaborately than do Hill and Boxill as a sort of "moral deference," a humility in the face of radically different and challenging moral experience.[43] Such humility is essential if whites are to know, understand, and act morally regarding racial injustice.

Taken together, these filmic and philosophical criticisms enhance each other's claims by confirming and amplifying separate diagnoses of the many cognitive problems surrounding race—especially anti-Black racism—in America. They also offer hopes of possible resolution by making clear the complexity of the difficulties on which they focus. Through such juxtapositions we might better grasp the relations between epistemology, race, and doing the right thing.

NOTES

1. See, e.g., Ed Guerrero, "A Circus of Dreams and Lies: The Black Film Wave at Middle Age," in *The New American Cinema*, ed. Jon Lewis (Durham: Duke University Press, 1998), 328–52; idem, "Black Violence as Cinema: From Cheap Thrills to Historical Agonies," in *Violence and American Cinema*, ed. J. David Slocum (New York: Routledge, 2001), 211–25.

2. See Manthia Diawara, "*Noir* by *Noirs*: Toward a New Realism in Black Cinema," in *Shades of Noir*, ed. Joan Copjec (London: Verso, 1993), 261–78; James Naremore, *More than Night: Film Noir in Its Contexts* (Berkeley: University of California Press, 1998), 246–53; Richard Martin, *Mean Streets and Raging Bulls: The Legacy of Film Noir in Contemporary American Cinema* (Lanham, Md.: Scarecrow Press, 1999), 137–42; Foster Hirsch, *Detours and Lost Highways: A Map of Neo-Noir* (New York: Limelight Editions, 1999), 289–304; Jans B. Wager, *Dangerous Dames: Women and Representation in the Weimar Street Film and Film Noir* (Athens: Ohio University Press, 1999),

124–27. African American appropriation of *film noir* has also received popular recognition. See, e.g., B. Ruby Rich, "Dumb Lugs and Femmes Fatales," *Sight and Sound* 5, no. 11 (November 1995): 6–10; Ed Guerrero, "Review of *Devil in a Blue Dress*," *Cineaste* 22, no. 1 (1996): 38, 40–41. Still, I would argue that its significance has been largely misunderstood, particularly its transformation of *noir*. For an especially striking example, see Hirsch, *Detours and Lost Highways*.

3. See, e.g., *Force of Evil* (Abraham Polonsky, 1948), *Raw Deal* (Anthony Mann, 1948), and *The Damned Don't Cry* (Vincent Sherman, 1950).

4. While generally I am in agreement with Eric Lott's claim in "The Whiteness of *Film Noir*," *American Literary History* 9 (1997): 542–66, that classical American *film noir* is marked by grievous racist exclusions, the problem is slightly more complicated that his generalization allows—something of which he shows some awareness in the last few pages of his essay. Lott is right to argue that overall classical *noir* is "the refuge of whiteness" (546), for its themes and obsessions are almost exclusively those of white culture. Yet there are exceptions that Lott dismisses too quickly, the most noteworthy of which are latecomers in the classical *noir* period, Orson Welles's *Touch of Evil* (1958) and Robert Wise's *Odds Against Tomorrow* (1959). I take up these and other complications relating to *film noir* and race in my *Philosophy, Black Film, Film Noir* (forthcoming).

5. See, e.g., Charles Mills, *The Racial Contract* (Ithaca, N.Y.: Cornell University Press, 1997), 17–19.

6. See my "Black on White: *Film Noir* and the Epistemology of Race in Recent African American Cinema," *Journal of Social Philosophy* 31 (2000): 82–116.

7. Chester Himes, *My Life of Absurdity: The Later Years* (New York: Paragon House, 1976).

8. And, for that matter, film. But that is a story that has already been well told. See, e.g., Thomas Cripps, *Slow Fade to Black: The Negro in American Film, 1900–1942* (New York: Oxford University Press, 1977); idem, *Making Movies Black: The Hollywood Message Movie from World War II to the Civil Rights Era* (New York: Oxford University Press, 1993); as well as essays in Daniel Bernardi, ed., *The Birth of Whiteness: Race and the Emergence of U.S. Cinema* (New Brunswick, N.J.: Rutgers University Press, 1996); Manthia Diawara, *Black American Cinema* (New York: Routledge, 1993).

9. See, e.g., John Rawls, *A Theory of Justice* (Cambridge, Mass.: Harvard University Press, 1971).

10. See, e.g., Robert Bernasconi, "Who Invented the Concept of Race? Kant's Role in the Enlightenment Construction of Race," in *Race*, ed. Robert Bernasconi (Oxford: Blackwell, 2001), 11–36; Richard H. Popkin, "Eighteenth Century Racism," in *The Columbia History of Western Philosophy*, ed. Richard H. Popkin (New York: Columbia University Press, 1999), 508–15; Mills, *The Racial Contract*, esp. 64–72; Emmanuel C. Eze, "The Color of Reason: The Idea of 'Race' in Kant's Anthropology," in *Postcolonial African Philosophy*, ed. Emmanuel C. Eze (London: Blackwell, 1997), 103–40; and the essays by these historical figures anthologized in Emmanuel C. Eze, ed., *Race and the Enlightenment* (London: Blackwell, 1997).

11. Mills, *The Racial Contract*, 17–19.

12. Ibid., 126–27.

13. Thomas E. Hill Jr. and Bernard Boxill, "Kant and Race," in *Race and Racism*, ed. Bernard Boxill (Oxford: Oxford University Press, 200¡), 448–47¡.

14. Ibid., 470.

15. Ibid., 469–70.

16. Lewis Gordon, *Fanon and the Crisis of European Man* (New York: Routledge, 1995), 62–63.

17. Lewis Gordon, *Bad Faith and Anti-Black Racism* (Atlantic Highlands, N.J.: Humanities Press, 1995), 182–84.

18. David Theo Goldberg, *Racist Culture* (London: Blackwell, 1993), esp. 144–45.

19. Jody David Armour, *Negrophobia and Reasonable Racism* (New York: New York University Press, 1997), 35–46.

20. Armour argues that *acting* on rationally based factual assessments such as those that Bayesian perspectives might offer would be unreasonable because it would fail to take into consideration other crucial factors, such as "the consequences of error if those factual judgments are mistaken" (ibid., 47). In other words, the cost of potential mistakes is too high for the threshold of *reasonably* acting on such beliefs to be breached. More generally, Armour explains that acting on these seemingly rationally justified racist beliefs ignores the value-laden dimension of reason (ibid., 55–57). The fact that being reasonable requires a balancing of different values, some of which are the costly potential harms that may arise if one is inaccurate about one's assessments, militate against these discriminatory beliefs' being endorsed by reason. Ultimately, he argues, such apparently rational assessments fall back on racial stereotypes for their foundation, rather than sound reasoning, so they may be rationally rejected (ibid., 51–54).

21. See Armour, *Negrophobia*, 1–46. See also Michael Levin, "Responses to Race Differences in Crime," in Boxill, *Race and Racism*, 145–79.

22. For this term I am mimicking, obviously, Laura Mulvey's description of what is now commonly called the "male gaze": see Laura Mulvey, "Visual Pleasure and Narrative Cinema," *Screen* 16, no. 3 (1975): 6–18.

23. Mills, *The Racial Contract*, 18; see also ibid., 91–109.

24. Ibid., 18.

25. See, e.g., Nino Frank, "The Crime Adventure Story: A New Kind of Detective Film," and Raymond Borde and Etienne Chaumeton, "Towards a Definition of *Film Noir*," both in *Perspectives on Film Noir*, ed. and trans. R. Barton Palmer (New York: G. K. Hall, 1996), 21–24, 59–65, respectively; Carlos Clarens, *Crime Movies* (New York: W. W. Norton, 1980), 191–233; Brian Neve, *Film and Politics in America: A Social Tradition* (New York: Routledge, 1992), 147–70; Mike Davis, *City of Quartz* (New York: Vintage, 1992), esp. 18–46.

26. Oddly, while this film explicitly condemns lynching, all its characters are white. This is strange because the history of lynching in America would lead one to believe that the lead characters who suffer this fate would be Black (see, e.g., James Allen et al., *Without Sanctuary: Lynching Photography in America* [Santa Fe, N.M.: Twin Palms, 2000]). Yet these roles are played by white actors (Lloyd Bridges and Frank Lovejoy) and no references to race are made in the narrative.

27. See Copjec, *Shades of Noir*, 261–78.

28. Ibid., 263.

29. Ibid., 262.

30. I want to note that the use of *noir* themes such as crime and transgression as "metaphors of resistance" to the values of the dominant white culture is something that the philosopher Tommy Lott has pinpointed as a key element in the success of rap and

hip-hop music: Tommy L. Lott, *The Invention of Race* (London: Blackwell, 1999), 121. By noting that the dominant media images of Black men are those of criminals and the ways in which hip-hop and rap work to invalidate those images by taking them on and recoding them for their own purposes, Lott explains that these musical forms convey different meanings to their intended audiences from those conveyed to individuals in power (ibid., 120–21). One result of this recoding is a transformation of what knowledge is: "to be *politically* astute" rather than in possession of empirical details (ibid., 122). Another is the value of defiance in the face of oppressive circumstances for the purpose of reinforcing a sense of self-respect, without necessarily endorsing the form that defiance takes (ibid.). Much like rappers who have exploited stereotypical gangster- and thug-life images to critique white power, makers of Black *film noir* have used and recoded the components of this form of film to expose and criticize white ways of knowing and acting. For a fuller explanation of how recent black films have borrowed from rap and hip-hop, see S. Craig Watkins, *Representing: Hip Hop Culture and the Production of Black Cinema* (Chicago: University of Chicago Press, 1998).

31. Regarding the former point, see Mark C. Taylor, "Malcolm's Conk and Danto's Colors; or, Four Logical Petitions Concerning Race, Beauty, and Aesthetics," in *Beauty Matters*, ed. Peg Zeglin Brand (Bloomington: Indiana University Press, 2000), 57–64; Mills, *The Racial Contract*, 61–62.

32. Gordon, *Bad Faith and Anti-Black Racism*, 114–15.

33. Ibid., 115.

34. Bernard Boxill, *Blacks and Social Justice*, rev. ed. (Lanham, Md.: Rowman and Littlefield, 1992), 139.

35. Mills, *The Racial Contract*, 81–87.

36. Ibid., 86.

37. Ibid., 87–88.

38. Ibid., 88.

39. See my "Black on White," esp. 90–106.

40. Perhaps, too, it is a response on Lee's part to critics such as bell hooks and Douglas Kellner, who have argued that one of the weaknesses of earlier Lee productions was that his critiques of race were too confined to single-issue or identity politics, and that he needed to incorporate a politics of otherness: see bell hooks, *Yearning: Race, Gender, and Cultural Politics* (Boston: South End Press, 1990), esp. 183–84; Douglas Kellner, "Aesthetics, Ethics, and Politics in the Films of Spike Lee," in *Spike Lee's "Do the Right Thing,"* ed. Mark A. Reid. (New York: Cambridge University Press, 1997), 73–106, esp. 98–99.

41. Hill and Boxill, "Kant and Race," 470.

42. See Adrian M. S. Piper, "Two Kinds of Discrimination," in Boxill, *Race and Racism*, esp. 231–37.

43. See Laurence Thomas, "Moral Deference," *Philosophical Forum* 24 (1992–93): 233–50.

Racial Kitsch and Black Performance

If kitsch is "ersatz culture," as the modernist art critic Clement Greenberg has proposed, then the racist kitsch that we still occasionally encounter in flea markets, on trips abroad, and in galleries and museums of contemporary art might be defined as failed humor. Kitsch, according to Greenberg, attempts to say something profound, but can utter only clichés. Its abject failure is an embarrassment. The sub-genre of racist kitsch, which was largely ignored by the modernists, attempts by contrast to say something banal. In its failed effort to move unobtrusively among the objects of our everyday encounter, racist kitsch unwittingly reveals itself to be profoundly laden with meaning. Attempting to remain ephemera at the periphery of our vision, racist kitsch in fact holds our gaze, stops our conversations, and in its demand for attention in spite of itself is an equal embarrassment.[1]

Racist kitsch is pretty disgusting. To well-meaning people today, and especially to those of us racialized as "others," the only pleasurable response to it is the pleasure of mastering the urge to laugh with the joke. Through disgust, we reassert our dignity and attain distance from the pleasure that the stereotype urges upon us. This oppositional distance places the racist object in a new frame, one in which the object is re-signified. From a token of mundane racist enjoyment, it becomes a totem of our racial survival.[2]

Tavia Nyong'o, "Racial Kitsch and Black Performance," *Yale Journal of Criticism* 15, no. 2 (2002): 371–91. © Yale University and the Johns Hopkins University Press. Reprinted with permission of the Johns Hopkins University Press.

Our disgust tells us that we are not the audience solicited by the object, that we are not the people who would find the object harmless fun. Disgust reasserts the boundaries of the body when it comes in potential contact with literal or metaphorical excrement.[3] The pleasure of disgust comes when we recover bodily integrity in the face of the dis-equilibrium presented by somebody else's shit. In the particular case of racist kitsch, disgust apprehends the object as a kind of body that we are not, or, at least, one that we are no longer. It draws a boundary, not only against the object's complicit audiences, but also against the object itself.

Strong disgust demands an immediate tactic or gesture to reassert dignity. The original response intended by the creators of racist kitsch, and now sedimented firmly into the unmemorialized pasts of white supremacy, is simply to laugh at the object. A more contemporary and oppositional tactic might be to destroy the object physically and thus end the intolerable question of its significance. In this vein, some recent critics have objected strongly to the curating or creating of racist kitsch, even with an oppositional gaze or intent. In different ways, two recent critics of "black memorabilia" reject the possibility that such an oppositional curating or creative practice could succeed. Racist kitsch is simply "visual terrorism," Robin Chandler observes, and Michael Harris, agreeing, suggests that because such kitsch "is linked to, and a product of, white imagination," the "attempt to invert and reconstruct another's dreams inevitably keeps one tied to and preoccupied with that other rather than the self."[4]

Such criticism amounts to a theoretical destruction of the kitsch object: It attempts to imagine or invent a discursive and cultural space in which the object of racist kitsch might no longer *matter*. The space produced through this imagined violence is occupied by an undifferentiated and collective black self, one that need never enter into relation with another. Such an approach solves the problem of history, and of racism, simply by wishing them away.

Another contemporary reaction, only superficially opposite, would be to curate the object, or to own it, and in these acts of curating and/or ownership, to modify the object in such a way as to render legible upon its surface the practices of our disgust. What happens when we attempt to collect or curate racist kitsch, to take ownership of it by modifying it so that it does not produce disgusting pleasure but a pleasurable disgust, or even an aesthetic experience on the order of the beautiful or the sublime?

What would be the consequence if an examination of such strategies of oppositional curating and ownership unexpectedly revealed that one key characteristic of the racist figure was its ability to retain, even under the powerfully revisionary gaze of disgust, the capacity to act as a scapegoat or effigy?[5] Could it be the case that our oppositional gaze and attendant practices depend upon the effigy's characteristic talent for absorbing blame, and thus, that they perpetuate our dependence upon scapegoating and its attendant cruelties?

In raising the issue of scapegoating, I am also seeking to provide a critique of the oppositional gaze from the standpoint of recent theoretical inquiry into shame.[6] The transformational powers of performance are available, this vein of criticism suggests, through resisting the pleasures of disgust and the temptation to reassert our bodies' imagined borders. Instead, queer criticism suggests, power might accrue from a confrontation with bordering work, from a dismantling of the protections of disgust, and from an embracing of shame and abjection as a point of departure.[7] It is through this suggestive new approach that I will attempt to reread the political and visual dynamics of racist kitsch, beginning in the nineteenth century, continuing with the film and television phenomenon, the *Little Rascals*, and culminating with a consideration of the recent film *Bamboozled* (2000), directed by Spike Lee.

Toward a Genealogy of Performing Black Children

Discussions of racist kitsch tend to notice especially the figures of Mammy and Uncle Tom.[8] Equally important to me is another invention of the nineteenth century: Topsy, the performing black child. In Harriet Beecher Stowe's novel *Uncle Tom's Cabin* (1852), Topsy is introduced as an example of the degraded condition into which children fall under the system of chattel slavery. When she is discovered by the kind-hearted plantation owner Augustine St. Clare she is dirty, parentless, abused, and without instruction in the gospel. St. Clare hears her screams as she is being beaten and buys her away from a cruel master to salve his conscience. Yet, unable to admit his sentimentality, St. Clare pretends to members of his family that he bought Topsy simply because she was "rather a funny specimen in the Jim Crow line."[9] Hearing a child being beaten, St. Clare replaces this with what psychoanalysis calls a "screen memory" of a child performing.[10]

Topsy enters the St. Clare household as surplus. The St. Clare residence is already teeming with numberless black children who are perpetually underfoot of their betters. St. Clare's abstemious visiting cousin from the North, Ophelia, is horrified at the extravagance of Topsy's purchase, especially given St. Clare's claim that it was a whim. She is even more distraught to be assigned the task of educating and Christianizing the irrepressible Topsy, who famously boasts of her natal alienation: "Never was born...never had no father nor mother, nor nothin'.... I spect I grow'd. Don't think nobody never made me."[11]

In the novel Topsy is eventually civilized, not by the harsh discipline of the compassionless woman she sarcastically calls "Feely," but instead by the sentimental power of Evangeline, the daughter of Marie and Augustine St. Clare. It is Little Eva's feeling for Topsy that precipitates the morally transformed character, who by novel's end is cleaned up, free, and off on a Christian mission to Africa.

Stage versions of *Uncle Tom's Cabin*, the indispensable play of the late–nineteenth-century American theater and para-theater, sometimes capitalized on Topsy's transformation from wild child to demure Christian. But more commonly they misread Stowe's novel and took St. Clare at his word when he claimed to have bought Topsy as entertainment, and left her laughably reprobate. On stage, she performed St. Clare's screen memory. As an entertainer, Topsy quickly became one of the most popular characters in the play, as necessary as Uncle Tom. Actors playing Topsy sometimes received top billing in mid–nineteenth-century productions, and Topsy's song was a hot seller in sheet music. Rival productions of *Uncle Tom's Cabin* were soon advertising two Topsies—double the fun, and fidelity to Stowe's novel be damned.[12]

Topsy's conquest of the landscape of U. S. popular culture makes her an inaugural figure in the genealogy of performing black children. She appears at a historical moment where a white-supremacist and slaveholding nation was actively debating "the character and destiny" of black folk. Within this debate were anxieties over the potential demographic explosion of a freed people of color, anxieties that manifested in the form of soberly scientific explanations about why the Negro would naturally die out if not under the pastoral care of slavery. This fantasy, also manifest in the counterfactual but common-sense belief that "hybrid" progeny between the races would be infertile (hence the echo of "mule" in the popular usage of "mulatto"), was belied by demographic reality. The Malthusian spectacle of a slavish class reproducing uncontrollably animated the popular consciousness that found in Topsy a scapegoat figure capable of resolving these tensions.[13]

In sharp contrast to the beloved Little Eva, whose angelic presence evoked tender memories for many bereaved white mothers and fathers (including Stowe herself, who had lost an infant son), Topsy is parentless and, in lacking Eva's qualities of feminine Christian sentiment, peculiarly genderless. Eva is not just well behaved, she is perfectly innocent, so perfect that her death from consumption was depicted on stage as a saint's apotheosis. She is literally too good for this world. Topsy, who is subjected to continuous physical abuse by Aunt Ophelia and the house slaves, is so hardy she is almost insensate. She is fun to kick; even she finds it fun. Eva is one of a precious few. Topsy is part of a disturbing and disgusting surplus. The violence done upon her is the performance of waste.[14]

The shiny, hard, and brittle surfaces of racist ceramic figurines reflect back upon the psychology of scapegoating black children. If the classical Hollywood techniques of film lighting seem peculiarly appropriate to the production of whiteness, as Richard Dyer has suggested, then the material form of the ceramic figurine seems, contrariwise, particularly apt for specifying blackness as a hardened form of subjectivity.[15] In this racial simile, a black skin is as hard as stone; not skin at all, but a mask, with perhaps nothing behind it. This invulnerability provides an alibi for racist violence, salving the guilt that accompanies the wish to punish the black child purposelessly.[16] This enjoyment completes the ideological ruse by finding within itself the occasion for a feeling of benevolence toward the scapegoat. Even moments of jarring violence are remembered as a charming encounter with a pickaninny. A bodily metaphor that people turn to in describing this pleasurable and guilty violence is eating. The performing black child is either hungry or eating or being eaten, or, ideally, all three.

The Story of Little Black Sambo, an odd and almost impossibly naive text, illustrates the edibility of the performing black child.[17] In the story, Sambo is set off for a walk in a set of colorful new clothes and accessories, which he is forced to give up, one by one, to a series of rapacious tigers. Having avoided being eaten through the performance of this strip tease, Sambo then witnesses the tigers fight ferociously until they melt into a pool of clarified butter, which is collected and used to fry up a delicious meal for Sambo and his parents. The story defers and ultimately disavows its desire to eat Sambo, making a visual meal of the threatening tigers instead. This popular story was made into at least one play for the children's theater, and is still in print today.[18]

If the cute black child is good enough to eat, she is also tough as nails. This toughness is suggested not so much in actual children, who are neither hard nor brittle nor invulnerable to pain, but rather in the materiality of the ceramic figurine. The racialized function of the figurine within consumer culture dates back to the dissemination in the late 1780s of the Jasperware Wedgewood medallion that famously portrayed a kneeling slave declaring, "Am I not a man and a brother?"[19] The historical and ideological links between this sort of abolitionist collectible and the commodification, beginning with the popular appropriation of Uncle Tom's Cabin, of the racist kitsch figurine, have yet to be fully traced. I want to suggest that the material dynamics of the figurine, which invite the enjoyable practices of abuse, and which also anticipate and accept the abuse that our revisionary and oppositional practices enact upon them, form the concrete obstacle to any utopian regime of non-racist visual enjoyment.[20]

Our Gang/Little Rascals

The difficulties intrinsic to any wished-for escape from the shame of America's racial past are evident in the shifting fortunes of the film and television phenomenon *Our Gang*, also known as the *Little Rascals*. In remarking upon this fixture of American childhood from my grandmother's day up to my own, I focus especially on the "peculiar" rascals: Ernie ("Booker T. Bacon," "Sorghum," "Sunshine Sammy") Morrison, Allen ("Farina," "Maple") Hoskins, Eugene ("Pineapple") Jackson, Jannie ("Mango") Hoskins, Matthew ("Stymie") Beard, Bobbie ("Cotton") Beard, and the three children named "Buckwheat": Carlena Beard, Willie Mae Taylor, and most famously, Billie Thomas.

What links these rascals, besides the fact that they are nearly all named after breakfast foods or exotic fruits, is their location in a racialized entertainment industry as performing black children. Although the culture industry they worked in undoubtedly participated in the establishment and maintenance of racial inequality, what is interesting about the black rascals is less their fit within then current racial policies of segregation and subordination as the lack of fit between the racial formation of the time, ideologically considered, and the general economy of innocent pleasures to which *Our Gang* caters. *Our Gang*—which ran from 1922 through 1944 in theaters and then, beginning in the 1950s, on television—played no specific ideological role within white-supremacist politics. The cultural work it seems to do is less a bolstering of claims to white supremacy, and more a production of the appropriate ambience for the insinuation of racially unmarked innocence, an innocence predicated upon a forgetfulness of the past that is one of the greatest privileges of whiteness.[21]

Something like the Blakean dialectic of innocence and experience is clearly at work in any contemporary encounter with *Our Gang*. The most exhaustive work of film scholarship on the series is also the product of a critic's love affair with the series.[22] In this exhaustive catalogue of every silent- and sound-era episode of the series, the critical vocabulary of film reviewing—discussions of technique, production anecdotes, and the crucial thumbs up or down summary judgment—provide the alibi for the critic to wish away the racial scapegoating that is nearly omnipresent.

The white rascals are not given edible names (Alfalfa is a possible exception). Gender distinction between them is essential to the parodies of adult heterosexual courtship and male bonding that delivered frequent laughs. By contrast, black children are edible and androgynous.[23] Farina was referred to with both male and female pronouns, even within a single episode. As Leonard Maltin explains,

> The studio had been deluged with mail inquiring whether Farina was a boy or a girl— a puzzled movie-going audience really didn't know, and for some reason wanted to find out. So Hal Roach seized upon this widespread curiosity as a publicity gimmick, resulting in news releases that failed to disclose the lad's real name, Allen Clayton Hoskins, and avoided the matter of sex, instead describing Farina with incredible appellations such as "that chocolate-coated fun drop of Hal Roach's Rascals."[24]

White little rascals, although homeless orphans, are not subjected to consistently imaginative punishments that frequently culminate in an implied off-screen death. This is the fate reserved for the younger of the two black rascals (there are typically two black rascals at any point in time, represented in the film as the siblings they in fact often were). Episode 6, "Saturday Morning" (December 3, 1922) ends with Farina accidentally submerged in a river by her brother. The same gag is repeated in episode 107, "Fly My Kite" (May 30, 1931). In episode 15, "Lodge Night" (July 29, 1923), the gang forms the "Cluck Cluck Klams," which Sunshine Sammy and Farina haplessly join, wear white sheets, and elect an "Xsalted Ruler." As an intertitle explains, Farina "doesn't know what the lodge is about—but is in favor of anything."[25] In episode 20, "No Noise" (September 23, 1923), Farina eats "nails, needles, and bits of tin and wire," which leads to the other rascals threatening to operate upon her.[26] She is drugged with chloroform and then shocked back awake with electricity. In episode 23, "Big Business," Mango chews on a razor. Episode 32, "Every Man for Himself" (October 19, 1924), ends with Farina covered with cactus needles from head to foot, which the gang "helpfully" removes. In episode 59, "Love My Dog" (April 17, 1927), Farina lets a white kid punch him in the face for two bits each time in order to raise five dollars to get his dog out of the pound.

Fans of the Little Rascals, or for that matter, the Three Stooges or the Marx Brothers, may remember this level of pleasurable punishment being inflicted on many white characters, not simply black ones.[27] But except for those who remember the Nickelodeon era, the Little Rascals we watched was already sanitized of its most brutal bits, which were inflicted with racial specificity on Farina, Buckwheat, and their functional equivalents.

Fredric Jameson has noted the prominence of pastiche in postmodern culture.[28] I want to build upon this insight in calling attention to the forms in which *Our Gang* has been restaged in American culture. Maltin's filmography provides an account of how, in the television series drawn almost entirely from the talkie era, the most objectionable episodes were silently taken out of circulation. In the form in which I first encountered the Little Rascals, as video-cassette compilations of their funniest moments, very few residues of racial scapegoating remain. Video pastiche is therefore in this case not random or eclectic fragmentation but is deeply patterned by a strategy of revising the Little Rascals continuously so as to rescue their innocent pleasures from the contagion of racist kitsch.[29] This is pastiche with a politics, a cultural logic in which racist enjoyment goes bad at a certain point in the stream of time, is suddenly revealed to be in poor taste. Like mold on a piece of cheese, offensive bits are trimmed and discarded while retaining as much of the originally wholesome commodity as we can stomach. By redefining racism as "not funny," value is preserved. Racism simply becomes bad business and is therefore shelved (in store perhaps for the day when it becomes good business once more?).

Maltin does not concur with this view. Race and racism are for him categories of experience, and, as such, are to be excluded from the enchanted worlds of innocent pleasure. The racial reader of *Our Gang*, in Maltin's view, simply cannot abandon her baggage of racial neuroses. This reader invents or produces race in an innocent text that is doing its best to get beyond, or outside, or before race. For episode 25, "Seein' Things" (April 6, 1924), it is worth quoting Maltin's synopsis at length:

> Every time Farina eats meat, he has strange nightmares. After being chased away from the gang's "barbercooe," he comes upon a toppled picnic basket in the street with enough food to fill an army. Farina downs it all, from fried chicken to ice cream, and that night he has a dream to end all dreams, being chased by giant-size versions of the gang kids through city streets, diving underwater, then returning to shore where a dynamite blast sends him flying through the air, landing on the ledge of a tall building, which he climbs to the top as the gang pursues him, following this with a shimmy up a roof-top flagpole, and after that's been chopped down, toppling precariously on a plank many stories above the pavement. Finally the gang manages to saw off the board, and Farina plummets to the ground—or rather, his bed, for at this point he awakens from his dream and vows, "Ah eat mush from now on!"[30]

Incredibly, this is for Maltin simply another example of "the non-malicious innocence with which *Our Gang* always treated the black–white situation."[31] Race, when it is considered at all, can only be understood as a "situation" that unhappily intrudes upon the world of the Little Rascals, one to which they are obliged occasionally to gesture. Lost in such an analysis is any awareness of the way visual culture actively produces racial consciousness, in addition to reflecting it. When, in episode 81, "Election Day" (January 12, 1929), Farina's parents, played by Louise Beavers and Clarence Muse, are driven out of town by a mob of angry whites, Maltin only comments on the "startling illusion" created by the "visual gag" of the dust cloud they raise.[32] When forced to admit that an episode is a little vulgar (the "Cluck Cluck Klams," for instance), he simply dismisses those films as inferior or in poor taste.

In so explaining away the distasteful elements of *Our Gang,* Maltin consigns the iconography of racist kitsch to "the great hole of history," to use Suzan-Lori Parks's emotive phrase.[33] It is hard not to imagine this process as akin to disposing of the evidence of a crime. This manufactured innocence is hard to bear for those who would still wish to act against racism in the contemporary world, which explains the somewhat paradoxical interest, among black and anti-racist artists, in reviving and refiguring the iconography of racist kitsch. The other option, it seems, is to let it all be consigned to the great hole of history.

From Racist Kitsch to Racial Kitsch

I find evidence for these claims in the reappearance of racist kitsch at the very moment where one would have supposed social and political transformations would have made it irrelevant. Spike Lee's film *Bamboozled* (2000) indexes and extends a long-standing practice of African-American curating of the racist kitsch figure. But in moving this practice from the less-accessible spaces of the private home or the art gallery to the much broader stage of contemporary cinema, Lee's film becomes a crucial site for the close analysis of this practice of oppositional curating. The film is trapped in the unhappy dynamic of disseminating an iconography that it cannot stop destroying, and which it therefore cannot stop producing. The alternative to the evacuated, innocent past proposed by Maltin is one populated only by racism, a Pandora's box of innumerate little black Sambos who, like vengeful spirits, arise to destroy all who unwisely invoke their name.

The film concerns the black television executive Pierre Delacroix, played by Damon Wayans, who proposes a neo-minstrel show to his white boss Thomas Dunwitty (Michael Rapaport) to protest the latter's patronizing attitude toward black culture. To Delacroix's seeming distress, Dunwitty takes the bait, and the show, shorn of Delacroix's intended irony, is an overnight success. *Bamboozled* ruthlessly satirizes in every direction. Neither condescending white media stars, nor ambitious black urban professionals, nor even race-conscious black nationalists escape the film's corrosive wit. Less moralistic than didactic, the script builds into the film the very dialogue about racism, authenticity, and entertainment that it wants to generate among its viewers. Ultimately, however, the film cannot escape its narrative destiny, which is to impose a judgment upon the intolerable web of ambiguities and inauthenticities it conjures. It does so through an extraordinarily melodramatic series of murders: first of Manray /Mantan (Savion Glover), the star of Delacroix's minstrel show, then of the black hip-hop collective who stage his televised execution, and, finally, of Delacroix himself, shot by his remorseful assistant Sloan Hopkins (Jada Pinkett Smith), the character whose moral authority is undercut the least in the film.

Bamboozled, as with all work by Spike Lee, provides much critical fodder.[34] Ironically, one of Lee's most interesting and astute critics, Manthia Diawara, has identified Lee's aesthetic as itself a form of kitsch. In a cryptic but essential essay, "Afro-kitsch," Diawara critiques the "kitsch of blackness," which he defines as the "imitation of a discourse of liberation" in the service of "mass identification."[35] Returning to the definition of kitsch as failed seriousness, he considers the difficulty of Lee's films to lie in their frustrated desire to achieve the impossible, to become a surrogate for a radical politics within the landscape of a demobilized and demoralized media culture. Nowhere is this dilemma more acute than in Bamboozled.

That a new reflexivity has been introduced into Lee's vision is evident in the intensely skeptical focus that Bamboozled brings to bear upon the black nationalist collective Mau Mau, led by Sloan Hopkins's brother Julius Hopkins, a.k.a. Big Blak Afrika (Mos Def). Sincere but somewhat hapless (as evidenced in their obviously white member, played by M.C. Serch of 3rd Bass), they react with holy anger against the neo-minstrel show, but are totally oblivious to the man behind the curtain, and therefore select Manray himself as the target of their vengeance. In a scene that visually parallels the opening of the film, in which Manray is dancing on a pallet, they set him dancing again to the rhythm of their gunfire.

A major point of Bamboozled seems to be to call attention to the immense skill trapped within minstrelized iconography—to the double injustice done to audience and performer by the demeaning legacies of slavery and racism. Thus, the film invests itself in producing as plausible a neo-minstrel show as possible, with as talented a cast of dancers and comedians as possible, led by Glover. This structural contradiction in the film, which Lee purposefully elicits in fusing Glover's culturally proud choreography with blackface's cultural profanity, is formally resolved by the unusual level of bloodletting at the film's end. In blacking up, Manray/Mantan becomes waste, and his violent death is literally a performance: it is broadcast on prime-time television.

A moment which prefigures the violence visited upon Manray/Mantan is a scene between him and Lil' Nigger Jim in which, frustrated by the child's

Bamboozled (2000). It's Showtime! Savion Glover as Manray/Mantan.

inability to learn choreography quickly enough, Manray verbally abuses him. This moment is understood as a watershed in Manray's dehumanization: He has begun to internalize Jim's status not as a human child but as a mechanized, senseless, performing doll, as a Topsy. We, on the other hand, protectively and humanely recognize Jim as an abused child. This scene of a child being beaten is doubly phobic: of Manray/Mantan's unmanly sadism *and* of Jim's helpless and childish non-masculinity. He alerts our protective instincts, but protection is not the same as, perhaps is even the opposite of, identification. Between Jim and the Mau Mau going out in a blaze of glory, there is no contest about where identification lies. To identify, contrapuntally, with the abashed and wounded child, rather than with our protective feelings for him, is to locate the abjection on screen and within ourselves that *Bamboozled* elicits but cannot tolerate.

The film seems to deliver a very pointed warning against black-on-black violence. But this critique of black-on-black violence does not extend to violence itself; rather, it is the focus, not the nature, of Mau Mau's wrath that is most questioned (i.e., the focus on Manray, not the white executive who shows his racist true colors in the moments before Manray is kidnapped by the Mau Mau). This seems to be because, while authenticity is subject to a great deal of skepticism in *Bamboozled*, the shamefulness of *in*authenticity is never questioned. The film's phobia for Pierre Delacroix is total. He has abandoned his name, his language, his family, his race, even his manhood (as is shown in his treatment of women). Depicted with over-the-top glee by the comic actor Damon Wayans, who uses the effeminate mannerisms he perfected in parodying a gay film reviewer on the television series *In Living Color,* Delacroix is the film's internal scapegoat, one upon whom we can credibly lay blame, and, therefore, additional violence. The odd, excessive repetition of carnage, in which Delacroix's death avenges the death of the Mau Mau (which is society's vengeance for their murder of Manray), shows that the film cannot find a way to exit the circuit of "an eye for an eye."

Conclusion: Becoming Modern, Becoming Innocent

The curating or ownership of racist kitsch is confounding to those who would rather forget it ever occurred. Thus, a film like *Bamboozled* is seen by some as "heavy-handed satire," an "endless polemic" that is only barely "endurable." For Maltin, the author of these judgments, to remember the racism within innocent pleasures is already to be polemical.[36] To pollute the American popular film—a form centered, as Richard Dyer argues, upon the romantic utopia of a white heterosexual couple in three-point lighting—with blackface is simple resentment. Twentieth-century postmodernity in the U.S. racial imagination is structured by a wish to move beyond and forget the scapegoating of blacks. Becoming modern involves the seemingly impossible task of becoming innocent, a project that in its more academic formulations announces itself as "post-race."

Manthia Diawara's provocative essay accompanying photographs of racist kitsch by David Levinthal discusses this difficulty with uncommon skill.[37] His comprehensive analysis of the visual and material culture of racist kitsch, and the specific resignifications that Levinthal's art photography works upon them, ends in an ambivalent anecdote regarding an interaction with his thirteen-year-old son, who innocently happens upon him as he is examining the photographs. His son's indifferent response to the images, Diawara reports, "is challenging me to stop being the custodian of these stereotypes, to distance myself from them, and to begin enjoying the humor in them. Only then will I, like him, become an individual and modern."[38]

Diawara's essay thus ends by taking the willfully ironic stance of an achieved innocence. Becoming modern means becoming innocent, a process that seems available only through the enlarging and revivifying energies of a child. Diawara's enjoyment of his son's insouciance—may I call it his invulnerability?—in the face of racist kitsch recapitulates the economy of pleasure I have been discussing, but in a way that should produce self-recognition in us rather than another round of scapegoating.

Although Diawara's wish to "begin enjoying the humor" again reminds us of Maltin's position regarding *Our Gang*, I want to suggest that it can have a different implication. I have repeatedly suggested that oppositional spectatorship to the figure of racist kitsch cannot overcome its ability to reproduce scapegoating, because these practices of opposition inevitably reinscribe the object as a target for hatred and scorn, and in doing so, draw other people into the suffering orbit of the ceramic doll, other people whose punishments can be understood not as cruelty but as fun. This is the fate of Manray and especially Delacroix in *Bamboozled*.

The transforming of shame this essay has been recommending cannot proceed programmatically. By definition, any project endorsing creativity cannot determine in advance what course such creativity might take. But it may be at least suggestive to explore a parallel here between queer theory and Descartes's famous "I think, therefore I am." At bottom, the shame of racist kitsch resides in the idea that "I am thought of as less than human." And yet, the very shame that floods through at that thought, a shame that, were we not human, we would have no capacity to feel, is our best internal evidence that the thought is wrong and vulgar: I feel (shame), therefore I am (human).

Acknowledging the permanence of our shame, and its usefulness, may mark the beginning Diawara wishes for but does not quite find in his call to "begin enjoying the humor" again. The point may not be to become individual and modern, to ever achieve a kind of prophylactic invulnerability to the object that says, "Shame on you! Shame on you for being black!" We do not, at this late date, need yet newer formulations of pride to negate this shame. The point may be to locate, within the transformations of our shame, a way out of scapegoating, and thus out of the bloodletting that accompanies with such monotonous reliability our attempts to regain our innocence.

NOTES

This essay first emerged at the solicitation of Laurie Essig, and I thank her and Sarah Chinn for encouragement and comment. Along the way toward its present incarnation, Robin Bernstein and Brian Herrera added their timely criticisms. Thanks also to Pearl James, Erika Rundle, and the editors of the *Yale Journal of Criticism* for their valuable help and comments.

1. On kitsch as ersatz culture, see Clement Greenberg, "Avant-Garde and Kitsch," in *Art in Theory: 1900–1990*, ed. Charles Harrison and Paul Wood (Oxford: Blackwell,

1992). See also Dennis Dutton, "Kitsch," in *Grove Dictionary of Art Online*, 1998 available online at http://www.groveart.com (accessed May 15, 2002). On what I am calling "racist kitsch," see Patricia A. Turner, *Ceramic Uncles and Celluloid Mammies: Black Images and their Influence on Culture* (New York: Anchor, 1994); Kenneth W. Goings, *Mammy and Uncle Mose: Black Collectibles and American Stereotyping* (Bloomington: Indiana University Press, 1994). On contemporary art that mimics and critiques racist kitsch, see Michael D. Harris, "Memories and Memorabilia, Art and Identity," *Third Text*, no. 44 (1998). Ferris State University in Big Rapids, Michigan, hosts the Jim Crow Museum of Racist Memorabilia, curated by Dr. David Pilgrim.

2. See bell hooks, "The Oppositional Gaze," in idem, *Black Looks: Race and Representation* (Boston: South End Press, 1992), 115–32. On the application of an oppositional gaze to interrupt sexist (and, implicitly, racist) pleasures, see Laura Mulvey, "Visual Pleasure and Narrative Cinema," *Screen* 16, no. 3 (1975): 6–18.

3. See William Ian Miller, *The Anatomy of Disgust* (Cambridge, Mass.: Harvard University Press, 1997). See also Norman O. Brown, "The Excremental Vision," in idem, *Life against Death: The Psychoanalytical Meaning of History* (Middletown, Conn.: Wesleyan University Press, 1959), 179–201.

4. Robin M. Chandler, "Xenophobes, Visual Terrorism and the African Subject," *Third Text,* no. 35 (1996): 17; Harris, "Memories and Memorabilia," 42.

5. The terms "scapegoat" and "effigy" are used somewhat interchangeably in this essay, although a longer account would need to restore their full complexity. An important account of the scapegoat is given in René Girard, *The Scapegoat*, trans. Yvonne Freccero (Baltimore: Johns Hopkins University Press, 1986). See also Joseph Roach, *Cities of the Dead: Circum-Atlantic Performance* (New York: Columbia University Press, 1996), esp. 36–41.

6. See Eve Kosofsky Sedgwick, "Queer Performativity: Henry James and the Art of the Novel," *GLQ* 1, no. 1 (1993): 1–16. See also idem and Adam Frank, eds., *Shame and Its Sisters: A Silvan Tomkins Reader* (Durham, N.C.: Duke University Press, 1995). A recent defense of politics conducted from the standpoint of abjection/shame is available in Michael Warner, *The Trouble with Normal: Sex, Politics and the Ethics of Queer Life* (New York: Free Press, 1999).

7. This argument is made powerfully throughout Robert Reid-Pharr, *Black Gay Man: Essays* (New York: New York University Press, 2001).

8. See, e. g., the titles (but not the exemplary content) of Turner, *Ceramic Uncles and Celluloid Mammies*; Donald Bogle, *Toms, Coons, Mulattoes, Mammies, and Bucks: An Interpretive History of Blacks in American Films*, 3rd ed. (New York: Continuum, 1994).

9. Harriet Beecher Stowe, *Uncle Tom's Cabin* (New York: Bantam, 1981), 237.

10. See Sigmund Freud, "'A Child Is Being Beaten': A Contribution to the Study of the Origin of Sexual Perversions [1919]," in *The Standard Edition of the Complete Psychological Works of Sigmund Freud*, vol. 17, trans. and ed. James Strachey et al. (London: Hogarth, 1955), 179–204. On the psychic traffic between beating and performance, see Eve Kosofsky Sedgwick, "A Poem Is Being Written," *Representations* 17 (1987): 110–43.

11. Stowe, *Uncle Tom's Cabin*, 238. On the concept of "natal alienation," see Orlando Patterson, *Slavery and Social Death* (Cambridge, Mass.: Harvard University Press, 1982).

12. On stage versions of *Uncle Tom's Cabin*, see Harry Birdoff, *The World's Greatest Hit* (New York: Vanni, 1947); Thomas F. Gossett, *Uncle Tom's Cabin and American Culture* (Dallas: Southern Methodist University Press, 1985). In "A Child Is Being Beaten," Freud notes, "In my patients' *milieu* it was almost always the same books whose contents gave a new stimulus to the beating-phantasies: those accessible to young people, such as what was known as the *'Bibliotèque rose,'* Uncle Tom's Cabin, etc." (Freud, "A Child Is Being Beaten," 180). This fragment suggests that Topsy, as one of the children being beaten in the novel, can actually be thought to contribute to the evidence on which Freud builds his theoretical account.

13. See George Fredrickson, *The Black Image in the White Mind: The Debate on Afro-American Character and Destiny, 1817–1914* (New York, Conn.: Harper and Row, 1972).

14. This definition of violence derives from the work of Georges Bataille on what he terms "general economy," which for Bataille is founded not upon the problem of scarcity but, rather, on the problematics of excess: excess of resources, excess of people: see Georges Bataille, *The Accursed Share: An Essay on General Economy* (New York: Zone Books, 1998). The exact phrasing is from Roach, *Cities of the Dead*, 41.

15. Richard Dyer, *White* (New York: Routledge, 1997).

16. The etiology of this guilt is a problem within psychoanalysis. In "A Child Is Being Beaten," Freud initially locates the origin of this guilt in the family romance (Freud, "A Child Is Being Beaten," 191). This is usually not the approach taken by theorists of oppositionality, who assume this guilt is of an *ethical* nature. While Freud later in his essay seemingly acknowledges the role of ethical or conscientious guilt (ibid., 194), it is sobering to ponder his first account of guilt, built entirely without reference to ethics. In other words, Freud finds it possible to theorize this guilt without depending upon any necessary ethical counterweight to sadism. Oppositional criticism, by contrast, is rhetorically dependent upon claiming this universal, if suppressed, hard-wired guilt.

17. Helen Bannerman, *The Story of Little Black Sambo* (New York: Stokes, [1900]). Although set in India, the race of Sambo is destabilized not only by his name, but by those of his parents, Mumbo and Jumbo. So while he may *literally* be a lower-caste Indian, *literarily* speaking he is of African descent. In fact, part of the "charm" of the book is to render such geographic niceties beside the point; the black pickaninny is nothing if not portable.

18. Hazel Sharrard Kaufman, *Little Black Sambo, a Play in Three Scenes for Pre-School Children* (New York City: Samuel French, 1928).

19. On the transformation of the Wedgewood icon from sculptural medallion to popular print, see Kirk Savage, *Standing Soldiers, Kneeling Slaves: Race, War, and Monument in Nineteenth-Century America* (Princeton, N.J.: Princeton University Press, 1997), 21–22. See also Marcus Wood, *Blind Memory: Visual Representations of Slavery in England and America* (New York: Routledge, 2000).

20. This paragraph is influenced by the arguments put forward in Saidiya Hartman, *Scenes of Subjection: Terror, Slavery, and Self-Making in Nineteenth-Century America* (New York: Oxford University Press, 1997).

21. Scott Malcolmson's recent account of the development of racial ideology in the United States is especially illuminating in drawing the connection between whiteness and innocence: see Scott L. Malcomson, *One Drop of Blood: The American Misadventure of Race* (New York: Farrar, Straus and Giroux, 2000).

22. Leonard Maltin and Richard W. Bann, *Our Gang: The Life and Times of the Little Rascals* (New York: Crown, 1977). In what follows, I am primarily reading this text rather than the filmic texts it refers to, some of which are no longer commercially available.

23. The non-importance of gender difference at the formative stage of the fantasy "a child is being beaten" is noted by Freud ("A Child Is Being Beaten," 185).

24. Maltin and Bann, *Our Gang*, 42.

25. Ibid., 33.

26. Ibid., 38.

27. Sarah E. Chinn reminds me that they are seen weekly on Comedy Central's *South Park*.

28. Fredric Jameson, *The Cultural Turn: Selected Writings on the Postmodern* (New York: Verso, 1998).

29. In "A Child Is Being Beaten," Freud refutes the simplistic sexualized accounts of repression adopted by other psychoanalysts, and instead insists on seeing repression as an historical process. "Man's archaic heritage forms the nucleus of the unconscious mind; and whatever part of that heritage has to be left behind in the advance to later phases of development, because it is unserviceable or incompatible with what is new and harmful to it, falls a victim to the process of repression" (Freud, "A Child Is Being Beaten," 203–204). See also idem, *Civilization and Its Discontents*, trans. James Strachey (New York: W. W. Norton, 1961).

30. Maltin and Bann, *Our Gang*, 42.

31. Ibid., 67.

32. Ibid., 93.

33. Suzan-Lori Parks, *The America Play, and Other Works* (New York: Theatre Communications Group, 1995). See also Joseph Roach, "The Great Hole of History: Liturgical Silence in Beckett, Osofisan, and Parks," *South Atlantic Quarterly* 100, no. 1 (2001): 307–17.

34. See the special issue of *Black Renaissance/Renaissance Noire* devoted to the film (Fall–Winter 2001).

35. Manthia Diawara, "Afro-Kitsch," in *Black Popular Culture: A Project*, ed. Gina Dent and Michele Wallace (Seattle: Bay Press, 1992), 287–89.

36. Maltin's review of *Bamboozled* can be found online at http://www.imdb.com.

37. David Levinthal and Manthia Diawara, *Blackface* (Santa Fe, N.M.: Arena, 1999).

38. Ibid., 17.

"I Be Smackin' My Hoes": Paradox and Authenticity in *Bamboozled*

Bamboozled paints a portrait of a corporate plantation where the slaves now have stock options.
—Duane Dudek, *Milwaukee Journal Sentinel*

Call him what you will—talented, stubborn, creative, didactic, hard-working, jackass, auteur—Shelton "Spike" Lee has been a cultural force for over twenty years. Many of his films are household names; others barely elicit recognition. Beyond *Do the Right Thing* (1989), the trajectory and evolution of Lee's literal production is nothing short of phenomenal. In the directing of over fifty fictional narrative films and videos, documentaries, commercials, and music videos, Lee has produced some of the most provocative and aesthetically sophisticated work around—especially in terms of screening black folks. No matter what one thinks of his filmmaking or him personally, his impact on American popular culture cannot be denied.

On college and university campuses, scholars use Lee's work across many disciplinary fronts. I know this because I've been teaching his films over the last several years and engage with professors from media studies and English to women's, Africana, and American studies who do the same. The field of media studies especially continues to be one of the most consistent places to find critical interrogation and inquiry of his work. Yet, opinions about Lee's narrative and aesthetic practices span the gamut. In his first work of the twenty-first century, *Bamboozled* (2000), Lee once again forces U.S. audiences to confront the product of their histories—legacies of slavery, racism, violence, and disdain.

Like most of Lee's works, *Bamboozled* is packed with myriad narrative threads. Briefly, the film finds Lee's characters engaged in a classic game of chicken: Black television writer is not black enough—not offering black enough stories according to his white, wannabe black, boss. Said writer tries to outfox this executive "wigga" by creating a black program—a minstrel show—so offensive and racist that he gets fired. In spite of the writer's intentions, the program becomes a hit. The writer is caught between the pain of his creation and the joy of his success. Amid this dilemma, other storylines include a lovers' triangle, a call for revolution, and a reification of American racist artifacts. These subplots support the principal story of the writer. But in typical Lee fashion, they take center stage in frequent and unexpected ways. In the end, black lives are lost, with others left in ruin. These are the broad strokes of *Bamboozled*'s story.

Within this minimal synopsis, Lee addresses the articulation and continuation of minstrelsy, the hegemonic structuring of entertainment (in this case television), the struggle between class and race, and the desperation for and of African American televisual recognition. While substantial critical scholarship has addressed the aforementioned subject matters, what has escaped significant commentary is *Bamboozled*'s internal and external paradoxes and its engagement with constructions of the real. Thus in this essay, I use the frameworks of paradox and authenticity to examine the ways in which Lee both forwards and undermines notions of black progress in twenty-first century visual culture and within real-lived actualities.

Like *Bamboozled*, which opens with a definition of satire, I look to Noah Webster's *New World Dictionary* for a definition of "paradox"—Webster's religious piety coupled with his tendency to craft words in ways that supported his religious positioning make this version apropos. Paradox is "a statement that seems contradictory, absurd, etc. but may be true in fact . . . a statement that contradicts itself and is false . . . a person, situation, etc. that seems inconsistent or full of contradictions."[1] This essay takes up the third definition. In the case of *Bamboozled*, paradox refers to situations and persons that are not only contradictory but also meaningfully detrimental to progressive, collective visions for African America. The definition encapsulates the intention, reflection, and refraction of the film.

Alongside paradox, the invocation of authenticity, of "keepin' it real," permeates almost every interaction, every scene in *Bamboozled*. The debate of authenticity in black popular culture has been raging in both consumer and scholarly communities for the past three decades (if not longer); the best discussion of it, perhaps, is Stuart Hall's "What Is This 'Black' in Black Popular Culture?"[2] In terms of Lee's work, scholars noticed and reiterated his claims of authenticity (and claims of others for him) ever since *Do the Right Thing*.[3] Returning to Webster, "authenticity" is defined as "that [which] can be believed; reliable . . . genuine; real . . . legally executed, as a deed."[4] In terms of popular culture, authenticity refers to the display, respect of, and/or aspirations of those from where you came. The anthropologist John H. Jackson Jr. writes that, instead of authenticity, what should be discussed is racial sincerity—"an attempt to talk about racial *subjects* and subjectivities. . . . Sincerity highlights the ever-fleeting 'liveness' of everyday racial performances that cannot be completely captured by authenticating mediations of any kind."[5] While sincerity offers a useful paradigm for real-lived subjects, authenticity seems to better situate representations of African American life within popular visual culture and their paradoxical relationship to that culture.

Minstrelsy

Before addressing how these frameworks of paradox and authenticity work in *Bamboozled*, I want to situate this film in the context of cultural and media scholarship. *Bamboozled*'s revival of minstrelsy has generated a deluge of scholarly and journalistic critique, including special journal editions of *Cineaste* and *Black Renaissance/Renaissance Noir*. The film provides examples of and attempts to unpack the legacy of minstrelsy historically, culturally, and visually. From minstrel history lessons given by Sloan (Jada Pinkett Smith) to the compelling montage of images that concludes the work, the overriding story trajectory (and thus maybe justified critical attention) is the evolution of minstrelsy and Lee's narrative insinuation that it continues into the twenty-first century.

The scholar Michele Wallace reasons that, "for many black cultural historians, blackface minstrelsy is assumed to be the paradigmatic instance of an inauthentic, racist, and hostile representation of blackness."[6] The minstrelsy ethos, if following the logic of *Bamboozled* and its not-so-veiled references to UPN and WB, is perpetuated in every aspect of contemporary visual exhibition.[7] No stranger to controversy, Lee refuses to ignore what he deems ignorant in contemporary culture. In the film, he addresses the preponderance of African American representations (mostly sitcoms) that appeared initially on Fox and migrated to UPN and the WB television networks beginning in the 1990s, and BET in the latter part of the decade. From advertisements to music videos, the grateful, humble, "shuckin and jivin" black is resurrected within these media offerings—ostensibly, but not exclusively—at the hands of whites but for the pleasure of all. *Bamboozled* imagines what the television and actual world might look like with the revival of an actual minstrel show in prime time.

Lee positions minstrelsy in variant ways—as horrific but also as deceptively entertaining. The critic Greg Tate suggests that the film seems to be mostly concerned with minstrelsy "as the currency of success in the African-American negotiations with white corporate America"[8] (minstrelsy making the opening epigraph viable and visible). Paradoxically, the scholar Michael H. Epp believes that the film's address of minstrelsy determines its effects, observing, "Just as minstrelsy can be used to serve racist ends so can it be used to revisit racist discourse—always remembering however, that [*The Birth of a Nation*'s] place in the blackface lore cycle is a forbidding one."[9] Says the critic Stuart Klawans: Lee has "shown that the entertainment *is* the wound—the louder the laughter, the worse the damage."[10] While Lee's usage of minstrelsy is not wrong, it is not quite right either.

Furthermore, Lee hedges the extent to which African Americans contribute to their continued visual degradation. He uses the well-documented "realities" of working in the entertainment industry as a departure point for an argument that posits continuity between working conditions in the past and the present (and continuities between the representative politics of the film and television industries). In an interview on *Bamboozled*, he maintains that actors such as Hattie McDaniel and Bill Bojangles Robinson acted in those parts because it was their only option to work.[11] In the film, audiences are instructed on the racist images that dominated mainstream culture and cultural production (and not so long ago), on lessons of blacking up, and on the legacy and intricacy of tap dance as demonstrated by Manray (Savion Glover).[12] This same point is reiterated in the struggles of Delacroix's (Damon Wayans) assistant Sloan and their working conditions within a sea of white faces.

Lee's own career provides an example of how artists must negotiate the entertainment industry. For instance, as part of the strategy to control and retain his vision, he produced a book to accompany each of his first five films. These "journals" chronicle the production processes and include commentary by cast and crew, photographs, and the script for each film. Additionally, he sold T-shirts, hats, and other paraphernalia emblazoned with his films' logo and/or ideology—all available from Spike's Joint retail outlets in Brooklyn and Los Angeles (both now closed). Lee remarks, "Somebody wearing your T-shirt is a walking billboard."[13] In his production of *Malcolm X*, Lee sold items with an X across them one year before the release of the film. With *Bamboozled*, a striking poster of an open-mouthed caricature in black face invites the audience into the depths of Dixie—an image that indicts multiple audiences.

Yet despite the racism and challenges of the entertainment industry, I submit that options always exist. Black actors' participation in early cinema brought minstrel performances from the stage to the screen in the same way that contemporary African American performers such as Cuba Gooding Jr., Kim Whitley, Lil' Kim, Tiny Lister, and frequently the Wayans brothers contemporarily choose to with many of the roles they assume. In other words, African Americans play a crucial role in the continued perpetuation of one-dimensional imagery of themselves. When Lee kills many of the black characters in the end, all of the white ones live on (including the one white Mau Mau) to replicate the Minstrel Show's success.

Moreover in the years since *Bamboozled*'s release, few critics or media makers—scholarly or otherwise—have grappled with the conundrums it poses. Certainly within HBO's *Da Ali G Show* (HBO, 2003), *Matrix Revolutions* (Andy and Larry Wachowski, 2003), *Crash* (Paul Haggis, 2004), *Black. White.* (FX, 2006), and the myriad discourses that circulate about these texts, one would expect to see/read some linkages made to minstrelsy, blackface, *Bamboozled*, something. But perhaps the paradox of *Bamboozled* for mainstream culture is its silencing illumination. The structured absence of mainstream/popular commentary beyond film review points to the ongoing celebration of post-ideologies alongside the false sense of (inter- and intra-) racial progress. This discussion of minstrelsy leads directly to the second most addressed aspect of this film, satire and its effectiveness.

Satire

Various writers have taken up *Bamboozled* in light of the first word uttered in the narrative beyond the sound track—"satire." Offering a voiceover definition of the term, the writer Pierre Delacroix, "Dela," dissects the word as a way to introduce the audience to what is to follow as well as to the purpose of the film. Referencing the perpetuation or negotiation of minstrelsy, film reviewers and scholars use satire as a jump-off point to assess the strengths and weaknesses, successes and failures of the film. And yes, *Bamboozled* is indeed satirical—casting its critical spotlight on everything from black television representation to the structure of the television industry to the role women occupy in entertainment (especially behind the scenes).

Yet while the scholar Jamie Barlowe concurs that *Bamboozled* is indeed a biting satire, the audience within the narrative as well as reviewers outside often misread it. She laments:

> The real satire—the real joke— . . . is on all of us in the United States, as a nation that cannot face its own history of colonialism, hegemony, cultural imperialism, slavery, discrimination, fear-based perceptions, and racism, but which professes as a nation to abhor the very violence that underpins and informs the society, its institutions and re-representations of the black Other.[14]

In opposition, others such as Tate believe that *Bamboozled* lacks "satirical nerve."[15] Generally, scholars and critics alike have valued Lee's satirical approach and, to varying degrees, agree with its success. While the scholarly lenses of minstrelsy and satire have been useful in thinking about *Bamboozled*'s impact, it seems to me that obvious, yet minimally explored, frameworks of paradox and authenticity in *Bamboozled* can yield some of the most useful insights into contemporary black progress.

Power of Paradox

An illustration of *Bamboozled*'s central paradox lies in its audition scene. Having received the green light from the CNS Network to create a pilot for the minstrel show, Delacroix, Sloan, and a casting director (Liza Jessie Peterson) begin the staffing process beyond the two main characters Manray/Mantan (Savion Glover) and Womack/Sleep-n-Eat (Tommy Davidson). At the beginning of this audition session, Dela bemoans the dearth of roles for African American actors as evidenced by the line around the building for this television minstrel show.

His voiceover informs the audience that just the smallest advertisement in *Backstage* brought African Americans of various levels of talent, experience, and appropriateness to the call. The Roots (well regarded for their cultural consciousness and racial sincerity) audition for the position of house band, the Alabama Porch Monkeys. When asked if they have a problem with the band's name and their role, the lead singer (Tariq Trotter, a.k.a. Black Thought) replies, "No sir"—implying that a lack of opportunities propel even entertainers like them to take roles that they may not otherwise.[16] From a didgeridoo player to interpretive dancer, black cultural workers bring whatever talents they have to resurrect life in a watermelon patch.

Yet it is a Luther Vandross/David Peaston wannabe's (Tuffy Questell) singing audition that really captures the essence of paradox *Bamboozled* embodies. He sings:

> I . . . I be smackin' them hoes. I be smackin' my hoes. Everyone knows it goes. Kick 'em to the ground. Step on 'em hard. Step on 'em hard. Kick 'em to the ground. Cause I . . . I be smackin' my hoes. I be smackin' my hoes. I be smackin' my hoes! Thank you.

Admittedly, this is both one of the funniest and most disturbing sequences in the entire film. In a mere thirty seconds, the black minstrel tradition is reified through the performance codes of rap and hip-hop. This scene moves beyond parody to demonstrate, through pastiche, historical continuities between the minstrel stage and contemporary music. While Sloan and the casting director watch his performance incredulously, the film positions this Generation X

Bamboozled (2000)."I Be Smackin' My Hoes" audition.Tuffy Questell as auditioning singer

singer (and his unseen promoters) as unknowledgeable, or at least not acknowledging anything problematic with his lyrics and presentation.

Transformations in rhythm and blues (R&B)and the larger industry more
generally have been ongoing since the early 1990s. The fluid sound and movement of "old school" R&B segued into the bump-n-grind of R. Kelly, where
even soul man Ron Isley becomes Mr. Big. The explosion of rap, hip-hop, and
technological innovation drove this transition. With these changes, we find an
R&B world once filled with great melodies and singers now replete with esca-
lated misogyny and pimp mantras, as illustrated by performers with awkward,
jerky moving bodies, marginal singing talent, and explicit lyrics—all promoted
as the embodiment of hip-hop cool.[17] *Bamboozled* addresses these overlapping shifts with the big balladeer. While Lee attacks the raiding of black culture by whites and others in many parts of the film, this example connects the
paradoxical nature of black success, commercialism, and racist/sexist thought
most clearly. In other words, the desire for access to mainstream audiences,
validation of a certain black cultural production, and critique of womanist
empowerment agendas become fully expressed in the soulful lyrics of "I Be
Smackin My Hoes," or more insidiously and real-world in the 2006 Oscar-
winning lyric, "It's Hard out Here for a Pimp."

Bamboozled demonstrates paradox further through the ads selling luxury
products ("Hilnigger") in impoverished black and brown communities and by

positioning Dela as someone radicalized enough to create a coon show but too committed to living out his American dream to quit. But paradox appears not only within the narrative of *Bamboozled* but also through Lee's representation thereof. In an example from an earlier work, Lee attacks the film industry for its misuses of women's bodies. Yet he provides the same services in a *Girl 6* (1996) audition scene. Fronting the white director as the culprit (Quentin Tarantino), the audience receives a long, hard look at the breasts of the auditioning actress (Theresa Randle). *Bamboozled* operates in the same way. Says Epp: "While the narrative bitterly indicts the racist stereotypes on which American television relies for its humour, and rejects satire as a cynical excuse for their repetition, *Bamboozled*'s own repetition of minstrel stereotype was itself marketed and justified as satirical."[18] The film offers the promise of African American success through Delacroix (and de facto Lee) but negates it via his choices and his greed.

The Road to Real

The scholar Wahneema Lubiano's seminal essay "But Compared to What? Reading Realism, Representation, and Essentialism in *School Daze, Do the Right Thing*, and the Spike Lee Discourse" foregrounds questions of authenticity in interpretations of and critical engagements with Lee's works. She argues that representations "are not 'reality'; simple, factual reproductions of selected aspects of vernacular culture are neither necessarily counterhegemonic art nor anything else."[19] Authenticity claims emerge in *Bamboozled* early with Mr. Dunwitty (Michael Rapaport) chastising Delacroix for submitting "booty" program ideas focusing on middle-class African Americans. Dunwitty suggests that since black folks are the "true" innovators of fashion, music, comedy, Dela, in his blackness, should be creating and pitching some "dope shit." When Dela defends his canceled program ideas aimed at a middle-class, formally educated sensibility, Dunwitty asserts, "The reason why these shows didn't get picked up is that nobody, and I mean no-motherfuckin'-body, niggers and crackers alike, want to see that junk. People want to be entertained." It is at this nexus of entertainment and authenticity that *Bamboozled* wages war on television and related media conglomerates. Borrowing words from Malcolm X, Lee argues that black folks have been fooled, bamboozled, with the promise of representation—and for Lee, only certain types of representation equal power and progress.

In the narrative, Dunwitty immerses himself in blackness—his office art, his intonation, his wife. Near the end of the film, he goes even further by donning blackface (like the diegetic audience) to view the minstrel show taping. With his representation, authenticity becomes embodiment without, as Greg

Tate intones, the burden.[20] Yet underneath it all Dunwitty's whiteness (and thus his privilege) remains; his black wipes off. The implication of *Bamboozled*'s assessment is that there exists, somewhere, a better, clearer, more authentic, more real representation than what the minstrel shows on contemporary television (and extendedly film) provide—an essentialism that Lubiano dissects well. But, questions Wallace, "If, indeed, black-face minstrelsy epitomizes inauthenticity, what did become of the authentic narratives and cultural artifacts, material and existential, of the slaves in the postbellum period by the time of the early decades of the twentieth century when film and commercial culture had really begun?"[21] What indeed? More to the point, what is/can be authentic in twenty-first–century visual culture? *Bamboozled* fails to answer this question, although it suggests that even if hidden, submerged, or appropriated by larger (white) mainstream culture, some nebulous black authenticity exists. Beyond the questioning, or at least invoking the idea of an authentic black persona, Lee also speaks to black folks' real-lived conditions and the representations of those in the narratives of *Bamboozled*.

Similar to most of his narratives, Lee infuses *Bamboozled* with elements of New York City's actualities. For example, the reality of New York City's homelessness comes to light (literally) with the raid on the tenement where Manray and Womack squat, barely avoiding police capture. In 1999, New York City Mayor Rudolph Giuliani made it a priority to transform New York into a safer, gentler, cleaner, and whiter place. This meant among other things that the homeless had to move—somewhere, anywhere—out of sight and out of viable commercial property. Beginning in January 2000, raids were conducted to make the homeless "safer" by having them hauled off to jail.

The actualities of New York City, including the longtime WLIB talk-show host Imhotep Gary Byrd, activist Al Sharpton, and attorney Johnnie Cochran as commentators on the Minstrel Show, and a soundtrack featuring Stevie Wonder's "Misrepresented People" (the song's addition being less about it and more about the status of Wonder in African America), all lend authenticity to this work through real-lived (re)presentation. In Wonder's case, not only has he achieved the status of a man with personal and professional conviction, but he also is noted for his lyrical critique of blacks' "living for the city." The use of digital video, although employed as much for financial reasons as aesthetic ones, provides a greater sense still of authenticity due to viewers' associations of video with documentary (since it is most commonly used in nonfiction filmmaking) and thus with actuality and truth. The move also illustrates Lee's willingness to exploit the form, to experiment, to take a chance. In Lee's usage of digital video, he illustrates not only the possibilities for more expansive filmmaking but also foreshadows the explosion of reality television in the new millennium and the latter's relationship to racially

charged content (can anyone say *Black. White.* or *Survivor: Cook Islands*?).[22]
Beyond painting New York with a requisite allure and ugliness and highlighting the beauty of black folks themselves, Lee infuses this narrative with the
markers of "it's a black thing-ness."

Southern black humor gets vetted by the character who becomes Honeycutt (Thomas Jefferson Byrd) in the Minstrel Show. Within his audition for
the program, he includes the ditty "Niggers Is a Beautiful Thang," which later
becomes a part of the crowd warm-up cadence. Honeycutt's performance becomes the representational embodiment of Delacroix's father Junebug (Paul
Mooney) who exists in the insular world of the derisively called Chitlin Circuit. This arena, begun in the 1920s, was/is a space for African American entertainment directed exclusively toward and produced for African American
audiences.

According to the scholar Marc Anthony Neal, the circuit "was a loose network of jook-joints, nightclubs, dance halls, bars, theatres and restaurants that
flourished during the pre–Civil Rights era. Because of recording industry [and
theater industry and film industry] apartheid . . . the Chitlin' Circuit was ab-
solutely critical for the economic survival of black artists who had not crossed-
over to mainstream audiences."[23] Arguably, the Chitlin Circuit serves almost
as a kind of postmodern Underground Railroad.[24] Disregarded as the circuit
remains, this same space has brought wealth to theater and film producers like
Shelly Garrett and Tyler Perry who continue the tradition of serving black-only
audiences in ways that mainstream theater, film, and music do not. Plus, it has
served as an employment vehicle for actors, comedians, singers, and other entertainment personnel who find that in addition to Summer Time, the living
ain't easy anytime of the year for African American cultural workers.

In *Bamboozled*, Junebug has made peace with the entertainment system—
its duplicity, its racism, its greed, its indifference. This character in many ways
reflects the life and choices of the actor who plays it. Paul Mooney has written
for Redd Foxx, Richard Pryor, Eddie Murphy, Dave Chappelle, *In Living Color,*
and *Saturday Night Live*. By all rights, Mooney should be a household name.
But his stance has always been that he refuses to compromise—to shuffle along
and play the good house nigger.[25] This posture gets turned on its head, however,
when Lee configures the Mau Mau as present-day black nationalists.

Blowin' Up the Spot because Blak Iz Blak

When Sloan's brother Julius (Mos Def), a.k.a, Big Blak Afrika, asks her to get
his group the Mau Mau a spot on CNS, their discussion deteriorates into a battle of the meaning of success. Presumably possessing the same middle-class
background (although this assertion is not verified), each pursues a different

route to personal Promised Lands. Sloan—in her conservatively appointed Harlem townhouse—calls the Mau Mau "pseudo-revolutionaries," "embarrassing," and "ignant." Julius—black bomber jacket, skull cap, and empty-handed—positions Sloan as a wanna-be blingin' plantation worker, a "house nigger." On that note, she shows him the door. But the central ideas of paradox and authenticity as roadmaps to black progress resonate here via class.

The outrage and regret of black exploitation is partly rendered moot/mute by the exaggeration of the Mau Mau. In their first appearance, we see them in the recording studio, drinking forties (Da Bomb), getting high, and congratulating themselves for some simplistic and old discovery of the world's racist ideological operations. The real-lived resistance of the Kenyan Mau Mau and other Africans against colonialism was not just against European ways of doing things but also in line with "African cosmologies, social systems, ideological constructions, and systems of justice."[26] Thus, taking on the name of the Kenyan Mau Mau rebellion collective represents a paradox—first, because the name is one of unidentified origin (perhaps constructed by the Europeans they fought), and second, because their fight for independence finds no counterpoint in *Bamboozled*'s Mau Mau impulse.

For example, in their audition for the Minstrel Show, the Mau Mau rap about "socialistic fallacies," reparations, and Darwin's theory. Yet, the most poignant and indicting line is voiced by Hard Black (Mums): "You lucky I ain't read *Wretched* yet." *Wretched of the Earth*, Frantz Fanon's 1963 revolutionary yet cautionary text on wrestling with colonialism and nationhood, has served as an intellectual roadmap for many independence and counter movements. While its invocation provides validation to their cause and vision, Hard Black's assertion of not having even read it makes their claims (and their cause) laughable. *Bamboozled*'s Mau Mau know some of the lingo and the rhetoric of revolution but virtually nothing of the substance. This assertion bears itself out in the actions they take in the latter part of the film.

Yet instead of this scenario serving as an outright illustration of the detriments of partial truths and limited vision, some argue that Lee himself forwards white supremacy and the elevation of bourgeoisie ruminations through this parody of, specifically, conscious rappers. For example, the online writer Greg Thomas argues:

During promotional interviews for *Bamboozled*, both filmmaker Lee and "conscious rapper" Mos Def . . . mocked the rap crew and dismissed them as "naïve" or misguided. They are therefore comic relief for Lee, who must make "minstrels" out of them ("savage" and "bestial") even though this is supposedly an "*anti*-minstrel" film. Yet only these Mau Mau's put an end to "minstrelsy" through action. . . . Lee's script goes on to execute the main Black character after massacring our Mau Mau via white police violence. The white puppeteers are left alone, tellingly. Lee can kill no white characters at the hands of Black folk, evidently, and get his film made in Hollywood.[27]

Thomas's commentary illustrates the centrality of paradox. Is the outing of minstrelsy—the wake-up—so tied to profit that it betrays its own impetus? In most of his films, Lee has tried to address what he deems non-progressive representations of African Americans as well as actions perpetuated by blacks themselves that fail to forward a certain progressive agenda. Yet despite his intentions, Lee frequently reinscribes the same -isms that he seeks to undermine—bringing me to the most contentious area for Lee's filmmaking.

Lee's Women

Probably the most consistent criticism of Lee's work has been the treatment of women in his narratives. The raped Nola Darling and her spurned lesbian friend Opal Gilstrap in *She's Gotta Have It* (1986); the mad, violent, and ineffectual mothers of *Do the Right Thing* (1989), *Jungle Fever* (1991), *Crooklyn* (1994), and *Clockers* (1995); the nondescript women hanging out in *Do the Right Thing* and *Get on the Bus* (1996); money-grabbing Lala, the prostitute, the university ambassadors, and the ghostly, dead mother in *He Got Game* (1998); and the controversial women of *She Hate Me* (2004)—all of Lee's female characters seem incapable of doing much more than occupying the space of narrative prop or, generously, traditional roles. The scholar bell hooks has regularly gotten in Lee's behind for the abysmal portrayal of his female characters. For example, in a critique of *She's Gotta Have It*, she writes: "Nola Darling's sexual desire is not depicted as an autonomous gesture, as an independent longing for sexual expression, satisfaction, and fulfillment. Instead, her assertive sexuality is most often portrayed as though her body, her sexually aroused being, is a reward or gift she bestows on the deserving male. . . . Men do not have to objectify Nola's sexuality because she objectifies it."[28] Beyond Nola, Lee's portrayals of women find problems at every turn.

Yet to provide balance, Lee is one of a very few male feature (or independent) filmmakers to create work that centers on women's stories (*She's Gotta Have It*, *Crooklyn*, and *Girl 6*). In a *Cineaste* interview, Lee professes:

> I'm married to a very intelligent woman—she's a lawyer—and since we've been married I've made a concerted effort to have a better understanding of female characters. In terms of the criticism of my earlier films, that's one thing that was true, that the female characters

were not as multilayered as the male characters. So it was a definite choice to have Jada Pinkett Smith's character, Sloan, be the most sympathetic and the most intelligent.[29]

Conceding this, his representations of women have been consistently anything (misogynistic, nonsensical, abused) but paradoxical. Yet, *Bamboozled* attempts to bring something different.

In this film Sloan, Delacroix's mother (Susan Batson), the staff writers, and even Myrna Goldfarb (Dina Pearlman) the "great Niggerologist" appear, at minimum, as part of the ebb and flow of the story—employing seeming intelligence, without ridiculous denigration, and a participatory ethos. Yet while Sloan is positioned as a smart, hardworking, go-getter sistah (albeit her invocation of this fact a little too often), the script undercuts the impact she makes by adding a previous sexual relationship with Dela, her boss. It could be argued that this narrative strand was added either to highlight an ongoing conundrum in the entertainment industry or to reflect the "what is"—again the need for authenticity—within the narrative. However, it actually serves to solidify the position and role of women in visual culture—horizontal. That particular storyline contributes nothing to the overall trajectory of Lee's engagement with the ravages of Hollywood on Black representation. It once again keeps Lee's representational track record pretty much intact regarding women. In the end, Sloan returns to the group of mad black women—both angry and crazy—as she threatens and then kills Delacroix. She runs from the act babbling "you never listen to me." Perhaps Lee should take Big Blak Afrika's lesson to heart: to always keep the wisdoms around—but as more than decoration and educated bed partners.

Conclusion

Lee positions himself in the vein of Martin Luther King Jr., who, the film implies, authorized civil-rights protests where dogs and hoses threatened in order to show the world (through television) the atrocities of the time. *Bamboozled* is offered as the same sort of audacious corrective. As I, and at least one filmmaker (Zeinabu irene Davis), have noted, *Bamboozled* draws you in early with humor and lightness.[30] But as it moves forward, the funny falls away. Thus, you find yourself in a screening room, auditorium, or at home, full of intense and uncomfortable silence—no one moves, no one sips a drink—you are alone. The compelling narrative and images, for good or for evil, render their audiences mute.

Through the frameworks of paradox and authenticity, I attempt to characterize the lessons Lee teaches within *Bamboozled* and what we, as audience, can learn from them. Never one to dwell on the measure of blackness—black authenticity—through its reality quotient, *Bamboozled* calls for this type of measurement as indicative of its truth-telling. In other words, *Bamboozled* requires its audiences to look at the past and present as mirrors of one another. The past's authentication of minstrelsy and blackface (already false constructions) returns according to Lee in contemporary television. Thus in many respects, *Bamboozled* presents a layering of reality and fiction across time, medium, and minds. The paradox of this project becomes that, as it desperately condemns these images—this attitude of externalized racism and internalized struggle—it promotes it in the name of progress. Black progress comes at a price—the price to see the show or the price to be the show. Either way, it seems from *Bamboozled*, someone has to pay.

NOTES

I thank the students of my Spike Lee classes (2000–2004) at the University of Arizona and the University of Houston. They, more than anyone, have helped me to continue grappling with Lee's work in productive ways. Additionally, I thank Karla Rae Fuller for both guidance and enthusiastic support of my Lee work and Daniel L. Bernardi for always having my back.

Epigraph: Duane Dudek, "Lee's 'Bamboozled' Pokes at TV Industry," *Milwaukee Sentinel Journal*, November 5, 2000.

1. "Paradox," in *Webster's New World Dictionary with Student Handbook* (Nashville: Southwestern Company, 1975), 541.

2. Stuart Hall, "What Is This 'Black' in Black Popular Culture?" Pp. 21–33 in *Black Popular Culture*, ed. Gina Dent (Seattle: Bay Press, 1992).

3. Clearly, Lee's assertions for this type of authenticity are evident in his films prior to *Do the Right Thing*, especially in *School Daze*. In this particular narrative, Lee offers a plethora of aesthetics and issues surrounding 1980s black college life. Unfortunately, most published scholars (and the public in general) are too unfamiliar with historically black colleges and universities to assess what is and what is not "authentic."

4. *Webster's New World Dictionary*, 49.

5. John L. Jackson Jr., *Real Black: Adventures in Racial Sincerity* (Chicago: University of Chicago Press, 2005), 18.

6. Michele Wallace, "*Bamboozled*: The Archive," *Black Renaissance/Renaissance Noire* 3, no .3 (Summer–Fall 2001), available online at http://www.nyu.edu/gsas/program/africana/blackrenaissance/vol3no3/main.html.

7. Black Entertainment Television (BET) is as guilty as either of those two, despite its limited original programming.

8. Greg Tate, "*Bamboozled*: White Supremacy and a Black Way of Being Human," *Cineaste* 26, no. 2 (2001): 16.

9. Michael Epp, "Raising Minstrelsy: Humour, Satire and the Stereotype in *The Birth of a Nation* and *Bamboozled*," *Canadian Review of American Studies* 33, no. 1 (2003): 25.

10. Stuart Klawans, "Amos, Andy 'n' You," *Nation*, November 6, 2000, 35.

11. As found in Allison Samuels, "Spike's Minstrel Show," *Newsweek*, October 2, 2000, 75.

12. In 1996, the tap dancer Savion Glover won a Tony Award in choreography for his work *Bring in da Noise, Bring in da Funk*. He has performed in other Broadway productions prior and since.

13. Comment in William Grant, "Reflecting the Times: *Do the Right Thing* Revisited," in *Spike Lee's 'Do the Right Thing,'* ed. Mark A. Reid. Cambridge Film Handbooks (Cambridge: Cambridge University Press, 1997).

14. Jamie Barlowe, "'You Must Never Be a Misrepresented People': Spike Lee's *Bamboozled*," *Canadian Review of American Studies* 33, no. 1 (2003): 12.

15. Tate, "Bamboozled: White Supremacy and a Black Way of Being Human," 15.

16. While the Roots are not cast in the film as themselves, the implication of their presence (and overt placement, if you are familiar with their music) refers to their non-diegetic musical stance. The same applies to the casting of Mos Def.

17. For more on the relationship of hip-hop and visual culture, see my *Pimpin' Ain't Easy: Selling Black Entertainment Television* (New York: Routledge, 2007); Mark Anthony Neal, *Soul Babies: Black Popular Culture and the Post-Soul Aesthetic* (New York: Routledge, 2002); idem, *Songs in the Key of Black Life: A Rhythm and Blues Nation* (New York: Routledge, 2003); S. Craig Watkins, *Hip Hop Matters: Politics, Pop Culture, and the Struggle for the Soul of a Movement* (Boston: Beacon Press, 2005).

18. Epp, "Raising Minstrelsy," 25.

19. Wahneema Lubiano, "But Compared to What? Reading Realism, Representation, and Essentialism in *School Daze, Do the Right Thing*, and the Spike Lee Discourse," in this volume.

20. See Greg Tate's edited text *Everything but the Burden: What White People Are Taking from Black Culture* (New York: Harlem Moon, 2003).

21. Wallace, "*Bamboozled*."

22. Both of these "reality" series attempted to center race as an element of the drama, or in the case of *Black. White.*, as the drama itself.

23. Marc Anthony Neal, "Chitlin' Circuit Soul," available online at http://www.popmatters.com/music/reviews/various–ChitlinCircuitSoul.shtml>.

24. Ibid.

25. Perhaps the comedian Dave Chappelle took a page out of Mooney's playbook when he walked away from a potential $35 million contract with Comedy Central, but I digress.

26. Ella Shohat and Robert Stam, *Unthinking Eurocentrism: Multiculturalism and the Media* (New York: Routledge, 1994), 79.

27. Greg Thomas, "Editorial: 'Mau Mau Music,'" *ProudFlesh* 3 (2004), available online at http://www.proudfleshjournal.com/issue3/thomas.html.

28. bell hooks, "whose pussy is this: a feminist comment," in this volume, and *Reel to Real: Race, Sex, and Class at the Movies* (New York: Routledge, 2006), 230. See also her article "*Crooklyn*: The Denial of Death" in the same text.

29. Spike Lee, quoted in Gary Crowdus and Dan Georgakas, "Thinking about the Power of Images: An Interview with Spike Lee," *Cineaste* 28, no. 2 (2001): 6.

30. See Zeinabu irene Davis, "Beautiful-Ugly Blackface: An Esthetic Appreciation of *Bamboozled*," *Cineaste* 26, no. 2 (2001): 16–17.

De Profundis: A Love Letter
from the Inside Man

My name is Dalton Russell. Pay strict attention to what I say because I choose my words carefully, and I never repeat myself. I've told you my name. That's the "who." The "where" could most readily be described as a prison cell. But there's a vast difference between being stuck in a tiny cell and being in prison. And I am not in prison. The "what" is easy. Recently, I planned, and set in motion events to execute the perfect bank robbery. That's also the "when." As for the "why," beyond the obvious financial motivation, it's exceedingly simple: Because I can. Which leaves us only with the "how." And therein, as the Bard would tell us, lies the rub.

—Russell Gerwitz, Inside Man

By the 1960s the French auteur theory had gained considerable currency among the literati of film school and Hollywood. The awareness of how one cinematically gestures within yet against an institutional system took powerful hold for those who wished to make, especially, narrative films that transgressed, slyly, the established order of things. If Howard Hawks, Alfred Hitchcock, and Douglas Sirk managed to bypass studio constraints through a unique style, young filmmakers, born into the cultural era identified by the "filmmaker-as-artist," or the "auteur," asserted their aesthetically raised consciousness of the histories and theories of cinema through a sometimes mannered but always determined mark that identified their individual signature. Institutions being what they are (and Hollywood the crowned jewel of that ideological industrial mode of homogenized production), the fashion of auteurism may have identified the sine qua non of the filmmaker's craft, but it also served as brilliant packaging for a generation of moviegoers starved for anything that smacked of individuality over establishment banality.[1]

Though Hollywood often placed its hot-property directors' names above the title of the film (John Ford, Alfred Hitchcock, and so on), auteur-generation product (Arthur Penn, Martin Scorsese, Robert Altman, Woody

Allen) proved lucrative both financially and creatively. (This period is also noteworthy for the lack of women and non-white directors on the Hollywood auteur short list.) Spike Lee enters the industry of Hollywood auteurism at a critical moment (the 1980s) when the industry (the production of the block-buster) and larger forces (the Reagan administration) were transforming the cultural landscape.[2]

As with all things Hollywood, the selling potential of any model is only as good as the profit it continues to generate. It appears—though it may be too early to know for sure—that the de-auteuring of filmmaking is under way as the sale of genre formulas more convincingly (and profitably) drives the in-dustry. The utterance of a director's name (and this is solely based on prelim-inary observations) indicates a de-auteuring phenomenon that occurs with individuals potentially identified as "box-office poison" and so threatens mass appeal. The reasons for this are many, and this is not the place to fully explore this tendency. Briefly, however, "auteurs" associated with urban subject mat-ter, over-intellectualized or contemplative narrative style, personal scandal, or political interests viewed as discomfiting to "mainstream audiences" are among those de-auteured (Spielberg, Scorsese, and Tarantino remain darlings of the industry and have thus far dodged, perhaps because of their distance from these reasons, the stripping of their auteur position and thus maintain their commercial viability).[3] Consider, for example, what I take to be Woody Allen's homage to Hitchcock's *Stranger on a Train* (1951), *Match Point* (2005), or Robert Altman's *A Prairie Home Companion* (2006). During the late-1970s and into the '90s, these filmmakers were identified by the industry as the very reason to see the film. Their stylistic signature, if not their literal presence in their films, thrilled young filmmakers who wished to "make a point" without bowing to the system. They also sold tickets. Though I am not stating that the director's name is entirely erased from Hollywood's sale pitch, films such as *Match Point* are not marketed in the same way as *Manhattan* (1979) or even *Hannah and Her Sisters* (1986); *A Prairie Home Companion* is not the "Altman" film once sold to us as recently as *Prêt-à-Porter* (1994) or during the height of American auterism, *3 Women* (1977).[4]

Spike Lee has not escaped this new formulation of generic Hollywood packaging fomenting around socially or artistically troublesome auteurs, espe-cially since the blockbuster 1980s.[5] If the controversial *Do the Right Thing* was unabashedly identified as a "Spike Lee Joint" (advertisements for the film even included the director's image), *Inside Man* buried the risk of low ticket sales by, well, burying the director's name and, for the most part, his face.[6] From the studio's perspective, marginalizing Lee's presence and involvement served well their bottom line. Certainly, Lee's association with a project is a blessing and a curse, since a sharp division cuts audiences' response to his films. I often hear from students, for example, that they find Lee as filmmaker as one who "hits them over the head" with a message. But it is not only my students who complain about the African American message kid.[7] Selling *Inside Man* more as a star vehicle (Denzel Washington, Clive Owens, Jodie Foster) makes institutional sense given the uneasy if not vituperative response to the mere mention of Lee's name. Yet champions of the auteur theory rightly argue that the unmistakable "how" of Lee (and Allen and Altman) nonetheless displays itself, institutional constraints notwithstanding. Indeed, a certain pleasure of the text is made available when the association between director and film is divorced by the institution, since the interpretive game to identify the marks of authorial presence is invariably set in motion. Indeed, "match point."

Undoubtedly, what makes *Inside Man* a pleasurable text, in part, is the locating of Lee-*isms* observed by the savvy viewer. More provocatively, I argue, the "how" of *Inside Man* discloses the very process of de-auteuring at work in contemporary Hollywood, if not culture itself. *Inside Man* makes explicit the environment of ideological containment operating during a more conservative era (one that Hollywood finds itself pandering to and in which the director must insist on his or her directorial signature). Therein "lies the rub." *Inside Man* announces, through style ("how") the way controversial ideas in American culture are stifled, ideas perceived as too offensive or combative for the general public to digest. Importantly, *Inside Man* suggests that a de-auteuring of the director's voice simultaneously parallels a de-auteuring of that of the viewer. This is to say, for Lee, the mark of the auteur is foremost a gesture of cinematic writing through which both director and spectator must participate in the making of meaning. (Recall Lee's imperative to "Wake up!" in *School Daze* and *Do the Right Thing*.)

Performing from the Inside

As the film's opening monologue recommends (cited in the epigraph), the distinction between "being stuck in a tiny cell and being in prison" is particularly acute in *Inside Man*, a "heist film" in which the central action occurs in a monumental Wall Street bank. *Inside Man* (screenplay by Russell Gerwitz) is the story of a performance of a bank heist. The "robbers," led by Dalton Russell (Clive Owens; the shared name of our thief and screenwriter should not go unnoticed), produce a spectacle that looks as if a traditional bank robbery of cash and jewels is under way. As becomes clear, our performance artists-cum-bank robbers are not interested in the money (a strategy that Detective Keith Frazier [Denzel Washington] suspects early on). Rather, their goal is to heist the capital that serves as the foundation of the banking system itself. In this instance, the bandits seek to reveal financial relationship of the bank's

CEO, Arthur Case (Christopher Plummer), to the Nazis, as well as the bags full of diamonds that have been historically mined on the back of slavery. These poisonous underpinnings of the capitalist structure are held by Case in a safety deposit box in the bowels of his bank.

The taking of the bank by the Dalton and crew follows Lee's introduction to the exterior location of the film (iconic shots of New York) as well as the interior place of the bank, where we see the routine activity of New Yorkers making transactions. Here, we see an array of New Yorkers composed of Lee's astutely rendered diversity of the city (Sikh, Jewish, Asian, African American, Latino, Italian American, and so on). And, as always, while Lee celebrates this cultural milieu, he also points to these New Yorkers' not-so-ideal qualities and idiosyncrasies (from sexism to racism to self-absorbed arrogance). As the New Yorkers wait in line idly, chatting on their cell phones, staring into space, objectifying one another (boys leering at girls), and listening to music through headphones, the robbers—costumed as painters (guerrilla performance artists?) with white masks covering their noses and mouths—lock up and shut down the bank. The thieves are now in charge of a large cache of hostages as well as crippling documentation hidden by the capitalists. Shocked into awareness of their surroundings by the violent coup, the bank's patrons are now human collateral. The distinctive qualities of humanity are thus subsumed in the interest of protecting the lies of the institutional apparatus (read here, economic). This point is made clear when Arthur Case is told of the robbery and deeply worries not about the hostages but about the whereabouts of a signed document that, if made public, will reveal his fifty-year-old secret pact with the Nazis to funnel money from Jewish estates into Swiss bank accounts. To maintain the secret relationship between the Nazis and the American capitalist, Case hires the unscrupulous Madeline *White* (Jodie Foster) to protect his secret.

Hence, the loss of difference (for Lee, I suspect this is understood as "humanity") is at the heart of *Inside Man*. I suggest that in the film the hostages-as-collateral are key to grasping Lee's pessimistic view of the state of New York's cultural diversity. Under the auspices of the Patriot Act and other state-sanctioned controls, Lee's New York is eerily made to shut up and exist in a zombie-like daze required of all good patriots. New York/the United States of 2006 is now a place where civil liberties are silenced and "cultural difference" suggests guilt instead of the uneasy dynamic of David Dinkins's "beautiful mosaic." The effect of this neo-state control is the homogenizing of culture where the veneer of good behavior/good patriotism is identified by an ideal of national sameness, a whiteness that erases the gradations of difference that have historically marked Manhattan and its surrounding boroughs. Perhaps most insidious in this de-democratizing moment is the acceptance of this ideological containment by a group of people usually associated with loud

Inside Man (2006). Lee's homogenous bank robbers.

and arrogant resistance: New Yorkers. *Inside Man* is the provocative styliza-
tion of the erasure of culture and its conflicting voices.

When Dalton rounds up his hostages, he demands they strip and don gray
industrial suits and white masks. The hostage's captors wear the same outfit.
In this way, the richness of cultural diversity that is simultaneously beautiful
and angry in Lee's traditional worldview is reduced to a culture of sameness.
It is an uneasy wake-up call for New Yorkers to hear, since they pride themselves on their unmistakable ethnic makeup. *Inside Man* reduces the city's
population to mere consumers who participate in an economy that steals not
only their money, but also their identity. In this way, an important cinematic
Lee signature is literally gagged in the film. In Lee's cinematic trope, the "bigotry rant" (*Do the Right Thing, 25th Hour*), characters articulate their racist,
sexist, and homophobic sentiment of their urban neighbors. It is a hallmark of
Lee's complicated view of New Yorkers' relations with one another. In a tracking shot that conjures this rehearsal of repressed anger, Lee, in *Inside Man*,
shows the captive New Yorkers gagged with white cloths, able to release only
muffled screams and cries. In the bowels of the bank, not far from Case's
safety box, the city's cultural differences are mocked and shown as an exploitation managed by the mechanisms of capitalist greed and self-interest.

In the bank (a central force of the city), the robbers, the clerks, the clients, the secretaries are collapsed into one. If the calls to "wake up" in *Do the Right Thing* were loud and clear, the volume is paradoxically turned up in *Inside Man* precisely by the revelation of forced silence. The heist that occurs in the film is a performance meant to bring to light the theft of difference and civil liberties. By remaining silent, the homogenized consumer supports, participates in, an economic system founded in historical terror.

Calling attention to this sameness, then using it, is thus key to the success of the heist, since it will allow Dalton Russell to exit as a free man through the purportedly impenetrable front doors of the bank. In the climactic scene when the threat to rush the bank by the authorities is imminent, Dalton's crew disperses among the hostages, en masse, by charging through the front doors, filling the street, and awaiting arrest, since everyone inside the bank is now a suspect. Flash-forward sequences reveal the "guilty-until-proven-otherwise" treatment all hostages are given after the event, especially by Detective Frazier. Since no distinction can be made between robber, hostage, and even Frazier, the flood of industrial-suited and masked bodies makes it impossible to identify the "good guys" from the "bad guys."[8] Indeed, the hostages and the audience, for most of the film, cannot identify who the "real" robbers are, because throughout the ordeal, the heist crew "performs" as hostages (that is, they dress in the gray suits and intermingle among the captives during feeding time).

The art of performance is thus extremely important to this heist. Prior to the explosive exit of hostages and robbers, the well-planned spectacle unfolds (a dummy, for example, is shot in lieu of an actual hostage, with all the spurting-blood effects that Lee pilfers from Hollywood). The centerpiece of the performance/heist is the construction of a fake room, a purloined closet, behind a supply closet—the "cell"—from where Dalton awaits the proper moment to escape (about a week after the drama in the bank concludes). With the dust settled and the police unable to determine the criminals, Dalton prepares his exit. Dressed in street clothes to blend in (the game of difference and sameness in Lee's hand never lets go of the complicated relationship between inside and outside, difference and sameness), he crosses the lobby to leave. As he does so, he purposely bumps into Detective Frazier, who, though he will ironically never have the opportunity to arrest Dalton, nevertheless connects with Dalton at this significant exchange. At this encounter between two figures of equivocal moral standing in their pursuit of justice, Dalton, in a final gesture of dramatic flare, drops a single, sparkling, yet historically tainted diamond in Frazier's pocket. (Later, of course, Frazier will discover the jewel and realize the "how" of Dalton's escape, as well as what the message of the heist was all about.) Once Dalton leaves, we see him reconnect with his crew and gather our first confirmed glimpse of the robbers (an unexpected mélange of characters). Before they depart, Dalton announces to his crew that he only has the Nazi–Case documents but not the diamonds. After all, the spectacle had nothing to do with profit and everything to do with principle.

Like narrative, like filmmaker. The moral ambiguity of good guy/bad guy in *Inside Man* is most apparent if we understand that is it Spike Lee who is unmasked as the impresario of this heist-as-spectacle. If the director's name has been sidelined in this Hollywood production, Lee's "how," albeit "gagged," has not been so easily silenced. Given Lee's penchant to include himself in his earlier film productions as both director and actor, it would be somewhat remarkable if he marked his presence *inside* this film by style alone. How is this masked presence inserted through something more than repetition of style? How is the authorial hand asserted in a way that complies with the framework of generic production yet resists its reductive affect? Through the maskings and masquerade of *Inside Man*, Lee inserts his performance through an act of doubling that is revealed in an iconic symbol directly associated with his presence in and vision of New York: a Yankees baseball cap.

When Dalton makes his casual escape, his everyday costume includes a Yankees baseball cap that is at once overwhelmingly American (baseball as pastime) and very New York/Lee (both often despised by many Americans). The tipping of his hat, as it were, at the moment of Dalton's escape from the confines of the cell aligns Lee with the character who creates the spectacle, a character who, we recall, importantly shares a name with the screenwriter. It is Lee/Russell who gets away with the heist, perhaps with the help of the other inside man, Detective Frazier.[9] Lee/Russell commits the perfect crime by appearing to do one thing (and in that they have succeeded—make a Hollywood genre film/steal the documents) while unfolding something entirely different. The bank robber(s) walks out the front door and are no worse for the wear.

Lee puts on display *Inside Man* as a production; the film is something made, sold, and packaged by the institution of Hollywood and financed by a bank that made decisions about when and why this film project would be made. These institutions also determined much of the "how" (genre format, stars, running time, and so on)—sort of. The "how" of production is nothing less than a dynamic of power relations. The homogenizing of film product from Hollywood and its pressure to erase, to gag the authorial hand and voice considered too dangerous to secure the gate keeping of meaning only works so far. Lee's *Inside Man* indeed recommends that the "how" has everything to do with a successful robbing of the bank.

Making One's Mark

If authorship serves and is served by a particular ideological system (Foucault's author-function), it is also a mode of cultural production, a process of relations through which the mark or signature of the author displays what Marx once called the "invisible threads" of capital.[10] The repetition of authorial style is thus significant to the extent that while it, on the one hand, makes invisible the threads of ideological production (here, Hollywood), this signature also, as Jacques Derrida puts it, is "no *pure* presence, but only chains of differential marks."[11] In order to locate these differential marks that disrupt a totalizing effect, it is worth recalling Lee's (and the two Russells') request at the opening of *Inside Man* to "pay strict attention to what I say" because the director of this performance chooses his "words carefully."

To center the action in a bank where the performance of a heist plays out raises two key tensions that Lee continually navigates in his work: New York and Hollywood. First: New York. A bank centered in the heart of the city's financial district puts into relief the economic heart of Hollywood film production. As all good historians of filmmaking know, New York is where the money comes from to make Hollywood films. On the one hand, New York is identified as the core of American and world finance and the place where directors and producers ultimately turn to get their films made. On the other hand, New York, especially as Lee shapes it in his "love letters" to the city, is an amalgam of peoples who share complicated histories and relationships with one another (relationships at risk, as I discussed earlier).[12] The opening sequence to *Inside Man* is thus critical because, in it, we see the enormous cross-section of New Yorkers intermingled with one another, often pleasantly, often annoyingly, in the monument to capitalism—the bank. At base, and though many romanticize the cultures of difference outside this economic institution, New Yorkers' lives revolve around the city's main preoccupation: money. Yet like the director who participates in the Hollywood *and* New York institution, it is important to recall that we are in a cell and not a prison. And there is a "vast difference" between the two.

Second: Hollywood. It is well known that Lee struggles to finance his films in a white-privileged industry. It is not that Lee is naive about what he must do to raise the necessary cash to produce his work. In typical Warholian fashion, Lee has sold his name and face to corporations such as Nike, the Gap, Barney's, and, most recently, Ford. Given these economic circumstances, the opportunity to raise capital (in all senses) for more desired projects by shooting "blockbuster" genre films that marshal the director's name to the promotional margins is expected (consider Gus Van Sant's career moves).[13] In this way, the New York bank central to *Inside Man* draws our attention to the director's position in the economy of Hollywood production in which he or she must inevitably turn. It is precisely the financial institution where contracts are signed and the promise to deliver a product that will generate a profit is made. Of course, the signature on the contract is no guarantee of box-office success, since the signature, of whatever stature, is always a tenuous thing that hinges on the memory of past successes. Yet the signature is the best the bank can do in its strategies to secure profit. The bank thus holds the director's name as collateral; he or she is held hostage to the bank note to the extent that his or her creative vision is subject to institutional containment ("gagged"). For Lee, signing with Hollywood is at once freeing (the largess of Hollywood's bankroll at his disposal) and constraining (the demands to make a generic product that sells tickets; the whitening of the product). The question is: Is it possible for the gagged director and spectator to walk out the front door of the bank, or the theater, free human beings? Possibly. If we pay strict attention to the "how" (the "rub," after all) and we don't neglect the "vast difference between being stuck in a tiny cell and being in prison," we may see just how *Inside Man* is Lee's troubled love letter to New York in the form of a Hollywood heist.

NOTES

For Janet Staiger. Also, I thank Charles Silver for access to the Museum of Modern Art's film-clip files on Lee, as well as my student Thomas Sentina for engaging discussions about the state of the "auteur" during the spring 2006 semester.

Epigraph: Russell Gerwitz, screenplay for *Inside Man*, dir. Spike Lee (Universal City, Calif., Universal Studios, 2006). The text of the monologue, spoken by Dalton Russell (Clive Owen), was transcribed from the film's DVD version.

1. For an overview of film authorship practices and approaches, see David A. Gerstner and Janet Staiger, *Authorship and Film* (New York: Routledge, 2002). On the Hollywood industry in the 1960s, see Paul Monaco, *The Sixties, 1960–1969* (Berkeley: University of California Press, 2001).

2. See Stephen Prince, *A New Pot of Gold: Hollywood under the Rainbow, 1980–1989* (Berkeley: University of California Press, 2000). On Hollywood's selling of the authorial stamp, see Timothy Corrigan, "The Commerce of Auteurism," in *Film and Authorship*, ed. Virginia Wexman (New Brunswick, N.J.: Rutgers University Press, 2003), 96–111.

3. I emphasize fictional filmmaking here since the spate of documentary films by controversial figures such as Michael Moore indicates a somewhat different emphasis in terms of Hollywood's look to the auteur/genre model. Indeed, Lee's recent foray into documentary filmmaking with *When the Levees Broke: A Requiem in Four Acts* (2006) confirms Hollywood's redirecting of "controversial" material through the more obvious genre (that is, the genre perceived as the appropriate venue for less palatable subject matter) where the filmmaker's voice is "meant" to be individual, political. This shift is

important since it again highlights the centrality of genre in Hollywood marketing (particularly by demographics) and the malleability of the auteur in this institutional practice.

4. The "death of the author" has again proved more contradictory than its utterance purports to reveal. Indeed, given Robert Altman's recent death, it is interesting to note the state of auteur interest in the twenty-first century. Certainly, academics will now be in a position to examine Altman's body of work. The IFC movie theater in Manhattan (only a few blocks from New York University's film school), for example, immediately commenced a "comprehensive" retrospective of the director's work. Thus, the claim I make for de-auteuring rests in the contemporary marketing of narrative film. The "major" directors will undoubtedly play a significant role for filmmakers and film scholars (one hopes). Hence, while we may expect film series for the likes of Altman at venues such as IFC and the Museum of Modern Art, a major theater chain such as AMC Theaters is less likely to do so. Yet a director considered less turgid (such as Steven Spielberg) might receive a very different reception from AMC upon his passing, given his less esoteric and confrontational aesthetic and politics.

5. Vince Leo raises this noteworthy condition: "The trailers and ads for *Inside Man* make little or no mention of Lee's involvement, probably because at this point in his career, you are either a Lee fan or you have learned to ignore his ambitious but sometimes overbearing output. In truth, this is easily his most accessible work, and like Woody Allen's *Match Point*, the auteur finds a way to take an average film and make it something special, weaving a complex, albeit messy, tapestry of many interesting ideas": Vince Leo, "Inside Man," available online at http://www.qwipster.net/insideman.htm (accessed June 18, 2006). As I point out, things are bit more complicated than either identifying as a "fan" or "ignoring" Lee's "overbearing output."

It is somewhat ironic, if not telling, that Lee, who was often compared to his New York colleague as the "black Woody Allen," finds himself in the same position of de-auteuring. In fact, Lee emphatically rejected the comparison in 1989: "The neighborhood [I create] will have a feel of the different cultures that make up the city, specifically Black American, Puerto Rican, West Indian, Korean, and Italian-American, unlike Woody Allen's portraits of New York": Spike Lee, quoted in Joe Wood, "Yes, and I Read the Book . . . Spike Lee Does the Write Thing," *Village Voice*, August 22, 1989, 59. Lee is mentioned as the "black Woody Allen" in "Spike's Sparks," 7 *Days* 2, no. 23 (June 14, 1989): 14; for an explicit comparison, see "Slow 'Action' Movie Aims at Brainier Set," March 30, 2006, available online at http://www.azle-news.net/news/get-news.asp?id=5950&catid=9&cpg=get-news.asp (accessed June 18, 2006).

6. Lee did appear in interviews on such venues as CNN's *American Morning*, where he stated, "Well, I don't want to make B.S. also, so you got to try to find that balance. And I think this script enabled me to put my personal touch and still do a film that hopefully is going to make money": CNN, *American Morning*, transcript, March 21, 2006, available online at http://transcripts.cnn.com/transcripts/0603/21/ltm.03.html (accessed June 11, 2006).

7. Note Leo's comment regarding "overbearing output." For many, such as Joe Klein of *New York* magazine, Lee is a "classic art-school dilettante when it comes to politics" and thus creates with "cavalier naïveté": Joe Klein, *New York*, June 26, 1989, 14–15. More to the point, in a letter to the editor one Al Reyes described Lee as the "Thought Police" and as an "angry, resentful (and, at best, minimally talented) little man

[with a] sleazy p.c. agenda" and suggested that the director's "big mouth only betrays [his] youth and reckless stupidity": *New York Press*, March 10–16, 1999, 3.

8. As with his other films, such as *Do the Right Thing* (1989), Lee sets a moral ambiguity in the New York of *Inside Man* when the bank's patrons are presented as nothing but collateral to protect the cornerstone of American capitalism: the bank. Lee's "good guys" and "bad guys," like the classic western and gangster films, are not easy to pin down, however. In an interview for *Do the Right Thing*, Lee comments on the "autobiographical resonances" that contributed to his performance as Mookie. Lee states that Mookie is the "'one black person that white people can identify with and who's not threatening . . . and then'—Lee laughs devilishly—'at the end of the movie he's the one that starts the riot.' He's laughing harder now, 'So the people who trusted him in the beginning, now their world's *really* fucked up'": Lee, quoted in "Spike's Sparks," 16). In *Inside Man*, it is never completely transparent whether Detective Frazier is guilty or not over some earlier money transaction during a drug bust, while Dalton Russell's motives are just as difficult to pin down entirely.

9. A longer essay would take up the complicated nexus of the "moral equivalence" the film's narrative suggests with regard to determining, once and for all, what is the "right thing to do" and *how* such a thing is achieved. (This equivalence irritates the Christian right: see http://www.christiananswers.net/spotlight/movies/2006/insideman2006 .html [accessed June 26, 2006]). Given the exchange of the diamond, however, and the morally ambiguous standing Lee assigns to Frazier *within* the police department, it is possible to argue for Frazier's insertion into the thieves' cadre and their performance, since he (unwittingly?) enables Dalton Russell's escape once he understands Arthur Case's and Madeleine White's main objectives. *Inside Man* is Lee's Hitchcockian play on doubled guilt (often via an exchanged object) that troubles the protagonist's motives in the outcome of the Hollywood narrative that is resolute on (moral) closure.

10. Karl Marx, *Grundrisse: Foundations of the Critique of Political Economy*, trans. Martin Nicolaus (London: Penguin Books, 1973), 304.

11. Jacques Derrida, "Signature, Event, Context," in idem, *Margins of Philosophy* (Chicago: University of Chicago Press, 1986 [1982]), 318.

12. Though all Lee's films have been love letters to the city, *25th Hour* is perhaps the most direct expression of the director's relationship to New York. Filmed following September 11, 2001, it suggests the complex tensions between diversity and homogenization developed in *Inside Man*. For more on this, see Paula J. Massood, "The Quintessential New Yorker and Global Citizen: An Interview with Spike Lee," *Cineaste* 29, no. 3 (Summer 2003): 4–6.

13. Van Sant comes to mind insofar as his trilogy (*Gerry, Elephant*, and *Last Days*) indicates not only the tremendous range of directorial style he successfully manages; these diversely formalized films significantly point to the ways filmmakers turn to major industry production (such as *Good Will Hunting* and *Finding Forrester*, in Van Sant's case) to help fund—or, at least, defray the costs of—smaller, personal projects. For a discussion of this phenomenon, see Douglas Singleton, "Reaching for Higher Ground," New York Foundation for the Arts website, available online at http://www.nyfa.org/ level3.asp?id=389&fid=4&sid=8 (accessed January 14, 2007).

Filmography

DIRECTOR

FEATURE FILMS

Inside Man (2006)
40 Acres & A Mule Filmworks/Universal Pictures/Imagine Entertainment, distributed by Universal, 35 mm color, 129 minutes. Screenplay by Russell Gewirtz; cinematography by Matthew Libatique; editing by Barry Alexander Brown; music by Terence Blanchard and A. R. Rahman (additional songs).

She Hate Me (2004)
40 Acres & A Mule Filmworks, distributed by Sony Pictures Classics, Super-16 mm and 35 mm color, 138 minutes. Screenplay by Michael Genet and Spike Lee; cinematography by Matthew Libatique; editing by Barry Alexander Brown; music by Terence Blanchard and Raul Midon.

25th Hour (2002)
40 Acres & A Mule Filmworks/Gamut Films/Industry Entertainment/Touchstone Pictures, distributed by Touchstone Pictures, Super-35 mm Technicolor, 135 minutes. Screenplay by David Benioff; cinematography by Rodrigo Prieto; editing by Barry Alexander Brown; music by Terence Blanchard.

Bamboozled (2000)
40 Acres & A Mule Filmworks/New Line Cinema, distributed by New Line Cinema, Super-16 mm and digital video color, 135 minutes. Screenplay by Spike Lee; cinematography by Ellen Kuras; editing by Sam Pollard; music by Terence Blanchard, Bruce Hornsby, Prince, Stevie Wonder.

The Original Kings of Comedy (2000)
40 Acres & A Mule Filmworks/Latham Entertainment/MTV Films, distributed by Paramount Pictures, 35mm, digital video color, 115 minutes. Screenplay by Cedric the Entertainer, Steve Harvey, D. L. Hughley, and Bernie Mac; cinematography by Malik Hassan Sayeed; editing by Barry Alexander Brown.

Summer of Sam (1999)
40 Acres & A Mule Filmworks/Touchstone Pictures, distributed by Buena Vista Pictures, 35 mm Technicolor, 142 minutes. Screenplay by Victor Colicchio, Michael Imperioli, and Spike Lee; cinematography by Ellen Kuras; editing by Barry Alexander Brown; music by Terence Blanchard.

He Got Game (1998)
40 Acres & A Mule Filmworks/Touchstone Pictures, distributed by Buena Vista Pictures, 35 mm Technicolor, 134 minutes. Screenplay by Spike Lee; cinematography by Ellen Kuras and Malik Hassan Sayeed; editing by Barry Alexander Brown; music by Scott Hardkiss and Aaron Copland; songs by Public Enemy.

4 Little Girls (1997)
40 Acres & A Mule Filmworks/Home Box Office, distributed by HBO Documentary; 16mm, 35 mm, black-and-white and color, 102 minutes. Cinematography by Ellen Kuras; editing by Sam Pollard; music by Terence Blanchard.

Get On the Bus (1996)
15 Black Men/40 Acres & A Mule Filmworks; distributed by Columbia Pictures; 16mm, 35 mm, color; 122 minutes. Screenplay by Reggie Rock Bythewood; cinematography by Elliot Davis; editing by Leander T. Sales; music by Terence Blanchard.

Girl 6 (1996)
40 Acres & A Mule Filmworks; distributed by Fox Searchlight Pictures; 35 mm, Technicolor; 107 minutes. Screenplay by Suzan-Lori Parks; cinematography by Malik Hassan Sayeet; editing by Sam Pollard.

Clockers (1995)
40 Acres & A Mule Filmworks/Universal Pictures; distributed by MCA/Universal Pictures; 35 mm, Technicolor; 128 minutes. Screenplay by Richard Price and Spike Lee; cinematography by Malik Hassan Sayeed; editing by Sam Pollard; music by Terence Blanchard.

Crooklyn (1994)
40 Acres & A Mule Filmworks/Childhood Pictures/Universal Pictures; distributed by Paramount Pictures, 35 mm, color; 110 minutes. Screenplay by Cinque Lee, Joie Lee, and Spike Lee; cinematography by Arthur Jafa; editing by Barry Alexander Brown; music by Terence Blanchard.

Malcolm X (1992)
40 Acres & A Mule Filmworks/JVC Entertainment/Largo International N.V.; distributed by Warner Brothers; 35 mm, color; 194 minutes. Screenplay by Arnold Perl and Spike Lee; cinematography by Ernest R. Dickerson; editing by Barry Alexander Brown; music by Terence Blanchard, Timothy Barnwell, and Speech.

Jungle Fever (1991)
40 Acres & A Mule Filmworks/Universal Pictures; distributed by Universal Pictures; 35 mm, color; 132 minutes. Screenplay by Spike Lee; cinematography by Ernest R. Dickerson; editing by Sam Pollard; music by Terence Blanchard.

Mo' Better Blues (1990)
40 Acres & A Mule Filmworks/Universal Pictures; distributed by Universal Pictures, 35 mm, color; 129 minutes. Screenplay by Spike Lee; cinematography by Ernest R. Dickerson; editing by Sam Pollard; music by Bill Lee and Terence Blanchard.

Do the Right Thing (1989)
40 Acres & A Mule Filmworks/Universal Pictures; distributed by MCA/Universal; 35 mm, color; 119 minutes. Screenplay by Spike Lee; cinematography by Ernest R. Dickerson; editing by Barry Alexander Brown; music by Cathy Block, David Hinds, James Weldon Johnson, Rosamond Johnson, Raymond Jones, Bill Lee, Sami McKinney, Michael O'Hara, and Lori Petty.

School Daze (1988)
40 Acres & A Mule Filmworks/Columbia Pictures; distributed by Columbia Pictures; 35 mm, color; 120 minutes. Screenplay by Spike Lee; cinematography by Ernest R. Dickerson; editing by Barry Alexander Brown; music by Bill Lee and Stevie Wonder.

She's Gotta Have It (1986)
40 Acres & A Mule Filmworks; distributed by Island Pictures; 16 mm, black-and-white (with color sequence); 84 minutes. Screenplay by Spike Lee; cinematography by Ernest R. Dickerson; editing by Spike Lee; music by Bill Lee.

Joe's Bed-Stuy Barbershop: We Cut Heads (1983)
40 Acres & A Mule Filmworks/New York University; distributed by First Run Features; 16 mm, color; 60 minutes. Screenplay by Spike Lee; cinematography by Ernest R. Dickerson; editing by Spike Lee; music by Bill Lee.

STUDENT FILMS

Sarah (1981)
The Answer (1980)
Last Hustle in Brooklyn (1977)

SHORTS AND SHORT SEGMENTS OF COMPILATION FILMS

All the Invisible Children (2005), segment entitled "Jesus Children of America."
MK Film Productions S.r.1./Rai Cinemafiction; no North American distribution. Includes segments by Mehdi Charef, Emir Kusturica, Spike Lee, Katia Lund, Jordon Scott, Ridley Scott, Stefano Veneruso, and John Woo.

Ten Minutes Older: The Trumpet (2002), segment titled "We Wuz Robbed."
Atom Films/Emotion Pictures/Filmforderungsanstalt (FFA)/JVC Entertainment/Kuzui Enterprises/Matador Pictures/Odyssey Films/Road Movies Filmproduktion/WGBH Boston; no North American distribution. Includes segments by Victor Erice, Werner Herzog, Jim Jarmusch, Aki Kaurismaki, Spike Lee, and Wim Wenders.

Lumiere et comagnie (1995)
Cneteve/La Sept-Arte/Igeldo Komunikazioa/Soren Staermose AB; distributed by Fox Lorber. Includes segments by forty international directors.

TELEVISION (INCLUDES MADE-FOR-TELEVISION FILMS AND EPISODES OF SHOWS)

"*M.O.N.Y.*" (2007), series pilot
"*Shark*" (2006), series pilot

When the Levees Broke: A Requiem in Four Acts (2006)
40 Acres & A Mule Filmworks/Home Box Office for HBO.

"*Miracle's Boys*" (2005), mini-series (episodes 1 and 6)
Feralfilms LLC/MTV Networks/On-Screen Entertainment.

Sucker Free City (2004)
40 Acres & A Mule Filmworks for Showtime Networks.

Jim Brown: All American (2002)
40 Acres & A Mule Filmworks/HBO Sports for HBO Sports.

The Concert for New York City (2001), segment "Come Rain or Come Shine"
VH1/ Television.

A Huey P. Newton Story (2001)
40 Acres & A Mule Filmworks/Luna Ray Films/Lyrical Knockout Entertainment.

"*Pavarotti & Friends '99 for Guatemala and Kosovo*" (1999)
"*Pavarotti & Friends for the Children of Liberia*" (1998)

Freak (1998)
HBO for HBO.

PRODUCER

The Goal (Art Sims, 2006), executive producer
Dream Street (Lonette McKee, 2005), executive producer
Good Fences (Ernest R. Dickerson, 2003, made for television), executive producer
Home Invaders (Gregory Wilson, 2001), executive producer
3 A.M. (Lee Davis, 2001), co-executive producer
Love and Basketball (Gina Prince-Bythewood, 2000), producer
The Best Man (Malcolm D. Lee, 1999), producer
Tales from the Hood (Rusty Cundieff, 1995), executive producer
New Jersey Drive (Nick Gomez, 1995), executive producer
Drop Squad (David C. Johnson, 1994), executive producer

Select Bibliography

Aftab, Kaleem. 2005. *Spike Lee: That's My Story and I'm Sticking to It*. New York: W. W. Norton.

Baker, Houston. 1993. "Spike Lee and the Commerce of Culture." Pp. 154–76 in *Black American Cinema*, ed. Manthia Diawara. New York: Routledge.

Banks, Adam. 2006. *Race, Rhetoric, and Technology*. Mahwah, N.J.: Lawrence Erlbaum Associates.

Barlowe, Jamie. 2003. "'You Must Never Be a Misrepresented People': Spike Lee's *Bamboozled*." *Canadian Review of American Studies* 33, no. 1: 1–15.

Bernotas, Bob. 1993. *Spike Lee: Filmmaker*. Hillside, N.J.: Enslow Publishers.

Blake, Richard Aloysius. 2005. *Street Smart: The New York of Lumet, Allen, Scorsese, and Lee*. Lexington: University Press of Kentucky.

Booker Morris, Susan. 2004. "*Bamboozled*: Political Parodic Postmodernism." *Philological Papers* 50: 67–76.

Boyd, Todd. 1991. "The Meaning of the Blues." *Wide Angle* 13, nos. 3–4 (July–October): 56–61.

Brouwer, Joel R. 1997. *Images of Community: Constructions of Ethnicity and Identity in Late Twentieth Century American Film (Spike Lee, Martin Scorsese, Wayne Wang)*. Ph.D. diss., Michigan State University, East Lansing.

Chan, Kenneth. 1998. "The Construction of Black Male Identity in Black Action Films of the Nineties." *Cinema Journal* 37, no. 2 (Winter): 35–48.

Christensen, Jerome. 1991. "Spike Lee, Corporate Populist." *Critical Inquiry* 17, no. 3 (Spring): 582–95.

Cole, C. L., and Samantha King. 2003. "New Politics of Urban Consumption: *Hoop Dreams*, *Clockers*, and America." Pp. 221–46 in *Sporting Dystopias: The Making and Meaning of Urban Sport Cultures*, ed. Ralph C. Wilcox. Albany: State University of New York Press.

Dabreo-Ramharack, Cheryl. 1999. "Uplifting the Black Race, Only Males Need Apply: Black Male Militancy in *Malcolm X, Panther, Boyz n the Hood,* and *Get on the Bus* (Spike Lee, Mario Van Peebles, John Singleton)." M.A. diss., Concordia University, Montreal.

Daileader, Celia R. 2001. *Racism, Misogyny, and the Othello Myth: Inter-Racial Couples from Shakespeare to Spike Lee.* New York: Cambridge University Press.

Denzin, Norman K. 2001. *Reading Race: Hollywood and the Cinema of Racial Violence.* London: Sage Publications.

Diawara, Manthia. 1994. "Malcolm X and the Black Public Sphere: Conversionists versus Culturalists," *Public Culture* 7, no. 1 (Fall): 35–48.

Diawara, Manthia, ed. 1994. *Black American Cinema.* New York: Routledge, 1993.

Doherty, Thomas. 2000. "Malcolm X: In Print, On Screen." *Biography* 23, no. 1 (Winter): 29–48.

Donaldson, Melvin. 2006. *Masculinity in the Interracial Buddy Film.* Jefferson, N.C.: McFarland and Company.

Dyson, Michael Eric. 1995. *Making Malcolm: The Myth and Meaning of Malcolm X.* New York: Oxford University Press.

———. 1993. *Reflecting Black: African-American Cultural Criticism.* Minneapolis: University of Minnesota Press.

Eitzen, Dirk. 1995. "When Is a Documentary? Documentary as a Mode of Reception." *Cinema Journal* 35, no. 1 (Fall): 81–102.

Epp, Michael H. 2003. "Raising Minstrelsy: Humour, Satire and the Stereotype in *The Birth of a Nation* and *Bamboozled.*" *Canadian Review of American Studies* 33, no. 1: 17–35.

Ferncase, Richard K. 1996. *Outsider Features: American Independent Films of the 1980s.* Westport, Conn.: Greenwood Press.

Flory, Dan. 2006. "Spike Lee and the Sympathetic Racist." *Journal of Aesthetics and Art Criticism* 64, no. 1 (Spring): 67–79.

Fuchs, Cynthia, ed. 2002. *Spike Lee: Interviews.* Jackson: University Press of Mississippi.

Gabbard, Krin. 1992. "Signifyin(g) the Phallus: *Mo' Better Blues* and Representations of the Jazz Trumpet." *Cinema Journal* 32, no. 1 (Fall): 43–62.

———. 2004. *Black Magic: White Hollywood and African American Culture.* New Brunswick, N.J.: Rutgers University Press.

Geiger, Jeffrey. 2004. "'The Game behind the Game': Spatial Politics and Spike Lee's *He Got Game.*" Pp. 83–106 in *Race and Ethnicity in New York City,* ed. Jerome Krase and Ray Hutchison. Boston: Elsevier.

Gerstner, David A., and Janet Staiger, eds. 2002. *Authorship and Film.* New York: Routledge.

Girgus, Sam B. 2002. *America on Film: Modernism, Documentary, and a Changing America.* New York: Cambridge University Press.

Gordon, Dexter. 1998. "Humor in African American Discourse: Speaking of Oppression." *Journal of Black Studies* 29, no. 2 (November): 254–76.

Gubar, Susan. 2006–2007. "Racial Camp in *The Producers* and *Bamboozled.*" *Film Quarterly* 60, no. 2 (Winter): 26–37.

Guerrero, Ed. 1993. *Framing Blackness: The African American Image in Film.* Philadelphia: Temple University Press.

————. 2001. *Do The Right Thing*. London: BFI Publishing.

Hanson, Philip. 2003. "The Politics of Inner City Identity in *Do the Right Thing*." *South Central Review* 20, nos. 2–4 (Summer–Winter): 47–66.

Harris, Keith M. 2006. *Boys, Boyz, Bois: The Ethics of Black Masculinity in Film and Popular Media*. Studies in African American History and Culture. London: Routledge.

Harris, William A. 1996. "Cultural Engineering and the Films of Spike Lee." Pp. 3–23 in *Mediated Messages and African-American Culture: Contemporary Issues*, ed. Venise T. Berry and Carmen L. Manning-Miller. Thousand Oaks, Calif.: Sage Publications.

Holt, Elvin, and William H. Jackson. 2004. "Reconstructing Black Manhood: Message and Meaning in Spike Lee's *Get on the Bus*." *CLA Journal* 47, no. 4 (June): 409–26.

hooks, bell. 1989. *Talking Back: Thinking Feminist, Thinking Black*. Boston: South End Press.

————. 1996. *Reel to Real: Race, Sex, and Class at the Movies*. New York: Routledge.

————. 2006. *Outlaw Culture: Resisting Representations*, 2nd ed. New York: Routledge.

Horne, Gerald. 1993. "'Myth' and the Making of *Malcolm X*." *American Historical Review* 98, no. 2 (April): 440–50.

Houston, Kerr. 2004. "Athletic Iconography in Spike Lee's Early Feature Films." *African American Review* 38, no. 4 (Winter): 637–49.

Hunter, Tera. 1989. "'It's a Man's Man's World': Specters of the Old Re-Newed in Afro-American Culture and Criticism." *Callaloo* 38 (Winter): 247–49.

Jacobsen, Kurt, ed. 2004. *Maverick Voices: Conversations with Political and Cultural Rebels*. Lanham, Md.: Rowman and Littlefield.

Jones, Bronwyn K. 2004. "Performing Psychopathology: Crime Scene Photography, Forensic Aesthetics, and Performative Knowledge in the Contemporary Serial Killer Narrative (David Fincher, Thomas Harris, James Frazer, Spike Lee, Bret Easton Ellis)." Ph.D. diss. Northwestern University, Evanston, Ill.

Lee, Jonathan Scott. 1995. "Spike Lee's *Malcolm X* as Tranformational Object." *American Imago* 52, no. 2: 155–67.

Lee, Spike. 1987. *Spike Lee's Gotta Have It: Inside Guerrilla Filmmaking*. New York: Fireside/Simon and Schuster.

————. 1999. "Dealing to Do Doable Films: Life as a Very Independent Filmmaker." Pp. 15–32 in *Black Genius: African American Solutions to African American Problems*, ed. Walter Mosley. New York: W. W. Norton.

Lee, Spike, ed. 1991. *Five for Five: The Films of Spike Lee*. New York: Stewart, Tabori, and Chang.

Lee, Spike, and Lisa Jones. 1988. *Uplift the Race: The Construction of School Daze*. New York: Simon and Schuster.

————. 1989. *Do the Right Thing*. New York: Fireside/Simon and Schuster.

Lee, Spike, and Ralph Wiley. 1992. *By Any Means Necessary: The Trials and Tribulations of the Making of Malcolm X*. New York: Hyperion.

Lott, Tommy. 1991. "A No-Theory Theory of Contemporary Black Cinema." *Black American Literature Forum* 25, no. 2 (Summer): 221–36.

Klotman, Phyllis R., and Janet K. Cutler, eds. 1999. *Struggles for Representation: African American Documentary Film and Video*. Bloomington: Indiana University Press.

Massood, Paula J. 2000. "*Summer of Sam*." *Cineaste* 25, no. 2 (Spring): 62–64.

————. 2003. *Black City Cinema: African American Urban Experiences in Film.* Philadelphia: Temple University Press.

————. 2003. "The Quintessential New York and Global Citizen: An Interview with Spike Lee." *Cineaste* 28, no. 3 (Summer): 4–6.

————. 2004. "*Boyz n the Hood* Chronotope: Spike Lee, Richard Price, and the Changing Authorship of *Clockers*." Pp. 191–207 in *Literature and Film: A Guide to the Theory and Practice of Film Adaptation*, ed. Robert Stam. London: Blackwell.

McWhorter, Diane. 2001. *Carry Me Home: Birmingham, Alabama, the Climactic Battle of the Civil Rights Revolution.* New York: Simon and Schuster.

Miller II, James Lee. 1998. "A Rhetorical Analysis of Four Selected Films by Spike Lee and John Singleton." Ph.D. diss., Bowling Green State University, Bowling Green, Ohio.

Patterson, Alex. 1992. *Spike Lee.* New York: Avon Books.

Perkins, Eric. 1990. "Renewing the African American Cinema: The Films of Spike Lee." *Cineaste* 17, no. 4: 4–8.

Plessinger, Alison Ann. 2000. "Race, Gender, and Spike Lee: An (R)Evolution in Filmmaking." Ph.D. diss., Pennsylvania State University, University Park, Penn.

Powell Jr., Gerald A. 2004. *A Rhetoric of Symbolic Identity: An Analysis of Spike Lee's X and Bamboozled.* Lanham, Md.: University Press of America.

Prince, Stephen. 2000. *A New Pot of Gold: Hollywood under the Rainbow, 1980–1989.* Berkeley: University of California Press.Ramsay, Guthrie P. 2002. "Muzing New Hoods, Making New Identities: Film, Hip-Hop Culture, and Jazz Music." *Callaloo* 25, no. 1 (Winter): 309–20.

Reid, Mark A. 1993. *Redefining Black Film.* Berkeley: University of California Press.

————. 2005. *Black Lenses, Black Voices: African American Film Now.* Lanham, Md.: Rowman and Littlefield.

Reid, Mark A., ed. 1997. *Spike Lee's Do the Right Thing.* Cambridge: Cambridge University Press.

Rhines, Jesse Algeron. 1996. *Black Film/White Money.* New Brunswick, N.J.: Rutgers University Press.

Rocchio, Vincent F. 2000. *Reel Racism: Confronting Hollywood's Construction of Afro-American Culture.* Boulder, Colo.: Westview Press.

Rome, Dennis. 2004. *Black Demons: Media's Depiction of the African American Male Criminal Stereotype.* Westport, Conn.: Praeger.

Simmonds, Felly Nkweto. 1988. "She's Gotta Have It: The Representation of Black Female Sexuality on Film." *Feminist Review* 29 (Spring): 10–22.

Smith, Valerie, ed. 1997. *Representing Blackness: Issues in Film and Video.* New Brunswick, N.J.: Rutgers University Press.

Sterritt, David. 2007. "He Cuts Heads: Spike Lee and the New York Experience." Pp. 137–49 in *City that Never Sleeps: New York and the Filmic Imagination*, ed. Murray Pomerance. New Brunswick, N.J.: Rutgers University Press, 2007.

Stevens, Maurice. 2002. "Subject to Counter-Memory: Disavowal and Black Manhood in Spike Lee's *Malcolm X*." *Signs* 28, no. 1 (Fall): 277–301.

Wallace, Michele. 1990. *Invisibility Blues: From Pop to Theory.* London: Verso.

————. 2001. "*Bamboozled*: The Legacy." *Black Renaissance/Renaissance Noire* 3, no. 3 (Summer–Fall 2001), available online at http://www.nyu.edu/gsas/program/africana/blackrenaissance/vol3no3/main.html.

———. 2004. *Dark Designs and Visual Culture*. Durham, N.C.: Duke University Press.

Watkins, S. Craig. 1998. *Representing: Hip Hop Culture and the Production of Black Cinema*. Chicago: University of Chicago Press.

———. 2006. *Hip Hop Matters: Politics, Pop Culture, and the Struggle for the Soul of a Movement*. Boston: Beacon Press.

Willis, Sharon. 1997. *High Contrast: Race and Gender in Contemporary Hollywood Films*. Durham, N.C.: Duke University Press.

———. 2005. "*Do the Right Thing*: A Theater of Interruptions." Pp. 776–93 in *Film Analysis: A Norton Reader*, ed. Jeffrey Geiger and R. L. Rutsky. New York: W. W. Norton.

X, Malcolm, with Alex Haley. 1992 (1965). *The Autobiography of Malcolm X*. New York: Ballantine Books.

Yearwood, Gladstone. 2000. *Black Film as a Signifying Practice*. Trenton, N.J.: African World Press.

Additional sources appear in individual essays.

Contributors

Christine Acham is Associate Professor in the African American and African Studies Program at the University of California, Davis. She is the author of *Revolution Televised: Prime Time and the Struggle for Black Power* (2004) and recently co-edited the inaugural issue of *Screening Noir: A Journal of Black, Film, Television and New Media Culture*, titled "Blaxploitation Revisited." She is a member of the editorial board of *Film Quarterly*.

Toni Cade Bambara is the author of a number of fiction works, including *Gorilla, My Love* (1972), *The Salt Eaters* (1981), and *If Blessing Comes* (1987). She edited two nonfiction collections, *The Black Woman: An Anthology* (1970) and *Deep Sightings and Rescue Missions: Fiction, Essays, and Conversations* (1996, published a year after her death). Her screenplays include *W. E. B. Du Bois: A Biography in Four Voices* (1996).

Mark D. Cunningham is a Ph.D. candidate in the Department of Radio–Television–Film at the University of Texas, Austin. His research interests include black popular culture, black masculinity, and depression in the black community. His dissertation focuses on John Singleton's hood trilogy *Boyz n the Hood*, *Poetic Justice*, and *Baby Boy*.

Anna Everett is Professor of Film Studies in the Film and Media Studies Department at the University of California, Santa Barbara. She is the author of *Returning the Gaze: A Genealogy of Black Film Criticism, 1909–1949* (2001) and is at work on two books, *Digital Diaspora: A Race for Cyberspace* and *Inside the Dark Museum: An Anthology of Black Film Criticism, 1909–1959*. She is the founder and managing editor of *Screening Noir*.

Dan Flory is Associate Professor of Philosophy in the Department of History, Philosophy, and Religious Studies at Montana State University. He is the author of *Philosophy, Black Film, Film Noir* (2007) and an associate editor of *Film and Philosophy*.

Krin Gabbard is Professor of Comparative Literature and Cultural Studies at Stony Brook University. He is the author of *Jammin' at the Margins: Jazz and the American Cinema* (1996) and *Black Magic: White Hollywood and African American Culture* (2004), co-author of *Psychiatry and the Cinema* (1999), and the editor of *Jazz among the Discourses* (1995) and *Representing Jazz* (1995).

David A. Gerstner is Associate Professor of Cinema Studies at the College of Staten Island and the Graduate Center, City University of New York. He is the author of *Manly Arts: Masculinity and Nation in Early American Cinema* (2006), editor of *The Routledge International Encyclopedia of Queer Culture* (2006), and co-editor of *Authorship and Film* (2002).

Ed Guerrero is an Associate Professor in the Cinema Studies Department at New York University's Tisch School of the Arts. He is the author of *Framing Blackness: The African American Image in Film* (1993) and *Do the Right Thing* (2001).

Keith M. Harris is Assistant Professor in the English Department at the University of California, Riverside. He is the author of *Boys, Boyz, Bois: An Ethics of Masculinity in Popular Film, Television and Video* (2006) and the editor of a special issue of *Wide Angle* (2004).

bell hooks is the author of numerous critically acclaimed and influential books on the politics of race, gender, class, and culture, including *Ain't I a Woman: Black Women and Feminism* (1981), *Teaching to Transgress: Education as the Practice of Freedom* (1994), *Reel to Real: Race, Sex, and Class at the Movies* (1996), *Feminism Is for Everybody: Passionate Politics* (2000), and *Teaching Community: A Pedagogy of Hope* (2003).

Wahneema Lubiano is Associate Professor of Literature at Duke University. She is the author of numerous articles on African American history and popular culture and the editor of *The House That Race Built: Black Americans, U.S. Terrain* (1997).

Paula J. Massood is Associate Professor of Film Studies in the Department of Film at Brooklyn College and the Graduate Center, City University of New York. She is the author of *Black City Cinema: African American Urban Experiences in Film* (2003).

James C. McKelly is Associate Professor in the English Department at Auburn University. He specializes in twentieth-century American cultural studies, film studies, and modernism. His articles have appeared in *Screen, African American Review,* and *Profession*.

Tavia Nyong'o is Assistant Professor in the Performance Studies Department at New York University's Tisch School of the Arts. His articles have appeared in *Social Text, Theater Journal, GLQ, TDR,* and *Women and Performance.* He is the author of *The Amalgamation Waltz: Antebellum Genealogies of the Hybrid Future* (forthcoming).

Beretta E. Smith-Shomade is Associate Professor in the Department of Media Arts at the University of Arizona. Her teaching and research focus on television and film critical studies, with particular attention to representations of race, gender, class, and generation. She is the author of *Shaded Lives: African-American Women and Television* (2002) and *Pimpin' Ain't Easy: Selling Black Entertainment Television* (2007).

Michele Wallace is Associate Professor of English and women's studies at City College of New York and the Graduate Center, City University of New York. She is the author of *Black Macho and the Myth of the Superwoman* (1978), *Invisibility Blues: From Pop to Theory* (1990), and *Dark Designs and Visual Culture* (2004).

S. Craig Watkins is Associate Professor in the Department of Radio–Television–Film at the University of Texas, Austin. He is the author of *Representing: Hip Hop Culture and the Production of Black Cinema* (1998) and *Hip Hop Matters: Politics, Pop Culture and the Struggle for the Soul of a Movement* (2005).

Index

Academy Awards, 97, 102, 176
Acham, Christine, xxiv, 159, 265
acting, 11
adulthood, 125–26
aesthetic: cinematic, 128; criticism, 89n5; influence of Lee, xix; judgments on, 2; persuasive, 134. *See also* Black Aesthetic
African American(s): ancestors of, 164; art by, 23, 38; as audience members, 156–57; *The Color Purple* depicting, 24; entrepreneurial dilemma of, 74; experience of, 138–39, 160; expression of, 15; as fiction writers, 53n19; in film, 133; *film noir* appropriated by, 208n3; history of, xxiv, 162; homophobia and, 51; identity of, xxi; music of, 177–78, 191–93; representation of, xxvi, 161; rhetoric of, 140n5; visual degradation of, 231; work of, 46
African American community(ies): in *Do the Right Thing*, 59–60; duty within, 124–25; gay men in, 153; male socialization in, 55n23; role of black men in, 144; in *School Daze*, 10
African American culture: contemporary, 59; discourse on, 43; pragmatism in, 98; production in, 45; representation of, 161; traditions of, 128
African American filmmakers, 146; in Hollywood, 15; *noir* conventions reinvigorated by, 198
African American filmmaking, xv–xvi; production in, 32; renewed interest in, xviii

African American resistance, 60–61
agenda: film, 12; of Lee, 14; of popular culture, 78
Alice in Wonderland (Carroll), xxii, 116–20
Allen, Ray, 176–77. *See also* "Jesus Shuttlesworth"
Allen, Woody, 91, 182, 244, 252n5
ambara, Toni Cade, xv
American classical music, 178–81
American dream, 165
"Angie," 85; "Flipper" relationship with, 81–85
anti-realism, 129–30, 140n2
apartheid, 50; theme in *School Daze*, 19–20
Armour, Jody David, 200, 210n20
art: African American, 23, 38; revolutionary, 181–85
"Arthur Case," 246
Arthur, Paul, 99–100
"Art *vs.* Ideology: The Debate over Positive Images" (Muwakkil), 2
"Aunt Song," 120–24
authenticity, 110, 241, 241n3
The Autobiography of Malcolm X (Haley), 95, 100
autonomy, 69; of Lee, xxiv

Bad Faith and Anti-Black Racism (Gordon), 205–6
Baker, Houston, 72; on Lee's films, 98
Bakhtin, Mikhail, xxi, 69, 70